The Global Japanese Restaurant

FOOD IN ASIA AND THE PACIFIC

Series Editors:

Christine R. Yano and Robert Ji-Song Ku

This series showcases new works focused on food in the Asia-Pacific region and its diasporic iterations, highlighting the commonalities that the area and cultures might bring to the subject. Books under this series are disciplinarily diverse, drawing from the fields of geography, sociology, anthropology, history, globalization studies, gender studies, science and technology studies, development studies, ethnic studies, and cultural studies. The Asia-Pacific region evokes particular global relationships and domestic infrastructures—center-periphery, post-colonialism, imperialisms, and politicized imaginaries. The goal of the series is to bring food to bear in considering these relationships and infrastructures. We see a regional focus—including the inherent mobility of transnational flows, migration, and global capitalism therein—as productive elements, rather than as reifying limitation. By bringing together books that have a general topic (food) and an area focus (Asia-Pacific), FAP locates mobility itself as the framework from which scholarship may enrich our understanding of this complexly globalized world.

The Global Japanese Restaurant

MOBILITIES, IMAGINARIES, AND POLITICS

Edited by
James Farrer and David L. Wank

University of Hawai'i Press | Honolulu

A subsidy for images came from Sophia University.

First printing, 2023

Library of Congress Cataloging-in-Publication Data

Names: Farrer, James (James C.), editor. | Wank, David L., editor.
Title: The global Japanese restaurant : mobilities, imaginaries, and
    politics / edited by James Farrer, David L. Wank.
Other titles: Food in Asia and the Pacific.
Description: Honolulu : University of Hawai'i Press, [2023] | Series: Food
    in Asia and the Pacific | Includes bibliographical references and index.
Identifiers: LCCN 2023004998 (print) | LCCN 2023004999 (ebook) |
    ISBN 9780824894269 (hardback) | ISBN 9780824895143 (paperback) |
    ISBN 9780824895273 (pdf) | ISBN 9780824895266 (epub) |
    ISBN 9780824895280 (kindle edition)
Subjects: LCSH: Japanese restaurants—History. | Cooking, Japanese—
    Social aspects.
Classification: LCC TX945.4 .G56 2023 (print) | LCC TX945.4 (ebook) |
    DDC 647.9552—dc23/eng/20230210
LC record available at https://lccn.loc.gov/2023004998
LC ebook record available at https://lccn.loc.gov/2023004999

Cover photos: *(Top)* Geishas attend to guests at the Rokusan Gardens at a garden party held for the Western and Japanese press on August 22, 1940. (Time/Life Inc.)

(Bottom) A Japanese restaurant stood in the center of the town of Cafelândia, in 1932, one of the early hubs of Japanese migration to Brazil. The Hirano colony was founded by Humpei Hirano in 1915. In 1934, it had more than 5,000 Japanese immigrants, making up most of the population. (Collection of the Historical Museum of Japanese Immigration in Brazil, photographer unknown, 1932)

Contents

Acknowledgments

This book has been a shared journey of six coauthors writing and researching together at Sophia University. Although James and David edited it as a whole, we all contributed to multiple chapters, and so the book is our collective "baby." We are happy to send it out in the world and thank the University of Hawai'i Press for making this possible. Our efforts have been greatly helped by many research assistants, most of them students at Sophia University. Without their linguistic, ethnographic, and other talents, we could not have accomplished the project on such a global scale. They include Alice Ashiwa, Rosa Barbaran, Viviane Chaubet, Karisa Djohan, Linda Dück, Yeonji Ghim, Yajun Lisa Hu, Shayani Jayasinghe, Guyeon Kang, Yijin Kang, Fumiko Kimura, Roran Kobayashi, Anne-Sophie König, Purity Mahugu, Aimi Muranaka, Hina Nakamura, Anna Wiemann, Heena Yang, Alixe Yoneyama, Mariya Yoshiyama, Hisako Yoshizawa, Yingyue Zhang, and Marika Zulch.

Along the way, we have received significant institutional support. We thank Michio Hayashi, Miwa Higashiura, David Slater, and Tak Watanabe from the Sophia Institute of Comparative Culture, which supported this project administratively and financially for over a decade. The research was generously funded by a Sophia University Special Grant for Research in Priority Areas and a Japanese Society for the Promotion of Science (*kaken*) grant.

Some materials and case studies used in the book have appeared in preliminary forms in other venues. Elements of the overall argument appeared in an article coauthored by all six of us titled "Japanese Culinary Mobilities Research: The Globalization of the Japanese Restaurant," *Foods & Food Ingredients Journal Japan* 222, no. 3 (2017): 257–266; and a coauthored chapter by five of us, titled "Culinary Mobilities: The Multiple Globalizations of Japanese Cuisine," in *Routledge Handbook of Food in Asia,* edited by Cecilia Leong-Salobir (Abingdon, UK: Routledge, 2019), 39–57. Some of the cases in Chapter 5 were published in a chapter coauthored by Wank and Farrer titled "Chinese Immigrants and Japanese Cuisine in the United States: A Case of Culinary Glocalization," in *The Globalization of Asian Cuisines: Transnational Networks and Contact Zones,* edited by James Farrer (New York: Palgrave Macmillan 2015), 79–99; and in an article coauthored by Farrer and Wang titled "Who Owns a Cuisine? The Grassroots Politics of Japanese Food in Europe," *Asian Anthropology* 20, no. 1 (2021): 12–29. Early versions of some research reported in Chapter 2 were published in Farrer, "Domesticating the Japanese Culinary Field in Shanghai," in *Feeding Japan: The Cultural and Political Issues of Dependency and Risk,* edited by Andreas Niehaus and Tine Walravens (New York: Palgrave Macmillan, 2017), 287–312. Our other previous publications that informed the theorizations in this volume are cited in the text.

We would like to acknowledge the feedback and support we have received from audiences in our presentations on the topic around the world. These would begin with our students at Sophia University who shared their experiences of Japanese food abroad. Farther afield, audiences and commentators raised searching questions and helpful criticism in public lectures and presentations made at the Asian Studies Conference Japan, the Carnegie Council for Ethics in International Affairs, City University of Hong Kong, Emory University, the Fashion Institute of Technology, Franklin and Marshall College, the Freie University Berlin, the Hebrew University of Jerusalem, the International Convention of Asian Scholars, the National University of Singapore, National Taiwan University, New York University, Sun Yat-sen University, Taipei Medical University, Università degli Studi Roma Tre, the University of North Carolina, and the University of San Francisco. The two thoughtful anonymous reviewers for the press and our editor Masako Ikeda helped us make critical improvements to the manuscript.

Most importantly, we would like to thank the hundreds of people in many countries who shared their stories with us. It was an amazing experience to see and taste the differences in Japanese restaurants and also realize the similarities and connections among these disparate venues. Many informants became guides to their local restaurant scenes, helping to fill in our understanding of the broader picture.

Finally, as a now-dispersed collective of six coauthors, we would like to acknowledge our collegiality as delightful and thoughtful companions over the years of conceiving, researching, and writing this book.

A Note on Style Conventions

In this book, non-English words that do not appear in *The Merriam-Webster Dictionary* are italicized and defined in first use in each chapter. We acknowledge that for many readers these are not foreign words; however, we want to make the book accessible to those unfamiliar with Japanese food terms. Also, after some deliberation, we have adopted a convention to write all names in the conventional English naming order, with the surname last. In East Asian languages, surnames typically come first. However, this book largely portrays transnational contexts in which the mobile culinary actors have lived their lives in multiple languages. Therefore, the name order (and even some names) changes depending on the language spoken. No single convention is ideal, but we decided to be consistent and conform to the language of the text, which is English. (Names in references, however, are in the original word order as in the published version.)

1 | Introducing the Global Japanese Restaurant

JAMES FARRER AND DAVID L. WANK

In 1938, former geisha Moto Saito arrived in Shanghai with plans to open a Japanese restaurant.[1] In itself, her concept was nothing new. Japanese, including many women, had been running restaurants in this city since the 1880s. However, her restaurant would be distinct in several ways. Its location avoided the teeming Japantown of Hongkou District, where most of Shanghai's fifty thousand Japanese lived and operated hundreds of businesses, including restaurants. Elsewhere in the world, Japanese restaurants were situated in such immigrant enclaves, where they served nostalgic dishes to Japanese settlers and sojourners. But Saito, flush with money from a divorce settlement, opened on Nanjing Road next to the Cathay Hotel in the heart of Shanghai's International Concession, an area dominated by British financial capital. Despite her background, she did not open a geisha house offering erotic companionship with Japanese food, typical in Japantowns around the empire, from Taipei to Seoul. Instead, she designed a modern open dining room that appealed to Western expatriates and wealthy Chinese alike. It served newly fashionable Japanese dishes—notably sukiyaki and tempura—that Saito had observed Westerners enjoying on an around-the-world cruise eight years earlier. Her establishment, immodestly named Restaurant Queen in bold neon English lettering, employed over a hundred Japanese, Chinese, and Russian staff.

For Saito, the restaurant would redeem what she saw as the poor image of Japanese food served abroad.[2] During her long career, her goal as a restaurateur was nothing less than uplifting the reputation of Japanese cuisine in the eyes of foreigners.[3] However, in 1945, facing the collapse of the Empire of Japan, Saito sold Restaurant Queen to a Russian employee and returned to Japan. She ran a hotel-restaurant in Tokyo before setting off

1

again, this time for New York. In 1957, she opened an eponymous restaurant in midtown Manhattan that, as in her Shanghai venture, focused on sukiyaki, a dish in vogue in the United States since the 1930s. Restaurant Saito was a hit with both curious New Yorkers and Japanese expatriates. She hired many migrant women, including Chinese and Koreans, as well as Japanese who had married American soldiers. The restaurant was one of the early places where these diverse Asian Americans became part of the story of global Japanese cuisine in the West.[4] By the time Saito closed shop and returned to Tokyo in 1985, non-Japanese Asian restaurateurs had taken the lead in spreading Japanese cuisine beyond global cities.

Saito's remarkable culinary journey spanning half a century points to themes that resonate throughout this book. One is the rise of a new type of "global Japanese restaurant," an open-ended term we use to describe Japanese eateries created abroad that serve innovative dishes to appeal to diverse clientele. While earlier exemplars were typically created by Japanese migrants such as Saito, since the later twentieth century, most have been opened by other migrants (usually Asians), many of whom learned the trade in places like Saito's restaurant in New York. A second theme in Saito's story is the centrality of culinary global cities, including Shanghai and New York, urban centers where culinary influences converge and new food fashions are defined. A third theme concerns the origins of global Japanese restaurant fashions. Saito's story illustrates that these fashions did not begin with the sushi boom of the 1980s, as is commonly believed, but much earlier, with such dishes as sukiyaki, accompanied by the stylish service of Japanese women who were central to the global imaginary of the Japanese restaurant. Finally, we see that restaurant owners are not just doing business but are also cultural intermediaries engaging in a type of grassroots culinary politics, spreading what they often regard as authentic Japanese cuisine and culture to non-Japanese audiences.[5] At the same time, we see them adapting these authentic menus for local tastes, setting up a dynamic dialogue between Japan-based notions of authenticity and an increasing emphasis on culinary innovation.[6]

Focus: The Global Japanese Restaurant

This book is about the globalization of Japanese cuisine as seen through restaurants.[7] The restaurant is a point of entry to understanding what and how we eat, how we socialize over food and drink, and the contexts in which we do so. Scholars have shown how restaurants are a central institution of modern city life, one in which critical social identities—such as class, gender, and ethnicity—are reconstituted through public rituals of consumption, service, and sociability. They are spaces of play and pleasure as well as work and politics.[8] However, scholarship on restaurants has typically treated Western restaurants, particularly the French restaurant, as the iconic representatives of this phenomenon.[9] Non-Western restaurant forms that have spread around the world are often studied more narrowly as immigrant businesses or as local urban amenities rather than more broadly as institutions and imaginaries with a global scope.[10] In this book, Japanese restaurants—no less than the classic French restaurant—are conveyors of global culinary fashions rather than linked to a single type of Japanese migrant experience. The overseas Japanese restaurant is an expression of ethnicity and nationality, as well as political power, social distinctions, gender, modern aesthetics, local community, and other themes explored in this book.

We examine the establishment of restaurants outside Japan from the late nineteenth century in Japan's East Asian empire up to the twenty-first century, when over 150,000 Japanese restaurants were operating on all six inhabited continents.[11] A shifting cast of Japanese and non-Japanese actors—chefs and restaurateurs, as well as states and corporations—have driven this spread in the context of colonialism, settler migration, Japanese expatriate communities, ethnic succession, corporatization, and contemporary fine dining. They have created new dishes, spaces for consuming them, and dining styles, including many that depart from what can be found within Japan even while shaping expectations around the world regarding Japanese cuisine. We show that Japanese restaurants have become urban institutions that express, depending on the context, imperial power, class distinctions, and the gendered and racialized character of culinary fashions.

What counts as a "Japanese" restaurant in this study? We refrain from passing judgment on what should be considered a Japanese cuisine for conceptual and methodological reasons. If a restaurant represents itself as a Japanese restaurant, we include it. Most restaurants have a Japanese name and serve something their menus describe as "Japanese cuisine." Most dishes would be recognizable as Japanese to those broadly familiar with foodways in Japan, though not always and certainly not by everyone. At the low end, we encountered Japanese restaurants serving Chinese-style fast food, with menu entries for *yakisoba* and *gyōza* being Chinese-style stir-fried noodles and fried dumplings. At the higher end, we visited uber-expensive Japanese restaurants serving what some label as Japanized French cuisine. Nevertheless, all are included in our sample as modalities of Japanese restaurants in the modern world.

The various modes of the global Japanese restaurant challenge the widespread assumption that Japanese cuisine is created in Japan and exported abroad by Japanese restaurateurs and corporations. While not denying the role of Japan and of Japanese actors, we decenter both in our narrative by recognizing how a multitude of non-Japanese actors and sites outside Japan have also shaped the idea of what constitutes Japanese cuisine for diners around the world. Of course, many scholars of Japanese cuisine recognize that, in some way, it has long been part of a broader world. Numerous studies document how, over a millennium, foreign culinary influences and food products from China and Europe have come to Japan.[12] Other studies examine the foodways and restaurants of Japanese immigrant communities abroad and the spread of Japanese food beyond them.[13] While we borrow from their findings for this book, most of these studies could be labeled Japan-centric: they assume that Japanese food is produced in Japan, though influenced by other cuisines. Japan-centrism is even seen in studies that use the concept of "globalization" because they focus on Japanese actors, including restaurateurs, and see the Japanese food consumed globally, such as sushi and ramen, as exports from Japan.

In this book, the term "global Japanese restaurant" refers to the commercial production and serving of Japanese cuisine that occurs largely outside Japan and mostly for non-Japanese consumers. It is not a singular idea but has multiple genealogies. It comprises service models created in Japan, such as the *ryōtei* (fine dining restaurants with entertainment), *izakaya* (pubs), and *sushiya* (sushi bars), which developed in the teeming Japanese cities in the early modern period, particularly Edo (now Tokyo). Edo's one million inhabitants in the early nineteenth century already supported over six thousand such restaurants, creating a diverse repertoire of templates for later restaurateurs.[14] But the genealogies also include the French "restaurant," which in the nineteenth century established the modern restaurant form with ordering from a printed menu and individualized table service by waiters.[15] Over the next century, these innovations were adopted by other types of eateries around the world, including in Japan. Influences also encompass deskilled forms of restaurants originating in the United States, such as the diner and the hamburger stand, that became global forms in the mid-twentieth century. Additionally, the global Japanese restaurant includes such newfangled forms as the ramen bar, invented in twentieth-century Yokohama and Tokyo, the "wok sushi" buffet, invented in Italy, and the *temakeria* from Brazil.[16] Over the 150 years covered in this book, new forms of the global Japanese restaurant have emerged, offering foods redesigned and even invented to appeal to specific markets of non-Japanese while engendering conversations about "Japaneseness." To view a phenomenon spanning decades and spreading to all corners of the world, a global perspective is necessary, though challenging.

Perspective: Culinary Global Cities

The global Japanese restaurant is a phenomenon produced mainly in a few global cities, defined as an urban area with outsize influence on world affairs due to its positioning in transnational movements and networks. We introduce the term "culinary global city" to describe cities that play a central role in the circulation and production of culinary culture. As described by Saskia Sassen, global cities are locales within nations that occupy the commanding heights of the global economy, concentrating and directing allocations of capital. Apex cities, such as Tokyo, New York, and London, have the largest aggregations of financial services, corporate headquarters, international organizations, cultural institutions (education, media, arts), sports, airports, and so forth. They also have the deepest transnational ties with other apex cities and exert disproportionate influence over a large region or hinterland. Other cities, such as São Paulo, Chicago, and Berlin, constitute second-tier cities with lesser aggregations, while many are ranked yet lower. Multiple transnational networks of people and capital run through global cities. This includes the circulation of elites—the highly paid personnel who run the financial industries, staff corporate headquarters, and manage world-class cultural institutions. It also includes the circulation of poor people, often migrants, to maintain the infrastructure of global cities by cleaning offices, repairing roads, serving as nannies, and preparing meals. These circulations are between apex cities and then to their hinterlands of lower-tier cities and outlying regions.[17] Globalized and highly interlinked restaurant service sectors have become a defining feature of the appeal and lifestyles of global cities.

Culinary global cities, as we define them, are cities that play a key role in the global culinary field, as nodes for the creation and dissemination of new culinary ideas, as well as spaces in which both restaurants and key cultural intermediaries—culinary media and rating agencies—are concentrated.[18] Based on our historical and ethnographic research, a map of culinary global cities would overlap significantly with one of the global financial cities described by Sassen because similar exchanges of information and concentrations of influence and resources to those in the financial sector occur in the culinary field. Culinary global cities have concentrations of highly skilled migrant chefs, culinary media and authorities (e.g., Michelin reviewers), specialized suppliers, and wealthy customers. Chefs exchange ideas through frequent job hopping, both within and between global cities. In our research, we see a concentration of high-end Japanese restaurants in cities that are also financial centers, with large numbers of midrange and fast-food Japanese restaurants also serving these local urban markets. Hong Kong in 2017, for example, had 1,380 Japanese restaurants out of a total of 16,000 restaurants.[19] And according to the global Tripadvisor online review site, in 2021, there were 284 Japanese restaurants in Dubai, 631 in New York City, 752 in London, 974 in Paris, 1,107 in São Paulo, 1,102 in Singapore, and 1,112 in Moscow.[20] Finally, according to a search on the most used Chinese restaurant review site, there were 4,449 Japanese restaurants in Shanghai, making it possibly the city outside Japan with the most Japanese restaurants.[21] Given that this is primarily a historical and ethnographic study, we do not attempt to rank culinary global cities in a quantitative fashion, but rather describe the sociocultural interactions that characterize these places.

Global cities matter as local sites, Sassen claims, because global processes are concentrated in them: "Recognizing that the global also dresses itself in the clothing of the local, reshaping it from the inside, opens up a vast research agenda. It means that studying globalization needs to include detailed local research—notably ethnographies—of multiple conditions and dynamics that are global or are shaped by it but function inside the national and are mostly experienced as national. Cities and neighborhoods, rather than national territory as such, are major sites for such entities . . ."[22] Similarly, this book brings together our numerous local investigations of restaurants that are mainly located in entertainment districts in major cities. Food media, food critics, and food tourism are also concentrated in these cities, as are chefs who move among restaurants borrowing and transmitting ideas. Trends for restaurants and dishes are established and then conveyed to lower-tier cities and outlying regions by these mobile chefs and restaurateurs. This book also follows restaurateurs deep into these hinterlands to illustrate their culinary links to trends in global cities.

Temporally, Sassen's global cities frame overlays our account of the globalization of Japanese cuisine. She argues that the 1980s was a watershed for the position of cities in the world. Before 1980, wealth was more dispersed within a country through industrial production, and the largest cities were sites to gather and allocate capital within nation-state boundaries. After the 1980s, "open border" neoliberal policies stimulated transfers of economic production from rich to developing countries and more extensive capital accumulations in the largest cities. At this point, "world cities," such as New York, London, and Hong Kong, became "global cities," allocating capital around the world and interacting with other global cities through increasingly dense networks.[23] This periodization fits our narrative of a shift from traditional Japanese immigrant enclaves to mobile actors in culinary global cities that define and spread the culinary and business models of the global Japanese restaurant. In the late twentieth century, chefs and restaurateurs working outside these communities, including many non-Japanese migrants, became the primary actors in setting up Japanese restaurants in movements proceeding along urban hierarchies. Globe-spanning networks of influence and investment fostered this spread of new restaurant forms. To the extent that Japanese people and organizations have remained important, this is less linked to their positions in Japan than to their experiences and networks in culinary global cities.

Analytic Concepts: Culinary Mobilities, Culinary Imaginaries, and Culinary Politics

Our analysis is guided by concepts of culinary mobilities, culinary imaginaries, and culinary politics. They are conceptually distinct, although empirically intertwined in analysis. "Culinary mobilities" refers to patterns in the movement of producers, consumers, suppliers, and products centered in cities and operating in networks and hierarchies. As with mobilities scholarship generally, this book primarily considers human mobility—in this case, the producers and consumers who support Japanese restaurants. These people also enable the mobilities of such objects as foodstuffs and interior design elements found in restaurants. Mobilities scholarship emphasizes the diverse patterns of people moving across borders. Patterns in this book include colonial migration, settler migration, business expatriation, transnational culinary career-making, circular migration, and rural-to-urban labor migration. We also focus on the short-term mobilities of chefs, critics, corporate trainers, and investors who hop from city to city, including usually brief but symbolically necessary culinary pilgrimages to Japan. These mobilities convey capital, political power, and culinary authority as they create global culinary infrastructure for Japanese restaurants.[24]

The mobilities of people in restaurant work can be labeled culinary migration.[25] The history of culinary migrations in Japanese cuisine parallels the shifting of central food cities, as described earlier, from Japanese colonial capitals and overseas migrant communities to culinary global cities, such as New York and Los Angeles. Before the 1980s, most Japanese restaurants around the world were operated by Japanese restaurateurs, were headed by Japanese chefs, and catered primarily to Japanese migrants. In these contexts, chefs used ingredients imported from Japan or local substitutes, laying the basis for such fusions as Peruvian Nikkei cuisine and the California roll. Some of these fusions appealed to non-Japanese customers, greatly expanding the market for Japanese cuisine. From the 1980s, non-Japanese actors became preponderant in all aspects of Japanese restaurants, including ownership, cooking, supply chain, and patronage. Our research traces the growing importance of global cities outside Japan as nodes of this culinary innovation and the role of non-Japanese ethnic networks in bringing Japanese dishes to smaller cities and even rural towns.[26]

The second concept is "culinary imaginaries." Broadly speaking, cuisines have come to be labeled in national (or sometimes regional and ethnic) terms as the association of particular tastes, ingredients, dishes, drinks, and etiquette with the people seen as living in a specific nationally defined space.[27] However, as argued by Arjun Appadurai in his study of cuisine in India, national cuisines are largely invented traditions. While Appadurai highlights the cookbook as the key marker of this national cuisine, one could also identify restaurants as the key modern institution conveying associations of certain dishes and dining etiquette with national identities.[28]

To explain globalizing cuisines as culinary imaginaries, we employ such concepts as "deterritorialization," "reterritorialization," and "hybridization." They describe ideas and products being detached from the places they are commonly associated with (deterritorialization) and manifested

FIGURE 1.1 Playing on European images of Japan and Asia, Kamikaze Sushi in Düsseldorf is a fashionable fast-service sushi restaurant opened by Vietnamese German restaurateur Tri Nyugen. Born in Germany, Nyugen appeals to a young urban clientele with the name "Kamikaze," a bold interior design, and the slogan "Japanese food for the brave!" His menu features spicy sushi rolls that deviate from the more traditional offerings in Japanese-owned restaurants in the city. (Photo by James Farrer, August 17, 2017)

elsewhere in new and surprising guises and meanings, including national ones (reterritorialization and hybridization).[29] Thus, restaurant cuisines in global cities may be identified with distant territories and nations, couched in the rhetoric of "authenticity." Japanese and other nationally defined cuisines are culinary practices that have been deterritorialized from households and face-to-face communities and reterritorialized in urban centers as "foreign" or "ethnic" cuisines on restaurant menus.[30] This process makes the global accessible to locals and the foreign familiar.[31]

Through the naming, tastes, and aesthetics of the dishes; the style of service; the décor and atmosphere; and staff behavior, restaurants produce such varied images of Japan as traditional, hip, exotic, Asian, rustic, ubermodern, healthy, clean, or efficient.[32] The investigation of imaginaries also brings us into the kitchen—a culinary contact zone where chefs and staff, increasingly of different backgrounds and ethnicities, exchange skills and ideas to produce food dishes that they present as "Japanese."[33] We are less concerned about how these dishes relate to what is actually found in Japan than about the imaginaries of "Japan" produced through them. While some imaginaries may be adaptations to consumers' expectations in particular locales, others are global imaginaries that appeal to consumers around the world, such as an *izakaya* in Berlin modeled on one in New York, itself modeled on one in Tokyo.

A central conveyer of these culinary imaginaries are the restaurant workers, particularly those directly facing the customers. Seen in a comparative context, Japanese eateries in the nineteenth century featured female servers, and also entertainers and sex workers, at a time when waitresses were a relative novelty in China, Europe, and the United States.[34] The Japanese café waitress became an iconic figure in the early twentieth century, and her eroticized interactions with male patrons were part of the popular fascination with these spaces both inside Japan and as they expanded overseas, particularly in Asia.[35] To be clear, by the twentieth century the sexualized waitress was not only a Japanese phenomenon, as seen in Frances Donovan's pioneering ethnography of waitresses in Chicago in the late 1910s. Donovan shows how these women, often rural-to-urban migrants, actively constructed their sexual personae through what she calls the "sex game" of exchanging flirtations and intimacies for tips and gifts.[36] Waitresses in "native costume" were marketed as a central attraction of foreign-themed restaurants that became popular in the United States in the 1920s and 30s.[37] Our story of the globalization of Japanese restaurants similarly shows the important role of female servers and entertainers in producing the atmosphere of the Japanese restaurant, especially in the early twentieth century. It also shows male servers and cooks performing masculinized and racialized displays of culinary skill, such as the knife-wielding hibachi chef. The restaurant worker, whether male or female, thus embodies and performs a gendered, racialized, and sexualized imaginary of the restaurant.

The third analytic concept is "culinary politics." From pop music to fashion, as a cultural phenomenon expands its geographic scope, struggles ensue over influence, boundaries, definitions, and social organization. There are conflicts over who has managerial authority and status within a cultural field and who lacks authority or is excluded from it—in other words, the "ownership" of a cultural product.[38] Regarding restaurant cuisine, recipes or restaurant concepts cannot easily be registered as intellectual property. Therefore, contestation happens in the space of public opinion. Contents often center on claims of "authenticity," a code word for battles over

FIGURE 1.2 Geishas drink with guests at a garden party at the Shanghai restaurant Roku-san Garden on August 22, 1940. The restaurant employed over sixty women as geishas. See Chapter 2 for more details. (Time/Life Inc.)

culinary ownership and authority, especially with a cuisine traveling beyond its "national" territory. Appadurai writes, "Authenticity is typically not the concern of the native participants in a culinary tradition, except when they (and the food) are far from home. It generally arises in the context of export, tourism, gourmandize, and exoticism. The concern with authenticity indicates some sort of doubt, and this sort of doubt is rarely part of the discourse of an undisturbed culinary tradition. It is the problem of the outsider."[39]

This ongoing concern with authenticity underscores the inherent tension in a globalized "national" cuisine.[40] As Japanese restaurants open around the world, they engender various questions and struggles in their new locations. Who defines the cuisine? Who gets to open a restaurant in a city or country? Whose cooking represents the highest levels of a cuisine? Who gets resources for expanding a restaurant business? In our analysis, answers to these questions lay in such varied factors as market competition, strategies of the Japanese state, and ethnic and racial stereotypes.

The primary arena of culinary politics is market competition. This includes mobilization and exploitation within ethnic communities of capital and cheap labor, competing claims of authenticity and status, ties to government officials for access to land and licenses, and urban gentrification and displacement. Market competition also occurs among chefs, consumers, and restaurant critics (both professional and self-styled) through negotiation and contestation over what is good food, the requisite skills to cook it, the standards of evaluation, and the price consumers pay for such distinctions. Producers of reterritorialized cuisines define and defend the authenticity of their foreign-sounding menus even while pragmatically localizing the dishes in terms of ingredients and taste. This often engenders a culinary identity politics fraught with cultural essentialism and ethnic and racial stereotyping.[41]

A prominent arena of this competition is the culinary field centered on fine dining restaurants where chefs vie for such accolades as Michelin stars and a place on the World's 50 Best Restaurants list. This is market competition, though with ultra-thin profit margins in fine dining, status seems more the issue. In the twenty-first century, a symbiosis of highly mobile star chefs and economic "one-percenters" (including customers and investors in restaurants) has propelled Japanese cuisine, or Japanese-inspired cuisine, to the lofty heights of fine dining once monopolized by French cuisine. This, in turn, addresses perhaps the most perplexing question regarding culinary globalization—namely, why some cuisines are more fashionable than others.[42]

International relations are a further arena of culinary politics. In the early twentieth century, the Japanese imperial state expressed its modernity and, therefore, the superiority of Japan through hybridized Japanese-Western food served in modern restaurants in the capital cities of its colonies. Then, decades later, Japanese restaurants became targets of the postcolonial politics of anti-imperialism in Asia, seen in attacks on Japanese restaurants in China and Korea. In the twenty-first century, the Japanese state has sought to exert control over the imaginary of its cuisine worldwide for the purposes of soft power, gastro-diplomacy, and culinary nation branding.[43] We also see actions by states that, while not directly concerned with cuisine, have dramatically affected it. An example is the internment of Japanese descendants in North America during World War II, which dispersed residents of the large Japantowns on the West Coast, setting in motion new culinary trends. To tie these all together, culinary mobilities produce global imaginaries, which are the focus of culinary politics, but the relationships may also be more complex than that, as seen throughout the book.

Collaborative Fieldwork and Writing

This book was jointly researched by its six author-researchers, all of whom were involved in writing multiple chapters. To investigate restaurants across time and space, we adopted a mixed-method multisited research design. One method was archival research, including newspaper accounts and reviews, memoirs, menus, and photographs, as well as such online documents as blogs, corporate websites, and restaurant review websites. We accessed archives in China, the United States, Germany, and Japan, and internet resources, particularly those created by overseas Japanese community historians. Menu collections, though fragmentary, gave a sense of the dishes available at certain times. For contemporary restaurants, online reviewing sites gave insights into customer authenticity claims. Of course, for a book with a view encompassing the globe over 150 years, we drew on the findings of other scholars, particularly for histories of Japanese communities in different cities.

The other method was fieldwork, including observation, participant observation, and multiple forms of interview (ethnographic, informational, casual). Each of the core researchers (the six authors) used various combinations of the two methods, sometimes with the aid of research assistants. We conducted fieldwork in North America (primarily the United States), South America (primarily Brazil), Europe (primarily Britain, Czechia, Denmark, France, Germany, Italy, and Ukraine), Asia (primarily China, Japan, Philippines, Sri Lanka, Taiwan, and Vietnam), Africa (primarily Kenya), and Australia.[44] Some crucial places for overseas Japanese cuisine (such as Hawai'i and Peru) are underrepresented, but given the broad scope of the study, the coverage of any given place is limited; our goal was to produce a global account rather than local case studies.

The fieldwork on restaurants was conducted from 2010 to 2020. In selecting restaurants to research in a location, we used various criteria, including the oldest, most popular, and most highly rated in the media, as well as those that informants identified as locally significant. In small towns in North America and Europe and large cities in lower-income countries with only a few Japanese restaurants, it was possible to visit almost all establishments. In larger cities, such as Paris or Hanoi, it was possible to visit a concentration of restaurants in specific districts over a relatively short time. In key cities in this book, including Asheville, North Carolina; Berlin; Colombo; Düsseldorf; Kyiv; Lancaster, Pennsylvania; London; Melbourne;

New York City; Paris; Prague; San Francisco; São Paulo; Shanghai; Tianjin; and Tokyo, fieldwork involved extensive interactions with the Japanese restaurant community over several weeks or months. In every locale, the sample combines elements of scientific selection and opportunism. A typical research visit to a restaurant began by investigating it online, then exploring the neighborhood, and finally visiting for a meal. While dining, we observed the menu, décor, customers, and service staff, taking notes and photos. The best time for a visit was the slower afternoon time between lunch and dinner, when we could talk at length with the service staff. Interviews ranged from chatting with the service people or the sushi chef while sitting at the bar to more formal sit-down interviews with staff, including owners and managers. In addition, we interviewed three other groups related to the global Japanese restaurant industry. One was Japanese government officials and businesspeople involved in research and the food industry. A second group was members of Japanese overseas communities, including local researchers, about the history and role of restaurants in these communities. Finally, we interviewed local food writers and ordinary consumers about their impressions and dining experiences.[45]

The data analysis and manuscript preparation were also a group effort involving all core researchers. Several steps were taken to ensure the sharing and integration of the data among project members. First, all data, including transcripts, notes, and online sources, were held in a single online data site accessible to all authors. Second, we held periodic workshops where the six authors and student research assistants presented research findings. Third, we jointly presented our research in progress in public presentations and scholarly articles. These measures enabled the authors to develop shared concerns that are expressed in the book's narrative. Thus, we consider it a jointly written work, with different authors taking the lead on specific chapters.

Organization of the Book

To craft a narrative consistent with our global perspective, we center each chapter on the matrix of culinary mobilities, imaginaries, and politics associated with a specific historical process (colonialism, settler migration, transnational business expansion, culinary fashions, etc.). The chapters are in rough chronological order, although each chapter traces its process up to the present (2022) to the extent possible. The early chapters start in the late nineteenth century, while the later chapters have more recent starting points. Though each chapter can be read on its own, their sequence is a history of how Japanese restaurants have been conveyed to all corners of the modern world. The mobilities, imaginaries, and politics described in earlier chapters constitute forms of the global Japanese restaurant that open up possibilities for innovations described in subsequent chapters.

The first three chapters (2, 3, 4) start from the nineteenth century and, perforce, describe the earliest Japanese actors bringing Japanese restaurants into the world. Chapter 2 describes the emergence of Japanese restaurant scenes in colonial cities of Japan's East Asian empire and their subsequent reevaluation in postcolonial China, Korea, and Taiwan. Chapter 3 focuses on the restaurants created by Japanese migrants from the early twentieth century in settler and expatriate enclaves in the Americas, Europe, and Southeast Asia and their transformation into touristic culinary districts in recent years. Chapter 4 is centered in major culinary global cities and describes successive global culinary fashions from the nineteenth to the twenty-first century that conveyed Japanese restaurant forms—tearooms, sukiyaki houses, teriyaki steak houses, sushi bars, ramen shops—far beyond Japanese migrant enclaves. Their promoters were cultural intermediaries, especially journalists and food writers, as well as Japanese restaurateurs, waitresses, and front house managers, who translated Japanese cuisine to foreigners.

The next four chapters (5, 6, 7, 8) start from the mid-twentieth century and later, describing the mobile actors—mostly migrants and corporations—who have significantly enlarged the presence of Japanese restaurants in the world. Chapter 5 describes migrants of other ethnicities, often Asian, who, beginning in the United States in the 1980s, established individually owned restaurants with sushi-roll-centered menus that vastly expanded the consumer market for Japanese cuisine. Chapter 6 examines the corporatized fast-food chains that, by the twenty-first century, had displaced individually owned restaurants as the driving force of the global Japanese restaurant industry. Chapter 7 considers one of the fastest-growing and most intriguing Japanese restaurant forms, the *izakaya*, with a media-driven culinary imaginary spreading through manga, television series, and social media. Chapter 8 describes the globalization of innovative Japanese fine dining in the twenty-first century driven by highly skilled chefs in a few global cities, notably Hong Kong, New York, Paris, São Paulo, and Tokyo.

Chapter 9 concludes by directly engaging the conceptual question running through the book: How is a national cuisine manifested in an increasingly globalized modern world? Here we consider the broader implications of the preceding chapters. A central finding is that the globally popular Japanese cuisine is increasingly created in restaurants around the world by people of many nationalities. This incorporation of Japanese cuisine into global society has not been a linear process but rather an emergent one over 150 years, as argued in every chapter of this book. We end by considering how the COVID-19 pandemic of 2020 may be affecting the global Japanese restaurant.

Notes

1. Saitō Moto (斎藤もと), *Nyūyōku no koinobori* (ニューヨークの鯉のぼり) [A carp flag in New York] (Tokyo: PHP Press, 1988). We use the English spelling of Saito's surname in this book, since this is what she used in her life in New York. As explained in the acknowledgments names in this book are written in the English naming order with surnames last.

2. Saitō, 87–148.

3. Saitō, 55–56.

4. Saitō, 149–217.

5. James Farrer and Chuanfei Wang, "Who Owns a Cuisine? The Grassroots Politics of Japanese Food in Europe," *Asian Anthropology* 20, no. 1 (2021): 12–29.

6. In Chapter 9, we discuss how innovation has come to be regarded itself as a marker of an authentic restaurant experience.

7. Although the term "restaurant" originates in the West, we adopt it generically to refer to eateries with menus, service, and seating, introducing particular Japanese forms of restaurants when they arise in the narrative. For a similarly encompassing use of the term "restaurant," see Katie Rawson and Elliott Shore, *Dining Out: A Global History of Restaurants* (London: Reaktion Books, 2019).

8. David Beriss and David Sutton, "Restaurants, Ideal Postmodern Institutions," in *The Restaurants Book: Ethnographies of Where We Eat,* ed. David Beriss and David Sutton (Oxford: Berg, 2007), 1–13; Gary Alan Fine, *Kitchens: The Culture of Restaurant Work* (Berkeley: University of California Press, 1996); Paul Freedman, *Ten Restaurants That Changed America* (New York: Liveright, 2016); Christel Lane, *The Cultivation of Taste: Chefs and the Organization of Fine Dining* (Oxford: Oxford University Press, 2014); Vanina Leschziner, *At the Chef's Table: Culinary Creativity in Elite Restaurants* (Stanford, CA: Stanford University Press, 2015); Alan Warde and Lydia Martens, *Eating Out: Social Differentiation, Consumption and Pleasure* (Cambridge: Cambridge University Press, 2000).

9. Priscilla Parkhurst Ferguson, "A Cultural Field in the Making: Gastronomy in 19th-Century France," *American Journal of Sociology* 104, no. 3 (1998): 597–641; Rebecca Spang, *The Invention of the Restaurant: Paris and Modern Gastronomic Culture,*

2nd ed. (Cambridge, MA: Harvard University Press, 2020); Amy B. Trubek, *Haute Cuisine: How the French Invented the Culinary Profession* (Philadelphia: University of Pennsylvania Press, 2000).

10. Some studies that take a broader scope are Bruce Makoto Arnold, Tanfer Emin Tunç, and Raymond Douglas Chong, eds., *Chop Suey and Sushi from Sea to Shining Sea: Chinese and Japanese Restaurants in the United States* (Little Rock: University of Arkansas Press, 2018); and Rawson and Shore, *Dining Out*.

11. This worldwide spread of Japanese cuisine is reflected in statistics compiled by the Japanese government on Japanese restaurants. In 2006, there were 24,000 outside Japan, a number that grew sevenfold to 156,000 by 2019. Ministry of Agriculture, Forestry and Fisheries, "Kaigai ni okeru nihon shoku resutoran no kazu" (海外における日本食レストランの数) [The number of Japanese restaurants abroad], 2019, http://www .maff.go.jp/j/press/shokusan/service/191213.html.

12. Katarzyna Joanna Cwiertka, *Modern Japanese Cuisine: Food, Power and National Identity* (London: Reaktion Books, 2006); Barak Kushner, *Slurp! A Social and Culinary History of Ramen—Japan's Favorite Noodle Soup* (London: Global Oriental, 2012); Eric C. Rath, *Japan's Cuisines: Food, Place and Identity* (London: Reaktion Books, 2016); Eric C. Rath, *Oishii: The History of Sushi* (London: Reaktion Books, 2021); George Solt, *The Untold History of Ramen: How Political Crisis in Japan Spawned a Global Food Craze* (Berkeley: University of California Press, 2014).

13. Katarzyna J. Cwiertka, "Eating the Homeland: Japanese Expatriates in the Netherlands," in *Asian Food: The Global and the Local,* ed. Katarzyna J. Cwiertka and Boudewijn C. C. Walraven (Abingdon, UK: Routledge, 2015), 133–152; Katarzyna J. Cwiertka, "From Ethnic to Hip: Circuits of Japanese Cuisine in Europe," *Food and Foodways: Explorations in the History and Culture of Human Nourishment* 13, no. 4 (2006): 241–272; Ikezawa Yasushi (池澤康), *Amerika nihonshoku uōzu* (アメリカ日本食ウォーズ) [American Japanese food wars] (Tokyo: Toshibaya, 2005); Ishige Naomichi (石毛直道) et al., *Rosuanjerusu no nihon ryōriten—sono bunka jinruigakuteki kenkyū* (ロスアンジェルスの日本料理店―その文化人類学的研究) [Japanese restaurants in Los Angeles—an anthropological research] (Tokyo: Domesu, 1985); Sasha Issenberg, *The Sushi Economy: Globalization and the Making of a Modern Delicacy* (New York: Penguin, 2007); Iwama Kazuhiro (岩間一弘), "Shanghai no nihonshokubunka: Menyū no genchika ni kansuru hiaringu chōsa hōkoku" (上海の日本食文化：メニューの現地化に関するヒアリング調査報告) [Shanghai's Japanese food culture: A hearing survey report of menu localization], *Chiba shōdai kiyō* 51, no. 1 (2013): 1–54; Kawabata Motoo (川端基夫), *Gaishoku kokusaika no dainamizumu: Atarashii "ekkyō no katachi"* (外食国際化のダイナミズム: 新しい "越境のかたち") [The dynamism of the internationalization of the restaurant industry: The new "pattern of transnationalism"] (Tokyo: Shinhyoron, 2016), 138–148; Sandra Keßler, "Japanisch, exotisch, kosmopolitisch, modern: Sushi als Global Food in Deutschland" [Japanese, exotic, cosmopolitan, modern: Sushi as global food in Germany], in *Interkulturalität und Alltag* [Interculturality and the everyday], ed. Judith Schmidt, Sandra Keßler, and Michael Simon (Münster: Waxmann, 2012), 148–161; Isao Kumakura, "The Globalization of Japanese Food Culture," *Food Culture* 1 (2000): 7–8; Dorothea Mladenova, "Sushi global: Zwischen J-branding und kulinarischem Nationalismus" [Sushi global: Between J-branding and culinary nationalism], in *Japan: Politik, Wirtschaft und Gesellschaft* [Japan: Politics, economy and society], ed. David Chiavacci and Iris Wieczorek (Berlin: Vereinigung für sozialwissenschaftliche

Japanforschung, 2013), 275–297; Lynn Nakano, "Eating One's Way to Sophistication: Japanese Food, Transnational Flows, and Social Mobility in Hong Kong," in *Transnational Trajectories in East Asia: Nation, Citizenship, and Region,* ed. Yasemin N. Soysal (Abingdon, UK: Routledge, 2014), 106–129; Wai-Ming Ng, "Popularization and Localization of Sushi in Singapore: An Ethnographic Survey," *New Zealand Journal of Asian Studies* 3, no. 1 (2001): 7–19; Nancy K. Stalker, "Introduction: Japanese Culinary Capital," in *Devouring Japan: Global Perspectives on Japanese Culinary Identity,* ed. Nancy K. Stalker (Oxford: Oxford University Press, 2018), 1–31; Noboru Toyoshima, "Japanese Restaurants in Thailand: Dining in the Ambience of Japanese Culture," *Journal of Asia-Pacific Studies* 19 (2013): 279–296; Christine R. Yano, "Side-Dish Kitchen," in Beriss and Sutton, *Restaurants Book,* 47–64.

14. Iino Ryōichi (飯野亮一), *Izakaya no tanjō: Edo no nomidaore bunka* (居酒屋の誕生: 江戸の呑みだおれ文化) [Birth of the *izakaya*: Edo's drinking culture] (Tokyo: Sakuma shobo, 2014), 16. For the history of the emergence of specific types of Japanese restaurants, see Okubo Hiroko (大久保洋子), *Edo no shoku kūkan—Yatai kara nihonryōri e* (江戸の食空間— 屋台から日本料理へ) [The eating spaces of Edo—from street stalls to Japanese cuisine] (Tokyo: Kodansha, 2012).

15. Spang, *Invention of the Restaurant;* Rawson and Shore, *Dining Out.*

16. These are discussed in Chapter 6.

17. See Saskia Sassen, *Global City: New York, London, Tokyo* (Princeton, NJ: Princeton University Press, 1991); and Saskia Sassen, "The Global City: Introducing a Concept," *Brown Journal of World Affairs* 11, no. 2 (2005): 27–43.

18. For evidence of how culinary creativity builds on the agglomeration effects of cities, see Leschziner, *At the Chef's Table.* For a discussion of the importance of transnational mobility in the careers of chefs, see James Farrer, "From Cooks to Chefs: Skilled Migrants in a Globalising Culinary Field," *Journal of Ethnic and Migration Studies* 47, no. 10 (2021): 2359–2375. For a discussion of agglomeration effects in urban culinary infrastructure see Jeffrey M. Pilcher, "Culinary Infrastructure: How Facilities and Technologies Create Value and Meaning Around Food." *Global Food History* 2, no. 2 (2016): 118.

19. Watson Baldwin, "The Restauranteurship of Hong Kong's Premium Japanese Restaurant Market," *International Hospitality Review* 32, no. 1 (2018): 8–25.

20. Tripadvisor.com, accessed August 13, 2021.

21. Dianping.com, accessed February 14, 2021. Note that these numbers are calculated differently by different websites, so they are not comparable.

22. Saskia Sassen, "Researching the Localizations of the Global," in *The Oxford Handbook of Global Studies,* ed. Mark Juergensmeyer, Saskia Sassen, and Manfred Steger (New York: Oxford University Press, 2018), 74.

23. See Sassen, *Global City.*

24. The "mobilities" label originates with John Urry, *Sociology beyond Societies: Mobilities for the Twenty-First Century* (Abingdon, UK: Routledge, 2012). We outline our ideas of "culinary mobilities" in James Farrer et al., "Japanese Culinary Mobilities: The Multiple Globalizations of Japanese Cuisine," in *Routledge Handbook of Food in Asia,* ed. Cecilia Leong-Salobir (Abingdon, UK: Routledge, 2019), 39–57.

25. See Farrer, "From Cooks to Chefs."

26. David L. Wank and James Farrer, "Chinese Immigrants and Japanese Cuisine in the United States: A Case of Culinary Glocalization," in *The Globalization of Asian Cuisines: Transnational Networks and Culinary Contact Zones,* ed. James Farrer (New York: Palgrave Macmillan, 2015), 79–99.

27. The concept of the "culinary imaginary" was developed by Jean Duruz in relation to food and travel writing. See Jean Duruz, "Adventuring and Belonging: An Appetite for Markets," *Space and Culture* 7, no. 4 (2004): 427–445; and Jean Duruz, "The Travels of Kitty's Love Cake: A Tale of Spices, 'Asian' Flavors, and Cuisine Sans Frontières?," in Farrer, *Globalization of Asian Cuisines,* 37–56. For discussion of the restaurant as a deterritorialized global imaginary, see Bill Grantham, "Craic in a Box: Commodifying and Exporting the Irish Pub," *Continuum* 23, no. 2 (2009): 257–267.

28. Arjun Appadurai, "How to Make a National Cuisine: Cookbooks in Contemporary India," *Comparative Studies in Society and History* 30, no. 1 (1988): 3–24.

29. John Tomlinson, *Globalization and Culture* (Chicago: University of Chicago Press, 1999); Ulf Hannerz, *Cultural Complexity: Studies in the Complexity of Meaning* (New York: Columbia University Press, 1993).

30. James Farrer, "Introduction: Travelling Cuisines in and out of Asia: Towards a Framework for Studying Culinary Globalization," in Farrer, *Globalization of Asian Cuisines,* 1–20.

31. Shun Lu and Gary Alan Fine, "The Presentation of Ethnic Authenticity: Chinese Food as a Social Accomplishment," *Sociological Quarterly* 36, no. 3 (1995): 535–553; Krishnendu Ray, *The Ethnic Restaurateur* (New York: Bloomsbury, 2016).

32. Cwiertka, "Eating the Homeland"; Irmela Hijiya-Kirschnereit, "Das Sushi-Sakrileg: Zur Verbreitung von Sushi in Mitteleuropa" [The sushi sacrilege: The spread of sushi in Central Europe], *Jahrbuch für Kulinaristik* 2 (2018): 134–165.

33. Farrer, "Introduction."

34. Rawson and Shore, *Dining Out,* 149–155, 161.

35. Elise K. Tipton, "Pink Collar Work: The Café Waitress in Early Twentieth Century Japan," *Intersections: Gender, History and Culture in the Asian Context,* no. 7 (2002), http://intersections.anu.edu.au/issue7/tipton.html.

36. Frances R. Donovan, *The Woman Who Waits* (Boston: Richard G. Badger, 1920), 211–220.

37. Audrey Russek, "Appetites Without Prejudice: U.S. Foreign Restaurants and the Globalization of American Food Between the Wars," *Food and Foodways* 19, no. 1–2 (2011): 34–55.

38. Farrer and Wang, "Who Owns a Cuisine?"

39. Arjun Appadurai, "On Culinary Authenticity," *Anthropology Today* 2 (1986): 25.

40. For discussions of the politics of national cuisines, see Atsuko Ichijo, Venetia Johannes, and Ronald Ranta, eds., *The Emergence of National Food: The Dynamics of Food and Nationalism* (New York: Bloomsbury, 2019); and Michelle King, ed., *Culinary Nationalism in Asia* (London: Bloomsbury Academic, 2019).

41. Hirose Akihiko and Kay Kei-Ho Pih, "'No Asians Working Here': Racialized Otherness and Authenticity in Gastronomical Orientalism," *Ethnic and Racial Studies* 34, no. 9 (2011): 1482–1501; Robert Ji-Song Ku, *Dubious Gastronomy: The Cultural Politics of Eating Asian in the USA* (Honolulu: University of Hawai'i Press, 2013).

42. See Ray, *Ethnic Restaurateur.* We address this issue in Chapters 4 and 5.

43. For "culinary soft power," see James Farrer, "Eating the West and Beating the Rest: Culinary Occidentalism and Urban Soft Power in Asia's Global Food Cities," in *Globalization, Food and Social Identities in the Asia Pacific Region,* ed. James Farrer (Tokyo: Sophia University Institute of Comparative Culture, 2010), 128–149; and Stephanie Assmann, "Global Engagement for Local and Indigenous Tastes: Culinary Globalization in East Asia," *Gastronomica* 17, no. 3 (2017): 1–3. For the related idea of

gastrodiplomacy, see Felice Farina, "Japan's Gastrodiplomacy as Soft Power: Global Washoku and National Food Security," *Journal of Contemporary Eastern Asia* 17, no. 1 (2018): 131–146; Theodore C. Bestor, "Most F(l)avored Nation Status: The Gastrodiplomacy of Japan's Global Promotion of Cuisine," *Public Diplomacy Magazine* 11 (2014): 57–60. For nation branding, see Katarzyna Joanna Cwiertka and Yasuhara Miho, *Branding Japanese Food: From Meibutsu to Washoku* (Honolulu: University of Hawai'i Press, 2020).

44. Interviews in some places (particularly Indonesia, Korea, Kenya, Mozambique, and Sri Lanka) were conducted primarily by research assistants. The research languages of core researchers included Chinese, Czech, English, French, German, Japanese, Portuguese, Russian, Spanish, and Ukrainian, while the research assistants contributed Danish, Indonesian, Korean, Sinhalese, Tagalog, Swahili, and Vietnamese.

45. For each restaurant, we asked three sorts of questions. One addressed the history and background of the restaurant and its owners, chefs, and other staff members. A second concerned the food offerings, including the menu and key dishes. A third focused on the operation of the restaurants, including customers, suppliers, operating hours, special features, and so forth. We also engaged in more general discussions concerning competition in the Japanese cuisine sector, long-term plans, and so on. After a research trip, we organized our notes and transcribed interviews.

2 | Imperialism and Its Culinary Legacies

Japanese Restaurants in East Asia

CHUANFEI WANG, JAMES FARRER,
AND CHRISTIAN A. HESS

J apanese restaurants first appeared outside Japan in East Asia, stimulating the most multifaceted culinary imaginaries and contentious culinary politics described in this book. This is intimately bound up with the colonial expansion of the Empire of Japan from the late nineteenth century until its disintegration in 1945 after World War II. During this period a modernized restaurant sector was among the many institutions that the Japanese created in the capital cities of their East Asian colonies—Taiwan, Korea, Manchuria—and their colonial-style concessions in cities on China's coast. The sector included the many varieties of restaurants also found in Japan during the same period, serving both traditional Japanese and new Japanese-Western cuisine (*yōshoku*). In the colonial capitals and concessions, Japanese restaurants were located in prestigious or central urban venues, making them highly visible symbols of Japanese imperial power and spaces of politics and business. Initially catering to Japanese colonists, they soon attracted diners from local middle and upper classes eager to experience modern urban culture. This embedding of Japanese restaurants and foodways among the colonized populations made them flashpoints of postcolonial politics in the successor states of Japan's overseas empire.

The four sections of this chapter trace the vicissitudes of Japanese restaurants in the colonial possessions and their successor states, with the first two encompassing the colonial period (1868–1945), and the last two concerning the postcolonial era (1945–). The focus is on the colonial cities of Taipei, Dalian, and Seoul and the concession areas of Shanghai and Tianjin.

21

Then as now, these cities had large numbers of Japanese restaurants. The first section shows how Japanese colonial restaurant scenes in these cities grew along with empire-building activities. The second section presents case studies of Japanese restaurants in Shanghai, and the rising anti-Japanese sentiment that targeted them. The third section examines the development of Japanese restaurants in these cities after 1945. The fourth section focuses on postcolonial culinary politics linked to competition among East Asian states since the late twentieth century.

Culinary Imperialism: Japanese Restaurants in Colonial Cities, 1870s–1945

The Japanese empire, more than just a political-economic endeavor, was a modernizing project that aimed to convey new ways of urban life from Japan, including restaurants, to "backward" colonies.[1] As in European colonies, imperialism proceeded through the coercive transmission of modern institutions—urban planning, transportation, sanitation, schools, bureaucratic administration, and commercial districts—imitating those recently created in Japanese cities.[2] A distinguishing characteristic of Japan's East Asian colonies in comparison with European ones was the far larger presence of colonizers relative to the local populations. In 1920 in Korea and Taiwan, Japanese were 2.5 and 4 percent of their respective populations, in contrast to the Dutch East Indies and British India, where European settlers were only about 0.01 to 0.03 percent of the population.[3] Furthermore, Japanese administrators, entrepreneurs, and settlers were more likely to bring their families and live in cities.[4] In 1920, Japanese residents represented 29 percent of the population of Korean cities, and by 1930, the thirty thousand Japanese residents in Shanghai's International Settlement far outnumbered Europeans and Americans.[5] These Japanese populations were large enough to support modern Japanese urban entertainment districts, including restaurants replicating those in Japan at the time. While created for the Japanese community, the restaurants served many local people, especially rising urban elites.

While cuisine was not imposed on colonial subjects in the way that language and government were, restaurants were closely associated with Japan's imperial expansion. They occupied all economic rungs, from high-class restaurants in hotels and department stores to family-run establishments in Japanese shopping areas to smaller cafés and bars in red-light districts. The earliest were small eateries often involving drinking and prostitution that were founded in the late 1880s. Throughout the colonial period, restaurants emphasized female servers and entertainers, including trained geishas, who were featured in contemporary Japanese tour guidebooks and celebrated in the Japanese and even local language media. The Japanese women who worked in these establishments, though exploited in the sex trade, thus were key cultural intermediaries establishing Japanese restaurants as an urban fashion. They became central figures in the culinary imaginaries associated with Japan.

Japanese also built luxurious modern restaurants in hotels in cities throughout the empire. Typically located near Japanese-built highways and railway stations, they enabled Japanese travelers in the colonies to experience a mix of the familiar and the exotic.[6] There were even guidebooks on the Japanese empire written for Western tourists, underscoring the degree to which both Japanese dishes and Japanese-Western cuisine (*yōshoku*) were already known among non-Japanese travelers by the early twentieth century. For example, a guidebook written by the Japan Department of Railways for English-speaking tourists praised the Yamato Hotel in Dalian as the only one regularly serving European meals.[7] It also mentioned several independent restaurants in the city, "noted for their excellent cuisine in pure Japanese style."[8] Another guidebook in English touted the Yamato hotel chain, owned by the South Manchuria Railway Company, in Manchurian cities. "The excellent Yamato Hotel is a link in a chain of hotels operated in Manchuria by the S.M.R. Railway Company, is conducted along American lines, and is recommended."[9]

In Seoul, the Sontag and Chosen Hotels, the leading Westernized hotels, were patronized by Japanese travelers and served Western and Japanese meals.[10] During this period, Japanese shipping and railway restaurants were also major purveyors of Western and Japanese cuisine, ranging from high-end sukiyaki and French cuisine on transpacific passenger ships to more mundane fare on railway restaurant cars.[11] For example, a trilingual Japanese-Chinese-English menu from the Manchurian Railway published around 1940 offered Japanese Western-style dishes, such as beef and pork cutlet, curry rice, and *oyako-donburi* (chicken and egg rice bowl), alongside coffee, cake, pickles, and steamed rice. In this way, restaurants of the

FIGURE 2.1 A wartime menu (1939–1942) from the dining car of the Japanese-run Manchurian railway asks diners to practice self-restraint in consumption to support Japanese soldiers. ("Kōa hōkōbi Lunch Menu in the Mantetsu Dining Car," Rare Book Division, New York Public Library Digital Collections)

Japanese empire promulgated not only new versions of Japanese cuisine but also Japanese versions of European foods and beverages that became an important culinary legacy in East Asia.[12]

Another key venue for modern restaurants was the department store. An example is the Mitsukoshi Department Store, Japan's first department store, established in Tokyo in 1904, which opened branches in Seoul in the 1920s and the 1930s. These branches featured restaurants serving Japanese-style Western dishes, such as curry, salads, and cutlets, to over a thousand customers daily. By the 1930s, eating in Japanese restaurants and Japanese-style Western restaurants was part of the daily life of middle-class urban Koreans. As in Japan, these restaurants often served a variety of Japanese, Western, and Chinese dishes.[13]

The rest of this section offers an overview of Japanese restaurants in this region. Our primary data are memoirs and guidebooks from the early 1900s to the 1940s; Chinese and English newspaper reports, especially from Shanghai archives; and a few surviving menus in public and private collections. This overview illustrates how Japanese restaurant scenes were a key feature of Japan's colonial cities in East Asia, as seen in Seoul, Tianjin, Dalian, and Taipei (Shanghai is covered in a separate section). These cities had different positions in the Japanese empire. Seoul and Taipei were colonial capitals. Dalian was a directly administered city, while Japanese controlled concession areas in Tianjin. Despite their different administrative statuses, they shared a common development as Japanese urban centers. We thus use case studies of these four cities to introduce common features of the Japanese restaurant scenes that developed in cities throughout the empire.

Shaping the Modern Urban Foodscape in Seoul

Korea was Japan's first imperialist venture, and its foodways were profoundly affected by colonialism. Japanese influences on Korean cuisine began when Japan established its first settlement in Busan in 1876, and Japanese began migrating to Korea, including Seoul, the capital (known as Keijō in Japanese). By the 1880s, *yojeong* (Japanese-style *ryōtei*, fine-dining restaurants) could be found in Seoul in areas where Japanese, Chinese, and other foreigners lived. These *yojeong* featured Japanese foods and alcohol served by Japanese women regarded as sex workers. One restaurant named Hyecheongwan ran a newspaper advertisement touting not only its alcohol, snacks, food, and *janggookbap* (rice in beef soup) but also baths and rooms for assignations. These became known as places where Japanese elites and their Korean associates discussed politics and consorted with prostitutes. In 1895, following the abolition of the hereditary caste of women known as *gisaeng*, many of these Korean entertainers and sex workers also began working at *yojeong*.[14] This pattern of a Japanese restaurant with female servers, sex workers, and entertainers was found throughout the empire.

As early as 1888, there were fourteen Japanese restaurants in the city. During the decade leading up to the annexation of Korea in 1910, the largest of the high-end Japanese restaurants in Seoul was Hwa-wol-ru, with thirty geisha entertainers.[15] All the high-end Japanese restaurants were located in the city center, today's Myeong-dong and Chung-mu-ro areas, where the majority of the Japanese lived and operated businesses.[16] By the 1930s, the Keijō Chamber of Commerce listed ninety-eight Japanese restaurants, including twenty-five eateries specializing in particular dishes, such as sukiyaki, sushi, and udon noodles.[17] These Japanese restaurants introduced dishes to Koreans that were already popular in Japan, such as *tonkatsu* (fried pork cutlets), udon, and soba, as well as Japanese-Chinese dishes, such as *gyōza* (dumplings) and *chanpon* (fried noodles with meat and vegetables).

The growing numbers of Japanese restaurants motivated Japanese entrepreneurs to establish businesses for making and supplying Japanese food ingredients in Korea. Most were small businesses in Japan that expanded to Korea. For example, Japanese entrepreneur Kazuyoshi Doi's food businesses ranged from tofu to poultry to hogs. Between 1907 and 1921, he supplied ingredients to Japanese restaurants and grocers in Seoul, including pork, chicken, tofu, and fruits. Japanese customers viewed the tofu produced in his factory as more hygienic than Korean-made tofu. Other Japanese ran factories producing soy sauce, wheat flour, starch, spirits, and even porcelain.[18] These developments established the foundations of a modern food industry in Korea.

Japanese restaurants also had a profound impact on commercial dining culture in Korea. They stimulated the practice of eating outside the home for pleasure and leisure in modern forms of eateries, including the restaurant, café, cafeteria, and bar. In Seoul, these forms became stratified. At the high end were the *yojeong* with geishas and restaurants situated in hotels and department stores, catering to Japanese expatriates and affluent Koreans. Their menus featured Japanese-style Western dishes, such as curry, salads, and cutlets, as well as Japanese and Chinese dishes.[19] The lower tier comprised mass market eateries, specializing in specific Japanese dishes. In short, Japanese colonial power brought with it a modern and stratified consumer dining scene.[20] Many dishes became popular among Koreans and have featured in Korean restaurant cuisine ever since.

More profoundly, Japanese restaurants shaped the basic tastes of what has come to be considered Korean cuisine.[21] Local foods were flavored by products from Ajinomoto, the Japanese food company. It set up factories in almost all of Japan's major colonies, with some of the earliest in Korea in 1910, thereby introducing industrial food production in the region.[22] The soy sauce they produced was distinguished from the locally made product by a slight sweetness that has been popular among Koreans ever since.[23] Koreans also took a liking to Ajinomoto's monosodium glutamate flavoring and began using it widely for cooking. However, such cultural impositions provoked a decolonizing culinary politics after 1945, as discussed later in the chapter.

Building Japanese Culinary Infrastructure in Tianjin

Japanese culinary imperialism involved the creation of a comprehensive culinary infrastructure that included supplies of labor as well as foodstuffs. This can be seen even in Japanese concession areas in China. Although Tianjin was not a colony, economic activities in the Japanese concession in this important port city in the early twentieth century were controlled by Japanese authorities. Japanese thus were able to build out a sizable restaurant scene supported by a Japanese-dominated culinary infrastructure of suppliers, importers, and labor brokers. Tianjin's Japanese population in the 1890s numbered only forty-eight people.[24] However, it grew rapidly when the First Sino-Japanese War ended in 1895 and a formal Japanese concession was established in Tianjin. A Japanese guidebook from 1901 lists eight Japanese eateries in the most prosperous area of the concession.[25] A decade later, a guidebook from 1912 describes eighteen Japanese restaurants, seven dessert shops, one tofu shop, and two fish shops—all run by Japanese in the concession. Statistics on the Japanese community show that 137 people operated food-related small businesses and thirteen were professional chefs.[26]

Transportation links to Japan were critical in the growth of the settlement and facilitated the migration of culinary labor from Japan. In 1905, a passenger ship route opened between Tianjin and Osaka, and by 1912, Tianjin's Japanese population had grown to 2,189. According to one guidebook for Japanese travelers, in 1912, Akebono-chō (today's Nenjiang Road) had ten Japanese *kaiseki* (formal cuisine) restaurants employing about sixty geishas and seventy waitresses, situated in two-or-three-floor Western-style buildings.[27] Customers paid 120 sen (the smallest unit of currency at the time) per hour as tips (*hanadai*) for each geisha who served them. The Japanese author of the guidebook was amazed by the prosperous scene, exclaiming that Japanese men in Tianjin were more self-indulgent than their counterparts in Japan because the small Japanese population of about two thousand people supported so many entertainment businesses. Beyond the high-end places he introduced in the guidebook, he notes there also were many other, cheaper places providing similar services by women.[28] Such commentary shows that the Japanese restaurant business in Tianjin was inseparable from the activities of female waiters and entertainers serving male travelers and sojourners.

The Japanese population of Tianjin grew steadily, reaching 17,811 by 1937.[29] The restaurant scene expanded with it, including suppliers. By 1928, there were thirty-two restaurants, as well as twenty-five food ingredient suppliers in Tianjin, mostly of tofu and fish, which constituted the majority of small businesses run by Japanese.[30] Many restaurants served sushi, soba, and Japanese sweets (*namagashi*).[31] One of the most prestigious was Shikishima, patronized by China's last emperor, Pu Yi, who dined there with Japanese diplomats. The high-end nightclub Asia Hall (Ajia Kaikan) served high-ranking Japanese military officers Japanese dishes such as tempura, eel (*unagi*), sushi, and sashimi flown in from Japan. These establishments also served Chinese elites living in the Japanese concession or doing business there.[32]

Japanese women migrants were key agents in creating this world of cuisine and entertainment. In 1912, of the 235 Japanese working in Tianjin's restaurants or food-related businesses, 182 were women, including 49 working in restaurants (*ryōriten*), 10 in cheap eateries (*yinshokuten*), 15 in sweets shops, 4 in fish shops, and 2 in tofu shops. In terms of profession, 5 women were listed as chefs, 58 as geishas, and 43 as waitresses.[33] By 1924, geisha was the most common occupation of Japanese women in Tianjin.[34] This overview of the restaurant scene in Tianjin conveys a growing Japanese culinary infrastructure, and the significant economic and cultural role of female culinary workers and entertainers.

Creating a Modern Urban *Sakariba* in Dalian

Japanese urban entertainments and a modern urban lifestyle were part of the colonial experience. Dalian's incorporation into the Japanese empire made it an "instant city" and showcase of modern urban development under

Japanese control. Dalian (Dairen in Japanese) was built out as a port city by Russians and named Port Arthur. After the Russo-Japanese War in 1905, it was ceded to Japan. By the 1940s, it had a large industrial sector and naval base with 225,000 Japanese residents, the largest urban population of Japanese outside Japan.[35] Most of them lived and shopped in a central district controlled by Japanese businesses and the military. The district had diverse Japanese restaurants oriented to the Japanese inhabitants, from expensive ones for entertaining dignitaries to smaller eateries. Dalian was especially known for its lively cafés and cabarets that offered flirtatious companionship from waitresses along with the food service.

A comprehensive guide to the city published in Japanese in 1931 includes a section called "Taste of Dalian" introducing its Japanese restaurants to Japanese readers. The guide estimated there were over ninety Japanese restaurants in the city, serving tempura, sushi, sukiyaki, and other dishes, as well as *yōshoku*.[36] For tempura, the guide noted that Tenkin was the oldest establishment, and that Torihiko served eel dishes in a rustic décor. It mentioned three sushi restaurants, all in the main Japanese shopping district. They served Osaka-style compressed sushi, as the chefs were from western Japan.[37] There were also exclusive sukiyaki restaurants, featuring all-female table service.[38]

The main institution in the city's dining scene in the 1930s was the café, with hundreds of such establishments employing over six hundred hostesses. The guidebook exuberantly called this "the golden age of the cafe, a flood of cafes!" The hostess bar/café, serving food and alcohol, was the most numerous and popular. These establishments were a key part of a colonial *sakariba*—a lively entertainment district, modeled on those in cities in Japan, that combined a tradition of female dance hostesses and waitresses with westernized forms of music, drink, and hospitality.[39] They were frequently shut down by the police for providing "lewd services"[40] during state campaigns to curb prostitution.[41] Due to their rich mix of traditional Japanese venues with geishas and cafés with jazz bands and Japanese dance hostesses, the colonial *sakariba* in Dalian, as well as other colonial cities, were a "global nightscape"—a modern panorama of drinking, dancing, and music venues familiar from the new medium of film and enjoyed by people of many nationalities and ethnicities.[42] Migrant Japanese women, as proprietors, waitresses, entertainers, and sex workers, were key agents in creating this lively Japanese culinary and entertainment scene in the empire.

Japanizing the Population through Cuisine in Taipei

Japanese restaurants had a deep impact on consumer practices throughout the empire and perhaps nowhere more than Taiwan. Taipei was the capital of Taiwan, the first colony of the Empire of Japan, which administered it from 1895 to 1945. The Japanese state aspired to make the island a model colony and shape Taiwanese people, especially the elites, into loyal Japanese subjects who identified with Japanese culture. Japanese colonization and infrastructure development radically transformed the island's economy and society.[43] Japanese settlers were concentrated in Taipei. In 1921, there were 171 restaurants in the city, with 145 operated by Japanese (a much higher proportion of Japanese ownership than in other cities of Taiwan, where fewer Japanese resided). Japanese restaurateurs in Taipei replicated the triad of Japanese, Chinese, and Western offerings already becoming popular in Japan. By 1928 a register of Japanese-owned businesses listed fifty-six Japanese restaurants, ten Western restaurants, and thirty-two Taiwanese or Chinese restaurants. Some served a mix of cuisines. For example, the Taiwan Lou was famed for both Western and Chinese dishes. Japanese officials and consumers also favored a new label of "Taiwanese cuisine" (*Taiwan liaoli*) for restaurants serving Chinese cuisine. This allowed them to distinguish the foods of the colonies from those of mainland China, even when many of the dishes (and many of the cooks producing them) were from mainland provinces, especially neighboring Fujian. "Taiwanese cuisine" restaurants also became common in Japan.[44]

As in other cities in the empire, in Taipei Japanese restaurants introduced new forms of dinner entertainment, centered in the entertainment district of Ximending near the areas of Japanese business and settlement. Young female entertainers danced, sang, and read poetry to entertain banqueters in these restaurants, and photos and brief biographies of these women were used in advertising.[45] For example, Ryokan Umeyashiki was renowned in the 1920s for its entertainment by geishas from Japan. Another prominent spot was Kishu An, an elaborate three-story restaurant (*ryōtei*) opened in 1917 in suburban Xindian by a migrant from Wakayama Prefecture. Guests arriving from the city by rickshaw joined geishas on boats in the nearby Danshui River to catch *ayu* (sweetfish). Then, they returned to the restaurant to bathe as their fresh catches were prepared for dinner.[46]

Japanese eateries introduced Japanese food into Taiwanese urban food culture by popularizing such dishes as sushi, tempura, *tonkatsu* (fried pork cutlets), and *oden* (stewed snacks), as well as sweets, including mochi (rice cakes) and *castella,* the Japanese-Portuguese cake.[47] Sukiyaki, in particular, became popular among educated Taiwanese. They saw the collective cooking method of sukiyaki—sharing a hotpot with peers—as representing modern values of freedom and equality.[48] Many lower-end Japanese eateries popularized items that are still known as Taiwanese street foods. Taiwanese ate *senbei* (rice crackers) and mochi (*jianbing* and *mashu* in Chinese) at Japanese-owned snack shops in Japanese residential districts. The Calpis brand yoghurt drink, developed in Japan in 1919, became popular among Taiwanese youths.[49] Fried sweet potato brought to Taiwan by Japanese from Kyushu was flavored with sweet-chili ketchup, commonly used in local food, and called *tianbula,* literally "sweet, not spicy," a transliteration of the Japanese word "tempura."[50] Other Japanese street foods that became popular included grilled squid (*kao huazhi* in Mandarin), wheel cakes (*chelunbing* in Mandarin) derived from Japanese *imagawayaki* (bean-paste cakes), and sushi rolls. Another imported foodway was the Japanese box meal *obento* (*biandang* in Mandarin). As in Japan, they were made by restaurants and specialty shops for delivery to offices, carried by children to school for lunch, or sold in train stations. During World War II, Taiwanese even consumed patriotic *hinomaru* box lunches that evoked the Japanese flag with a red pickled plum (*umeboshi*) on a bed of white rice.[51] These colonial foodways left an indelible mark on Taiwanese food culture that became part of localist identity politics in post-1949 Taiwan, discussed later.

A Culinary Contact Zone at the Confluence of Empires

All of the elements of Japan's culinary imperialism described in the previous section came together in Shanghai, alongside the additional element of Shanghai's emerging status as a culinary global city. Shanghai in the early twentieth century, more than any city in Asia, and possibly the world, was a contact zone between competing empires and social forces, with all the major powers and their citizens present. In the years leading up to World War II, it had a highly variegated culinary scene with elegant hotel restaurants, independent French restaurants operated by Russian and Georgian émigrés, Viennese cafés run by Jewish refugees from Nazi-controlled

Europe, and American cafés and bars. It was also a place in which many Westerners and Chinese encountered Japanese cuisine.

Unlike in Tianjin, in Shanghai there was no formal Japanese concession under consular authority. However, with the formation of the Shanghai International Settlement in 1863, Shanghai was open to Japanese migration and business as well. In 1871, only 7 Japanese lived in Shanghai, but by 1890, the number had increased to 337 men and 302 women.[52] Many of the earliest residents were female sex workers from Nagasaki and its poor hinterlands. Their activities were linked to an emerging Japanese restaurant scene. In the early 1880s, there was a fad for Japanese teahouses (*dongyang chaguan*) featuring a mix of food, entertainment, and prostitution. The first Japanese teahouse was opened in the late 1870s by Takenaka Bunsaku, a former cook from the Japanese consulate. He sold tea and snacks (*kashi*), at first imported from Nagasaki and later made in Shanghai by two workers he hired. He also hired young Japanese waitresses and staged nightly dance performances to attract Chinese customers. The Japanese teahouse proved to be a successful business model that attracted imitators. One enterprising Japanese courtesan opened a teahouse with prostitutes, and neighboring proprietors copied her.[53]

Soon, "Japanese teahouse" became a generic term for a restaurant serving Japanese and Western snacks along with the companionship of young Japanese women. By 1883, there were more than ten Japanese teahouses on Sima Road (now Fuzhou Road), the emerging center of Shanghai nightlife, each with a Japanese owner and staff of half a dozen young women. Given the small Japanese population, most customers were Chinese and Western male sojourners in the city. Chagrined by the low-class image that these rowdy businesses created for Japan, Japanese authorities in Shanghai brought over four constables from Japan to police the district and curtail the trafficking and migration of women into the city.[54] With the outbreak of the First Sino-Japanese War in 1894, the city's Japanese nightlife boom came to a halt. Most members of the Japanese community temporarily took refuge in Japan.[55] However, Japanese restaurants with female servers, entertainers, and prostitutes would become a prominent feature of Shanghai's urban scene for decades to come.

In 1895, after Japan's victory in the First Sino-Japanese War, Japanese returned to Shanghai. Japanese restaurants reappeared, but now increasingly focused on serving the rapidly growing Japanese population. Attracted by lower rents, the restaurants, along with other Japanese businesses, concentrated in the Hongkou District, which became known as Shanghai's

（下）圖三六（景二十海上）
道藏る當に西の園公新端北の諸川四北
る在てし・築建本日純に側西の路鐵

（街人本日）（上）路崧呉（景二十海上）
の閣今るあて過座河の街本日海上ら即て路道の心中の城地口虹
の跡細本日らかだのたし下游が帶塊の兵邪支に近附此て愛事
るあて事ろれかづなう らた見て！像相た學塊の座梁京車は狀搏

FIGURE 2.2 Shanghai's prewar Japantown was centered on the central streets of Tibet Road and Wusong Road *(top left)*. Rokusan Garden *(bottom right)* with its large Japanese teahouse was an urban landmark. (Postcard from the late 1930s mailed back to Japan by a soldier, owned by James Farrer)

Japantown. By the 1910s, the area had over fifty restaurants run by Japanese, with about half featuring the companionship of geishas along with alcohol and food.[56] In 1909, there were 57 Japanese women working as geishas or prostitutes in Hongkou, but by 1923, there were 563 women, including bar hostesses.[57] Many of them worked in restaurants on Wusong Road and North Sichuan Road, north of Suzhou Creek, which separated the Japanese-dominated Hongkou from other areas of the International Settlement. By 1930, Japanese formed two-thirds of Hongkou's foreign population, while 665 of the 703 businesses along bustling Sichuan North Road were Japanese run and built mostly in Japanese style.[58] Daily shipments of vegetables and fish arrived from Nagasaki, which was also the most significant home region for Japanese residents in Shanghai. Among Japanese, the city was jokingly called "Shanghai City in Nagasaki Prefecture" (Nagasaki-ken, Shanhai-shi). With the advent of regular steamer service between Nagasaki and Shanghai in 1926, the journey only took twenty-six hours and cost

7.5 yen (USD 14 in 1930 currency). Even people with few resources could head to Shanghai to try their luck.[59]

The most prominent restaurant in the district was Rokusantei, which opened on Boone Road (now Tangu Road) in 1900, near the future Japanese Club (which opened in 1904). By the 1920s, Rokusantei was a large establishment boasting sixty geishas from Nagasaki and a spacious second-floor tatami-covered room with *tokonoma* (alcoves) featuring Japanese flower arrangements.[60] Its owner, Nagasaki native Rokusaburō Shiraishi, became known as the "geisha king" of Shanghai. In 1912, farther north in Hongkou, he opened Rokusan Garden, a large wooden Japanese-style teahouse serving Japanese and Chinese food. Its expansive grounds included a lawn for garden parties, a Shinto shrine (the *Shanhai jinja*), and a Japanese garden with seasonal blossoms. Geishas performed elaborate music and dance routines at banquets. It served as a community space for the Japanese residents of Shanghai, including meetings of the Japanese Residents Association (Nihonjinkai). It was also a space of economic and political activity. Japanese officials held banquets there for visiting Japanese and leading Chinese dignitaries, including Sun Yat-sen in 1912 and Chiang Kai-shek in 1928. Its patrons included Chinese cultural figures, such as writer Lu Xun and painter Wu Changshuo, who exhibited there.[61] Rokusan Garden became a Shanghai landmark among the Chinese, who knew it by its name as pronounced in the local Shanghainese dialect. Other prominent Japanese restaurateurs in Shanghai also opened imitation garden eateries in the suburbs.[62] As discussed in Chapter 4, Japanese teahouses became a worldwide fashion in the early twentieth century, often situated in Japanese-style gardens or mimicking a garden in the interior design.

Chinese Customer Reactions to Japanese Restaurants in Colonial Shanghai

The early Chinese reactions to Japanese restaurants in the Chinese-language press were generally skeptical in tone. Some regarded Japanese food as strange, even disgusting. Others who visited Japanese restaurants were unimpressed by the food but liked the exotic décor and attentive service by Japanese women. One hurdle was the raw seafood. A 1917 commentary in the Chinese-language newspaper *Xiaoshibao* dismissed Japanese food as unhygienic. "In terms of food, Japanese are far behind Chinese. It costs each person five to six yuan, which is expensive, but we do not see how it is better

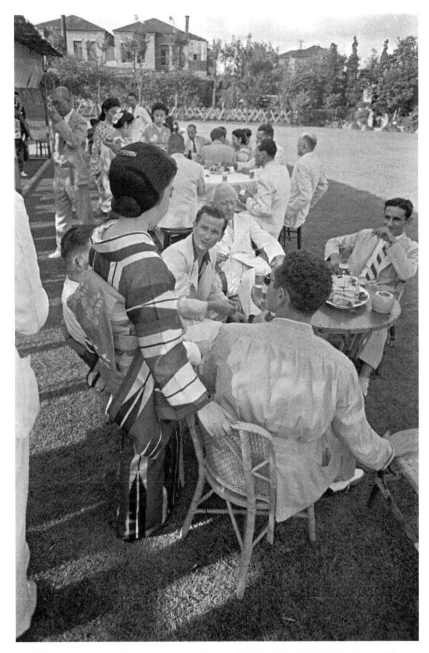

FIGURE 2.3 Geishas attend to guests at Rokusan Garden at a garden party hosted by the Japanese consulate for the Western and Japanese press on August 22, 1940. Rokusan Garden frequently hosted Japanese diplomatic and community events. (Time/Life Inc.)

[than Chinese food]. The chopsticks are neither sterilized before use nor disposed afterwards. The raw fish may have microbes, so they are not sanitary."[63] Even sukiyaki was disparaged by Chinese before becoming popular. In 1928, a Chinese author wrote in a Chinese newspaper of his experience of eating sukiyaki with his Chinese friend at a Japanese restaurant. "Sukiyaki is made with raw beef boiled in hot water with a lot of sugar. Before eating, the cooked beef should be dipped in raw eggs. The beef smells strange and is hard to eat." The author and his friend eschewed the sukiyaki in favor of the beer, getting very drunk over dinner.[64]

By the 1930s, however, increasing familiarity appears to have overcome this initial aversion to sukiyaki. Its global popularity, as described in Chapter 4, undoubtedly influenced cosmopolitan Shanghainese elites. In 1935, an article in a Chinese newspaper described the author's dining experience with friends at a Japanese restaurant in Hongkou. He wrote, "The owner is an old Japanese woman. She can only speak Japanese. But we can't. So she called a young waitress, who could speak some Shanghai-English [pidgin]. She said to us, 'you are welcome to our restaurant. We feel pleasure to serve you. I'm sorry you have to take off shoes and sit on the ground to eat.' We could not read the Japanese menu, but we knew sukiyaki was not raw, so we ordered it. Two Japanese waitresses made food for us during the meal. They put raw fish, chicken and beef into a hot pot." The author and his friends were unaccustomed to eating raw eggs but appreciated the freshness of the food, the spare use of oil, and especially the attentive Japanese waitresses. The author tipped a waitress one yuan and was impressed by her gratitude. He was also impressed that she had graduated from Tokyo Women's Middle School.[65] Such young, attentive Japanese waitresses attracted Chinese men to Japanese restaurants. With professional geisha entertainers and prostitutes working in the larger ones, the women attending a table often outnumbered the customers.[66]

By the 1940s, an expansive Japanese restaurant scene had developed in Shanghai, with expensive establishments found in the International Settlement and cheaper locales still concentrated in Hongkou. According to a 1944 Chinese-language periodical, Chinese considered Japanese restaurants in Hongkou inexpensive and delicious. These restaurants were largely divided into those serving Japanese cuisine and those serving Japanese-Western dishes. The latter, such as Morinaga, Meiji, and New Shanghai in Hongkou, sold cooked dishes, as well as coffee and milk, and did not expect tips, unlike the more expensive Japanese cuisine restaurants in the city center. A meal was about forty yuan, which, as the author noted, was reasonable for a middle-class Shanghai patron. Additionally, there were establishments for drinking Japanese tea.[67] The sukiyaki house, as discussed later, was the type of restaurant most widely patronized by Chinese customers.

After the war, the one hundred thousand Japanese residing in Shanghai were repatriated to Japan, and ownership of their restaurants shifted to Chinese, as well as a few Russians,[68] with only a few Japanese employees staying on as cooks and waitresses. These restaurants dwindled in number, enhancing the appeal of those remaining.[69] Some new owners went to great lengths to acquire control of them. One man named Tehmin Liu (Liu Demin in *pinyin* romanization and Chinese name order) impersonated a general of the ruling Nationalist Party (Guomindang) in order to take over two famous restaurants in Hongkou, Saloon Sukiyaki House and Tsukinoya.[70] Before Liu's arrest in 1948, the latter establishment, renamed Salon Yeuji (Shalongyanji in Mandarin), had become a popular Japanese restaurant whose patrons included Nationalist military officers. The restaurant was described variously in the Chinese press as a "mysterious" place where Japanese hostesses served customers, and one of the few remaining authentic Japanese restaurants.[71] Its menu included sashimi, sukiyaki, teriyaki fish, grilled fish, fried shrimp, miso soup, rice, and fruits. Over forty women served as hostesses, a third of whom were Japanese. One Chinese writer described it as "Shanghai's paradise": "He [the owner] took me for a tour of the restaurant. There were seven or eight small rooms. Some were separated by curtains, others by glass. . . . At this time, all the small rooms were full of guests. Some sat on the floor, accompanied by women with heavy makeup. Some rooms were occupied by Western men, accompanied by enchanting 'White Russian' women who were eating and laughing. Two things were indispensable here, alcohol and women!"[72] After World War II, Chinese patrons lamented the decline of these Japanese restaurants less in terms of the food than the dearth of these Japanese waitresses.

This Japanese restaurant scene persisted briefly after the founding of the People's Republic of China (PRC) in 1949. In May 1950, the Runo Sukiyaki restaurant still advertised its "polite Japanese waitresses" in the *North China Daily News*, the most influential English-language newspaper (closed by the new government in the following year).[73] In 1952, as relations between the PRC and capitalist countries rapidly deteriorated in the buildup to the Korean War (1950–1953), Japanese restaurants were also shut down. For the next three decades, Japanese restaurants disappeared from mainland China.

Anti-Japanese Politics and Attacks on Japanese Restaurants

During the colonial era, Chinese viewed the presence of the Japanese colonizers with a deep ambivalence that extended to their cultural artifacts, such as restaurants. On the one hand, they saw Japanese as fellow Asians who had successfully modernized and, on the other, as colonizers and invaders of China. This led to anti-Japanese protests, in which restaurants, as visible symbols of Japan, were frequent targets. In 1925, the *China Press* reported an attack by "Chinese rioters" on Mangestu, a Japanese restaurant on Linching Road, causing damages of $16,472.[74] "A mob comprised principally of mill coolies led the attack. Windowpanes, vegetable beds, woodwork, crockery and everything else on which members of the mob could lay their hands were destroyed, and a considerable quantity of clothing and valuables carried off."[75]

Boycotts of Japanese businesses were another form of protest. In 1927, the Nanking Road Anti-Japanese Boycott Union and the Association for the Severance of Diplomatic Relations with Japan sent letters to Chinese restaurants, urging them not to use Japanese food products, which were imported into the city daily: "Everybody else has joined the anti-Japanese boycott movement, but the restaurants are lagging, so we hope that you, too, will join. Should any 'cold-blooded' customers come and demand from you 'inferior' dishes, it is your duty to remind them of the sufferings that China has sustained at the hands of Japan and to urge them not to eat any more such dishes."[76]

In 1936, an article in the tabloid *Jingbao* framed a call for Chinese to resist Japanese restaurants and products by contrasting the attitudes of Chinese and Japanese consumers. "The Japanese invasion is bad, but its people's patriotism is admirable. If you go to Hongkou, you will find dozens of Japanese restaurants, furniture shops and foodstuff. All of the products sold are from Japan. They are three or four times more expensive than those produced in our country. But our people [Chinese] would like to buy them."[77] The author noted that Japanese refused to import Chinese fruits, so Chinese should not import Japanese ones.

In the same year, the *Shanghaibao* newspaper described Japanese restaurants as a highly lucrative business that profited from prostitutes, food, and alcohol in Japan's occupied territories in northeast China's Qiqihaer. The Chinese public was urged to boycott them.[78] However, politically motivated attacks and calls for boycotts by Chinese of Japanese restaurants were sporadic, and many Chinese continued to patronize them. These episodes foreshadowed similar protests and boycotts decades after the colonial era. As shown below whenever political tension between China and Japan increased, the Japanese restaurant was easily attacked as a highly visible outpost of Japanese influence and culture.

Sukiyaki: The Earliest Global Japanese Cuisine

Shanghai, more than any other city in Asia, was a cosmopolitan metropolis, and a culinary contact zone not just for Chinese encountering Japanese restaurants but also for other foreigners encountering Japanese (and other) foodways. In the 1920s, the Shanghai English press began publishing articles about the popularity of sukiyaki in the United States.[79] In the prewar period, this dish served as a kind of national dish for Japan, since it was palatable to foreigners and offered an interactive and exotic dining experience (see Chapter 4). In 1930, the Japanese Club in Shanghai, which represented Japanese business interests in the city, treated foreign guests to sukiyaki, in an early example of sukiyaki diplomacy.[80] However, this food fad seems to have been promulgated as much by Westerners, especially Americans, as by Japanese themselves. Notices of "sukiyaki parties" began appearing frequently in the society pages of Shanghai's flourishing English-language press. One 1936 article notes that "sukiyaki parties are proving to be the rage among a certain set of social Shanghai, as hostesses are giving one after another of these Japanese dinners which are most conducive to hospitality, good fellowship and 'breaking of the ice' for some guests."[81] US Navy sailors seem to have been particularly fond of sukiyaki dinners, with massive sukiyaki parties for visiting sailors reported well into the late 1930s, even as tensions with Japan were rising.[82] While many of these parties were held at social clubs or private residences, sukiyaki specialty restaurants also opened up in the International Settlement and French Concession, catering to their wealthy Western and Chinese residents.

Despite the vicious fighting between Japan and the West, the sukiyaki boom survived World War II. Even during wartime, Shanghai's famed Cathay Hotel offered sukiyaki, with the dish written in Japanese katakana on the otherwise English and French menu. For example, the menu from May 12, 1943, offered sukiyaki alongside "Veal Chop Vichy"—probably a nod to the collaborationist French regime in Vichy, France. Sukiyaki parties continued, and sukiyaki restaurants operated in the fashionable areas of the city. The popularity of the dish even persisted during the first few years of communist rule beginning in 1949. In 1950, Japanese Restaurant Runo, most likely owned by Russian refugees, advertised sukiyaki, as well as Russian and Georgian dishes, along with "Real Indian Chicken Curry."[83] In March 1951, the Togo Sukiyaki House in the sumptuous Palace Hotel still advertised sukiyaki, tempura, sashimi, and *kabayaki* (grilled eel).[84] This restaurant likely closed in 1952, along with the hotel. Shanghai's suki-yaki era had ended, even as the boom continued in the United States and Europe (see Chapter 4).

After Empire: Japanese Culinary Legacies

The colonial history of Japanese restaurants and foodways in the cities de-scribed thus far profoundly shaped the development of their Japanese cu-linary scenes in the postwar era. Ambivalence toward Japanese colonialism reappeared in popular memories of the colonial experience, colored by po-litical efforts at culinary identity building in Korea, Taiwan, and mainland China. The rest of this chapter examines the interactions of Japanese food-ways with these popular memories as reflected in local reception of Japa-nese restaurants. We will first examine Taipei and Seoul, which offer clear contrasts in local receptions. Then we shall examine Dalian and Shanghai, the two cities in mainland China that had the largest prewar population of Japanese residents and, subsequently, the densest economic and cultural in-teractions with Japan.

Taiwan and Korea: Diverging Paths of Postcolonial Culinary Politics

The different geopolitical contexts of postcolonial states in Korea and Tai-wan have shaped their divergent approaches to the culinary legacies of Japa-nese colonialism. In Taiwan, the main line of geopolitical conflict was with the Communist Party of China in the PRC, thus deflecting attention from Japan's colonial occupation. In contrast, the harshness of colonial rule in Korea and subsequent political rivalry between North and South Korea led to competing claims over which was the legitimate successor to the anti-Japanese resistance of the colonial period. This created very different pat-terns of culinary politics in regard to defining a cuisine representing their own ethnic identities. In Korea, this process meant denying or downplaying Japanese influences, while in Taiwan aspects of the culinary legacies of Japanese colonialism helped define a "Taiwanese" cuisine as distinct from the regional cuisines of mainland China.

From Nostalgia to Localist Imaginary in Taipei. The politics of Japanese cuisine in Taipei can be divided into two periods. The first period was characterized by martial law that spanned from the late 1940s until its lifting in 1987, which began the second period, characterized by democratic politics. After the end of the Japanese occupation in 1945, Taiwan almost immediately became the base for the retreating army and government of the Nationalist Party of China and, from 1949, the government's only sovereign territory in China. Within Taiwan, a distinction emerged between the Mandarin-speakers from the mainland (usually called "outside province people," *waishengren*) and mostly Taiwanese-speaking locals ("Taiwan provincials," *benshengren*). Resentment that locals might have directed toward the former Japanese colonizers became oriented toward the mainlanders, who included the new military and government elites. In the late 1940s, the Nationalist Party of China brutally repressed suspected communist sympathizers in Taiwan and imposed cultural policies reminiscent of the Japanese colonial government, such as banning the local dialect in favor of Mandarin in school.

The distinction between mainlanders and locals also played out in culinary politics. As anthropologist David Wu points out, Taiwanese elites made class distinctions by consuming Japanese-style foods, while mainlanders sought American-style products.[85] Japanese foodways became an element of a collective local identity. In referring to local Chinese-style dishes, Taiwanese also embraced the label "Taiwanese cuisine," a category created by the Japanese colonists to distinguish foods in Taiwan from those in mainland China. As Yu-Jen Chen's research shows, there was no term "Taiwanese cuisine" before the Japanese arrived.[86] Whether from habit or nostalgia, Taiwanese urban elites, especially in Taipei, continued to consume Japanese-style foods, such as sukiyaki.[87] They continued to eat their school *obento* boxes cold in the Japanese fashion. But now the school system was dominated by mainlanders who imposed the Chinese norm of eating hot foods by insisting that all school lunches be heated in steamers before being consumed. This steaming mixed the flavors and tastes in ways that locals considered unpleasant.[88] Despite these tensions, Japanese culture was not banned, unlike in Korea, and Japanese cuisine remained popular, appearing on menus and in markets under the names coined for them in the colonial period. Thus, *tianbula* was widely sold, called by the same term from the colonial period, in contrast to Korea, where names were changed to Koreanized versions. New Japanese restaurants were founded, often by former assistant cooks who had worked in Japanese restaurants during the colonial period. They ran stalls and mom-and-pop canteen-style eateries serving *omuraisu* (rice and omelet), fried noodles, and other simple dishes that would become part of Taipei's vibrant side streets and night markets.

One of the oldest such eateries is Meiguanyuan (Bikanen in Japanese). It was founded in 1946 by Langtie Zhang, a southern Taiwan native who had come to Taipei a decade earlier to make a living. He worked as an assistant chef at a Japanese restaurant, most likely a cafeteria (*shokudō*, or *shitang* in Mandarin), where he learned his trade. He then served in the Japanese army during World War II. In 1946, he returned to Taipei and opened Meiguan Shitang (Meiguan Cafeteria), soon renaming it Meiguanyuan (Meiguan Garden) and moving it to Ximending, an entertainment district in the heart of the old Japanese city. The restaurant had a functional interior with tables and a small counter, and it served a wide range of dishes, including cutlets, curry, and sushi. It prospered and expanded. Then, in 1999, the owner's sons, who had inherited the business, had a falling out, apparently over changing the original menu. The older brother set up a new Meiguanyuan directly across the street from the old one. Guidebooks and online blogs referred to them as nostalgic remnants of Old Taipei.[89] When we visited in 2018, Taiwanese people in their eighties and older still came to eat Japanese food and speak Japanese with each other.[90]

The acceptance of Japanese cuisine as nostalgia reflects the degree to which "Taiwaneseness" has become a politicized identity in the face of the increasing determination of the Chinese government to reunify Taiwan with the People's Republic of China (PRC). In this context, the colonial past has become incorporated into Taiwanese history, less as a period of brutal subjugation (as in Korea) than as a part of Taiwan's history that underscores its distinctiveness from the PRC. This has stimulated efforts to preserve remnants of Japanese culture in Taipei as the heritage of Taiwan, often with an eye to tourism.[91] One such remnant is the previously described Kishu An, said to be the last Japanese-style wooden *ryōtei* structure in Taipei and declared protected urban heritage in 2004.[92]

An Elite Culture in Korea. The situation in Korea contrasts sharply with that in Taiwan. Immediately following the dissolution of the Japanese empire, the new Korean government banned Japanese popular culture, including Japanese-language theater performances, movies, radio broadcasts, and publications, and demolished houses and other buildings associated with the Japanese empire. It was only in 1998 that this ban on Japanese cultural imports was lifted, even though Korea and Japan had established diplomatic relations over three decades earlier.[93]

Only a few prewar Japanese restaurants survived the Japanese withdrawal and the devastation of the Korean War. One was Dae Seong Am Bon Ga, opened in 1920 by a Japanese in Gimcheon City on the major land transportation routes between Seoul and Busan. After World War II, its first Korean owner was Hongryeong Jeong. He had started working there in 1942, assumed ownership immediately after the war, and passed it on to his grandson in 1998. The menu remained practically unchanged over the decades, offering such Japanese dishes as soba, *maeuntang* (spicy fish stew), sushi, *hwe* (Korean-style sashimi), and others.[94] *Hwe* illustrates how some Japanese dishes from the colonial era were modified due to anti-Japanese sentiment after 1945. For example, rather than serve the Japanese-style sushi taught by his Japanese master, Jeong served *hwe*, with fish slices cut thinner than Japanese sashimi.[95]

The example of *hwe* underscores how the Korean language purification movement that swept Korea after World War II affected Japanese cuisine there. Although Japanese dishes were still served in restaurants, their names were modified or replaced by Korean words. For example, udon became *garak* noodle, tempura became *twigim,* soba became *memil* noodles, *donburi* (rice bowl) became *deopbap, tonkatsu* became *jaeyook twigim,* and sukiyaki became *we jeongol.*[96] Many linguistically Koreanized dishes also assumed a more typically Korean flavor profile even while remaining visually similar to the original Japanese dish. For example, *gimbap,* the Korean version of Japanese *norimaki* (sushi rolls wrapped in laver), contains more ingredients than the Japanese version and is seasoned with sesame oil rather than vinegar.[97] Disputes about the origins of these dishes are also part of this politics.

In the early postwar era, as most Koreans could not afford to eat out, the few remaining Japanese restaurants were exclusively associated with elite politicians and businessmen, many of whom were educated in Japan.

They patronized high-end Japanese-style *ryōriya* renamed by the Korean word *"yoriok,"* despite the departure of most of their Japanese cooks and other food workers. *Yoriok* were places for men to talk politics and business while accompanied by young women serving them alcohol and singing and dancing. Just as in the colonial era, a meal began with alcoholic beverages and paired side dishes, moved on to the main meal, and finished with tea, dessert, and socializing between customers and hostesses.[98] *Yoriok* remained fashionable up to the 1970s, when they were displaced by newer mass market restaurants catering to the growing middle classes.[99]

Some of these cheaper restaurants also specialized in Japanese-style foods. In the 1960s, Japanese-style *tonkatsu* shops opened in the Myeong-dong area of Seoul where previously there had been many Japanese restaurants. By the 1980s, there also were restaurants specializing in udon and soba. At the same time, expensive Japanese restaurants opened in affluent areas of Seoul, especially Gangnam, including one that imported a sushi chef from Japan. In the 1990s, Japanese-influenced bars called *nobadayaki* and Japanese ramen noodle restaurants proliferated.[100] In the 1990s, Japanese restaurants selling various Japanese foods opened in university districts, many run by Koreans who had studied in Japan. The formerly upscale *yoriok,* having fallen out of fashion, broadened their consumer appeal by offering *hanjeongsik,* featuring ample amounts of food.[101]

The juxtaposition of Taiwan and Korea highlights their very different postcolonial culinary politics. In Taiwan, the association of Chinese restaurants with the Nationalist regime and the tense political relationship with mainland China legitimated an imagined and romanticized type of postcolonial nostalgia. In Korea, nationalism defined by opposition to the Japanese colonialism spurred the erasure of colonial foodways by imparting a "Korean" character to localized Japanese dishes. Even in Korea, however, proximity to Japan and familiarity with Japanese foodways led to a strong revival of the Japanese restaurant sector in later decades.

China: From Erasing the Japanese Colonial Past to Embracing Japanese Restaurants

Japanese and other foreign-cuisine restaurants disappeared from the PRC in the 1950s.[102] Then, after the 1979 reforms to create a market economy, some foreign-cuisine restaurants began to reappear, though most Chinese were initially too poor to afford them. Only in the 1990s did such restaurants, including Japanese, reemerge in significant numbers. Consumers became reacquainted with Japanese cuisine, but after a gap of nearly forty years, the meanings and associations of Japanese restaurants had little to do with those of the colonial era described earlier. Instead, Japanese cuisine emerged as a new foreign food fashion associated with business expatriates, the high-class lifestyles of a rising urban elite, and the internationalization of Chinese cities.

In this section, we look at how Japanese restaurants reappeared in China in the late twentieth century. Since then, they have become the most popular foreign restaurants in Chinese cities, even as disputes have emerged over the legacies of Japanese colonialization and wartime activities in China. Here we revisit Dalian and Shanghai, two Chinese cities examined earlier in this chapter, drawing on fieldwork throughout the 2010s. Since 1990, Dalian has emerged as a center of Japanese corporate activities, and Shanghai has become China's most dynamic global city, with one of the largest overseas Japanese communities in the world. In both cities, Japanese cuisine has become entrenched in urban foodways, while the Japanese restaurant business has become dominated by Chinese actors.

Dalian. The resurgence of Japanese restaurants in Dalian closely followed China's economic liberalization and new flows of people and capital between Japan and Dalian.[103] Japanese restaurants reappeared in the early 1990s when Japanese investment capital, along with Japanese managers and employees, came to the city. Since then, the customer base for most Japanese restaurants has included a significant number of Japanese expats and tourists, a pattern that distinguishes Dalian from Chinese cities with a relatively smaller Japanese expatriate presence.[104] The city's proximity to Japan and historical links attracted a return of Japanese capital and expats in the 1980s.[105] By the mid-2000s, there were approximately thirty thousand Japanese, including tourists, in the city on any given day.[106] This led to a Japan-centric nightlife and restaurant scene, with fewer European-style restaurants than other major cities in China, and a bar scene catering to Japanese men.[107] Our fieldwork found three primary kinds of ownership among the restaurants in the city: restaurants owned by Japanese but managed by Chinese, family-operated eateries run by Japanese-Chinese married couples, and restaurants and bars owned by local Chinese who had lived in Japan.[108] Our interviews with local restaurant owners also revealed the importance for Japanese restaurateurs to have Chinese partners or managers, because the locals were better than the Japanese at understanding local business regulations and customers, handling sourcing of cheaper real estate (location fixing), and obtaining a steady labor supply from rural areas.

Unlike in Shanghai, high-end Japanese restaurants have struggled in Dalian. Its relatively small population of six million, and a less robust economy, means that there are fewer high-spending local Chinese. Also, since the 2000s, the spending power of the Japanese clientele declined as managerial expatriates gave way to younger Japanese working in the growing technology and call-service outsourcing sectors. They were hired as skilled temporaries on local contract pay scales, driving the growth of midrange restaurants catering to these younger Japanese on modest incomes.[109]

At the time of our fieldwork in 2017 and 2018, the most successful Japanese restaurants were the popular *izakayas* clustered in the Dalian Economic Development Zone and downtown Dalian near the Japanese consulate and Hotel Nikko. These pub-like establishments had a steady customer base of Japanese regulars who brought Chinese coworkers, as well as young Chinese on dates (see Chapter 7 for a discussion of the *izakaya*). The *izakayas* followed the Japanese tradition of bottle keep—serving regular drinkers from personal bottles of whiskey with their names on them that were kept behind the bar. Many were large establishments with multiple dining areas and screens featuring Japanese movies or television programming.

A typical *izakaya* was Akiyoshi, located near the Hotel Nikko in a complex that was purpose-built for Japanese restaurants, bars, and massage parlors. Akiyoshi's first floor had a long dining counter for customers to sit and chat with Chinese waitresses who had learned Japanese while working in Japan or in language schools in Dalian. Overhead screens played Japanese dramas and sports events. Upstairs was for group dining, including office parties. About 80 percent of the customers were Japanese, including salarymen who were regulars stopping in for Suntory highballs or beer and a quick bite. They ordered from an omnibus menu containing many Japanese comfort foods, including sushi, ramen, tempura, and curry, as well as such standard *izakaya* fare as grilled meat and fish.[110] Other Japanese eateries in Dalian were attuned to global trends in Japanese cuisine, such as the ramen boom or the California sushi roll trend. For example, Sushi Luck was a small chain with two branches in downtown Dalian that featured minimalist, modern interiors and sushi rolls made with exotic sauces and spices.[111]

Shanghai. The flourishing globalized restaurant scene in pre-1949 Shanghai was decimated by the disappearance of the foreign population, collectivization of private businesses, and especially during the Cultural Revolution (1966–1976), when fine dining restaurants became cafeterias for the proletariat. After 1979, a few famous Western restaurants in Shanghai still survived (all as state-owned enterprises), but none of the former Japanese restaurants remained.[112] By the 1990s, only a few elderly residents of Shanghai likely remembered the once-famed Rokusantei, and in the early twenty-first century, even the physical remains of Japanese Hongkou were razed by urban redevelopment. A new Japantown emerged in suburban Hongqiao near the international airport, far from Hongkou.

Among the first Japanese-cuisine restaurants were the two at the Okura Garden Hotel that opened in 1990 on the premises of the former French Club of Shanghai, fronted by manicured formal gardens. The Garden Hotel was the top hotel in Shanghai in the 1990s, and its illustrious surroundings enhanced the association of Japanese cuisine with luxury. Japanese restaurants at the hotel pioneered the import of Japanese food products to make high-quality Japanese cuisine, many of which were no longer known in Shanghai.[113] Head chefs from Japan trained the first generation of local chefs, such as Chef Tang, introduced below. These chefs went on to open Japanese restaurants later in the decade. The customers of Japanese restaurants in the 1990s were mostly business travelers from Japan and their Chinese business clients.[114]

A report from the Japan External Trade Organization states that this early boom was driven by three types of actors: individual Japanese entrepreneurs, Japanese companies, and individual Chinese entrepreneurs.[115] Independent Japanese entrepreneurs were the early entrants into the market. According to a 2005 survey of thirty Japanese restaurants, thirteen had Japanese owners, and seventeen had Chinese owners. Half of the restaurants served a clientele that was more than 50 percent Japanese, and only nine had a customer base of less than 30 percent Japanese.[116] In the 2000s, Japanese corporate chains popularized Japanese tastes in China by introducing Japanese foodways to a far larger market segment of middle-class Chinese consumers.[117] These chains included Watami, Gatten Sushi, Ajisen Ramen, Genroku Sushi, Matsuko Japanese Restaurant, Saizeriya, Yoshinoya, Sukiya, and Matsuya (see Chapters 6 and 7).[118]

Japanese expatriate entrepreneurs played a large role in the early development of this culinary scene as investors, operators, and customers. Hongqiao, the city's thriving new Japanese business hub, became the center for Japanese restaurants. It had many small venues for Japanese white-collar workers to unwind after work, and fancier venues for business meals. Many establishments were for after-party (*nijikai*) drinking sessions with Chinese hostesses, perhaps not unlike the geisha services of prior decades. In addition, an enormous nighttime economy of saunas, bars, and massage parlors for Japanese men grew next to these restaurants. Unlike in the 1930s, however, very few of the women in such places were Japanese. Nearly all women working in these sex establishments were Chinese who had learned Japanese from their clients or by working in Japan. Although not restaurants, these sex establishments were part of the nighttime geography of Hongqiao.[119]

Other restaurants in Hongqiao were community eateries for expatriates. An example is Ajikura, founded in 2002 by Teruo Katayama. A native of Osaka, he had run a small chain of *takoyaki* shops in Japan since the 1970s. As competition increased in Japan, he came to Shanghai in the 1990s seeking business opportunities and opened Ajikura. An *izakaya* specializing in *okonomiyaki* (savory pancake) and alcohol, Ajikura was a home away from home for expat salarymen. Almost 70 percent of his customers were Japanese, Katayama said, and the rest Chinese. Business boomed and he invested in two new restaurants. However, in the 2010s, business suffered due to rising rent and labor costs, as well as mismanagement. According to his acquaintances, Katayama was more interested in nightlife than minding the shop. He delegated management of the new branches to a Shanghainese business partner, who soon seized ownership of them.[120] Despite this loss, Katayama's original restaurant in Hongqiao continued to thrive, and he still controlled it. When we last visited in January 2020, all tables were occupied or reserved, with hundreds of bottle-keep *shōchū* (distilled spirits) testifying to the popularity of the restaurant as a drinking establishment that stayed open until three o'clock in the morning. Katayama's long-term manager from Anhui Province still was managing the business on a daily basis.[121] Katayama's story illustrates the common dilemmas for independent foreign restaurateurs of navigating relationships with local Chinese business partners. While partnerships were desirable for local market knowledge and government relations, they were widely regarded as risky for foreign restaurateurs in China.[122]

The first decade of the 2000s was a period of rapid growth, diversification, and transition in the Japanese restaurant market. In the early 2000s, Japanese culinary culture in Shanghai still was expatriate driven (similar to such cities as Düsseldorf and Hanoi, described in Chapter 3). By 2005, over five thousand Japanese companies had registered in the city, where more than forty thousand Japanese resided long-term. Many Japanese in the restaurant industry spoke no English or Chinese, relying entirely on employees with Japanese language ability. But increasingly, rich and middle-income Chinese became the new dominant consumers. Japanese restaurants proliferated in Shanghai, from the extreme high to the low end. Expensive sushi restaurants and *kaiseki* restaurants emerged in 2004 (see Chapter 8), and cheaper sushi restaurants followed.[123] In May 2016, the most popular Chinese restaurant website, Dianping, listed 3,464 Japanese restaurants in the city in the following categories: 1,702 offering fine dining cuisine, including *kaiseki*, regional *nabe* (hotpot), Japanese beef, crab, *fugu* (blowfish), sashimi, and tempura (fine style); 689 serving fast food, including ramen, revolving sushi, and tempura; and 321 grill restaurants, including teppanyaki and *okonomiyaki*.[124] By this count, Shanghai had become the city outside Japan with the largest number of Japanese restaurants in the world.

On the producer side, Chinese restaurateurs with years of experience working in Japanese kitchens in Shanghai became the driving force in the Japanese restaurant scene, catering to the increasing Chinese market. Tao Tang (Tang Tao in Chinese naming order), about fifty years old, was one of the earliest Chinese restaurateurs who helped create this market.[125] We met in January 2020 at Takumi, Tang's high-end *robatayaki* (charcoal grill) restaurant, located on the fourth floor of International Financial Center Mall—one of the landmarks of the Lujiazui financial hub, with a high-end shopping mall in its base.[126] While describing the development of his restaurant group, Tang quickly ordered a selection of items from Takumi's menu: fresh sashimi from Japan, grilled fish, and other delicacies that could have been served up in a Tokyo restaurant. The average bill in the evening was about CNY 550 (USD 80) a person, he said. It was luxurious, but by Shanghai's Japanese restaurant standards, not an exclusive price.

Tang was among the first generation of Chinese chefs trained by chefs from Japan in China. His story of rising from the position of an entry-level chef in Shanghai's first international Japanese hotel, the Okura Garden Hotel, in 1990 to ownership of a chain of Japanese restaurants reflects how a group of working-class Shanghainese laboring in Japanese restaurants in Shanghai from the 1990s became transnational restaurateurs. In 1993, after three years working at the Okura, Tang invested in opening a fancy Japanese restaurant called Oedo on Donghu Road in the former French Concession, an area of the city favored by Western expatriates and wealthy

FIGURE 2.4 Customers sitting at the counter in Takumi's flagship restaurant in the center of Shanghai's financial district can watch the chefs cooking fish and fresh vegetables on the *robata* grill. (Photo by James Farrer, January 8, 2020)

overseas Chinese just as it had been in the 1930s. In the 1990s, Japanese were still half of the customers at Oedo, and other foreigners were a large part of the rest. At the time, there were only six Japanese restaurants and a handful of Japanese expatriate chefs working in the city.[127]

By the time of our interview at Takumi in 2020, most customers were Chinese. Authentic Japanese taste was an important principle for Tang, and he has always hired a Japanese executive chef who decides recipes and trains other chefs. At one point he had five Japanese chefs working in multiple restaurants, but it was hard to work with them, he said, because "they were very stubborn." Many Chinese bosses also were very stubborn, he joked, and thus could not work well with the Japanese. Tang said that unlike most Chinese owners, he gave his executive chef a lot of decision-making authority.[128] The most important principle at Takumi, he explained, was to present the "authentic" tastes of Japan to the customers, who were increasingly familiar with them from their travels to Japan.

In the eyes of Tang, Japanese restaurant groups were not successful in the Chinese market largely due to their indecisive management. He gave a personal example of a Japanese company that coinvested with him in Ta-kumi but then pulled out in 2011 when the Great East Kanto earthquake struck, leaving him high and dry. Takumi saw this as an inability of Japa-nese management to deal with uncertainty. Many of the successful Japanese brands in Shanghai were run by Hong Kong companies, he said, notably Maxim Group (the largest food and beverage company in Hong Kong).[129] In contrast, Tang said that Chinese entrepreneurs like himself have cre-ated many midsize restaurant companies purveying Japanese cuisine in the city. Their advantages lay in social relationships that gave them access to key resources. One resource was prime locations. For him, this came from friendships with Hong Kong and Singapore developers who dined at Oedo in the 1990s. When these developers opened malls in Shanghai, they offered good locations to well-connected restaurateurs, such as Tang. Through our research, we see ties to developers as key to developing res-taurant chains in countries throughout Asia (see Chapter 6).

Another advantage for local operators relative to Japanese and other foreign restaurant owners was connections to the local labor market. By 2020, restaurant labor had become costly and difficult to recruit and re-tain. Pressured by rising living costs for workers and competition among restaurants for their services, wages had risen. In Shanghai in 2020, a well-trained and experienced head chef hired locally could fetch CNY 20,000 (about USD 3,000) a month. To promote loyalty, Tang took his top chefs to Japan every year to experience good Japanese food and train their pal-ates. He maintained a loyal upper-level staff, while the younger ones turned over after about three years. Entry-level staff lived in dormitories about half an hour from the restaurant, underscoring the necessity to offer a dormitory to recruit employees, most of whom were rural-to-urban migrants (see Chapter 5).[130]

Increasingly, Shanghai's restaurant sector became dominated by corpo-rate restaurant groups. Most were owned by local Chinese or overseas Chi-nese. For example, Zhengxian Sushi and Zhengxian Teishoku were owned by a Taiwanese, and Jiangtaiwuer by a Canadian Chinese. A few chains were directly operated by a parent company from Japan. However, most oper-ated under licensing agreements, or as joint ventures, offering openings for local investors without knowledge of Japanese cuisine (see Chapter 6). This has led to the rapid growth of Japanese chain restaurants run by local entrepreneurs. Through their blend of local knowledge and managerial capacities, Chinese-owned chains thrived, while Japanese chefs and restaurateurs survived in the specialized market niche of expensive and "authentic" cuisine for the wealthiest local consumers who frequently travel to Japan.

Postcolonial Culinary Politics

Japanese restaurants and cuisine have become entangled in the contentious international relations of East Asia over claims regarding "national" cuisines. This culinary politics has two faces. The more cordial face, often labeled gastrodiplomacy, involves the deployment overseas of restaurants and national cuisine as cultural export promotion and nation branding. A more virulent face can be seen when restaurants, or culinary products and practices, are regarded as symbols of rival countries and come under attack in the context of broader political conflicts. Neither of these forms of culinary politics is purely (or even mainly) about food, but both highlight restaurants as public national symbols. An earlier example of such culinary politics is the attacks on Japanese restaurants in prewar Shanghai that were already described. This section examines culinary politics in Shanghai in the 2000s and the culinary rivalry between Japan and Korea.

Targeting Japanese Restaurants in Shanghai's Anti-Japanese Protest

While Japanese restaurants in Shanghai from the 1990s seemed unconnected to the Japanese presence in the colonial period, they were entangled in increasingly fraught relations with Japan. Political tensions often centered on what the Chinese and Japanese both referred to as the "history problem." The "Anti-Japanese War"—the label in the PRC for Japan's invasion of China from 1937 to 1945—and the accompanying Japanese atrocities were a constant theme in political rhetoric, classroom history education, and entertainment media from the 1990s onward. None of this was helped by the Japanese government's obfuscation and denial of wartime history. Restaurants, while not topically related to these issues, became a convenient target for protesters, just as they had been in the 1920s.

The largest street demonstration to hit Shanghai was the Anti-Japanese Protest of April 16, 2005. Around twenty to thirty thousand mostly young protesters marched from People's Square in central Shanghai to the Japanese consulate shouting anti-Japanese slogans. Two events triggered the protest. One was the Japanese state's attempt to become a permanent member of the United Nations Security Council. The second was the approval by the Japanese Ministry of Education of school textbooks that denied or downplayed Japanese wartime atrocities in China. Protesters carried signs referring to the historical and territorial disputes. Many threw rocks at the consulate and other Japan-affiliated targets ranging from Japanese cars to businesses. Since they were highly visible, Japanese restaurants became a major target, with several near the consulate severely damaged. We observed the protest from the sidelines.[131]

The *izakaya* Ajikura, described earlier, was near the consulate and became a convenient target. It was severely damaged. Its owner, Teruo Katayama, became an unwitting celebrity in China and Japan following the protests. He was not in the restaurant at the time but heard from employees that fifteen people attacked it with rocks, broke windows, and threw furniture out in front of the shop and set fire to it. Police did not stop the protesters from assaulting the building, although they arrived after six men entered a third-floor office and started destroying equipment. Four were arrested and charged. A day after the demonstration, a group of journalists from Japan, along with a German journalist and a member of our team, met with Teruo Katayama and Emi, his daughter, at a Japanese cocktail bar for an interview. The attitude was somber, and Emi cried throughout the interview, overwhelmed by the rage of the Shanghai residents against Japan.[132]

Katayama's responses represent how one expatriate restaurateur came to terms with this conflict. Despite his shock at the damage to Ajikura and the Hongqiao District, Katayama opined that Shanghai was not a city where Japanese had to be frightened. He distinguished between the demonstration and the violent behavior against his shop, which he called a "riot" (*bōdō*). He felt that most of the young people did not support the riot. "Demonstrations are normal. They happen everywhere in the world," he said. The Chinese demonstrators had a point, he said, speaking to a young German reporter in the group. "Look at Germany. They apologized for the war. Japan hasn't done that. I regret that, but it is no excuse for a riot." Two weeks later, the same journalists and friends of Katayama met for the reopening of his restaurant. It was filled with Japanese customers, all regulars. Katayama said he was gratified that some brought their families to show they felt safe in Shanghai. He also said that he expected to be compensated for his losses by the Changning District government, whose representatives had met with Japanese business owners to reassure them that they were still welcome. Within a few months, a sense of normalcy returned to the area, but Katayama only received CNY 5,000 in compensation, a tiny fraction of the CNY 580,000 he claimed in damages. While very disappointed, he stayed in business, seeking to put the demonstration behind him.[133] (The restaurant was still open when we visited in 2020.)

The 2005 demonstration put Japanese companies on notice of increased political risks, and larger manufacturers began moving operations out of China to Southeast Asia, decreasing the number of Japanese expatriates in Shanghai. Then, after another round of nationwide anti-Japanese demonstrations in 2012 over the sovereignty of the islands called Senkaku in Japanese and Diaoyu in Chinese, Japanese companies, including restaurants, were again attacked (though on a smaller scale). This accelerated the departure of Japanese businesses and expatriates from Shanghai. Restaurant owners moved to Malaysia and other countries in Southeast Asia to escape the political risks, as well as the rising costs, of doing business in Shanghai. According to one Japanese report, monthly rent and wages rose fivefold from 1998 to 2010, greatly outpacing increases in menu prices.[134] The shrinking profit margins hit small restaurateurs the hardest.[135] The Japanese-cuisine restaurants most able to operate profitably were restaurant chains with access to cheap labor from distant provinces in western China and favorable deals with major real estate developers. These were mostly Chinese-owned restaurant groups. As in the late 1940s, the new masters of the Japanese food scene became Chinese companies. This helped insulate the restaurants from culinary protest politics, enabling the Japanese food boom to continue.[136]

Culinary Soft Power Competition: Japan versus Korea

In Japan and South Korea, food is often employed by the state as a cultural symbol to compete for soft power.[137] In the late 1990s, a "kimchi war" erupted between Japan and South Korea as both countries competed for recognition as the country producing authentic kimchi (in Korean), or *kimuchi* (romanized according to Japanese pronunciation). Kimchi is a daily dish on the Korean dining table; however, Japan had been producing Japanese-style kimchi and expanding its share in the world kimchi market (South Korea, Japan, and China remain the major kimchi producers and exporters). Reacting to the success of Japanese kimchi makers, the South Korean government applied to the World Health Organization and the Food and Agriculture Organization's Codex Alimentarius commission to establish an international standard of making kimchi, claiming that Japanese-style kimchi is less tasty and healthy because its flavor is produced less from fermentation than from artificial sour flavorings. Although the Japanese government accused South Korea of simple trade protectionism, the Korean-style kimchi was designated the international standard in 2001[138] and the craft of kimchi making obtained recognition as a UNESCO Intangible Heritage in 2013.[139] (In the 2010s, this kimchi battle was resumed between South Korea and China, with similar arguments about the labeling and origins of pickled cabbage. Consequently, in July 2022, the South Korean government proposed again to the Codex Alimentarius Commission for the revision of the name of the main ingredient from "Chinese cabbage" to "kimchi cabbage."[140])

In the 2010s, South Korea and Japan switched their culinary soft power competition from cabbage to cuisine. In 2010, the South Korean government began globally promoting *hansik*—traditional Korean cuisine—as its national cuisine. It aimed to make *hansik* among the world's top five cuisines by 2017.[141] In Japan, food culture was one of the four cultural goods included in a Japanese government program called Cool Japan, designed to promote Japanese culture abroad. One successful effort was the listing of Japanese *washoku* (described as "the traditional dietary cultures of the Japanese, notably for the celebration of New Year") as an Intangible Cultural Heritage by UNESCO in 2013, viewed by the Japanese government as a nation-branding victory. This outcome represented both imitation of and competition with South Korea. According to some accounts, Japan's application benefited from the lessons of the failed application by the Korean government the previous year for UNESCO recognition of Korean court cuisine as the cultural heritage of South Korea. The application was rejected on the grounds that court cuisine was an elite practice that did not represent common South Korean foodways. The Japanese application committee, seeing the failure of the Korean application, reworked their own application originally based on *kaiseki*, Japan's own haute cuisine. The revised application successfully submitted to UNESCO downplayed the refined aspects of *kaiseki* to present it as *washoku*. Even though this idea of *washoku* is considered incoherent and ahistorical by some scholars, it is widely used in the government's promotion of Japanese restaurant cuisine abroad.[142]

Another face of geopolitical competition in the culinary field is efforts by nonstate actors, such as media commentators, to sway public opinion. This occurred in Korea in 2013 after Japan's successful UNESCO listing of *washoku*. Some online media insisted on using the Korean word *"asik"* to refer to Japanese food instead of *"washoku."* According to a discussion in the South Korean *JoongAng Ilbo* some Koreans were offended by the word *"washoku"* because the character *"wa"* refers to the spirit of the Japanese people, which to Koreans implies Japanese claims of superiority. Some Korean internet commentators, when considering the history of Japanese invasion and colonization of Korea during the early twentieth century, suggested that Japanese cuisine be called *waesik,* with the character *"wae"* being intended as a hostile reference to Japan.[143] This was an echo of earlier Korean resentment regarding Japanese colonialism after World War II.

Japanese restaurants have also been dragged into other political disputes unrelated to cuisine. In a 2019 trade spat between South Korea and Japan over the issue of forced labor in the colonial period,[144] Japanese restaurants run by local Korean proprietors in South Korea became targets of the "No Japan" boycott movement. As in Shanghai, businesses responded by drawing a sharp line between what is on the menu and who serves the cuisine. In particular, brand names that sounded Japanese, such as Fukuoka Hambageu (hamburger steak), Tokyo Deungsim (barbecue), and Tokyo Suljip (pub), coped by publicizing that they were actually domestic brands.[145]

Culinary Imperialism and Its Postcolonial Culinary Imaginaries in East Asia

From the late nineteenth century until Japan's defeat in 1945, Japan's colonial presence catalyzed the spread of Japanese cuisine throughout a broad swath of Asia, influencing urban foodscapes from a position of power that Japan would neither occupy anywhere else nor ever again. For over half a century, Japanese restaurants introduced local people in colonial cities, willingly or not, to new food varieties and modern consumption style. And again, in the late twentieth century, Japanese investments in the region resurrected the image of Japanese restaurants as spaces of modernity and the urban high life. In both periods, Japan represented an alternative, non-Western modernity in which its distinct restaurant spaces played an important public role.

As Japanese businesses returned to Asia in the postwar period, the post-colonial imaginaries of the colonial era took very different forms for Japanese and for the populations of the former colonies. To Japanese, the colonial legacy served as an incentive for many Japanese companies and individuals to seek their fortunes in East Asia. As Koichi Iwabuchi argues Japanese in the late twentieth century saw the region as a type of time machine where Japan's energetic high-growth past could be relived.[146] Some restaurateurs (especially men) saw nearby Asian countries as a space of erotic and personal adventure, not only for launching a new business but starting a new life, perhaps with a younger partner from the local population. We met many such restaurateurs in our fieldwork in China and elsewhere in Asia.

To people in the former colonies, the resurgence of Japanese cuisine had more complex and ambivalent connotations. Only in Taiwan do we see a genuine postcolonial nostalgia, which includes a Taiwanese (i.e., anti–mainland Chinese) nationalist or localist agenda. Elsewhere in East Asia, with history issues still regarded as "unresolved" by the Chinese and Koreans, the pursuit of Japanese cuisine did not reflect postcolonial nostalgia but rather a search for new lifestyles and fashions associated with cosmopolitan, modern, and healthy living, ideas reflected in subsequent chapters of this book. This view of Japanese cuisine was particularly widespread among young Chinese who view contemporary Japan as an alternative for building modern civilization, including cosmopolitan lifestyles and the cultural and ethical "quality" (*suzhi*) of citizens. Food was part of this imaginary.[147] Despite Japan's declining political and economic power in the twenty-first century, Japanese culinary culture in general was influential both as a way of pursuing a modern life and as a component of local culinary diversity. Nowhere else in the world was the depth of knowledge and interest in Japanese cuisine greater than among Japan's closest neighbors, yet nowhere else did culinary politics more strongly affect its reception.

Notes

1. Bill Sewell, "Reconsidering the Modern in Japanese History: Modernity in the Service of the Prewar Japanese Empire," *Japan Review* 16 (2004): 213–258.

2. Ikegami Akira (池上彰), *Sō datta no ka! Chūgoku* (そうだったのか！中国) [Is that so! China] (Tokyo: Shūeisha, 2010), 170–172.

3. Dennis L. McNamara, "Comparative Colonial Response: Korea and Taiwan," *Korean Studies* 10 (1986): 54–68.

4. In 1920, 347,000 Japanese lived in Korea, growing to 712,000 in 1945, 64 percent of whom lived in cities. Yamamoto Takatsugu (山元貴継), "Nihon tōchi jidai no chōsenhantō ni okeru nihonhondo shusshinsha no tenkai—tochi shoyū to no kakawari o chūshin ni" (日本統治時代の朝鮮半島における日本本土出身者の展開— 土地所有との関わりを中心に) [Development of people from Mainland Japan on the Korean Peninsula during the Japanese colonial era—focusing on the relationship with land ownership], *Rekishi chiri gaku* 45, no. 1 (2003): 3–19.

5. Joshua A. Fogel, "'Shanghai-Japan': The Japanese Residents' Association of Shanghai," *Journal of Asian Studies* 59, no. 4 (2000): 927–950.

6. See, for example, Kate Smith, *Travel and the Social Imagination in Imperial Japan* (Berkeley: University of California Press, 2017); and Kenneth Rouff, "Japanese Tourism to Mukden, Nanjing, and Qufu, 1938–1943," *Japan Review* 27 (2014): 171–200.

7. Yoshinobu Oikawa, *An Official Guide to Eastern Asia: Trans-continental Connections between Europe and Asia* (Imperial Japanese Government Railways, 1906; repr., Tokyo: Edition Synapse, 2009), 152.

8. Yoshinobu, 152.

9. T. Philip Terry, *Terry's Guide to the Japanese Empire: Including Korea and Formosa, with Chapters on Manchuria, the Trans-Siberian Railway, and the Chief Ocean Routes*, rev. ed. (Boston: Houghton Mifflin, 1930), 757.

10. Katarzyna Joanna Cwiertka, *Cuisine, Colonialism and Cold War: Food in Twentieth-Century Korea* (London: Reaktion Books, 2012), 40–42.

11. Robert Hegwood, "Sukiyaki and the Prewar Japanese Community in New York" (unpublished paper presented at the Columbia Graduate Student Conference, 2014).

12. "'Kōa hōkōbi': Lunch Menu in the Mantetsu Dining Car," ca. 1939–1942, Rare Book Division, New York Public Library, New York Public Library Digital Collections, http://digitalcollections.nypl.org/items/a7df6659-147f-9ed8-e040-e00a18063c70.

13. Cwiertka, *Cuisine, Colonialism and Cold War,* 44–47.

14. Ha Wonho, "Yeogsasanchaeg: Yorijip baengnyeon" (역사산책] 요리집 백년) [History: 100 years of restaurants], Korean History Society, June 5, 2004, http://www.koreanhistory.org/4031.

15. Joo Young-ha (주영하), *Sigtag wiui Hangugsa: Menyuro bon 20 segi Hangug eumsig munhwasa* (식탁 위의 한국사: 메뉴로 본 20 세기 한국음식문화사) [History of Korea on the table: Understanding Korean food cultural history of the 20th century through menu] (Seoul: Humanist, 2013), 169–170. The main building of the restaurant was located in Bon-jeong 2-jeong-mok, Gyeongseong (Gyeongseong is the old name of Seoul in imperial Korea; the location is what is now Chung-mu-ro 2-ga, Seoul) and the grand banquet hall was also located in the same area (what is now Chung-mu-ro 3-ga, Seoul).

16. Joo, *Sigtag wiui Hangugsa,* 55. According to Joo, in 1906, the high-end Japanese restaurants in Seoul were Hwa-wol-ru, Guk-chwi-ru, Cheong-hwa-jeong, Song-yeop, Myeong-wol, and Gwang-seung.

17. Cwiertka, *Cuisine, Colonialism and Cold War,* 36.

18. Joo, *Sigtag wiui Hangugsa,* 50–53.

19. Chinese migrants also built Chinese restaurants in colonial Seoul and were successful enough to inspire Japanese to run Chinese eateries. Cwiertka, *Cuisine, Colonialism and Cold War,* 38.

20. Cwiertka, 38–47.

21. Cwiertka, 40–42.

22. Its factories were also built in Taiwan around the same period. "Ajinomoto Group History," Ajinomoto, April 3, 2020, https://www.ajinomoto.com/aboutus/history/ajinomoto-group-history.

23. Yeong Iu, "History of Food Exchanges between Korea and Japan," *Korea Herald,* December 10, 2015, http://www.koreaherald.com/view.php?ud=20151210001173.

24. Wan Lujian (万鲁健), *Jindai Tianjin riben qiaomin yanjiu* (近代天津日本侨民研究) [Research on Japanese migrants in modern Tianjin] (Tianjin: Tianjin renmin chubanshe, 2010), 71.

25. Yamaguchi Tsutomu (山口勗), *Shinkoku yūreki annai* (清国遊歴案内) [Travel guidebook of Qing China] (1902), 64, https://dl.ndl.go.jp/info:ndljp/pid/767032/8?tocOpened=1.

26. Tominari Ichiji (富成一二), *Tenshin annai* (天津案内) [Tianjin guidebook] (Tianjin: Chūtō sekiyin kyoku, 1913), 188–193.

27. Their names were Shikijima, Kobekan, Marusei, Roharo, Heirakuen, Hanaya, Machiyoi, Kikuya, Itansachi, and Nakaya. Tominari, 231.

28. Tominari, 231.

29. Wan, *Jindai Tianjin,* 76–77.

30. Tianjin's Japanese Society (天津居留民団), *Tenshin kyoryū mindan nijū shūnen kinen shi* (天津居留民団二十周年記念誌) [Special Issue of 20th Anniversary of Tianjin's Japanese Society] (Tianjin: Tenshin kyoryū mindan, 1930), 616–20.

31. Kishida Kunio (岸田國士), *Kitashi Monojō* (北支物情) [About northern China] (Tokyo: Hakushasuisha, 1938), 64.

32. Matsumura Mitsunobu (松村光庸). "1930-nendai ni okeru Tenshin Nihon sokai kyoryūmin no kōzōteki tokushitsu" (年代における天津日本租界居留民の構造的特質) [Structural features of Tianjin Japanese concession residents in the 1930s], *Kaikō toshikenkyū* 6 (2011): 76; Wan, *Jindai Tianjin,* 92–94.

33. In the source, chef, geisha, and waitress are three independent categories. It does not clarify whether they were owners or employees in those businesses. Tominari, *Tenshin annai,* 188–193.

34. Wan, *Jindai Tianjin,* 102.

35. Christian A. Hess, "From Colonial Port to Socialist Metropolis: Imperialist Legacies and the Making of 'New Dalian,'" *Urban History* 38, no. 3 (2011): 373–390.

36. Takahashi Hayato (高橋勇人), ed., *Dairenshi* (大連市) [The city of Dalian] (Dalian, China: Tairiku shuppan kyōkai, 1931), 1292.

37. Takahashi, 541–542.

38. Takahashi, 542.

39. Merry White, *Coffee Life in Japan* (Berkeley: University of California Press, 2012), 11–12.

40. Takahashi, *Dairenshi,* 543–544.

41. "Dairen's Strict Blue Laws," *North-China Herald and Supreme Court and Consular Gazette,* August 16, 1939.

42. See James Farrer and Andrew David Field, *Shanghai Nightscapes: A Nocturnal Biography of a Global City* (Chicago: University of Chicago Press, 2015).

43. Leo T. S. Ching, *Becoming Japanese: Colonial Taiwan and the Politics of Identity Formation* (Berkeley: University of California Press, 2001).

44. Chen Yu-Jen (陳玉箴), *Taiwan cai de wenhuashi: Shiwu xiaofei zhong de guojia tixian* (台灣菜的文化史：食物消費中的國家體現) [The cultural history of "Taiwanese cuisine": Expressing the nation through food consumption] (Taipei: Lianjing chuban-

she, 2020), Kindle loc. 442–1193; Chen Yu-Jen (陳玉箴), "Shiwu xiaofei zhong de guojia, jieji yu wenhua zhanyan, rizhi yu zhanhou chuqi de 'Taiwan cai'" (食物消費中的國家, 階級與文化展演: 日治與戰後初期的臺灣菜) [National, class, and cultural expression in food consumption: Japanese occupation and "Taiwanese cuisine" in the early postwar era], *Taiwan shi yanjiu* 15, no. 39 (2008): 141–188.

45. Chen, *Taiwan cai de wenhuashi*, Kindle loc. 808.

46. The restaurant was a branch of an earlier Kishu An opened in 1897 in central Taipei. About Kishu An, see Jizhou an wenxuesenlin (紀州庵文學森林) [Kishuan literary forest], accessed November 27, 2022, https://kishuan.org.tw/aboutus_detail.htm.

47. David Y. H. Wu, "Cultural Nostalgia and Global Imagination: Japanese Cuisine in Taiwan," in *Re-Orienting Cuisine: East Asian Foodways in the Twenty-First Century*, ed. Kwang Ok Kim (New York: Berghahn Books, 2015), 119–122.

48. Wu, 110–111.

49. Chen, *Taiwan cai de wenhuashi*, Kindle loc. 1894.

50. Katakura Yoshifumi (片倉佳史), "Kōwan toshi kiryū wo tazune" (港湾都市基隆を訪ね) [Visit the port city of Keelung], *Nihon Taiwan kōryū kyōkai* 1, no. 898 (2016): 26.

51. Steven Crook and Katy Hui-Wen Hung, "The Biandang from Japanese Days to the Present," *Taiwan Business Topics,* January 19, 2019, https://topics.amcham.com.tw/2019/01/the-biandang-from-japanese-days-to-the-present.

52. Fogel, "'Shanghai-Japan,'" 928.

53. Ikeda Tōsen (池田桃川), *Shanhai hyakuwa* (上海百話) [A hundred tales of Shanghai] (Shanghai: Nihontō, 1926), 12.

54. Ikeda, 11–16; Yokoyama Hiroaki (横山宏章), *Shanhai no nihonjinmachi—Honkō: Mōhitotsu no Nagasaki* (上海の日本人街― 虹口: もう一つの長崎) [Shanghai's Japantown: Another Nagasaki] (Tokyo: Sairyusha, 2017), 71–84; Joshua A. Fogel, *Articulating the Sinosphere* (Cambridge, MA: Harvard University Press, 2009), 73–74. For a discussion of the popularity of Western food in the Sima Road nightlife district, see Mark Swislocki, *Culinary Nostalgia: Regional Food Culture and the Urban Experience in Shanghai* (Stanford, CA: Stanford University Press, 2008), 97–99.

55. Iwama Kazuhiro (岩間一弘), "Shanghai no nihonshoku bunka: Menyū no genchika ni kansuru hiaringu chōsa hōkoku" (上海の日本食文化：メニューの現地化に関するヒアリング調査報告) [Shanghai's Japanese food culture: A hearing survey report of menu localization], *Chiba shōdai kiyō* 51, no. 1 (2013): 1.

56. Iwama, 2.

57. Yokoyama, *Shanhai no nihonjinmachi—Honkō*, 34–38.

58. Yokoyama, 43; Miyake Koken (三宅孤軒), *Shanhai inshōki* (上海印象記) [Shanghai retrospective] (Tokyo: Ryōri shinbunsha, 1923).

59. Yokoyama, *Shanhai no nihonjinmachi—Honkō*, 45–46; Fogel, "'Shanghai-Japan,'" 930.

60. The building was used for housing after the war but was demolished sometime after 2015 to make room for a hotel complex. Interior and exterior photos of the contemporary building can be found at "Rokusantei kara miru sekai" (六三亭から見る世界) [The world seen from Rokusantei] Mikyō: Shanghaijōhō (blog), October 5, 2016, https://ekobiiki888.hatenablog.com/entry/20161005/1475610724.

61. We leave these four names in Chinese name order since they are famous historical figures whose names are always written this way.

62. Miyaji Kandō (宮地貫道), "Dōraku" (道楽) [Entertainment], *Shanghai nichinichi shinbun* (October 1929), reprinted in *Seiminshū—Shanhai nichinichi shinbun ronsetsushū* (成民集—上海日日新聞論説集) [Citizens collection—Shanghai nichinichi shinbun editorial collection] (Tokyo: Ōmu sha, 2019), 122; Matsumura Shigeki (松村茂樹), "Rokusanen ibun" (六三園逸聞) [Memories of Rokusan], *Otsuma kokubun* 28 (1997): 195–206.

63. Wang Xian (忘闲), "Riben liaoli" (日本料理) [Japanese cuisine], *Xiaoshibao*, December 29, 1917, 4.

64. Shou Ou (瘦鸥), "Dongyang liaoli changshiji" (东洋料理尝试记) [The experience of trying Japanese cuisine], *Shanghaihuabao* no. 350, 1928, 1.

65. Lun Xin (伦新), "Dongyang liaoliguan de sumiao" (东洋料理馆的素描) [Sketch of a Japanese restaurant], *Shuihuo* 1, no. 1, May 1935, 11.

66. Su Guangcheng (苏广成), "Zai hongkou chi riben liaoli" (在虹口吃日本料理) [Eating Japanese cuisine in Hongkou], *Haixing (Shanghai)* no. 5, 1945, 2.; Qianshi Shi, "Hongkou de riben liaoli dian" (虹口的日本料理店) [Japanese cuisine in Hongkou], *Shehuiribao*, July 24, 1945, 3.

67. Wang Bo (王渤), "Jialianwumei de riben liaoli dian" (价廉物美的日本料理店) [Cheap and good Japanese restaurants], *Haibao*, March 19, 1944, 1.

68. La Shou (辣手), "Jinri Hongkou" (今日虹口) [Today's Hongkou], *Xinshanghai*, no. 6, 1946, 10.

69. Lu Xi (露西), "Riben wei de canting" (日本味的餐厅) [A restaurant with Japanese flavor], *Feibao*, August 16, 1947, 2.

70. "Sukiyaki House Sealed by SWG," *North-China Daily News*, June 11, 1948, 3; "Quiz Army Rank of Sukiyaki Man," *Shanghai Post*, June 11, 1948, 1.

71. Feng Du (风度), "Shalong yanji he gonghong liangjia ribenfeng caiguan" (沙龙燕集和恭弘两家日本风菜馆) [Two Japanese restaurants: Shalongyanji and Gonghong], *Heping ribao*, August 22, 1947, 4; Bin, "Shalongyanji fazhe yanguang xiyin ni qu tanqi" (沙龙燕集发着艳光吸引你进去探奇) [The lights of the Salon Yanji entice you to explore inside], *Shishi xinbao*, September 18, 1947, 2.

72. Ding Yi (丁翼), "Shanghai de shiwaitaoyuan riben liaoli dian" (上海的世外桃源日本料理店) [Japanese restaurants as paradise in Shanghai], *Libao*, August 14, 1947, 2. The term "White Russian" refers to the refugees who came to Shanghai fleeing the Soviet Union. Many women worked in the entertainment industry.

73. Ad in the *North China Daily News*, May 22, 1950, 2.

74. There were many currencies in use in China in the 1920s, a period of political disunity. This most likely refers to the silver dollars that circulated at the time, often from Mexico.

75. "$18,000 Damage Done by Rioters in Yangtsuepoo: Japanese Restaurant and Kindergarden [sic] Lose Heavily, Statement Shows," *China Press*, June 20, 1925, 1.

76. "The Anti-Japanese Boycott: A Warning to Chinese Restaurant Keepers," *North-China Daily News*, July 13, 1927, 12.

77. Kan Kan (侃侃), "Riben liaoli dian yu rihuo" (日本料理店与日货) [Japanese restaurants and Japanese goods], *Jingbao*, August 5, 1936, 2.

78. Jiang Pan (江畔), "Qiqihaer riben liaoli dian: Qunian huajiu shouru baiyuwan" (齐齐哈尔日本料理店: 去年花酒收入百余万) [Japanese restaurants in Qiqihaer: More than one million yuan income last year], *Shanghaibao*, March 17, 1936, 3.

79. "Japanese at the Table: Flesh-Pots of the West, the Origin of Sukiyaki," *North-China Daily News*, December 21, 1920, 5; "Sukiyaki Joins Rank of Chop Suey Dishes: Sliced Onion, Pork Fat and Other Delicacies in It," *China Press*, January 22, 1927, 2.

80. "Sukiyaki Party Big Success at Japanese Club: Friendship Society at Dinner Entertains Mixed Gathering," *China Press,* December 12, 1930, 2.

81. "Sukiyaki Party Is the Rage for Certain Set," *China Press,* February 9, 1936, 2.

82. "Sailor 'Y' Plays Host to Big Crowd: Usual Sunday Evening Sukiyaki, Social Meeting Held," *China Press,* section 2, January 11, 1932, 1.

83. Ad in the *North-China Daily News,* May 22, 1950, 2. The name Runo means "Golden Fleece" in Russian; see Katya Knyazeva, "Just How Cosmopolitan Can You Get?," Livejournal, February 10, 2018, https://avezink.livejournal.com/77166.html.

84. *North-China Daily News,* March 26, 1951, 2. The owner of a restaurant in that building wrote that she sold it to a Russian in 1945 (see her story in Chapter 4).

85. Wu, "Cultural Nostalgia."

86. Chen Yu-Jen, *Taiwan cai de wenhuashi,* chap. 3.

87. Ceng Pingcang (曾品沧), "Rishi liaoli zai Taiwan: Chushao yu Taiwan zhishi jieceng de shequn shenghuo" (日式料理在台湾：锄烧与台湾知识阶层的社群生活) [Japanese cuisine in Taiwan: Sukiyaki and social life of the Taiwan intellectual class], *Taiwan shi yanjiu* 22, no. 4 (2015): 1–34.

88. Crook and Hung, "Biandang."

89. Fieldwork by Chuanfei Wang, May 13, 2018.

90. Fieldwork by Chuanfei Wang, May 10, 2018.

91. Shannon Lin, "Taiwanese Rediscovering Their History in the Streets of Taipei," *News Lens,* July 13, 2017, https://international.thenewslens.com/article/73429.

92. Jizhou an wenxue senlin.

93. Kim Bora, "Jeonbeomgieob paegteu chekeu: Keobseupeu·milkeukalamele nogadeun bulpyeonhan jinsil)" (전범기업 팩트체크:컵스프·밀크카라멜에 녹아든 불편한 진실) [War crime companies fact check: The uncomfortable truth about cup soup and milk caramel], Business Watch, September 27, 2019, http://news.bizwatch.co.kr/article/policy/2019/09/23/0023.

94. Jeon Junho, "Gimcheon daeseongam bonga leul asinayo" (김천 '대성암 본가'를 아시나요) [Do you know Daeseongam Bonga in Gimcheon], *Hangook Ilbo,* June 12, 2017, https://www.hankookilbo.com/News/Read/201706121112739671.

95. Joo, *Sigtag wiui Hangugsa,* 168–169.

96. Hwang Gyoik, "2012 nyeon, Illyuga seouleul jibaehanda" (2012 년, 일류 (日流) 가 서울을 지배한다) [In 2012, Japan wave dominates Seoul], *Sisa In,* March 2, 2012, https://www.sisain.co.kr/news/articleView.html?idxno=12469.

97. Changzoo Song, "Transcultural Business Practices of Korean Diaspora and Identity Politics: Korean Sushi Business and the Emergence of 'Asian' Identity," *Studies of Koreans Abroad* 32, no. 3 (2014): 1–23.

98. Joo, *Sigtag wiui Hangugsa,* 168–169.

99. Kwon Hyeryeon, "[Eumsig (eumsig) eulo bon 70 nyeon] Ilbonsig danpatppang, silhyangmin naengmyeon, geuligo lamyeonui chueog" ([음식(飲食)으로 본 70년] 일본식 단팥빵, 실향민의 냉면, 그리고 라면의 추억) [Seventy years seen through food: Memories of Japanese style *anpan,* cold noodles of refugees, and *ramyeon*], *Chosun Ilbo,* August 12, 2015, https://news.chosun.com/site/data/html_dir/2015/08/11/2015081100849.html.

100. Hwang Gyoik, "Hanguge on ilboneumsigeun jjagtung" (한국에 온 일본 음식은 짝퉁) [Japanese food that came to Korea is not authentic], *Weekly Donga,* August 28, 2006, https://weekly.donga.com/3/search/11/80016/1.

101. Hwang, "2012 nyeon, Illyuga seouleul jibaehanda."

102. In the cities, most Western restaurants and all Japanese ones were closed down in the 1950s. In Shanghai, which had had by far the most foreign restaurants, the number dwindled to twenty-one by 1963, and only thirteen by the Cultural Revolution. See James Farrer, "Culinary Globalization from Above and Below: Culinary Migrants in Urban Place Making in Shanghai," in *Destination China: Immigration to China in the Post-reform Era,* ed. Angela Lehmann and Pauline Leonard (New York: Palgrave Macmillan, 2019), 175–199.

103. Japanese firms brought young IT workers from Japan to Dalian on local contracts. See Kumiko Kawashima, "Service Outsourcing and Labour Mobility in a Digital Age: Transnational Linkages between Japan and Dalian, China," *Global Networks* 17, no. 4 (2017): 483–499.

104. Interviews and fieldwork by Zhang Yinyue, September 2018.

105. See Yukiko Koga, *Inheritance of Loss: China, Japan, and the Political Economy of Redemption after Empire* (Chicago: University of Chicago Press, 2016).

106. Sasha Issenberg, *The Sushi Economy: Globalization and the Making of a Modern Delicacy* (New York: Gotham Books, 2007), chap. 11.

107. Tiantian Zheng, *Red Lights: The Lives of Sex Workers in China* (Minneapolis: University of Minnesota Press, 2009).

108. Fieldwork by Zhang Yinyue, September 2018.

109. Kumiko Kawashima, "Japanese Labour Migration to China and IT Service Outsourcing: The Case of Dalian," in Lehmann and Leonard, *Destination China,* 123–145.

110. Fieldwork by Christian Hess, March 2017.

111. Fieldwork by Zhang Yinyue, September 2018.

112. See James Farrer, "Imported Culinary Heritage: The Case of Localized Western Cuisine in Shanghai," in *Rethinking Asian Food Heritage,* ed. Sidney Cheung (Taipei: Foundation of Chinese Dietary Culture, 2014), 75–104.

113. James Farrer, "Domesticating the Japanese Culinary Field in Shanghai," in *Feeding Japan: The Cultural and Political Issues of Dependency and Risk,* ed. Andreas Niehaus and Tine Walravens (New York: Palgrave Macmillan, 2017), 287–312.

114. Iwama, "Shanghai no nihonshokubunka," 7.

115. JETRO, "Kaigai yūbō shijō shōryū chōsa (chūgoku)" (海外有望市場商流調査 (中国)) [Promising overseas market commercial distribution research (China)], Japan External Trade Organization, March 24, 2022, https://www.jetro.go.jp/world/reports/2022/02/36177d79e5c45062.html.

116. *Shanghai ryōriten chōsa hōkoku* (上海料理店調査報告) [A research report on Shanghai Japanese restaurants], Asahi Research Center, 2005, http://www.hokutou.jp/report/image/china_report20051102.pdf.

117. Iwama, "Shanghai no nihonshokubunka," 5.

118. JETRO, "Kaigai yūbō shijō shōryū chōsa."

119. The types of sexual services ranged from conversation to sexual intercourse and were detailed in guidebooks such as Oguchi Hideaki et al., *Shanghai & Guangzhou: Yoru no arukikata* (上海&広州: 夜のあるき方) [Shanghai & Guangzhou: Getting around at night] (Tokyo: Datahouse, 2003). Many long-term relationships also developed between Japanese expatriates and women working in these establishments. Fieldwork by James Farrer in Shanghai, 2005–2020.

120. The details of the story are unclear, but since the manager was designated a legal representative of Katayama, seizing ownership would not have been difficult. In the 1990s and early 2000s, foreign direct ownership of restaurants required larger investments than many owners could afford. Therefore, expatriate-invested small businesses were often registered under the names of local partners (often a spouse or a manager). This also eased interactions with corrupt regulators. If a struggle over ownership ensued, however, the foreign partner often had little legal recourse.

121. The current manager blamed Katayama's problems on his placing too much trust in the "Shanghainese" (as opposed to migrants from other regions like herself), a type of local ethnic politics. Conversations and fieldwork by James Farrer in 2005, 2010, and January 2020.

122. Himeta Konatsu (姫田小夏), "Shanhai ni mikiri wo tsukeru nihonjin inshokuten keieisha ga ato wo tatanai riyū" (上海に見切りをつける日本人飲食店経営者が後を絶たない理由) [Reasons why Japanese restaurant owners give up on Shanghai are endless], Diamond Online, August 23, 2019, https://diamond.jp/articles/-/212569.

123. Wang Haofan (王昊凡), "Shanhai no taishū sushiten ni okeru rōkaruka to 'sushishokunin' no seiritu oyobi sono yakuwari" (上海の大衆寿司店におけるローカル化と寿司職人の成立及びその役割) [Localization in Shanghai's popular sushi restaurants and the establishment of "sushi chefs" and their roles], *Nihon rōdō shakai gakkai nenpō* 27 (2016): 138.

124. Dianping.com, 2017.

125. Tang Tao, interview by James Farrer, January 8, 2020.

126. The International Financial Center Mall is a multilevel shopping mall with a huge variety of Japanese-themed places—about one-third of them were Japanese based on our observation. An entire basement appendage is devoted to trendy Japanese fast foods.

127. Tang Tao, interview by James Farrer, January 8, 2020.

128. This statement reflects a common view among informants in the industry that Chinese restaurant management tends to be owner-centric, and chefs typically have less autonomy than in Western or Japanese restaurants.

129. "Corporate Overview," Maxim's, https://www.maxims.com.hk/en/milestone. Accessed on November 20, 2022.

130. Wang Haofan, "Shanghai no taishū sushiten," 139.

131. This section of the chapter is based on James Farrer's fieldwork observing the protest and interviewing both protesters and Japanese residents in April 2005. See also James Farrer, "Nationalism Pits Shanghai against Its Global Ambition," YaleGlobal Online, April 29, 2005, https://archive-yaleglobal.yale.edu/content/nationalism-pits-shanghai-against-its-global-ambition; James Farrer, "The Multiple Contexts of Protest: Reflections on the Reception of the MIT Visualizing Cultures Project and the Anti-Right Japanese Demonstration in Shanghai," *Positions: East Asian Cultural Critique* 23, no. 1 (2015): 59–90.

132. Fieldwork by James Farrer, January 9, 2020.

133. Ralph Jennings, "Gingerly, Japanese Business in Shanghai Resumes," *Kyodo*, December 22, 2005; "Wakamono ni ima mo hannichi kanjō: Shanghai no demo kara ichinen" (若者に今も反日感情: 上海のデモから一年) [Young Chinese still hate Japan: One

year after the Shanghai demonstration], Excite Blog, April 16, 2006, https://juniversal
.exblog.jp/4408067/.

134. Himeta, "Shanhai ni mikiri."

135. Christopher St Cavish, "The Real Cost of Running a Restaurant in Shanghai:
A Detailed Look at One Restaurant's Books," Smart Shanghai, June 5, 2015, https://
www.smartshanghai.com/articles/dining/the-real-cost-of-running-a-restaurant-in
-shanghai.

136. Farrer, "Domesticating the Japanese Culinary Field."

137. James Farrer, "Introduction: Travelling Cuisines in and out of Asia: Towards a
Framework for Studying Culinary Globalization," in *The Globalization of Asian Cui-
sines: Transnational Networks and Contact Zones,* ed. James Farrer (New York: Palgrave
Macmillan, 2015), 1–20.

138. Calvin Sims, "Cabbage Is Cabbage? Not to Kimchi Lovers; Koreans Take Issue
With a Rendition Of Their National Dish Made in Japan," *The New York Times*, February 5, 2000, https://www.nytimes.com/2000/02/05/business/cabbage-cabbage
-not-kimchi-lovers-koreans-take-issue-with-rendition-their.html; "Codex Alimentarius: International Food Standards, STANDARD FOR KIMCHI CXS 223-2001," Food
and Agriculture Organization of the United Nations, accessed December 1, 2022,
https://www.fao.org/fao-who-codexalimentarius/sh-proxy/en/?lnk=1&url
=https%253A%252F%252Fworkspace.fao.org%252Fsites%252Fcodex%252FStandard
s%252FCXS%2B223-2001%252FCXS_223e.pdf.

139. Toshio Asakura, "Cultural Heritage in Korea—from a Japanese Perspective,"
in *Reconsidering Cultural Heritage in East Asia,* ed. A. Matsuda and L. E. Mengoni
(London: Ubiquity Press, 2016), 105–106.

140. "Codex Alimentarius: International Food Standards, Request for comments on a
proposal for revision of the Standard for Kimchi (CXS 223- 2001)," Food and Agriculture
Organization of the United Nations, accessed December 1, 2022, https://www.fao.org/fao
-who-codexalimentarius/sh-proxy/en/?lnk=1&url=https%253A%252F%252Fworkspace
.fao.org%252Fsites%252Fcodex%252FCircular%252520Letters%252FCL%2525202021
-91-OCS%252Fcl21_91e.pdf.

141. Gaik Cheng Khoo, "The Hansik Globalization Campaign: A Malaysian Critique," *Gastronomica: The Journal for Food Studies* 19, no. 1 (Spring 2019): 65–78.

142. Eric Rath, *Japan's Cuisines: Food, Place and Identity* (London: Reaktion
Books, 2016); Katarzyna Joanna Cwiertka and Yasuhara Miho, *Branding Japanese Food:
From Meibutsu to Washoku* (Honolulu: University of Hawai'i Press, 2020). See our dis-
cussion of the Washoku World Challenge in Chapter 8.

143. Lee Taekhee, "Itaeghuiui masttalagi keugi·mas 'kkamnol' hohwa gimbab mas-
jib beullogeu 1sedaeui ilsigjib naseu" (이택희의 맛따라기 크기·맛 '깜놀' 호화 김밥 맛집 블
로그 1세대의 일식집 나스) [The first generation Japanese restaurant Nasu serving luxury *kimbap* with amazing taste and the size], *JoongAng Ilbo*, December 22, 2017,
http://news.joins.com/article/22226155.

144. "South Korea and Japan's Feud Explained," BBC, December 2, 2019, https://
www.bbc.com/news/world-asia-49330531.

145. Choe Sanghyeon and Min Yeongbin, "Wulin Hangug tojonginde: Dokyo, Hu-
kuoka, Osaka ileumsseossdaga banilseubgyeog" (우린 한국 토종인데:도쿄·후쿠오카·오사
카 이름썼다가 반일 습격) [We are Korean born: Being a target of anti-Japan for having

Tokyo, Fukuoka, and Osaka in brand names], *Chosun Ilbo,* August 4, 2019, https://www.chosun.com/site/data/html_dir/2019/08/04/2019080400658.html.

146. Koichi Iwabuchi, *Recentering Globalization: Popular Culture and Japanese Transnationalism* (Durham, NC: Duke University Press, 2002), 177–181.

147. Jamie Coates, "Between Product and Cuisine: The Moral Economies of Food among Young Chinese People in Japan," *Journal of Current Chinese Affairs* 48, no. 3 (2020): 1–19.

3 | Japantown Restaurants

From Community Spaces
to Touristic Imaginaries

Christian A. Hess, James Farrer,
David L. Wank, Mônica R. de Carvalho,
Lenka Vyletalova, and Chuanfei Wang

In the late nineteenth century, migrants from Japan began heading far beyond the boundaries of the Empire of Japan to regions of the world
where they lacked status, resources, and the support of the Japanese state.
In cities around the world, they formed ethnic enclaves that became known
as Japantowns. Within them, a shifting cast of Japanese settlers, sojourners, and entrepreneurs created Japanese restaurants that defined Japanese
cuisine for generations of consumers. This chapter narrates a century and
a half of immigrant culinary politics reflecting discrimination against migrants, the rising status of Japanese cuisine linked to corporate expatriate
communities, and most recently the creation of gentrified Japanese culinary
districts largely bereft of Japanese residents. Over the decades we see restaurants shifting in their menus and décors from producing culinary nostalgia
for Japanese migrants and sojourners to creating spaces to market connoisseurship and fantasies of Japan to a growing non-Japanese clientele.

We document three kinds of Japantowns, each with its characteristic
forms of Japanese restaurants. The first section examines the poor migrants
from Japan who migrated to the Americas beginning in the 1870s, first to
Hawai'i and later to the US West Coast, Brazil, and Peru. In their migrant
enclaves in Los Angeles, São Paulo, and other cities, they established restaurants that served their communities as a home away from home. The second section examines the sojourner communities of elite Japanese. While
some were founded in the early twentieth century, the heyday of corporate-
linked Japantowns was after World War II as expatriates dispatched by

Japanese corporations created enclaves in cities around the world. Expensive restaurants founded to serve expatriates in these cities contributed to an imaginary of Japanese cuisine as exclusive and refined. The third section describes the commercialized Japantowns that emerged during the global boom in Japanese cuisine beginning in the late twentieth century. They are "Disneyfied" or themed culinary districts, much like the French Quarter in New Orleans or Little India in Singapore, organized for sustaining tourism rather than serving Japanese residents.[1] Within them, entrepreneurs of diverse ethnic backgrounds and chain restaurants experiment with Japanese culinary imaginaries constructed to appeal to tourists. The rise and decline of these Japantowns reflect various factors, including the changing character of out-migration from Japan, the shifting status of Japan internationally, and views of Japan and Japanese culture in the broader receiving societies.

Creating Japanese Restaurants in the Americas

The first section of this chapter explains the rise and decline of restaurant businesses among the new Japanese migrants in the Americas. It describes US West Coast enclaves, then Japanese community restaurants in Chicago, and finally the largest Japanese community in the Americas, in São Paulo, Brazil. The common thread in these stories is the formation of an ethnic Japanese restaurant industry serving Japanese migrant communities that was shaped by the dual politics of coping with white hostility and a desire to interact with and integrate into the larger society.

Japanese Eateries as Community Spaces on the US West Coast, 1890s–1941

In the United States, the high point of Japanese immigration was between 1900 and 1930, when over 250,000 people arrived.[2] The first Japanese restaurants appeared on the West Coast in cities like Los Angeles in the late 1890s, the region of the world that—not incidentally—would become an epicenter of the global Japanese food boom a century later.[3] The story of Japanese restaurants in Japanese settler communities on the West Coast is closely tied to intertwined experiences of racism, exclusion, and internment, and to the types of business opportunities settlers could carve out in this changing ethnic and economic landscape. The fortunes of Japanese eateries, from the makeup of their clientele to their size and location, likewise followed the rise and fall of Japantowns. Japanese restaurants in early settler communities served their fellow countrymen comfort food and entertainment from the home culture. They were immigrant third places needed in a hostile society.[4] By the 1930s, however, new food fashions, most notably sukiyaki, allowed Japanese restaurateurs to attract more diverse and middle-class patronage to Japantown restaurants.

Starting in the late 1800s, the West Coast experienced an influx of Japanese migrants, mostly men who came to work in agriculture, fisheries, railways, and mines.[5] Due to the rural orientation of migrants and their labor, Japanese communities in urban centers were relatively small compared with well-established Chinatowns.[6] In the early 1920s, the estimated Japanese population in California was about seventy-five thousand people.[7] By 1930, 75 percent of the Japanese population in the United States lived in California.[8] Los Angeles, for example, was home to over twenty thousand Japanese in 1935, half of them first-generation migrants.[9] Large Japanese settlements were also found in Seattle, Portland, Tacoma, and Vancouver. These cities provide important historical glimpses into the early restaurant scene in Japantowns before the 1940s.

Like many other migrants, Japanese entered the hospitality trade because of the low start-up costs and discrimination in the broader labor market. In the late nineteenth century, the earliest Japanese male migrants often worked as "house boys" in the homes of white people, and beginning in the 1890s, they started opened cafeterias serving Western-style food. Others found jobs in Chinese restaurants in Chinatown, learned culinary techniques, and opened their own Chinese restaurants. Outside the larger Japantowns, most Japanese-owned restaurants in California actually served standard American fare or Chinese cuisine, the latter usually labeled "chop suey." (The Chinese chop suey fashion was ignited by Chinese immigrant restaurateurs at the turn of the twentieth century.)[10] Before the sukiyaki boom of the 1930s, Japanese-cuisine restaurants operated almost exclusively in Japanese enclaves with enough residents to support them. The first may have been the Yamato, opened in San Francisco in 1887, followed by the Miharashitei in Los Angeles in 1893, both serving growing Japanese communities.[11]

West Coast Japantowns were immigrant enclaves both culturally and economically. Until the 1920s, the majority of urban businesses run by

Japanese served other Japanese migrants.[12] Given the large number of seasonal laborers flowing through cities like San Francisco, Fresno, Sacramento, Portland, and Seattle, some of the first urban businesses run by Japanese before the 1920s were boardinghouses, hotels, pool halls, and "bar-restaurants," basically small pubs serving food, alcohol, and female companionship to solitary, mostly male, Japanese migrant laborers. In 1912, Sacramento, for example, had twenty-five bar-restaurants, Stockton and Fresno had eleven each, and Los Angeles had thirty. Often these were native-place-oriented establishments, something we also see in some of the restaurants in colonial cities.[13] The economic development of a Japantown could be measured by the increase in Japanese-owned restaurants. For example, the number of Japanese restaurants in Seattle rose from one in the 1890s, to seven by 1907, to thirty-nine by 1916, including specialty shops purveying sushi and soba.[14]

Japantown restaurants in the 1920s had eclectic menus and clientele, serving everything from American-style breakfasts to chop suey and Japanese dinners.[15] One of the largest restaurants in Seattle's Japantown was, in fact, a Chinese restaurant, run by Yoshiji Wakamatsu, that could seat three hundred people. There was also the Nikko Low restaurant, a popular drinking spot for Japanese businessmen, which was noted for serving both Chinese and Japanese food. Lower-end establishments, like Seattle Japantown's Jackson Cafe, established in 1928 by Ichiro Egashira, relied heavily on Chinese customers. The café was open at night, and the patrons were mostly Chinese laborers. This nighttime flow of customers dried up after the Japanese invasion of Manchuria in 1931, when Chinese boycotted Japanese restaurants in the United States.[16] Nevertheless, these details indicate how Japanese not only brought their own cuisine to the US restaurant scene but were pioneers of pan-Asian cuisines (a pattern mirrored by other Asian restaurateurs in later decades).

The size of Japanese restaurants ranged from small family-run spaces to restaurants that could handle hundreds of customers. The Gyokkoken restaurant in Seattle, run by Jyusaburo Fuji, could serve three hundred. Smaller "high-class" restaurants, such as Maneki and Maruman, served well-to-do Japanese expats. These were "traditional" drinking and entertainment spots for men, offering the décor of home and the company of hostesses. A key feature of these restaurants, as in the Japanese colonies in Asia, was the role played by women, as managers, waitresses, or barmaids (*shakujō*, who doubled as hostesses, since there seem to have been few, if any, professionally trained geishas). According to one contemporary observer, Shizu (Yone) Kaida, "The mistress [manager] at the Japanese restaurant Maneki, is an unforgettable figure in postwar Japanese restaurants in Seattle. She came from Osaka, and though not really beautiful, she was a kindly woman and treated her husband with respect."[17] Maneki was a spot for eating, playing poker, and carousing with waitresses, and it even functioned as a picnic spot for families on Sunday. Hideo Miyazaki, originally from Tokyo, recalls the scene: "At restaurants, gentlemen enjoyed playing poker, dice, mahjong. Since I didn't drink sake I got together with my friends at Gyokkoken and played games. The sake drinkers went to Nikko Low where both Chinese and Japanese foods were served, and to Maneki and Shinpuken, traditional Japanese restaurants. There were no [trained] geishas of any sort in Japanese town, so at each restaurant, the mistress and a couple of waitresses in ordinary Western dresses entertained the customers by playing shamisen [a three-stringed lute]. I especially remember Shizu Hirao of Nikko Low and chubby Kimichan at Shinpuken." Miyazaki continues, "What was interesting was the maids who entertained us. They were all married and ranged in age from twenty-seven [to] fifty, most were once daughters of priests at Buddhist temples or of liquor store owners. They made good wages, working from four p.m. to midnight."[18]

Working-class Japanese employed in sawmills and railroads could not afford the high-end establishments but still flocked to Japantown in Seattle to enjoy themselves at cheaper spots. One popular destination was Ichiro Egashira's Jackson Cafe. Egashira's son, who took over the business, recalled, "Our Jackson Cafe and places like it were good for handling customers who stayed clear up to closing time. Often a waitress brought her customers from another place after hours, ate the best dishes, and took out food to go. We were open twenty-four hours and made a considerable profit. Today people have cars and don't stay at cafes too long."[19] Thus, before World War II, high- and low-end eateries were places of leisure for Japanese migrants and Japanese Americans who whiled away an evening between work and home.

Japanese-run restaurants were also a focus of racial tensions in places like California. As minority-owned businesses, Japanese restaurants became targets of racialized labor politics. Starting in the late 1890s, Japanese migrants opened many American-style cafeterias throughout California, serving "ten-cent meals" that undercut the prices of white-run establishments.[20] In San Francisco, tensions erupted between 1905 and 1907, when a series of racist attacks flared up against Japanese and their businesses. Japanese-run restaurants were a principal target. It appears that Japanese proprietors had angered the mostly white members of the Cooks and Waiters Union in San Francisco for price cutting in Japanese-run cafeterias. So the union took action by launching a three-week boycott of Japanese-run establishments.[21] These and other incidents of discrimination and violence deepened the insularity of Japantowns even as they grew larger.[22]

From Dens of Illegality to Culinary Craftsmanship, 1910s–1930s

In the early twentieth century, Japanese American community restaurants were far from the trendsetters that they would later become. Japanese culture, including cuisine, did receive positive appraisals in some travelers' accounts in the wake of Japan's victory in the Russo-Japanese War in 1905. However, due to anti-immigrant sentiment, local Japanese restaurants in the United States, much like their Chinese counterparts, were viewed suspiciously by local and state officials and the press.[23] In early Japantowns the boundaries between restaurant, bar, and brothel were often blurred, and US press reportage often associated Japanese restaurants with crime. During the early twentieth century, for example, Japanese restaurant owners in Hawaiʻi and on the West Coast increased their profits by bootlegging liquor or selling alcohol without a bar license. A 1908 *Los Angeles Times* article noted that "forty Japanese eating places here violate the liquor laws about every time they serve a meal."[24] Japanese-owned restaurants in Los Angeles were closed in a mass police action in 1908 for violating liquor licensing regulations. Other raids followed, creating fear and consternation among Japanese restaurant owners and employees.[25] Although the licensing issue seems to have been resolved, related conflicts persisted for years. During the Prohibition era (1920–1933), Seattle patrons of Japanese hotels could enjoy *shōchū*, a strong, distilled liquor, which was smuggled from Japanese restaurants directly to hotel rooms in hot water bottles.[26] Similar bootlegging incidents, often involving Japanese restaurants, were uncovered by reporters in Hawaiʻi from 1908 through the 1920s.[27]

The relationship between restaurants, bars, and the sex trade was an early feature of Japantowns on the West Coast, a fact lamented by Japanese officials like Masanao Hanihara, the secretary of the Japanese embassy. In 1908, Hanihara investigated the living conditions of Japanese in Washington, Oregon, Idaho, Utah, Colorado, California, and Texas. His view of Japanese migrant communities was highly negative, as evident in the report he wrote on conditions in Seattle's Japantown. "Streets are lined with Japanese restaurants, barbershops, pool halls, and boarding houses," he writes. "It means that the scene of the busiest part of the Japanese community is a row of shabby houses, dubious-looking posters and numbers of paper lanterns shamelessly hung at doors." He noted that "at night obscene sights and words are frequently glimpsed and overheard by passers-by. It is indeed far from a community of civilized people." He finished his description by bluntly stating that "a further undesirable phenomenon for Japanese in Seattle is a relatively larger number of barmaids, prostitutes and the like among the Japanese women in Seattle."[28] Although prostitution in eateries would disappear after World War II, the image of the Japanese female server as a geisha figure in a kimono would continue as part of the appeal of Japanese restaurants in the mid-twentieth century. The disparaging views of immigrant-run restaurants also would persist among elite Japanese expatriates, who felt these working-class immigrants were creating a backward image for the rising Japanese nation.

It was only with sukiyaki's growing popularity that Japanese restaurants began to be regarded as culinary destinations by white Americans. The late 1920s were a turning point, led partly by positive reports about Japanese cuisine on the East Coast, where there was less animosity toward Japanese migrants (see Chapter 4). Led by New Yorkers, the 1920s and 30s saw a rising interest in foreign-themed restaurants among white Americans, attracted by their exotic atmosphere and servers dressed in "native" attire.[29] Japantown restaurants benefited from this trend. Throughout the 1930s, from Seattle to Los Angeles, Japanese restaurants specializing in tempura and sukiyaki started attracting non-Japanese customers. Tenkin Tempura House was one of the largest and most popular tempura restaurants in San Francisco's Japantown, which was home to nearly nine thousand Japanese migrants and their families in the late 1930s. In 1940, Tenkin was even featured in a travel book touting the city's cosmopolitan cultural scene for (presumably white) tourists.[30] Tenkin was a large operation and featured home delivery with trucks. Noboru Hanyu recalled his time working there as a high school student in the 1930s, "driving the delivery truck and working butterflying shrimp, washing rice and making *tsukemono* [pickles]."[31]

However, even more than tempura, sukiyaki made Japanese cuisine visible to white customers, much as chop suey already had done for Chinese

FIGURE 3.1 Seattle's Bush Gardens was one of the preeminent Japanese restaurants on the US West Coast. It sat up to five hundred guests. As in most sukiyaki restaurants of the 1950s, kimono-clad waitresses helped prepare the sukiyaki tableside. (Postcard circa 1960, owned by James Farrer)

food. Sukiyaki restaurants experienced steady growth in popularity from the late 1920s through the 1930s. In larger Japantowns, sukiyaki was a high-class affair. Among the first sukiyaki restaurants were those established in such high-end hotels as the Yamato Hotel, reflecting the dish's elite status on the other side of the Pacific in the Japanese empire and on the menus of the ocean liners traveling between Japan and the United States. In the late 1920s, migrant restaurateurs began opening more elaborate restaurants to appeal to this new market, including some outside traditional Japantowns. A new sukiyaki restaurant in Mountain View, California, was described in the *Japanese American News* as "a pavilion gracing the highway to beckon all those who enjoy a delicious Japanese dinner served piping hot by Nippon maids in native costumes."[32] In 1936, during the Great Depression, there even was an ambitious (though unrealized) plan by a Japanese business-man to open a nationwide chain of five hundred sukiyaki restaurants to provide work for second-generation Japanese American youths facing an exclusionary "color barrier" in the US labor market.[33] As discussed in more detail in Chapter 4, sukiyaki's popularity positioned Japanese cuisine rela-tively high in the culinary hierarchy and gave Japanese cooks recognition as "culinary artists and skilled craftsmen."[34] But a less positive factor in this boom was racism in the larger society, so that few other employment opportunities existed for Japanese Americans in this era.

Wartime Internment and the Rise of Midwest Japantowns, 1942–1980s

The outbreak of war in the Pacific in 1941 and Japanese Americans' mass internment brought about the destruction or permanent diminishment of the West Coast Japantowns. With entire communities sent to remote internment camps, Japanese lost their homes and businesses. However, the impact in the cities of the Midwest, where few Japanese had previously lived, was radically different. In 1941, the War Relocation Authority permitted Japanese Americans to leave the internment camps if they relocated to designated locations in the Midwest and on the East Coast. Chicago was the first city open to resettle Japanese Americans.[35] Chicago's prewar population of about four hundred ethnic Japanese exploded as twenty thousand Japanese Americans came to work in textiles, book binding, and other light manufacturing industries. After the war, about fifteen thousand remained in Chicago, consolidating on the Near North Side at Clark and Division Streets, a neighborhood previously known for rowdy nightlife and vice. Over the next two decades, the North Side Japantown shifted three miles north to Lakeview, near Wrigley Field baseball stadium. The heyday of Lakeview Japantown was the 1960s and 1970s, when it supported 150 religious, commercial, and cultural Japanese-owned establishments, including forty restaurants, many clustered along Clark Street and Broadway Street.[36]

Chicago had Japanese restaurants since at least the 1910s, serving a mixed clientele, but their concentration into a Japantown was new.[37] During its flourishing in the 1960s, the restaurants were tightly woven into the community's fabric, much like the prewar Japantowns on the West Coast. This can be seen in an account of growing up in Chicago's Japantown by a resident interviewed for an oral history project on the community:

> Because there were so many families that knew each other in some way or another, there was a sense of safety in that there was always someone, some neighbor or friend of the family, who lived nearby. . . . This also provided a sense of self-policing, as none of us dared do anything to bring shame upon our families. That pressure to "not bring shame upon your race" kept most

Nikkei in line. Social pressure was also instrumental in other areas. As a child, I remember my parents talking about a Nisei man who beat his wife. When he walked into Nisei Lounge, a local tavern, everyone turned their backs to him and let him know that "wife beaters were not welcome there" and that he could return when he began treating his wife properly. . . . It was always nice to know that if you needed to stop to rest, or you felt uncomfortable by someone following you, there were numerous Japanese-owned businesses on Clark Street where you could seek safe haven.[38]

This interview illustrates how restaurants were both places where community norms and sanctions could be enforced and also refuges for Japanese Americans to eat and socialize free from worries of prejudice.

There were in fact several types of restaurants in Chicago's Japantown. We interviewed Stuart Mizuta, a Japanese American who grew up in Lakeview and shared his own classification of its restaurants as homestyle, fusion, authentic, and corporate (upscale).[39] The first three kinds in his homegrown typology developed largely in Chicago's Japanese American community in the early postwar decades, whereas the last type represents the more diverse boom in Japanese cuisine since the 1980s that has largely passed over Japantown. Indeed, including this last category of restaurant allows us to see how the Japanese cuisine business has now largely bypassed traditional Japanese American community restaurants, which always have struggled with an image of inauthenticity (among both non-Japanese food critics and elite Japanese visitors and expatriates).

First, Mizuta said, homestyle Japanese restaurants were spaces where Japanese Americans could feel comfortable, and they were only patronized by Japanese Americans. The décor was simple, and the owners cooked and waited on tables and lived upstairs. The menus featured home cooking and no sushi. By the 1990s, all had closed except for Sunshine Café, started in 1994 by a Japanese migrant couple, Joni and John Ishida. Joni had trained as a chef in Nagoya and ran a tea garden in Chicago in the 1960s catering to Japanese businesspeople. However, she found it stressful because of patrons' exacting demands, so she opened a casual restaurant called Cho Cho San's, while her husband, John, ran Johnny's Three-Decker Sandwich Shop. Then, gentrification and fires at their restaurants forced them to close and find jobs as cooks for United Airlines. However, their friends encouraged them to start another Japanese restaurant, as all the other homestyle ones had shut down, so they opened Sunshine Café.[40] It served homestyle dishes, such as croquettes (described as deep-fried Japanese mashed potatoes), hot and cold soba and udon noodle dishes, and such *donburi* (rice) bowls as *oyakodon* (chicken cutlet and egg over rice), *katsudon* (pork cutlet over rice), and beef *teridon* (teriyaki beef over rice). It also featured dinner-plate entrées, such as fresh mackerel, grilled teriyaki chicken, and vegetable stir-fry. A restaurant reviewer in 2017 raved about the "massive" bowls of sukiyaki and the homemade *gyōza* (dumplings).[41]

Second, there were Japanese American fusion restaurants serving inexpensive hybrid dishes. An example is Hamburger King, opened in the mid-1950s near Wrigley Field. In an interview for a community oral history, the daughter of its founder described the cuisine as follows: "Except for the hamburgers and grilled cheese, just about everything on the menu could be ordered with rice—Polish sausage, eggs, and rice; bacon and eggs and rice; flank steak and rice; chili mac and rice; and of course, rice and gravy." Its signature dish Akutagawa, named after a customer, consisted of ground hamburger, bean sprouts, eggs, and onions fried on a flat-top grill and served with rice.[42] Its clientele consisted mainly of Japanese American bachelors, a rough crowd that appreciated its late hours and inexpensive dishes, but it grew to include baseball coaching staff from Wrigley Field, as well as non-Japanese artists possibly attracted by its edgy vibe and low prices. Lacking Japanese-style décor, it was basically a "greasy spoon" diner where customers paid upfront when ordering. Its front window had a neon sign of a yellow and green bowl surrounded by the red words "Chicken teriyaki" and "Noodles." In 2010, the restaurant was sold to a Korean couple who kept the diner atmosphere but renamed it Rice 'N' Bread and added Korean dishes to the menu.

Third, the "authentic" Japanese restaurants described by Mizuta can be located on the American dining map as "neighborhood" restaurants. Authentic restaurants differ from homestyle ones because they have contemporary, but not upscale, décor; a hired waitstaff; and a menu including sushi and fewer overtly fusion dishes. A typical one was Matsuya, opened in the 1970s in Lakeview. Its sign announced its name in Japanese and English, indicating takeout and *obento* (Japanese box meal) delivery. Its menu featured meal sets with such entrées as chicken teriyaki, spicy salmon roll, and *nigiri* (hand-pressed) sushi, and sides and appetizers, such as *gyōza*, yakitori, fried oyster, *ika shogayaki* (squid sautéed with ginger), cold sashimi, *tako-su* (marinated octopus), seaweed salad, and sea urchin and quail egg in ponzu sauce. Matsuya sat about fifty people at four-person tables and an eight-person sushi counter, and it had Japanese wall decorations and television with Japanese programming.

Fourth, Mizuta mentioned upscale restaurants organized around sushi bars that showcased the chef's skill, with a clientele of Japanese business expatriates and non-Japanese with money and discerning tastes. Among the first was Katsu, opened in 1988 in Rogers Park, outside Chicago's Japantown. It was owned by Katsu and Haruko Imamura, immigrants from Japan who previously had worked in the textile industry. In 2013, *Zagat Guide* rated it the number two restaurant in Chicago. It featured four-course *omakase* (chef's choice) sushi and sashimi menus that, at about USD 130, were far more expensive than the community restaurants mentioned earlier. The sushi was traditional Japanese style, and Katsu refused customer requests to add cream cheese, spicy mayo, and other American-style ingredients.[43] Also, all dishes were served on Japanese-style ceramics, unlike in the other kinds of restaurants. Although Katsu embodies a type of restaurant now regarded by foodies as more "authentic" than many older restaurants in Japantown, this idea of authenticity valorizes practices in Japan while disavowing the culinary innovations and localizations typical of Japanese American restaurants. Moreover, Japanese restaurants such as Katsu are often not centered in any identifiable Japantown. This illustrates how the boom in Japanese restaurant cuisine from the late twentieth century—whether at the high or low end—has largely bypassed traditional Japantown restaurants in Chicago, San Francisco, and elsewhere. In contrast to cuisine regarded as "from Japan," Japanese American restaurant cuisine (like Chinese American cuisine) has had difficulty establishing its authenticity and status among consumers and critics (see Chapter 4).

The Redevelopment and Corporatization of West Coast Japantowns, 1960s–Present

West Coast Japantowns have been transformed by demographic shifts and urban renewal. Japantowns in San Francisco and Los Angeles were depopulated by internment and after 1945 struggled to revive as communities. In a sense, these communities were "defeated" four times. First was by internment. Second, postwar urbanization and development processes dominated by white elites enabled corporate-led urban renewal schemes of the 1950s–1970s to grab land from the Japanese community. Third was the influx of Japanese capital in the 1960s, sidelining locally owned businesses. Some Japantowns were destroyed, while a few live on as sites of culinary tourism and nostalgia. Fourth, in the 1990s, as Japanese Americans aged and moved away, migrants from other parts of Asia began taking up ownership of many Japantown restaurants, a development seen by some as a new threat to the community identity.

In the 1960s, starting in Little Tokyo in Los Angeles, the arrival of Japanese capital and expatriates affected the development of restaurants in the remnants of the Japantowns that had survived the war. For example, in 1964, the Tokyo Eiwa Group invested in a large two-story restaurant for five hundred customers called the Tokyo Kaikan with a Polynesian-themed all-you-can-eat Chinese buffet. This style of service violated health codes, so the restaurant switched to tempura, teppanyaki, Chinese, and sushi counters, with each in one corner of the restaurant. Later, the restaurant's piano bar became a popular Japanese-themed discotheque called Tokyo A-Go-Go, attracting Audrey Hepburn, Rock Hudson, and other stars. As will be discussed in Chapter 4, Tokyo Kaikan's sushi bar was possibly the first in the city, and where the California roll was reputedly invented.[44] The success of this development signaled that new trends in Japanese restaurants would be driven by the influx of Japanese corporate expatriates and trendsetting non-Japanese customers. By the 1970s, there were two Japanese communities in Los Angeles, an aging settler community centered in Little Tokyo and a transient expatriate community concentrated in suburban South Bay.[45] Japanese restaurants, which had previously been concentrated in Little Tokyo, began opening around the city, including in affluent neighborhoods in West Los Angeles and Orange County.[46] In the 1980s, non-Japanese customers became the fastest-growing market. Little Tokyo would hang on as a tourist destination but with increasingly fewer restaurants owned by its Japanese American residents.[47]

San Francisco's main Japantown experienced a more drastic postwar fate, with corporate-led urban renewal schemes razing a neighborhood now stigmatically labeled as "blighted" in postwar urban development plans. This "blight" largely referred to black Americans who moved into the neighborhood during the war. This stigma was reflected in a *New York Times* article on the 1968 launch of San Francisco's new Japan Center that gushed, "The old Nihonmachi [Japantown], long deteriorating, has won the promise of new life with the aid from private capital and the city's Redevelopment Agency."[48] Powerful corporations allied with the city government to steamroller opposition from the local Japanese American community. The mall-like Japan Center would occupy five acres in the heart of Japantown. In San Francisco, as in Los Angeles, these development plans were pushed by investments from Japan. Japan Center's biggest partner was Kintetsu Enterprises, which was owned by the Kinki Nippon Railway Company. In 1960, San Francisco's redevelopment agency selected National-Braemar to lead the design and development of the Japan Center project. National-Braemar was headed by Issei financier Masayuki Tokioka of Hawai'i and Los Angeles developer Paul Broman. Half of Japantown was seized by eminent domain and the homes of almost ten thousand people and hundreds of businesses were demolished.[49] The completed Japan Center buildings were allocated among four corporate investors. The Japan Center mall, which had displaced so many family-run businesses and restaurants, featured a new force in the restaurant scene—the corporate-run Japanese restaurant.[50]

Tenants in the new project included the first US branch of Japanese chain Suehiro, a three-hundred-seat steak restaurant featuring "beer and rice-fed Kobe-Matsusaka beef steaks flown in from Japan on special order."[51] The main dish at Suehiro was sukiyaki, the invention of which is sometimes attributed to Suehiro in Japan in the nineteenth century. In the 1980s, the space occupied by Suehiro was taken over by an outlet of the popular Benihana steak chain (see Chapter 4). There also were independent restaurants like Fuki-ya, advertised as the first *robatayaki* (open charcoal grill) restaurant in the United States. It was opened in 1978 by Richard Diran and his Japanese wife, Junko, who met in Kyoto and then moved to San Francisco.[52] As the community aged, the number of ethnic Japanese-owned restaurants slowly declined. By 2019, long-term residents we spoke with expressed dissatisfaction that Japan Center was now dominated by chain restaurants and Japanese-themed restaurants owned by Korean and Chinese entrepreneurs.[53]

In 2019, we joined a food tour of San Francisco, one of the ways this type of neighborhood is now sustained and marketed.[54] According to the guide, many of the traditional Japanese-owned restaurants in the neighborhood were struggling or closed. Only a small number of restaurants, grocers, tea shops, and *obento* shops were still owned by long-term Japantown families. There were a few trendy new restaurants, including Ichi Sando, specializing in gourmet Japanese *tamago sando* (egg sandwiches), started by chef Euijin Kim-Wright, who moved to San Francisco after working in fine dining restaurants in New York City. Reflecting the nationwide ramen boom, three shops in the neighborhood serve various styles of ramen, including Marufuku's chicken *paitan* (white broth) ramen, Yamadaya's slow-cooked *tonkotsu* (pork bone) broth ramen, and Hinodeya's light dashi-based ramen with whole wheat noodles. All of these shops, however, were brought to Japantown by outside restaurant groups. Marufuku was founded by Bay Area restaurateurs Eiichi Mochizuki and Koji Kikura, who started with the shabu-shabu restaurant Shabuway in San Mateo.[55] Hinodeya is the first foreign venture of a restaurant group from Utsunomiya, Japan.[56] Yamadaya is a chain begun in Torrance, California, by Yamada Jin, a graduate of Tokyo's Sophia University.[57]

A highpoint of the Japantown culinary tour was Benkyodo, one of the last remaining family owned Japantown institutions. A Japanese American family-owned confectionary founded in 1906, its owners were interned during World War II but returned to reopen the shop in 1951. Benkyodo, along with some other old Japanese shops in the neighborhood, still attracted a loyal following of ethnic Japanese customers—including American-born ones, new migrants, and Japanese expats—who still regarded the neighborhood, despite its radical changes, as their cultural home base.[58] Benkyodo was the last place in Japantown to sell locally made Japanese sweets, including over a dozen varieties of colorful *manjū* (stuffed flour cakes) and mochi (rice cakes), popular with foodie tourists. It was not just a sweet shop, however. Regulars still occupied the spinning stools along the counter to consume American-style deli fare, including a deviled egg sandwich and "hot dog sandwich."[59] With its third-generation owners retiring and no family members willing to take over, Benkyodo closed in March 2022. This closure symbolized the ongoing decline of the Japanese American family business presence in Japantown.[60]

San Francisco's Japantown may still be the nostalgic heart of the Japanese community, a place cherished by Japan-born migrants as well as those whose ancestors arrived a century ago. A search on Yelp in 2021 still found thirty Japanese restaurants in the Japantown area; however, it has lost its position as the center of Japanese food fashions in the city. Culinary innovation in Japanese foodways is now associated with San Francisco's dispersed fine dining scene, one that is no longer located in distinct Japanese neighborhoods, nor primarily concerned with Japanese customers, nor necessarily run by ethnic Japanese restaurateurs. We discuss these evolving culinary fashions in subsequent chapters.

The Formation of South America's Largest Japantown, 1908–Present

Between 1908 and the early 1940s, over 180,000 Japanese migrated to Brazil.[61] The largest Japantown formed by these migrants was in the Liberdade neighborhood in São Paulo. Its Japanese restaurants developed along broadly similar lines as those in North America, including the rise of community restaurants serving an ethnic enclave and their more recent eclipse by trendy Japanese restaurants established in other areas of the city. However, the development of Japantown restaurants in São Paulo also reflects differences from the United States in terms of the migration and settlement patterns of the Japanese population in Brazil.

Japanese migration to Brazil began and peaked later than on the US West Coast. The arrival of immigrants started in 1908 and reached a high point during the years between 1924 and 1933, when 130,000 people came.[62] This surge was partly a response to the 1924 Immigration Act in the United States, which virtually halted immigration from Japan. It was also spurred by Japanese government efforts to solve its domestic unemployment and population problems by funding emigration to the state of São Paulo and establishing companies there to broker jobs for the migrants.[63] Japanese immigration to Brazil continued after World War II, reaching approximately 180,000 people by 1959.[64] By 2020, there were nearly 2 million Japanese descendants, constituting almost 1 percent of the national population, and the largest of any country outside Japan, followed by the United States, with 1 million Japanese descendants.

The historical development of Japanese restaurants in Brazil differs from that in North America in several key respects. First, in comparison to the United States, the scale of the internment of Brazil's Japanese population during World War II was more limited (though still oppressive), so the dislocation of Japanese communities and their businesses was not as drastic. Second, while racist land laws in the United States prohibited Japanese from owning and farming rural land and pushed the community into cities, Japanese immigrants to Brazil remained primarily rural before World War II. In 1934, there were 120,811 Japanese working in the São Paulo countryside, and only 10,828 Japanese living in the city.[65] By 2020, in contrast, about 90 percent of the Japanese Brazilian community lived in cities, with the largest urban population in São Paulo.

The history of Japanese restaurants in São Paulo can be traced to the early 1910s when boardinghouses for immigrants started running restaurants, a pattern similar to that on the US West Coast. These establishments were clustered around Liberdade, a neighborhood close to the Municipal Market in Cantareira Street, where many Japanese businesses concentrated because of their roles as producers and buyers of agricultural products. As early as the 1920s, boardinghouses offered both Brazilian and Japanese cuisine (including coffee and bread for breakfast), showing how some young immigrants were adapting to Brazilian tastes.[66] In 1914, Uechi Ryokan, the first restaurant serving Japanese cuisine, opened in the Conde de Sarzedas area, the heart of Liberdade. It provided guests with a meal of white rice (probably long-grain indica), miso soup, *tsukemono* (pickles), and fusion homestyle dishes. Throughout the pre–World War II era, the typical Japanese eatery was a simple dining room offering basic dishes such as udon, bowl dishes, *inari* sushi (rice stuffed in a fried tofu pouch), and set meals. Many side dishes were Brazilian-style recipes familiar among migrants from the coffee plantations, such as *tempero*, a pickled chopped vegetable mixture. By the 1920s, fancier full-service restaurants (*ryōtei*) began to appear in São Paulo, replete with attractive female servers. One such restaurant was Ume no Ie, which advertised the companionship of the "beautiful Haruko" in a Japanese newspaper in 1929. The patrons were nearly all Japanese migrants.[67]

In the early twentieth century, these various inns and pensions with restaurants and "bars" (small eateries) offered a taste of home to rural migrants passing through the city. Shizue Arai, a second-generation Nissei whose parents owned a small restaurant just after World War II, recalled, "Many of those who came from the rural regions would watch several Japanese movies in a row and eat sushi and hand-kneaded udon noodles before returning backcountry."[68] The rural migrants greatly valued this chance to taste home and socialize with compatriots. A 1926 study of Japanese migrants in Brazil described a scene in an udon restaurant called Gyo-yoshi where the author recalled an "unforgettable encounter" with a young rural worker. The worker said that once a year he came to the city to eat a real udon meal, which gave him the patience to work in the countryside for another year.[69]

The development of full-service restaurants with elaborate dining rooms occurred later in Brazil than in the United States, and they were comparatively scarce. With a less urbanized population and fewer restaurants,

Japanese grocers and supply chains also developed more slowly than in North America. Though a Japanese migrant opened a soy sauce factory in 1914, most migrant families in Brazil made their own key ingredients, including miso.[70] As late as the 1980s, provisioning a restaurant with Japanese ingredients was difficult. One chef, whose family operated Japanese restaurants in Brazil for over fifty years, recalled making several trips a year back to Japan to obtain key ingredients in bulk (including *konbu* [dried seaweed]) because they were too expensive to source locally.[71]

Still, by the mid-1930s, there were over ten restaurants in the Japantown (*Nihonjingai*) in Liberdade.[72] The largest employed women as servers or

FIGURE 3.2 Confeitaria Motomu, founded by Minesaku Matsuzaki circa 1930, was famous for its sweets and ice cream, and was frequented by São Paulo society in the Liberdade neighborhood. (Hildegarde Rosenthal, Instituto Moreira Salles, circa 1940)

barmaids who often became public faces of the restaurants. For example, a float at a 1935 carnival parade carried waitresses from a popular Japanese restaurant, which also shows that Japanese Brazilians were participating in the broader urban culture of Brazil.[73] As in the United States, World War II dealt a blow to the flourishing Japantown. Following Brazil's declaration of war on Japan in 1942, the Brazilian government initiated discriminatory policies against Japanese Brazilians, including freezing their assets and prohibiting them from speaking Japanese outdoors. There were incidents of violence as well, including looting of shops along Conde de Sarzedas, the main street of Japantown in São Paulo. As a result, all communal spaces, such as street restaurants and eateries in inns and pensions, were, in effect, forced to close. At the end of 1942, the Japanese residents around Conde de Sarzedas were forcibly evacuated, many to farm settlements where their movements were closely monitored by police.[74]

The Japanese community in Liberdade began rebuilding when World War II ended. In 1945, two Japanese restaurants, Hisago Shokudo and Sakurai Shokudo, opened on Conde de Sarzedas and in Liberdade Square. Subsequently, restaurants were opened in nearby locations, including the Cantareira Municipal Market, Galvão Bueno Street, and smaller Japanese settlements, such as Pinheiros district. Still, until the mid-1950s, more than half the Japanese restaurants in São Paulo were located in inns and boardinghouses, indicating the continuing focus on travelers from rural areas.[75] By the early 1950s, there were twenty-eight Japanese hotels and pensions, and twenty-three Japanese restaurants (including simple cafeterias [*shokudō*] and fancier restaurants [*ryōtei*]) in São Paulo.

From the 1950s to the 1970s, a revitalized Japantown emerged in the neighborhood of Galvão Bueno Street in Liberdade, where several Japanese restaurants already existed. It was modeled on Little Tokyo in Los Angeles, with decorative streetlamps shaped like lilies of the valley and a large red torii (the gate of a Shinto temple).[76] More Japanese businesses opened in the area, including stores, restaurants, cinemas, and hotels, as well as the offices of various prefectural associations (*kenjinkai*), which were core institutions of the local Japanese society. A new Little Tokyo development plan for Liberdade, sponsored by the São Paulo City Tourism Board, included a subway station just underneath Liberdade Square in 1975. The vigorous revival of the neighborhood covered up the humiliating treatment of the community during World War II. Japanese restaurants increased substantially in the "New Japantown" (*Shin-Nihonjingai*) area. Japanese Brazilians owned restaurants ranging from places specializing in eel, oysters, or beef to one restaurant, Galvão Bueno, that featured "Tokyo style *tonkatsu,* Italian cuisine and *teishoku* [set meals]." They also operated Indian curry and Chinese restaurants, though the majority offered some Japanese cuisine. In 1978, the Liberdade Chamber of Commerce had sixty-three restaurants among its three hundred members.[77]

The arrival of Japanese corporate migrants in the 1950s challenged the centrality of the traditional migrant enclave economy, as in the United States. Some restaurateurs sought to cater to these new migrants by moving to areas like Bela Vista, a former Italian enclave favored by these expatriate families. In 1971 the Japanese beverage company Suntory, which had begun opening restaurants in the United States, opened one in the Jardins area, an upper-middle-class neighborhood. The Suntory restaurant became a symbol of an affluent, globalizing Japan, where top executives gathered for recreation and business. It also became a space that, to non-Japanese Brazilians, reflected the sophistication of the Japanese business world. By the late 1970s, Japanese cuisine had started to become more popular among non-Japanese Brazilians, a food fashion trend that began later than in the United States.[78]

The arrival of Japanese expatriates and the popularization of Japanese cuisine beyond the Japanese community created both opportunities and challenges for Liberdade's restaurants. High-end restaurants continued to open in trendy areas of the city favored by Japanese expatriates and the Brazilian elite rather than in Japantown. In 1988, 47 of São Paulo's 75 Japanese restaurants were in Liberdade, but by 2009, the neighborhood contained only 37 of the city's 319 Japanese restaurants.[79] Also, by this later time, many Nikkei owners of restaurants in the city complained that Liberdade had become increasingly dominated by migrants from other Asian countries profiting from the popularity of Japanese cuisine, a situation found in Japantowns around the world. One Nikkei restaurateur we spoke to in 2018 called this the "Orientalization" of Japanese cuisine.[80] The rise of Korean and Chinese restaurateurs was also linked to Nikkei Brazilians' declining interest in the restaurant trade. This reflected various trends, including the migration of many Nikkei Brazilians back to Japan beginning in the 1980s and the changing professional aspirations among young Nikkei in Brazil. Also, workers in Japanese restaurants were now increasingly non-Asian internal migrants from poorer regions of Northeast Brazil (*Nordestinos*). They

FIGURE 3.3 Galvão Bueno Street, the main shopping street in São Paulo's Liberdade neighborhood, is crowded with visitors on a national holiday afternoon. A man dressed as a samurai performs in front of the Azuki emporium, a Japanese shop. (Photo by Kevin Del Papa, November 15, 2021)

even came to dominate traditional culinary artisanal work, such as handmade tofu and Japanese confections.[81] As in Los Angeles and San Francisco, a few older restaurants endured, and the tourists still came, but Liberdade no longer defined the fashions for Japanese cuisine in São Paulo, and Japanese migrants less completely defined Liberdade.

Expatriate Japantowns

With the growth of an export-led economy after World War II, a new type of Japantown based on corporate expatriates on temporary assignments began appearing in cities around the world. In a few cases—such as Los Angeles and São Paulo—these communities partially overlapped with existing immigrant communities, though these old and new immigrants often interacted very little. In other cases—such as London and New York—substantial Japanese business communities already existed before the war.

But there are many business-led Japantowns—such as the large one in Düsseldorf or the smaller one in Hanoi—that were entirely the product of postwar corporate expatriation.

Despite their diversity in size and other details, Japanese expatriate communities have some common features. One is the corporate dominance of social life and even residential settlement patterns.[82] Japanese expatriates tend to self-segregate, a pattern driven by a lack of language skills, advice from companies, and the use of Japanese real estate agents (e.g., in Shanghai, London, and Düsseldorf), as well as a need for proximity to Japanese schools (e.g., Prague and Singapore), the central business districts (e.g., Singapore and Düsseldorf), commuter lines (e.g., London), or the main airport serving Japan (e.g., Shanghai). Japanese expatriates thus often reside in one suburban neighborhood and commute to a city center, and the Japanese restaurants serving them may be concentrated in both these residential and business centers (though more in the latter). Despite their insularity, in many cities around the world these expatriate communities have been gateways for introducing Japanese foodways to new markets. Restaurants serving these communities range from prestige projects meant to assert Japan's culinary soft power, to small community eateries used as refuges for corporate migrants and travelers. However, as expatriate communities have declined (many since the 1990s), even these restaurants have had to reorient toward non-Japanese customers.

Pre–World War II Expatriate Communities, 1900s–1945

The earliest expatriate restaurants were supported by small expatriate communities in a few capital cities. London hosted the first European Japanese community, making the city the center of Japanese culinary influences throughout Europe ever since.[83] From the 1860s, as the Meiji government opened Japan to the world, the core of this community was educated and urbanized individuals dispatched by Japanese government and corporations—students, officials, business leaders, and others seeking to learn Western knowledge and technologies and find opportunities for the expanding Japanese economy. These elite sojourners were accompanied to The United Kingdom by other Japanese immigrants who worked for them. Therefore, the initial Japanese community in London consisted of elite Japanese and their staff.[84] It was the latter group who stayed on to operate guest houses and eateries.

London in the 1930s had nearly one thousand Japanese residents. The size and affluence of the community created a market for Japanese restaurants. The earliest Japanese restaurant in London was the Miyako-tei, owned by Mantaro Uno, which was established around 1900. By 1924, there were six Japanese restaurants. Three of them—Hinode-ya, Miyako Club, and Tokiwa—stayed in business until the late 1930s.[85] The relationship between these Japanese restaurants and their customers was intracommunal. All of the establishments were located in Soho (considered by Japanese to be the Japanese neighborhood), were owned by Japanese, and mainly served Japanese residents and visitors. They mostly featured Japanese food; however, some offered hybridized cuisine. For example, Tokiwa hired a Chinese chef in 1924 and served Chinese food in addition to Japanese. Ikuine offered Western-style dishes such as curry rice and Spanish omelets.[86] Migrant chefs often learned at one restaurant and then opened a new one, or a branch, on their own with financial support from former employers.[87] Furthermore, some restaurateurs with experience in London tried their luck in other capitals, such as Paris, Hamburg, or Berlin, thereby extending the influence of London-based Japanese restaurants throughout Europe, a pattern still occurring a century later.

After London, the largest prewar Japanese business presence was in Germany, with Japanese business associations founded in both Hamburg and Berlin. The Berlin Japanese community consisted mostly of diplomats, representatives of trading companies, and students.[88] Already by 1902, three modest Japanese eateries operated in Berlin: Nippon Ba (Japan granny), Atami-ya, and Nihon Anagura (Japan cellar). They served grilled eel, sashimi, sushi, *suimono* (broth), *yakinori* (grilled laver), and other Japanese dishes "no different from those back home," according to author Sazanami Iwaya, who resided in Berlin from 1900 to 1902.[89]

In the 1930s, Berlin still supported three Japanese restaurants.[90] The most prominent was Akebono, opened around 1935 by Kuichi Sugimoto. Born in 1883 in Kure, he married but at age thirty-five left his wife and child and traveled to London to learn the hotel business. After several years in London and Cardiff, he moved to Berlin, possibly to open a branch of the prominent London Japanese restaurant Tokiwa. This venture apparently failed, and he opened his own restaurant, Akebono, in 1935.[91] A photo from 1941 survives of Akebono's exterior, with the prominent lettering "Japanisches Restaurant" and the name Sugimoto, and visible Japanese national and naval flags.[92] Akebono was popular with Japanese residents and travelers.

Sukiyaki seems to have been a popular specialty. The restaurant also catered for official embassy functions. This included a tasting dinner organized by the Japanese embassy in April 1943 to introduce a party of high-ranking military officers of Nazi Germany's Wehrmacht to soy products such as tofu, miso, and soy sauce as a solution to meat shortages. Soybeans presumably would be imported from Manchukuo (Japanese-controlled Manchuria). This event thus was a last gasp of Japanese colonial culinary politics married to new ideas of vegetarian eating. The knowledge that Adolf Hitler was a vegetarian may have factored into this fanciful scenario.[93]

In the prewar and wartime years, Berlin's Japanese restaurants were relatively expensive and were supported mostly by the Japanese expatriate community. They were situated in the affluent neighborhood of Wilmersdorf, an area with several Japanese-owned businesses and shops, that Japanese expatriates called "Japan village" (*Nihon mura*).[94] This prewar community never exceeded six hundred people and shrank during the war.[95] So given these small numbers, the three Japanese restaurants also must have had some German patrons. A 1927 report in the *Munich Illustrated Press* stated, "In Berlin, in Paris, in London, people can now eat according to the ways of foreign peoples. It began [in Germany] with Italian restaurants, Viennese cakes and American bars. But people no longer can satisfy themselves with just these. Now you can dine in a Japanese restaurant, have the original Japanese language menu presented and try one's hand clumsily with the customary chopsticks."[96] Nazism and the war ended this cosmopolitan scene. With much of the area of the Japan village destroyed in the massive British air raids in late November 1943, none of these Japanese restaurants survived.[97]

In comparison with Berlin and London, the Japanese community in Paris developed more through artistic and scholarly circles than business elites. The first Japanese restaurant in Paris was likely the Tomoe-tei in the Latin Quarter, which was opened in 1900 by a Japanese woman, Tomoe Itahara, who served Japanese dishes such as *nasu denraku* (miso eggplant) and *iwashi no shioyaki* (grilled salted sardines) to Japanese visitors to the 1900 Paris Universal Exposition (see Chapter 4). A visitor noted that the restaurant was decorated in a Japanese style and the dishes were served on Japanese ceramics by a young Japanese woman in a kimono.[98]

By 1936, there were four Japanese restaurants scattered through the city: Miyako and Botanya in the central sixteenth arrondissement, near many tourist attractions; Fouji (Fuji) in the fifth arrondissement, home of Sorbonne University; and the Japan Club in the eighth arrondissement, which is centered on the Champs Elysees. The restaurants served sukiyaki, tempura, and sashimi.[99] Japanese migrants faced linguistic, financial, and legal obstacles to opening restaurants in prewar France. The Japanese founders of Miyako and Botanya were both married to French women who jointly managed the restaurants and seem to have been the legal owners. Running a Japanese restaurant in Europe also was expensive. Restaurateurs in Paris could buy some supplies, such as soy sauce, from a Japanese shop near the Église de la Madeleine in central Paris but had to directly import other ingredients from Japan. They also grew some Japanese vegetables themselves. Additionally, expanding the market was difficult. Europeans remained unfamiliar with Japanese tastes, so Japanese restaurants in Paris, as in Berlin, relied on the regular patronage of a small community of fewer than five hundred Japanese, Japanese travelers, and occasional European curiosity-seekers.[100]

The most famous prewar Paris restaurant was Botanya, a Japanese-style *ryōkan* (establishment offering food and lodging), opened in 1928 by Satoshi Shimodaira near the Bois de Boulogne. It served as a community center for Japanese expatriates throughout the wartime years and into the mid-1950s. It was also a gathering spot for Japanese artists and literati. *Sake* and wine flowed freely at these parties, and it seems some French dishes also were served.[101] However, travelers were not always impressed. Moto Saito, a Japanese geisha, while on an around-the-world cruise in 1930, visited Botanya with a group of wealthy Japanese travelers eager for Japanese food after weeks of travel. According to Saito, the group found a sadly run-down establishment with foul-smelling soy sauce and rustic dishes. Saito, used to the cuisine in fine *ryōtei* in Japan, regarded her meal at Botanya as a "national shame," motivating her to open her own restaurants in Shanghai and New York (see her story in Chapters 1 and 4).[102]

Sustaining Europe's Largest Japanese Corporate Expatriate Community, 1960s–Present

During the heyday of Japan's overseas business expansion in the 1970s and 1980s, Japanese communities in Europe greatly surpassed their prewar predecessors in scale. However, with the decline of Japanese overseas investment in the 1990s, they began shrinking. Other than London, the one city in Western Europe where the Japanese expatriate business community was strong enough to sustain a flourishing restaurant scene into the twenty-first century was Düsseldorf, where the German city's Klein-Tokio (Little Tokyo) has occupied a prominent place near the main train station. With Berlin divided and isolated after World War II, Düsseldorf was the choice for Japanese investments due to its proximity to the new capital in Bonn and the industrial Rhineland, as well as its central location within Western Europe. In 1964, there were eight hundred Japanese residents and sixty Japanese companies in the city, surpassing those of Hamburg. By the 1980s, Düsseldorf had become the second-largest Japanese expatriate community in Europe, after London, with about 8,500 long-term residents and four hundred Japanese firms.[103] Düsseldorf's Japanese community developed along with the Japanese Club (1964), the Japanese Chamber of Commerce (1966), the Japanese School (1971), and the German-Japanese Centre (1978), creating an institutional Japanese network not found in other German cities.[104] In 2018, Little Tokyo still had the largest concentration of Japanese-owned restaurants in Western Europe, attracting Japanese expatriates from the region and non-Japanese foodies (including many Asians) wanting an "authentic taste." Its restaurants ranged from traditional sushi at the old-school Kikaku or Yabase, to ramen at Naniwa or Takumi, to Nobu-style fusion dining in Nagaya, the only Michelin-starred Japanese restaurant in Germany.

In 1997, of the roughly two hundred sushi restaurants in Germany, about a quarter were in Düsseldorf. Food historian Maren Möhring suggests that Japanese cuisine enjoyed high social status because the Japanese migrants were usually skilled professionals who lived in enclaves in the wealthiest areas of the city. Their high status influenced not only the price structure of Japanese food in Germany but also the position of Japanese food in the German culinary hierarchy. Even the tendency of the Japanese "colony" in Düsseldorf to isolate itself from the surrounding local society fed the conviction that Düsseldorf was the home of authentic Japanese cuisine, untouched by German influences.[105] Within Düsseldorf itself, the Japanese enjoyed a remarkable visibility in public representations of the city's culture and diversity. By the twenty-first century, however, the profile of the Japanese population was changing as it diversified into a shrinking corporate expatriate population and growing group of long-term settlers and their second-generation offspring now rooted in the city.[106] Moreover, by the 2010s, the flourishing Japanese gastronomy sector attracted an increasing number of low-income Japanese migrants willing to work in restaurants, with many being lifestyle migrants looking for a new start in Europe or just a break from life in Japan.[107] Cozy relations between Japan and the North Rhine-Westphalia government still meant that work visas were relatively easy to obtain for Japanese in comparison with people from other regions of Europe.[108]

Japanese restaurants became central to the public culture of the expatriate community in Düsseldorf, beginning with the one-hundred-seat restaurant Tokyo, which opened in 1963.[109] The following year, Nippon-Kan opened, which went on to become the most prominent Japanese restaurant in the city. As one frequent customer wrote years after it opened, "It was conceived not only as a place that served Japanese food but was meant to represent Japanese culture and serve as a place to establish good German-Japanese relations."[110] In short, it was a prestige project of Japanese industry and state to establish a presence in Germany to serve the Japanese community while presenting Japan in a good light to German society. We can see it as a transition to corporate-led culinary diplomacy.

Nippon-Kan was pushed by industry leaders, including the former head of Keidanren (the main Japanese industry association), Yoshihiro Inayama. The capital investment came from a group of major Japanese companies in Düsseldorf. The first head of the company managing Nippon-Kan was the former secretary of Nobusuke Kishi while he was Japan's prime minister (1957–1960). All materials for the Japanese interiors, including tatami mats, were imported and installed or built by workers brought over from Japan. The restaurant was partly staffed by people sent from the famous Tokyo restaurant Ryūkōtei in Yanagibashi. The waitresses were graduates from top Japanese universities who competed for this rare opportunity for women to work abroad. Later, in 1978, the restaurant imported the first generation of karaoke machines (using eight-track tapes), most likely becoming the first Japanese karaoke bar in Germany.[111] Over the next two decades, Japanese shops and restaurants would grow into the Little Tokyo around the Nippon-Kan and the adjacent Japan Center office building.

Nippon-Kan established the first supply chains for Japanese foods in Germany, illustrating the role of Japantown restaurants in creating a culinary infrastructure that later served a much larger Japanese restaurant industry.[112] According to a 1990 interview with Michio Morozumi, who came to work at the restaurant in 1968, many of the supplies initially came from an Asian food market in the city called Ost Shop, which sold rice, shoyu, ramen, miso, and some imported frozen foods. Nippon-Kan started using California-grown Japanese-style rice in 1968 (replacing Italian rice, which also was obtainable only at a pricey department store, since Germans rarely ate rice at that time).[113] By the late 1980s some Japanese vegetables, such as Chinese cabbage (*hakusai* or bok choy), daikon radish, and kabocha pumpkin, could be procured locally, but in the 1960s none of these were available. The cooks made do with local vegetables and canned and packaged goods. Also, Düsseldorfers were not big consumers of seafood. While the fish market in the nearby Old City sold mackerel, herring, and flounder, it was not fresh enough for sushi.

A supply of fresh fish was created when Nippon-Kan began regular runs to the famed Rungis market in Paris, which offered tuna, snapper, squid, horse mackerel, saury, sea bass, sardines, and, later on, scallops, Asian clams, and sea urchin. In the beginning, the restaurant sent a truck weekly between Düsseldorf and Paris, but border delays caused spoilage, so the team switched to air freight. Fish was purchased at Rungis at 3 a.m. and could arrive in Düsseldorf by 10 a.m. on Air France. In the late 1960s, Nippon-Kan started a fresh fish shop in the suburb of Oberkassel, where many Japanese expatriates lived. "There, we taught many Germans about eating raw tuna," Morozumi said in the 1990 interview. Fumio Ito, the first sushi chef at Nippon-Kan, noted that non-Japanese customers at the sushi counter were mostly brought by Japanese businesspeople, and some had eaten in Japan before. Sushi was still a luxury item in the 1960s, with only small amounts served, even at banquets.[114]

Additionally, Nippon-Kan was an incubator for Japanese restaurateurs in Düsseldorf. One old-timer is Kikaku, founded by Ito in 1977 in the center of Little Tokyo. A trained sushi master, Ito had initially worked abroad in Hong Kong. He came to Germany in 1964 as the first chef at Nippon-Kan. After working at the sushi counter for seven years, he spent four years at the Nippon-Kan seafood business in Oberkassel, where he drove the truck on the Paris runs. Still, his dream was to open his own sushi restaurant, so he sought the blessing of Nippon-Kan management and opened Kikaku in 1977.

Ito's unfiltered description to a Japanese journalist of his difficulties managing German guests is a window into the cultural negotiations over the space of the restaurant:

> Now [in 1989] it has been twelve years since I opened Kikaku. I don't know how many guests I have welcomed. Even in the days of Nippon-Kan I had

gotten to know quite a few foreigners [*gaijin,* meaning Europeans]. Now there are nights when the most people are not Japanese. On the one hand, I am happy about this, but German customers like to stay a long time, and there are nights when I regret that I must turn away Japanese guests. Japanese people are flexible and considerate, but Germans, when they sit down, they feel it is their right to stay there, even if it is crowded. Sometimes they will be as late as an hour for a reservation and still will insist that they made a reservation. I would like to tell them that if they are late for a reservation, it will be cancelled, but many of the staff don't speak very good German so it is difficult. Also, if you give them special treatment on one occasion because it is a slow night, Germans will take this for granted. "It was okay before, so why is not okay today" they would insist. You cannot make any exceptions. Sometimes there are Germans who will just squeeze themselves into a table where others are already sitting and create their own space. Because she has dealt with this on a daily basis, I think my wife [who worked the front of the house] has really gotten used to these [German] personality traits. If you want to do business in Germany, you just have to get used to it.[115]

It is clear from Ito's remarks that even in 1989, Little Tokyo was a Japanese cultural space, and he struggled to accept working according to German social norms. Japan's high-flying "bubble economy" of the 1980s was the high point of Ito's career. As the premier sushi chef in Düsseldorf, he was invited to make sushi at official functions all over Europe, including a visit to Eastern Europe by the prince (later Heisei emperor) and princess of Japan.[116]

Another Düsseldorf Little Tokyo institution that owes its origins to Nippon-Kan was the restaurant chain Maruyasu. It was founded by Akio Ando and his wife, Kimiko, who met in Germany and married in 1968. Unlike most of the elite Japanese expatriates coming to Düsseldorf at the time, they came as so-called guest workers employed in Germany to fill labor shortages (this wave of migrants included far more Koreans, some of whom later opened Asian grocery stores around Little Tokyo). Kimiko came to Düsseldorf in 1966 with three other Japanese women to work as nurses. Like many other "guest workers" (mostly from developing countries), all of them stayed on in Germany. Akio Ando arrived with other Japanese in 1965 to work in the coal mines. After a coal mine accident that killed three coworkers, Ando quit the mines and in 1970 got a job in the warehouse of Nippon-Kan, working there for eleven years. As members of the Buddhist sect Soka Gakkai, the Andos initially wanted to stay in Germany to spread Buddhism. (The Buddhist cause is still important to them, and about a third of the employees at Maruyasu are Soka Gakkai members.)[117]

The couple started with a small food-delivery service in Little Tokyo that did door-to-door sales. Kimiko quit her nursing job to work in the kitchen. In the 1990s, with the business struggling, they decided to make sushi to sell to both Japanese and Germans. They were offered a spot in the Shadow Arcade, a high-end shopping mall opening near Little Tokyo in Düsseldorf. At first, business was difficult, and they almost went bankrupt. "In Düsseldorf no one knew what sushi was," Hiroaki Ando (their youngest son) said in an interview. "One elderly lady came by and asked, 'are those pralines?' I replied, 'no that is raw fish.' She said, 'no, I can't eat something like that!'"[118]

Hiroaki, who manages the Little Tokyo branch of the restaurant, is a manga artist who studied and worked for seven years in Japan before returning to the family business. Rather than importing an expensive sushi master, he explained, Maruyasu built up its business by doing the opposite— creating machine-made sushi that was standardized, packaged in cellophane, and easily reproduced across chain outlets. In 2018, the young female head chef, who was Hiroaki's fiancée, was creating standardized recipes for use in all twelve sushi shops under the Maruyasu brand. Many of the chain's workers were young Japanese right out of college or high school with little kitchen experience. The market they aim at is now the German one, and not the expatriate Japanese.

In 2010, the iconic Nippon-Kan closed after forty-six years of business, part of the decline of expatriate-oriented restaurants in Little Tokyo. However, a decade later, Little Tokyo in Düsseldorf was still the largest neighborhood of Japanese eateries in continental Europe, with over thirty Japanese restaurants. The area remained packed with tourists and residents on the weekends. However, alongside the Japanese expatriate families, we saw many more German manga and anime fans, second-generation Asian German youths, and Chinese expatriate employees of Huawei and other Chinese firms. They, too, came to Little Tokyo for a taste of Japan, but their requirements and tastes were different. They lined up for ramen or bubble tea (a confection sometimes associated with Japan, though originally Taiwanese), or headed to the new Eat Tokyo chain restaurant owned by Japanese but employing Chinese workers and offering lower prices (see Chapter 4).

Especially painful for many older Japanese expatriates was the takeover of the Nippon-Kan location by an all-you-can-eat chain called Okinii. Its main attraction for the young German clientele was ordering simple Japanese and Chinese dishes from a tablet computer (a trendy feature that also allowed for the hiring of many service staff with limited German skills).

Okinii was owned by a second-generation ethnic Chinese restaurateur whose father operated Chinese restaurants in the Netherlands before moving in 1994 to Krefeld (near Düsseldorf) to open a Chinese restaurant. As will be described in Chapter 5, second-generation ethnic Asian restaurateurs in Europe (and the United States) used their economic and social capital, experience in midrange gastronomy, and understanding of European customers to move into the lucrative Japanese restaurant sector.[119]

Despite their "insular" character, the role of Japanese expatriate Japantowns in the spread of Japanese cuisine has been significant. Politically, they have been places for projecting Japanese culinary soft power, representing Japanese cuisine as elite and expensive, traditional and modern. Their restaurants established a culinary infrastructure and logistics for Japanese foods that extended far beyond these enclaves. They trained hundreds of chefs who went on to open restaurants in nearby markets, and they educated early consumers who first experienced Japanese foods in restaurants like Nippon-Kan. Finally, as seen in Düsseldorf, the restaurants have continued to attract an increasing number of non-Japanese consumers through their reputation for authenticity and quality, even while making difficult adjustments to serve such consumers.

Community Restaurants as Nostalgic Refuges and Transnational Imaginaries

Beyond fancy establishments for business entertainment, nearly all Japanese communities abroad reproduced a recognizable imaginary of a community restaurant, one that sojourners experienced as a transnational home away from home that was connected both to Japan and to the local Japanese community.[120] Most had omnibus and affordable menus and informal service. Yasushi Ikezawa, a pioneer in the post–World War II Japanese restaurant scene in the United States, characterized the typical overseas Japanese restaurant before the late 1960s as "refuge for the homesick" (*bōkyō no tomariba*). Before corporate Japanese arrived with all their cash, Ikezawa continues, these Japanese community restaurants on the US West Coast were "common man's canteens" (*taishū shokudō*) that served Kansai-style dishes, including *futomaki* (thick sushi rolls).[121] These places fed nostalgia as much as they filled stomachs, and most customers were male sojourners unable to cook for themselves.

An image of the restaurant as a transnational culinary and cultural refuge can be seen in the following description of the Berlin restaurant Tōyōkan, which the Japanese writer Kiyoe Saito visited in 1936 before the Berlin Olympics: "I took my dinner that night at the neighboring Japanese restaurant called Tōyōkan. When I entered, the first things that caught my eye were the Japanese newspapers. While I was waiting for the waitress to bring the items I ordered, I was able to read Japanese print for the first time in a long time, though the news was from seventeen or eighteen days before. Despite the fact that the newspaper was out-of-date, and although seated at a European table, while devouring the Japanese food I could forget for a second that I was in Berlin."[122] In his memoir, Saito emphasized the copresence of a Japanese cultural environment, especially in newspapers. He also remarked that the menu was extraordinarily varied, resembling the menus of restaurants in Japan, and offered yakitori, sashimi, various rice bowls, hot and cold soba, tempura, several types of hot pot, and sukiyaki. The restaurant was expensive but tasty, he wrote.[123] Younger travelers typically found cheaper refueling spots, such as Paris's Fouji (Fuji), located near the Sorbonne. French literature scholar Yoshizō Kawamori became a regular there while a student in the late 1920s. It was "small and dirty," he wrote, but he was attracted by the Japanese magazines and newspapers. "Even out of a sense of duty, you couldn't say the cuisine was excellent," he writes. He went there because it was cheaper than the two other Japanese restaurants in Paris.[124]

Based on our fieldwork in the 2010s, such culinary and cultural refueling spots can still be found in most Japanese enclaves around the world, especially corporate expatriate communities, which remain heavily male. What they share is, first, a nostalgia for homey Japanese foodways, and second, a sense of belonging to a local but also transnational Japanese community. Expansive menus of noodles, rice, fish, tofu, and snacks, and often Chinese dishes and fried rice, ensure that anybody can find their favorite comfort food. The décors are cluttered and eclectic, with walls plastered with advertising posters (often provided by Japanese beer companies) and mementos conveying connections both to Japan and to the local Japanese community: fading photos of regulars or art projects from the local Japanese school. Shelves often are crammed with Japanese-language media such as newspapers, books, or manga, and (in recent decades) television screens show Japanese programming. Such nostalgic imaginaries shared among restaurants around the world make this a transnational as well as local social space.

For example, we can see such places in Prague, which became a center of Japanese investment after the country's democratic transition in the 1990s. With over 250 Japanese corporations running their businesses in the Czech Republic and employing fifty thousand people, Japan was the second-biggest foreign investor and employer in the country, just after Germany.[125] In 2017, there were more than two thousand Japanese expatriates living in the city,[126] and as in Düsseldorf, they established such institutions as a Japanese Chamber of Commerce, Czech-Japanese Association, and Japanese school. The restaurant where the local Japanese community met regularly was Katsura, located in a four-star hotel for Japanese business travelers and tourists. The restaurant, in the windowless basement, was a large open space with movable partitions and large tables that imparted a casual canteen-like (*shokudō*) atmosphere. It was founded in 2006 by chef Hachiro Tsuda, who came to the Czech Republic after the 1989 Velvet Revolution to assist the opening of several Japanese restaurants in Prague. According to Tsuda, he never wanted to create a fine-dining spot, but rather an *izakaya* (pub) style venue where both locals and Japanese living in the city could relax and enjoy homestyle food.

Japanese families came to Katsura for weekend getaways, salarymen came for evening drinking sessions, and the Japanese community used its catering for gatherings of the Japanese soccer club and purchased its lunch boxes for sport matches and Japanese school events. Japanese programming played on wall-hung television screens, and shelves were full of Japanese manga, books for kids, and Japanese newspapers and magazines. Chef-owner Tsuda was usually standing behind the circle-shaped sushi bar counter, greeting the hotel guests and locals while preparing dishes. The restaurant's informal atmosphere and multilingual staff speaking Japanese, English, and Czech made the restaurant especially accessible and welcoming for all. Japanese customers typically passed over sushi on the menu—a favorite of the Czechs—to order the homestyle dishes such as *tonkatsu*, rice bowls, *okonomiyaki* (savory pancakes), and smaller snack plates. As for alcohol, most guests ordered Japanese beer or *shōchū,* and the restaurant had a bottle-keep system for repeat customers. During our last visit on a Friday evening in February 2020, just before the COVID-19 pandemic started to affect life in Prague, the restaurant was fully packed, the crowd divided equally between Japanese and locals.[127]

In the 2010s, a similar pattern of growing Japanese corporate investment and expatriate community in the Vietnamese capital of Hanoi made the city a center of Japanese gastronomy in the country (along with Ho Chi Minh City). During this period Hanoi's Japanese population doubled to over twenty thousand.[128] The first Japanese restaurants were founded in the city center in the 2000s, on Trieu Viet Vuong Street near government institutions, consulates, and the offices of many Japanese companies. The street became well known for its Japanese restaurants, which soon numbered nearly twenty. A few earlier restaurants were Japanese owned, but new ones were run by Vietnamese. Although many claimed to specialize in a particular dish, such as yakitori, sushi, *izakaya,* and other concepts, they all served many types of Japanese dishes, including fancy California rolls covered with decorative squiggly lines of spicy mayonnaise-based sauces. The street also had shops selling Japanese groceries and retail goods, karaoke bars, massage parlors, and Japanese language schools for Vietnamese students who planned to study and work in Japan. By the end of the 2010s, Hanoi's Japantown was visibly transforming from a neighborhood oriented toward Japanese expatriates to a lifestyle destination for Vietnamese interested in Japan.

One early restaurant was Ky Y on Trieu Viet Vuong Street, which opened in the early 2000s.[129] Unlike the flashy new restaurants created by Vietnamese owners, with their fake cherry trees and Japanese lamps, Ky Y was located in an old building, and when we visited in 2018, it retained a homey atmosphere, both Hanoi-like and Japanese. There was a long counter where the mostly male customers ate lunch alone or in small groups, and a large upstairs area with private rooms. According to the manager, 70 percent of the customers were Japanese, with the remainder being non-Japanese foreigners and Vietnamese. During our visit, many customers were Vietnamese men who, judging from the company badges hanging from their necks, worked at nearby Japanese companies. The menu featured Japanese set meals (*teishoku*) of grilled fish and were not localized for Vietnamese tastes. One Japanese visitor even complained to us during our fieldwork that the offerings were "too old fashioned." Japanese generally ordered flounder (*hirame*) and tuna, the waitress said, while Vietnamese preferred salmon. Other popular items were pork belly (*buta kakuni*) and grilled chicken, both served with rice, side dishes, and miso soup.[130]

Staff in these restaurants included Japanese and locals, many with complex migration histories. In Ky Y the Japanese cook was married to a Vietnamese woman. (The Japanese cooks are all married to Vietnamese women, otherwise they wouldn't stay here, a waitress joked.) The Japanese owner, Kojiro Kobayashi—who had been in Vietnam for thirty years—was often away from the restaurant. It was managed by a twenty-three-year-old Vietnamese woman who was keenly interested in Japanese cuisine and was sent by her boss to Japan for one year to study Japanese. Due to her outgoing nature, she quickly learned Japanese and, since coming back to Vietnam, had continued to study at a nearby Japanese language school.[131]

Restaurants like Fouji in 1920s Paris or Ky Y in contemporary Hanoi illustrate both the transnational and local nature of the community canteen style of restaurant. For those who could appreciate them—Japanese and locals familiar with Japan—they were islands of culinary and cultural nostalgia. For over a century, these nostalgic "refuges for the homesick" have served as defining local social institutions in Japantowns as well as been transnational imaginaries of Japaneseness aimed at Japanese migrants themselves. They are thus distinct from the touristic imaginaries aimed at outsiders, but which are increasingly prevalent in surviving Japantowns.

Themed Japantowns as Global Foodie Destinations

Since the 1990s, multiple forces have caused the decline of Japantowns as centers of Japanese communities created by Japanese settlers and sojourners to serve their needs. One was the demographic decrease in Japanese immigrant communities, as the descendants of migrants dispersed to new neighborhoods, and as inbound movements of corporate expatriates waned. Simultaneously there was increased interest in Japan and Japanese foods among non-Japanese customers in most regions. This even led to the rise of new Japantowns entirely geared to touristic consumption and with no strong associations among migrant Japanese populations. These could be described as "Disneyfied" or themed food districts in which Japaneseness served more as a marketing tool than as an ethnic boundary marker.[132]

Reinventing Paris Japantown as a Touristic Imaginary, 1970s–Present

The Quartier Japonais (Japanese Quarter) in Paris was founded as an expatriate-oriented neighborhood, but in the 2000s it was taken over by French young people and international tourists, especially from Asia, interested in Japanese popular culture. Its roots go back to the late 1950s, when

Japanese salarymen started coming to Paris. They often stayed in the area between the Opera Garnier and the Palais Royal, then an inexpensive neighborhood known for its gay bars, drugs, and prostitution. The Japanese Quarter formed in the 1970s as major Japanese corporations began reestablishing offices in the area. It consisted of businesses serving Japanese expatriates on Rue Saint-Anne near the Opera House.[133] In 1971, Mitsukoshi Paris, the first Japanese department store in Europe, opened to cater to Japanese tourists and expatriates who were flocking to the area. In 1975, the Bank of Tokyo's Paris branch, established in 1962, moved to Rue Saint-Anne.[134] Japanese restaurateurs moved in to meet the demand of the growing numbers of Japanese for homeland food.[135]

The oldest restaurant in the Japanese Quarter was Takara, first opened in 1958 by Takumi Ashibe near the Pantheon in the fifth arrondissement. In 1963, it moved to what later was to become the Japanese Quarter.[136] Ashibe was born in Nagano Prefecture in 1934. In a 1998 interview, he described how a neighbor arranged for him to travel to Paris to work in his hotel (probably the Botanya described previously). After that establishment closed, he struck out on his own and opened a small restaurant in 1958 called Takara. In 1963, seeking a bigger space, he opened Takara in the current location on Rue Moliere. Business picked up after 1964, the year of the Tokyo Olympics, when it became easier for Japanese to obtain passports for foreign travel, and Paris became a popular destination.[137] During the 1970s and 1980s, the restaurant was frequented by Japanese corporate expatriates stationed in Paris, who dined on corporate expense accounts. They were gradually replaced by French lovers of Japanese cuisine, who became the main clientele.[138]

In 1994 Ashibe's son Isao took over as chef, and in 2007 he sold the restaurant to Yukio Yamakoshi, who had been running Japanese restaurants in Germany for twenty years. Under Yamakoshi's direction, Takara retained its original elegant style, with woodwork, screens, and traditional woodblock prints. With the corporate executives now scarce, the menu felt more nostalgic than luxurious, including the traditional sukiyaki and shabu-shabu but also a broad selection of set meals from sushi to tempura that would be familiar to any Japanese traveler. Takara also began offering a few newfangled California rolls and tempura rolls to appeal to French customers. Yamakoshi explained with an undertone of resignation that French customers expected these items because of their dining experiences in Paris's numerous Chinese-owned restaurants. However, his personal goal was to continue to serve "family style" comfort food, much like the Japanese community restaurants in other cities described in the previous section.[139]

By the 2010s, Japanese restaurants such as Takara, which catered to Japanese expatriates and tourists, no longer typified area establishments. As demand grew in the Japanese Quarter, a growing number of Japanese restaurants hired workers from the Asian refugee community—Cambodians, Chinese, and Laotians—because young Japanese had difficulty getting work permits. Some new hires learned how to cook Japanese food and opened their own Japanese restaurants. In this way, many of the restaurants that opened in the Japanese Quarter and elsewhere in Paris from the 1980s were operated by non-Japanese restaurateur-chefs. These establishments illustrate the pattern of ethnic succession in the Japanese restaurant sector (described further in Chapter 5).[140]

Although long-term Japanese restaurateurs such as Yamakoshi lamented the impact of these newcomers on the taste for Japanese cuisine, they also admitted that the influx of non-Japanese restaurateurs and customers sustained the Japanese Quarter. In 1992, Japan's real estate and stock speculation "bubble economy" burst, drastically cutting the capital available for further expansion abroad. During the 1990s, Japanese expatriate communities shrank as Japanese corporations reduced or sold off overseas investments. The economic shock also depressed Japanese tourism to Europe, which adversely affected the sales of Japanese department stores and their retail ecology, such as small gift shops catering to Japanese tourists and services for residential Japanese. Many Japanese-owned businesses closed down, including the Mitsukoshi Department Store in 2010, which had anchored the Japanese Quarter.[141]

The Japanese Quarter, however, thrived on new customers. Among the most important non-Japanese restaurateurs sustaining it through these changes was the Korean French restaurateur Serge Lee, who immigrated to France with his family at age six. After studying art at university, he said he was inspired by the movie *Tampopo* to open his own ramen shop in 1989. Called Sapporo, it featured ramen made with a chicken broth similar to what would be served in Japan.[142] In 2000, he opened Aki Cafe, featuring Japanese sweets. Most were similar to those found in Japan, such as *meronpan* (melon-shaped sweet roll, often called "melon pan" in English) and *dorayaki* (bean-paste filled pancake sandwiches), while some were fusion, such as French cakes with yuzu peel. By 2018, he was one of Paris' most successful Asian restaurateurs, with five Japanese and two Korean restaurants.[143]

During the 2000s, ramen and udon noodle dishes became popular in the Japanese Quarter, as did curry rice, *katsudon,* and Japanese sweets. Driving the change was the strong interest in Japanese anime and manga among French youths. Many young fans of the anime *Naruto* became eager to try ramen, which was often eaten by its ninja protagonist. Similarly, *Yakitate!! Japan* and Naomi Kawase's Japanese film *Sweet Bean* sparked interest in Japanese sweets. During the 2010s, social media rapidly spread these new Japanese pop-culture trends. One example is the web magazine *Culture du Japon,* dedicated mainly to "J-hobbies," including manga, japanimation, literature, J-music, cinema, and video games, but also encompassing Japanese gastronomy and its promotion in France. During our fieldwork, we witnessed the impact of the portrayal of Japanese cuisine in pop culture consumed by French young people. Japanese manager Ono of Aki Cafe told us that French customers were often amazed at the similarity of his sweets to those portrayed in manga and anime.[144] The transformation of Paris' Japanese Quarter into a tourist center represented the emergence of a new type of themed Japantown, which we also see in New York.

A Gentrifying Little Tokyo in New York's East Village, 1990s–Present

Beginning in the early twentieth century, New York became home to an eclectic and economically stratified Japanese expatriate population. Whereas on the US West Coast Japanese settler migrants created Japanese enclaves in the face of hostility from the white population, New York, in contrast, was a destination for smaller and more diverse flows of migrants, comprising business expatriates, diplomats, students, independent scholars, and also working-class migrants. Therefore, New York never developed the kind of bounded immigrant enclave seen on the West Coast.[145]

In the 1930s, there were about thirteen Japanese restaurants in the city, supported by fewer than three thousand Japanese residents, Japanese travelers, and an indefinite number of non-Japanese curiosity seekers.[146] In the decades before and after World War II, Japanese restaurants were concentrated in Midtown, where Japanese banks and trading companies were located.[147] By 1974 there were 150 Japanese restaurants in the city, and a growing Japanese expatriate population, estimated at forty-five thousand, provided the big spenders needed to support these restaurants. Japanese financial capital began pouring into the city, and even Toyota invested in a branch of the restaurant Inagiku in the Waldorf Astoria Hotel. Its opening in 1974 helped solidify the association of Japanese cuisine with the highest level of luxury consumption in the city.[148] By 1990, there were over five hundred Japanese restaurants scattered around the city, reflecting both the spending power of Japanese expatriates and the growing interest in Japanese cuisine among ordinary New Yorkers.[149]

The first truly visible New York Japantown developed in the 1990s in downtown East Village, around St. Mark's Place. It was established not by corporate expatriates but by Japanese lifestyle migrants, adventurers seeking a new start in the United States and attracted by the cheaper rents and the bohemian vibe of Lower Manhattan in the 1970s. The encounter of New York's cultural avant-garde with Japanese culinary culture predates the creation of the current Little Tokyo centered on St. Mark's Place. One central place in this history was the restaurant Omen, opened in 1981 in Soho by Mikio Shinagawa, a former Buddhist monk from Kyoto. By the 1980s, Soho was a flourishing artistic center, and Shinagawa wanted to create a space to enjoy both "Japanese country food" and intellectual discourse.[150] The artistic scene at Omen was described to us by Michio Hayashi, a regular there who studied art history at Columbia University in the 1980s:

> It is a sort of out-of-mode place now but played a very important role in spreading an alternative Japanese food in the art community in New York back in the '80s. Clientele included John Cage, David Byrne (two I actually encountered there), and other numerous celebrities in the art/avant-garde culture community. In addition to their signature udon, they served Japanese sake back in the '80s already and functioned as a sort of high-end *izakaya*. . . . With the opening of many other Japanese restaurants with hip or arty taste/environment after the 1990s, this place lost the prestige it once had in the art community in New York. But for some time, this was the only Japanese restaurant in New York where you could enjoy the combination of creative Japanese *otsumami* [snacks for drinking] menus (without sushi or sukiyaki), good sake (imported from Japan), and a quiet and sophisticated artistic atmosphere.[151]

Following the shift of New York's avant-garde cultural scene from Soho to the East Village in the 1980s, many Japanese restaurants began opening in the East Village. Unlike Japantowns on the West Coast, this area had no connection with historical flows of Japanese migrants to the United States. It developed from the efforts of a few small-scale Japanese entrepreneurs who expanded their businesses to satisfy urban trendsetters' growing interest in Japanese cuisine. From the start, the East Village Little Tokyo was oriented to non-Japanese consumers, including adventurous gentrifying artists and intellectuals in the 1980s, wealthy new residents in the 1990s, and boisterous crowds of students and tourists from the 2010s. By 2016, a local food researcher counted sixty-one Japanese eateries in a four-block area centered on St. Mark's Place.[152]

The East Village Little Tokyo was established by a handful of Japanese migrants who arrived in the area when it was known more for crime than cuisine. An important figure in this story is Tony Yoshida, who grew up in Yokohama, moved to the United States in the late 1960s, and became a serial entrepreneur in the Japanese restaurant industry. In 1971, he opened his first venture, an ice cream parlor called Ice Cream Connection that used Japanese flavors in its ice cream. Yoshida became a local character in the East Village, wearing wooden sandals (*geta*) while pushing an ice cream cart around the neighborhood. Next, he opened a Japanese-style hamburger restaurant in St. Mark's Place called Dojo, featuring tofu burgers with carrot ginger dressing, and a twenty-four-hour American diner called Around the Clock Cafe that included Japanese comfort foods such as *yakisoba* (fried noodles) and udon alongside American diner food. In 1982, he opened Shiraku, an *izakaya*-cum-sushi bar, among the first *izakaya* in the area. In 1993, the space occupied by Shiraku was divided into an informal *izakaya* renamed Village Yokocho and a "speakeasy-style" hidden bar called Angel Share. The mostly non-Japanese clientele could eat dinner in the *izakaya* or drink while waiting to enter Angel Share through an inconspicuous door with no sign or marking. This unique combination of speakeasy cocktail bar and a Japanese *izakaya* proved spectacularly successful. It pioneered both the "Japanese cocktail" and *izakaya* booms in the United States, as drinkers coming to Angel Share for cocktails discovered the *izakaya* on their way in or out (see Chapter 7). Tony's daughter Erina Yoshida was born in 1987, and after studying at Waseda University in Tokyo, she returned to work in the family business. She subsequently managed the expansion of the Yoshida Japanese food empire into a multifaceted Japan Village complex in Industry City, a major commercial and retail development in Brooklyn.[153]

Another serial entrepreneur in the development of Japanese cuisine in the East Village was Bon Yagi, nicknamed the "mayor of Little Tokyo." His career paralleled Tony Yoshida's, and the businesses of these two families have dominated the neighborhood. In 1968, Yagi came to the United States and worked his way up in a diner in Philadelphia from dishwasher to short-order cook. This sparked his idea to purvey Japanese food in the United States. In 1976, he began a vegetable business in the East Village. Soon he had saved enough money to start a twenty-four-hour American-style diner called 103 Second Avenue that became a hot spot for artists like Keith Haring, Madonna, and Andy Warhol. In 1984, Yagi opened one of the first sushi bars in Lower Manhattan, named Hasaki after the town where his father was born. Over the next two decades, he opened more than a dozen restaurants, each featuring a different type of Japanese cuisine and distinctive Japanese-style décor.[154] In 1993, he founded the underground *sake* bar Decibel and, in 1996, Sakagura, both of which were early promoters of *sake* in New York City.[155] In quick succession these were followed by Sobaya, specializing in housemade soba noodles, Rai Rai Ken for ramen and *gyōza* dishes, Curry-ya for Japanese curry, Shabu-Tatsu for shabu-shabu hot pots, and the teahouse and dessert shop Cha-An. The most recent venues were informal settings serving street-style food, be it Otafuku x Medetai for *okonomiyaki* and *takoyaki* (octopus balls), or Yonekichi for rice burgers. As of spring 2020, Yagi's T.I.C. Restaurant Group numbered eighteen restaurants.[156] In his marketing, Yagi frames dining in his restaurants as "enjoying Japan without airfare."[157]

When asked why he chose to develop his culinary empire in the East Village, Yagi painted his business as part of a New York story of migration, noting that "Jewish people started here, and Polish and Ukrainians, and then the Japanese. Everybody was accepted, and we never felt strange." He also cheekily mentioned that Commodore Matthew Perry, who "opened up" Japan with his fleet of "black shops" in 1854, was buried right down the street, and Yagi wanted to return the favor by opening up New York to Japanese culture.[158] Along with Yoshida and other restaurateurs, Yagi also supported the development of the East Village Little Tokyo by organizing local events, such as a Japanese-style *matsuri* (neighborhood festival).[159] Now both patriarchs were stepping back from daily operations. Like Erina Yoshida, whose offices were a stone's throw away, Yagi's daughter Sakura Yagi had taken over many of the day-to-day operations of the company.

Although created by migrant entrepreneurs, Little Tokyo in New York and the Japanese Quarter in Paris were never significant Japanese immigrant residential enclaves. Instead, the founding entrepreneurs were, from the beginning, cultural intermediaries interpreting Japanese restaurant culture for non-Japanese consumers, as explored further in Chapter 4. Moreover, many subsequent restaurant owners in the area were not Japanese but immigrants from elsewhere in Asia. They were part of the transformation of these areas of the city into touristic foodscapes. The dishes that one finds in such places reflect global trends in the 2010s of marketing ramen, Japanese crepes, bubble tea, and other items that appealed to the growing clientele of young culinary tourists. These themed Japantowns are, thus, grounded in touristic imaginaries rather than the nostalgic imaginaries fostered in residential Japanese communities.

The Fading Japantown Restaurant

In major cities around the world, Japantown restaurants created a culinary infrastructure for the subsequent global spread of Japanese cuisine into both high-end and mass markets. They supported the livelihoods of thousands of migrants, including chefs, farmers, waitresses, and many other workers in these enclave economies. They also provided community spaces for Japanese migrants of all types, from working-class settlers to elite transients. However, in practice, the localized and hybridized restaurant cuisine of early Japantown restaurants has remained largely uncelebrated and unremembered, with a few exceptions, such as Benkyodo in San Francisco, which after 115 years in business now also has closed.

The evolution of Japantown restaurants provides a window onto the changing culinary politics of Japantown. Early prewar Japantown communities could be characterized as simultaneously nostalgic and assimilationist, in that they strove to preserve emotional ties to Japan for migrants while also meeting the expectations and tastes of the non-Japanese majority. As Japanese migrants adopted local culinary and social norms, so did the restaurateurs, producing a cuisine attuned to the tastes of a growing second and third generation of Japanese Americans and Brazilians. In the corporate Japantowns after World War II, we see a more clearly Japan-centric stance by restaurateurs backed by industry groups. They considered cuisine a projection of national pride and soft power, as seen in such prestige projects as Düsseldorf's Nippon-Kan. These projects represented authenticity through direct ties to Japan, bypassing local migrant foodways, a dismissive attitude long seen among elite expatriates and among many elite white critics. Most recently, touristic Japantowns can be regarded as part of a more flexible and open-ended marketing strategy that aims to attract consumers by using the "Japan brand" regardless of the origins of the owners and customers and even the foods. This development illustrates the ongoing decentering of migrant community foodways in defining Japanese cuisine overseas.

Overall, traditional Japantown restaurants are in decline. Whether in centers of Japanese immigration in the Americas or new centers of Japanese expatriate migration in Asia, Japantown restaurants have steadily lost their leading position in the Japanese food booms of the postwar period. New leading restaurants are opened in the more affluent neighborhoods of global cities and targeted at wealthy locals and travelers. These global Japanese food fashions that outgrew the Japantowns that nurtured them are the subjects of subsequent chapters.

Notes

1. Mark J. Souther, "The Disneyfication of New Orleans: The French Quarter as Facade in a Divided City," *Journal of American History* 94, no. 3 (2007): 804–811; Tou Chuang Chang, "Theming Cities, Taming Places: Insights from Singapore," *Geografiska Annaler: Series B, Human Geography* 82, no. 1 (2000): 35–54.

2. US Immigration and Naturalization Service, *Statistical Yearbook of the Immigration and Naturalization Service, 1997* (Washington, DC: US Government Printing Office, 1999), 25; Nitaya Onozawa, "Immigration from Japan to the U.S.A., Historical Trends and Background," *Tokyo Home Economics Bulletin/Tsukuba Women's University Bulletin*, no. 7 (2003): 115–125.

3. Ishige Naomichi (石毛直道) et al., *Rosuanjerusu no nihon ryōriten—sono bunka jinruigakuteki kenkyū* (ロスアンジェルスの日本料理店—その文化人類学的研究) [Japanese restaurants in Los Angeles—an anthropological research] (Tokyo: Domesu, 1985), 28.

4. The "third place" is an urban space for socializing between work and home. See Ray Oldenburg, *The Great Good Place: Cafes, Coffee Shops, Bookstores, Bars, Hair Salons, and Other Hangouts at the Heart of a Community* (Boston: Da Capo, 1999).

5. Kazuo Ito, *Issei: A History of Japanese Immigrants in North America* (Seattle: Japanese Community Service, 1973), 798.

6. Ivan H. Light, *Ethnic Enterprise in America: Business and Welfare among Chinese, Japanese, and Blacks* (Berkeley: University of California Press, 1972), 9–10; Ishige et al., *Rosuanjerusu*, 26.

7. Shichiro Matsui, "Economic Aspects of the Japanese Situation in California" (MA thesis, University of California at Berkeley, 1922), 7–8.

8. Kevin Wildie, *Sacramento's Historic Japantown: Legacy of a Lost Neighborhood* (Charleston: History Press, 2013), 15–16.

9. Isamu Nodera, "A Survey of the Vocational Activities of the Japanese in the City of Los Angeles" (PhD. diss., University of Southern California, 1936), 66–67.

10. Andrew Coe, *Chop Suey: A Cultural History of Chinese Food in the United States* (Oxford: Oxford University Press, 2009).

11. Ishige et al., *Rosuanjerusu*, 17–47. Ishige's team discovered that Japanese-cuisine restaurants could only be found in communities with at least five hundred Japanese residents, meaning that they largely served the Japanese community. Ishige et al., *Rosuanjerusu*, 35.

12. This is in terms of overall retail trends—in 1909, 63 percent of Japanese retail businesses were conducted with other Japanese, and it was not until 1924 that the percentage of "American trade" exceeded Japanese for the first time. Light, *Ethnic Enterprise in America*, 15.

13. Yuji Ichioka, *The Issei: The World of the First Generation Japanese Immigrants, 1895–1924* (New York: Free Press, 1988), 89.

14. Ito, *Issei*, 798–800.

15. Gary Kawaguchi and Shizue Seigel, "San Francisco's Japantown: The Shaping of a Community," *Nikkei Heritage* 12, no. 3 (Summer 2000): 7; Ishige et al., *Rosuanjerusu*, 34.

16. Ito, *Issei*, 828–831.

17. Ito, 828.

18. Ito, 828–829. The term "maid" probably refers to *shakujō*, barmaids who served customers and entertained them with conversation in most Japanese restaurants of this era.

19. Ito, 828.

20. Ishige et al., *Rosuanjerusu*, 27.

21. *Japanese in the City of San Francisco, California: Message from the President of the United States Transmitting the Final Report of Secretary Metcalf on the Situation Affecting the Japanese in the City of San Francisco California*, Senate Document No. 147, 59th Congress, 2nd Session, 1906.

22. David P. Conklin, "The Traditional and the Modern: The History of Japanese Food Culture in Oregon and How It Did and Did Not Integrate with American Food Culture" (MA thesis, Portland State University, 2009), 96–97.

23. Frank Jacob, "'Foreign, Brackish, and Exotic': Japanese Food in the American Press, 1853–1918," in *Chop Suey and Sushi from Sea to Shining Sea: Chinese and Japanese Restaurants in the United States*, ed. Bruce Makoto Arnold, Tanfer Emin Tunç, and Raymond Douglas Chong (Little Rock: University of Arkansas Press, 2018), 162; Gabriel J. Chin and John Ormonde, "The War against Chinese Restaurants," *Duke Law Journal* 67, no. 4 (2018): 681–741; H. D. Miller, "The Great Sushi Craze of 1905, Part 1," *An Eccentric Culinary History* (blog), accessed November 20, 2020, http://eccentric culinary.com/the-great-sushi-craze-of-1905-part-1/.

24. "Special Law for Japanese: May Be Favored in the New Liquor Ordinance," *Los Angeles Times*, August 26, 1908, II2.

25. "Ryōtei to meshiya no zen heisa" (料亭と飯屋の全閉鎖) [Complete closure of all restaurants and meal shops], *Shinsekai*, October 19, 1908, 4.

26. Ito, *Issei,* 768.

27. Jacob, "'Foreign, Brackish, and Exotic,'" 163.

28. Ito, *Issei,* 788.

29. Audrey Russek, "Appetites Without Prejudice: U.S. Foreign Restaurants and the Globalization of American Food Between the Wars," *Food and Foodways* 19, no. 1–2 (2011): 34–55.

30. Leonard Austin, *Around the World in San Francisco* (Stanford, CA: James Ladd, 1940), 50.

31. Noboru Hanyu, "Japantown in the 20s and 30s," *Nikkei Heritage* 12, no. 3 (2000): 15.

32. "Sukiyaki Pavilion Planned," *Japanese American News,* August 26, 1928, 1.

33. "Chain of 500 Sukiyaki Houses Planned in U.S. to Give Work to American-Born Young Folk," *Nippu Jiji,* October 8, 1936, 5.

34. "Kitchen Door of Japan Opens Wide, Discloses Culinary Artists at Work," *Washington Post,* June 14, 1934.

35. Erik Matsunaga, "30 Years of Lakeview: Chicago's Japanese American Community 1960s–1990s—Part 1," Discover Nikkei, December 23, 2014, http://www.discover nikkei.org/en/journal/2014/12/23/lakeview-1/.

36. Matsunaga.

37. Takako Day, "The Chicago Shoyu Story—Shinsaku Nagano and the Japanese Entrepreneurs," Discover Nikkei, March 2, 2020, http://www.discovernikkei.org/en /journal/2020/3/2/chicago-shoyu-3/.

38. Matsunaga, "30 Years of Lakeview."

39. Stuart Mizuta, interview by David Wank, March 2, 2017.

40. Neil Pollack, "Restaurant Tours: Sunshine Cafe Rises from the East," *Chicago Reader,* February 17, 2000, https://www.chicagoreader.com/chicago/restaurant-tours -sunshine-cafe-rises-from-the-east/Content?oid=901482.

41. Lindsey Howald Patton, "Swap Sushi for Hearty Homestyle Japanese at Sunshine Café," Serious Eats, March 9, 2017, http://chicago.seriouseats.com/2014/04/this-week -on-serious-eats-chicago-81.html.

42. Matsunaga, "30 Years of Lakeview."

43. Kevin Pang, "At Katsu, a Quarter Century of Sushi as Theatre," *Chicago Tribune,* October 4, 2012, https://www.chicagotribune.com/dining/ct-xpm-2012–10–04-ct -dining-1004-home-plate-katsu-20121004-story.html.

44. Sasha Issenberg, *The Sushi Economy: Globalization and the Making of a Modern Delicacy* (New York: Gotham Books, 2007), 87–91.

45. Takashi Machimura, "Living in a Transnational Community within a Multi-ethnic City," in *Global Japan: The Experience of Japan's New Immigrant and Overseas Communities,* ed. Roger Goodman et al. (Abingdon, UK: Routledge, 2005), 147–156.

46. Ishige et al., *Rosuanjerusu,* 37–44.

47. Bradford Pearson, "After Internment, a Store Was Born. It's Still an L.A. Staple," *New York Times,* July 1, 2020, https://nyti.ms/2VxZZa6.

48. Lawrence E. Davies, "San Francisco's New Japanese Touch," *New York Times,* March 3, 1968, 13.

49. Shizue Seigel, "Nihonmachi and Urban Renewal," *Nikkei Heritage* 12, no. 4 (2000): 6–10.

50. Page & Turnbull, *JAPAN CENTER REPORT,* San Francisco Planning Agency, May 2009, http://sfplanning.org/sites/default/files/FileCenter/Documents/1790-Japan%20 Center.pdf.

51. Davies, "San Francisco's New Japanese Touch."

52. "Gourmet Gemstones Are the Specialty of the House," *Goldsmith,* November 1983, http://www.diranart.com/web/images/stories/news/07.jpg.

53. Fieldwork by James Farrer, summer 2019.

54. Edible Tours Japantown Tour, fieldwork by James Farrer, June 21, 2019.

55. Amy Sherman, "The Newest Bowls of Ramen in Town," 7X7, April 9, 2013, https://www.7x7.com/the-newest-bowls-of-ramen-in-town-1786237281.html.

56. Hinodeya Ramen homepage, accessed November 14, 2022, http://hinodeyaramen.com/?page_id=1058.

57. Edwin Goei, "Ramen Yamadaya Offers Oink Noodle," OC Weekly, February 24, 2012, https://ocweekly.com/ramen-yamadaya-offers-oink-noodle-6421264/.

58. Benkyodo homepage, accessed November 20, 2020, http://www.benkyodocompany.com/; fieldwork by James Farrer, October 20, 2019.

59. Ryan Basso, "Go Eat This Now: Deviled Egg Sandwich at Benkyodo," *SF Weekly,* January 8, 2019, https://www.sfweekly.com/dining/go-eat-this-now-deviled-egg-sandwich-at-benkyodo-co/.

60. "San Francisco Manju-ya Benkyodo Closing After 115 Years," *Rafu Shimpo,* March 26, 2022, https://rafu.com/2022/03/san-francisco-manju-ya-benkyodo-closing-after-115-years/.

61. Christopher A. Reichl, "Stages in the Historical Process of Ethnicity: The Japanese in Brazil, 1908–1988," *Ethnohistory* 42, no. 1 (1995): 31–62.

62. Stewart Lone, *The Japanese Community in Brazil, 1908–1940: Between Samurai and Carnival* (New York: Palgrave Macmillan, 2001), 107.

63. "Emigration Incentives as a Means of Solving Population and Unemployment Problems," in *100 Years of Japanese Emigration to Brazil* (Tokyo: National Diet Library, 2014), https://www.ndl.go.jp/brasil/e/s4/s4_1.html.

64. Instituto Brasileiro de Geografia e Estatística, accessed September 15, 2020, https://www.ibge.gov.br.

65. Arlinda Rocha Nogueira, "São Paulo, Algodão e o Japonês na Década de 1930" [São Paulo, cotton and the Japanese in the 1930s], *Revista do Instituto de Estudos Brasileiros* 26 (1986): 9–26.

66. Lone, *Japanese Community in Brazil,* 48–49.

67. Mori Koichi (森幸一), "Sanpauroshi ni okeru nihonryōri(ten) no ichi, imēji, juyō no katachi" (サンパウロ市における日本料理 (店)の位置, イメージ, 受容のかたち) [Japanese restaurants in Saõ Paulo City: The market, image and the forms of acceptance], *JICA: Yokohama kaigai iju shiryōkan kiyō* 9 (2014): 21–57; Koichi Mori, "As condições de aceitação da culinária japonesa na cidade de São Paulo—por que os brasileiros começaram a apreciar a culinária japonesa?" [Conditions for acceptance of Japanese cuisine in the city of São Paulo—why did Brazilians begin to appreciate Japanese cuisine?], *Estudos Japoneses* 23 (2003): 7–22.

68. Shigeru Kojima, "The Immigrants Who Introduced Japanese Cuisine to the Americas (Part 2: South America)," *Food Culture: Journal of the Kikkoman Institute for International Food Culture,* no. 23 (2013): 3–4.

69. Mori, "Sanpauroshi ni okeru nihonryōri(ten)," 21.

70. Lone, *Japanese Community in Brazil,* 48.

71. Mori, "Sanpauroshi ni okeru nihonryōri(ten)," 26.

72. Kojima, "Immigrants," 6.

73. Lone, *Japanese Community in Brazil,* 127–128.

74. "Japanese Community Situations before and after the Outbreak of the War between Japan and the U.S.," in *100 Years of Japanese Emigration to Brazil* (Tokyo: National Diet Library, 2014), https://www.ndl.go.jp/brasil/e/s5/s5_2.html.

75. Mori, "As condições de aceitação da culinária japonesa."

76. Kojima, "Immigrants," 4.

77. Mori, "Sanpauroshi ni okeru nihonryōri(ten)," 23.

78. Mori, 26.

79. Mori, 28.

80. Cecilia Nagayama, interview by Mônica R. de Carvalho, August 2018.

81. Kojima, "Immigrants," 4.

82. Harumi Befu, "The Global Context of Japan Outside Japan," in *Globalizing Japan: Ethnography of the Japanese Presence in Asia, Europe, and America,* ed. Harumi Befu and Sylvie Guichard-Anguis (London: Routledge, 2003), 25–44; Nora Kottman, "Japanese Women on the Move: Working and (Not) Belonging in Düsseldorf's Japanese (Food) Community," in *Food Identities at Home and on the Move: Explorations at the Intersection of Food, Belonging and Dwelling,* ed. Raul Matta, Charles-Edouard de Suremain, and Chantal Crenn (Abingdon, UK: Routledge, 2020), 175–187; Paul White, "The Japanese in London: From Transience to Settlement?," in Goodman et al., *Global Japan,* 79–97; Günther Glebe, "Segregation and the Ethnoscape: The Japanese Business Community in Düsseldorf," in Goodman et al., *Global Japan,* 110–127.

83. Keiko Itoh, *The Japanese Community in Prewar Britain: From Integration to Disintegration* (Abingdon, UK: Routledge, 2001).

84. Itoh, *Japanese Community;* Katarzyna Cwiertka, *Modern Japanese Cuisine: Food, Power and National Identity* (London: Reaktion Books, 2006).

85. Itoh, *Japanese Community,* 69–70. Writer Iwaya Sazanami reports dining at two Japanese restaurants in London in 1902, including Miyako. See Iwaya Sazanami (巌谷小波), *Sazanami yōkōmiyage (gekan)* (小波洋行土産 下巻) [Sazanami Western tour memoir Volume 2] (Tokyo: Hakubunkan, 1905), 183–191.

86. Itoh, *Japanese Community,* 68.

87. Itoh, 67.

88. Düsseldorf Japan Club, *Rain no nagare: Shakai, rekishi hen* (ラインの流れ: 社会, 歴史編) [The flow of the Rhine: Society and history volume] (Düsseldorf: Japan Club, 1990), 119–121.

89. Iwaya, *Sazanami yōkōmiyage,* 75–76.

90. Ōhori Sō (大堀聰), "Senjika Doitsu no nipponshoku resutoran 'Akebono' no shashin hakken" (戦時下ドイツの日本食レストラン 'あけぼの' の写真発見) [Discovery of photograph of Japanese restaurant "Akebono" in Germany during the war], Nichizui kankei no pēji (日瑞関係のページ) [Japan Switzerland relations page], March 22, 2014, http://www.saturn.dti.ne.jp/~ohori/sub-akebono.htm.

91. Sugimoto died in Berlin in December 1941, and the restaurant was taken over by Fumi Hirata the head cook. Sō Ōhori's research suggests that the restaurant was registered under the name of Sugimoto's German wife (or possibly Hirata's), who spoke Japanese. Ōhori Sō, "'Akebono' no keieisha, Sugimoto Kuichi no atoashi wo ou" ('あけぼの' の経営者、杉本久市の足跡を追う) [Looking for traces of the operator of "Akebono," Sugimoto Kuichi], Nichizui kankei no pēji (日瑞関係のページ)[Japan Switzerland relations page], May 15, 2019, http://www.saturn.dti.ne.jp/~ohori/sub-2akebono.htm.

92. Tanabe Hiragaku (田辺平学), *Doitsu: Bōkū kagaku kokumin seikatsu* (ドイツ: 防空, 科学, 国民生活) [Germany: Air defense, science, national life] (Tokyo: Sagami shobo, 1942), 358.

93. Ōhori Sō (大堀聰), *Dainijisekaitaisenka no ōshū hōjin (doitsu suisu)* (第二次世界大戦下の欧州邦人[ドイツ・スイス]) [The Japanese in Europe in World War II (Germany and Switzerland)] (Tokyo: Ginga shoseki, 2021), 86–89.

94. Saitō Kiyoe (斉藤清衛), *Tōyōjin no tabi: Yōroppa kikō* (東洋人の旅: 欧羅巴紀行) [A trip to Europe: A journey of an Oriental person] (Tokyo: Shun'yō-dō shoten, 1937), 72.

95. Düsseldorf Japan Club, *Rain no nagare*, 119–121.

96. *Münchner Illustrierte Presse*, 1927, cited in Maren Möhring, *Fremdes Essen: Die Geschichte der ausländischen Gastronomie in der Bundesrepublik Deutschland* [Strange foods: The history of foreign gastronomy in the Federal Republic of Germany] (Berlin: Walter de Gruyter, 2012), 53.

97. Ōhori, "Senjika Doitsu."

98. Kawamori Yoshizō (河盛好蔵), *Pari kōjitsu* (巴里好日) [Good days in Paris] (Tokyo: Kawade bunko, 1984), 82.

99. Jim Chevallier, *A History of the Food of Paris: From Roast Mammoth to Steak Frites* (New York: Rowman and Littlefield, 2018), 130.

100. Ōhori Sō (大堀聰), "Pari no nihonryōriten botanya wo megutte" (パリの日本料理店 牡丹屋をめぐって) [About Botanya, a Japanese restaurant in Paris], Nichizui kankei no pēji (日瑞関係のページ) [Japan Switzerland relations page], August 19, 2021, http://www.saturn.dti.ne.jp/~ohori/sub-botanya.htm.

101. Shimodaira repatriated to Japan after the war. His French wife kept the restaurant going until his return around 1950. Ōhori, "Pari no nihonryōriten botanya wo megutte."

102. Saitō Moto (斎藤もと), *Nyūyōku no koinobori* (ニューヨークの鯉のぼり) [A carp flag in New York] (Tokyo: PHP Press, 1988), 55–56. Other travelers left more positive appraisals. See Ōhori, "Pari no nihonryōriten botanya wo megutte."

103. Japanisches Generalkonsulat Düsseldorf homepage, accessed September 1, 2021, https://www.dus.emb-japan.go.jp/itprtop_ja/index.html.

104. Düsseldorf Japan Club, *Rain no nagare*, 119–121.

105. Möhring, *Fremdes Essen*, 109.

106. Glebe, "Segregation and the Ethnoscape."

107. Kottman, "Japanese Women on the Move," 175–187.

108. Sebastian Schmidt (researcher at the Japan External Trade Organization) and Takayasu Fukui (director of the Japan External Trade Organization), interview by James Farrer in the Düsseldorf Japan External Trade Organization office, August 29, 2019.

109. Düsseldorf Japan Club, *Rain no nagare*, 37.

110. Nishimura Sanzen (西村三千), "Doitsu Nihon-kan no misejimai" (ドイツ日本館の店じまい) [The German Nippon-kan closes], *Yodan: Doitsu kagaku-shi no tabi*, no. 19, August 4, 2010, https://isomers.ismr.us/isomers2010/annex319.htm.

111. Düsseldorf Japan Club, *Rain no nagare*, 140–142 (interview with Nippon-kan nightlclub manager Suzuki Mayumi).

112. The role of culinary infrastructure in promulgating and sustaining a cuisine is described in Jeffrey M. Pilcher, "Culinary Infrastructure: How Facilities and Technologies Create Value and Meaning around Food," *Global Food History* 2, no. 2 (2016): 105–131.

113. Düsseldorf Japan Club, *Rain no nagare*, 82–84 (interview with Morozumi Michio), 66–67 (interview with Ito Fumio).

114. Düsseldorf Japan Club, 66–67.

115. Düsseldorf Japan Club, 66–67.

116. Düsseldorf Japan Club, 66–67.

117. Hiroaki Ando, interview by James Farrer, August 21, 2017.

118. Hiroaki Ando, interview.

119. Okinii was founded in Saarbrücken (with the name Oishii), but the family moved the company headquarters to Düsseldorf after they took over the prestigious Immermannstrasse location. For the family's history in Chinese gastronomy, see Peking Garden, accessed November 14, 2020, https://www.peking-garden-krefeld.de/über-uns.

120. Ishige et al., *Rosuanjerusu,* 45.

121. Ikezawa Yasushi (池澤康), *Amerika nihonshoku uōzu* (アメリカ日本食ウォーズ) [America Japanese food wars] (Tokyo: Toshibaya, 2005), 15.

122. Saitō, *Tōyō hito no tabi,* 72.

123. Saitō, 73–74.

124. Kawamori, *Pari kōjitsu,* 82–83.

125. "The Czech Republic Is an Attractive Location for Japanese Investment," Government of the Czech Republic, June 28, 2017, https://www.vlada.cz/en/media-centrum/aktualne/the-czech-republic-is-an-attractive-location-for-japanese-investments-158081.

126. Kaigai zairyū hōjin-sū chōsa tōkei (海外在留法人数調査統計) [Annual report of statistics on Japanese nationals overseas], Ministry of Foreign Affairs, Government of Japan, October 1, 2018, https://www.mofa.go.jp/mofaj/toko/page22_003338.html.

127. Fieldwork by Lenka Vyletalova, August 2017, September 2018, and February 2020; "Katsura je japonská hospoda s domácí kuchyní" [Katsura is a Japanese pub with home cooking], Hospodarske Noviny, February 20, 2012, https://vikend.hn.cz/c1-54717090-sake-se-v-evrope-pit-neda-z-konzervantu-boli-hlava.

128. Kaigai zairyū hōjin-sū chōsa tōkei (海外在留法人数調査統計) [Annual report of statistics on Japanese nationals overseas], Ministry of Foreign Affairs, Government of Japan, October 1, 2018, https://www.mofa.go.jp/mofaj/toko/page22_003338.html.

129. Fieldwork by James Farrer, February 8–11, 2018.

130. Fieldwork by James Farrer, February 8–11, 2018.

131. Fieldwork by James Farrer, February 8–11, 2018.

132. Souther, "Disneyfication of New Orleans."

133. "Enquête: Les restaurants japonais à Paris," *Jipango*, November 1998, www.jipango.com/jipango2001/jipango_98/jaap_hp2.html.

134. Chambre de Commerce et d'Industrie Japonaise en France, accessed November 7, 2018, http://www.ccijf.asso.fr/ja/committee/committee-08.

135. Kei Okijima (沖島景), "Sengo, opera nihonjinmachi keisei no kiseki" (戦後, オペラ日本人街形成の軌跡) [Postwar history of the formation of the Opera Japan Quarter], *News Digest* (France) no. 910 (August 19, 2010; no longer online, last accessed November 20, 2020) http://www.newsdigest.fr/newsfr/features/4119-history-of-quartier-japonais-opera.html.

136. Adrian Forlan, "Pourquoi Takara est toujours le meilleur restaurant japonais de Paris" [Why Takara is still the best Japanese restaurant in Paris], *L'Officiel,* March 3, 2018, https://www.lofficiel.com/food/voici-le-meilleur-restaurant-japonais-de-paris; "Un peu d'histoire," Takara, accessed November 20, 2020, http://isaora.free.fr/histoire.htm.

137. "Un peu d'histoire"; Ōhori, "Pari no nihonryōriten botanya wo megutte."

138. Yamakoshi Yukio (owner of Takara), interview by Chuanfei Wang and James Farrer, February 21, 2017.

139. "TAKARA, le plus ancien restaurant japonais de Paris," *First Luxe Magazine*, January 10, 2013, https://www.firstluxemag.com/takara-tradition-rime-avec-qualite.

140. See also James Farrer and Chuanfei Wang, "Who Owns a Cuisine? The Grassroots Politics of Japanese Food in Europe," *Asian Anthropology* 20, no. 1 (2021): 12–29.

141. Kyodo, "Mitsukoshi Shutters Flagship Paris Store," *The Japan Times* (Oct. 2, 2010) https://www.japantimes.co.jp/news/2010/10/02/business/mitsukoshi-shutters-flagship-paris-store/.

142. Tina Kempter, "Les faces cachées de la cuisine japonaise en France" [The hidden faces of Japanese cuisine in France]," *Wasabi* 34 (2013): 14–25.

143. Fieldwork by Chuanfei Wang, August 2018.

144. Ono, interview by Chuanfei Wang, August 2018.

145. Daniel H. Inouye, *Distant Islands: The Japanese American Community in New York City, 1876–1930s* (Boulder: University Press of Colorado, 2018).

146. Inouye, 154–156.

147. Matsumoto Hirotaka (松本紘宇), *Nyūyōku Take Sushi monogatari* (ニューヨーク竹寿司物語) [New York Take Sushi tale] (Tokyo: Asahi shinbunsha, 1995), 28–29.

148. Matsumoto, 79.

149. Matsumoto, 192.

150. Patti Smith, "The Regulars," *New York Times*, April 13, 2020, https://www.nytimes.com/interactive/2020/04/13/t-magazine/omen-restaurant-nyc.html.

151. Michio Hayashi, email correspondence with James Farrer, November 22, 2019.

152. Cathy Kaufman, "If You Build It, They Will Come: The Self-Conscious Creation of the East Village's Little Tokyo," *NYFoodStory: The Journal of the Culinary Historians of New York*, 2019, http://www.nyfoodstory.com/articles/if-you-build-it-they-will-come.

153. Erina Yoshida, interview by James Farrer, September 26, 2019.

154. Bon Yagi and Sakura Yagi, interview by James Farrer, April 17, 2019; Nancy Matsumoto, "Bon Yagi: Emperor of New York's Japanese East Village—Part 1," Discover Nikkei, November 5, 2015, http://www.discovernikkei.org/en/journal/2015/11/5/bon-yagi-1/.

155. Bon Yagi and Sakura Yagi, interview by James Farrer, April 17, 2019, and field visit to Sakagura; Sakagura homepage, accessed April 19, 2019, https://www.tic-nyc.com/sakagura.

156. Bon Yagi and Sakura Yagi, interview by James Farrer, April 17, 2019.

157. T.I.C. Restaurant Group homepage, accessed April 19, 2019, https://www.tic-nyc.com.

158. Bon Yagi and Sakura Yagi, interview by James Farrer, April 17, 2019.

159. For his social and intercultural activities, Yagi received the Order of the Rising Sun, Gold and Silver Rays; "Mr. Shuji Yagi (Shuho Bon Yagi)," Consulate General of Japan in New York, accessed September 1, 2020, https://www.ny.us.emb-japan.go.jp/decorations/2019/2/Yagi.html.

4 | Global Food Fashions and Their Cultural Intermediaries

Lenka Vyletalova, James Farrer,
Chuanfei Wang, and Christian A. Hess

Japanese cuisine inspired food fashions far beyond the boundaries of the overseas Japanese communities documented in previous chapters, changing how people around the world experienced urban dining. This chapter traces five global Japanese food fashions: the tearoom, sukiyaki house, Japanese steak house, sushi bar, and ramen bar. Each fashion involved a distinct restaurant form that spread across cities on multiple continents, accompanied by a spate of media attention. These trends rippled out from geographic and social centers to peripheral regions where they dissipated, with remnants flourishing in "culinary backwaters" less beholden to metropolitan food fashions. In this process, Japanese restaurateurs appealed to new consumers via aesthetics and service rather than simply taste. The restaurant as a whole is implicated in these food fashions, not just the menu items for which they are best known.

Fashion, avers sociologist Georg Simmel, involves two contradictory impulses: a desire to be part of the crowd by following an existing trend, and another to distinguish oneself from the masses by following new ones.[1] Geographically, food fashions spread to hinterlands as new ones rise in metropoles, the places we describe as "culinary global cities." All stories of Japanese restaurant forms in this chapter illustrate how a food fashion starts among trendsetters in global cities and then becomes a broader consumer pattern that we call a global food fashion. The trend broadens in reception, gradually becoming accessible to almost everyone. Such accessibility—massification or democratization—eventually renders the trend unfashionable, as is clearly seen with the tearoom, sukiyaki house, and steak house booms.[2] In the early 2010s, food bloggers proclaimed that "ramen is the new sushi," but by 2020, we already see the "new ramen" in the poke bowl and the *izakaya* (a Japanese pub).[3]

All these fashions have moved from an exclusive community to the broader public through the agency of cultural intermediaries—actors involved in the dissemination, evaluation, and legitimation of products, behaviors, and ideas. These intermediaries range from government officials serving as culinary ambassadors to journalists critiquing restaurants to waitresses interacting with new customers.[4] This chapter examines the innovative culinary imaginaries promulgated by these cultural intermediaries. While the success of Japanese foodways is often attributed to the unique qualities of the cuisine and artisanship of chefs, this chapter focuses on the restaurant as an imaginatively designed and socially constructed space. Thus, the "taste" of a Japanese restaurant goes beyond the foods served, with a large part of the consumer experience occurring on a semiotic level—ideas conveyed through a visually and acoustically rich social space that includes the performances of staff.

The first part of the chapter is organized chronologically by food fashions. While each has variable periods of gestation and decline, a rough sequence of their heydays is the teahouse in the 1890s–1920s, the sukiyaki house in the 1930s–1950s, the steak house in the 1970s–1980s, the sushi bar in the 1980s–2010s, and the ramen bar from the 2010s. Our narrative highlights continuities and changes in the types of cultural intermediaries who helped produce each boom. This shifting cast of characters includes government agents and exhibition organizers in the late nineteenth century, food critics and writers in the twentieth, and celebrity chefs and bloggers in the twenty-first century.[5] However, in all periods, individual restaurateurs and their usually female service staff have been the grassroots cultural intermediaries representing Japanese cuisine to newcomers.[6] In the second part of this chapter, we further highlight the role played by women owners and front-of-house managers as key cultural intermediaries in spreading Japanese restaurant culture.

These cultural intermediaries also became central participants in the culinary politics of articulating what exactly is valuable or desirable in the production of "Japanese cuisine." Some evangelized an ideal of "authenticity" based on standards in Japan, while others promoted creative expression or adaptation to new palates and environments. In conclusion, we look at the tension in these booms between ideals of authenticity and creativity that underlie the packaging of a national cuisine as global food fashions, a tension between the territorial basis of culinary culture and the deterritorialization of globalization.

The Japanese Tearoom and Culinary *Japonisme*

The Japanese tearoom was the first global Japanese culinary fashion. It featured imaginaries that would characterize subsequent Japanese restaurant booms. The tearoom's importance lies not in the food and drink itself but rather in introducing an image of the Japanese eatery as a refined social space. It laid the foundation for consumer perceptions of Japanese restaurants as not being simply a curious "ethnic" space but one associated with intrinsic aesthetic values of refinement, femininity, and the beauty of stylized nature.

This aesthetic globalization was closely tied to world expositions (or fairs), a form of cultural diplomacy that had begun already in the last years of the Tokugawa shogunate and continued into the next century. Japan's first participation was with a pavilion in the Paris International Exposition of 1867, formally headed by a child brother of the shogun.[7] World expositions were where new trends were born, as countries used them to showcase products and ideas. Culinary novelties introduced at world expositions over the decades included the cafeteria, the *Michelin Guide*, the automat, the sushi conveyor belt, and Chinese restaurants (new for Europeans).[8] In this sense, fair organizers acted as lifestyle experts and the state officials as cultural ambassadors for their societies. The Japanese state and industry emissaries used fairs to show off both traditional crafts and new industries, establishing Japan as both a cultured and modern nation. Significantly, most of Japan's displays included tearooms, almost always associated with Japanese gardens, beginning with a traditional teahouse in the 1867 Paris International Exposition.

The Paris teahouse was a hit with fair attendees. It was built of bamboo and white wood, and a counter served liquor and tea in small cups, the latter sweetened with sugar plums. Its salon featured three geishas from Japan in elaborate kimonos and, for Europeans, remarkable hairstyles. These three women, whose geisha names were recorded by a British journalist as

O-Kane, O-Sato, and O-Soumi (literally, Money, Sugar, and Ink), intrigued and charmed visitors by smoking, drinking tea, demonstrating Japanese parlor games, and singing the Japanese national anthem.[9] These nineteenth-century Japanese women were some of the first cultural intermediaries conveying the appeal of Japanese consumer style to Europeans. Far from passive objects of a male gaze, they performed and, in some ways, invented Japanese culture for Europeans.

The 1867 Paris International Exposition established an appreciation for Japanese interior design and arts that became known as *Japonisme,* which would shape the reception of Japanese culture and, eventually, cuisine. *Japonisme* was not only exotic but associated with the cutting edge of French art and design. After the 1867 exposition, the painter and ceramist Félix Bracquemond, together with other admirers of Japanese art, founded an art society called Jinglar, which met for monthly dinners in the salon of a member in Sèvres between August 1868 and March 1869.[10] Attendees came in kimonos and ate rice using chopsticks while drinking Japanese *sake* around a table where, reportedly, "apart from the cigars and ashtrays, all was Japanese."[11] Bracquemond created between 1866 and 1870 a large porcelain service inspired by the *kacho-ga* (literally bird and flower painting) engravings of fish by Hokusai and graphic studies of flowers by Hiroshige. This tableware, decorated with floral motifs featuring birds, fish, or insects, is one of the first concrete expressions of *Japonisme* in France.[12] Due to his knowledge of Japanese visual arts acquired by decorating such items of daily use as tableware, Bracquemond acted as a cultural intermediary, introducing Japanese arts, fashion, and even dining culture to the leading lights of the French impressionist movement.

After the political and commercial success in Paris, the Japanese tearooms at world exhibitions became more elaborate. Some were tearooms inside larger structures, while others were self-standing teahouses with gardens. For example, the 1876 Philadelphia Centennial Exposition featured a Japanese teahouse and a bazaar situated alongside the Chinese pavilion.[13] The 1893 Columbian Exposition in Chicago also included the elaborate Phoenix Palace (Hōōden), a careful reconstruction of the Byōdōin Temple in Uji, Kyoto Prefecture, with an open-air teahouse that fronted the lagoon on Wooded Isle, one of the most prominent positions on the fairgrounds. (The Japanese garden from the exhibit survives on the island in today's Jackson Park.)[14] The teahouse was run by the Japanese Central Tea Association, an industry organization in Tokyo, and served "light lunches and

FIGURE 4.1 The Japanese Tea Garden at Chicago's 1893 Columbian Exposition was located on Wooded Isle (now Jackson Park). Such teahouses were featured in nearly all Japanese exhibits in expositions in the late nineteenth and early twentieth centuries. (From C. D. Arnold and H. D. Higinbotham, *Official Views of the World's Columbian Exposition* [Chicago: World's Columbian Exposition, 1893])

samples of high-priced teas."[15] Similarly, in 1894, a Japanese teahouse and garden were built to showcase a Japanese village for the California Midwinter International Exposition (later called the World's Fair). It remained open in Golden Gate Park until 1942, and a reconstructed version has remained a major tourist attraction.[16] Next, the 1900 Paris Universal Exposition offered elaborate tea and *sake* pavilions featuring tastings. The expo also hosted performances by former geisha Sada Yacco (Sadayakko Kawakami) and the Japanese Court Company, the first Japanese theatrical troupe to tour Europe.[17] These exhibits fostered a widespread and growing interest in Japanese aesthetics. In this way, the combination of Japanese tea, the tearoom, and the tea garden became a global trend by the turn of the century. Furthermore, the tearoom culture was associated with Japanese women, who usually staffed them, and the Japanese tea culture became regarded as feminized.[18]

The popularity of tearooms in exhibitions helped set the stage for their spread as commercial restaurants. Some early restaurants were founded by Japanese migrants. In 1897, after the Columbian Exhibition, the Japan Central Tea Traders Association opened a Chicago office to promote Japanese green tea. In 1899, it opened a tearoom in Sans Souci Amusement Park on Cottage Grove Avenue, not far from the fair site. The tearoom hired a Japanese chef from Tokyo to prepare Japanese food. Kahei Ohtani, director of the Japan Central Tea Traders Association, visited the tearoom just after its opening and wrote, "It is very impressive to sit in a Japanese style room and enjoy Japanese food, thousands of miles from Japan."[19] This tearoom was among the first that served Japanese rather than Western food. Tearooms were a long-lived fashion in Chicago. Even in the years after World War II, one could find the Wisteria Tea Room on North Wabash in Chicago, run by a Ms. S. Okimoto, where kimono-clad Japanese women served sukiyaki, which by this time was already a global fad (as discussed in the next section).[20]

Outside overseas Japanese communities, Japanese tearooms were part of a broader fashion for tearooms, supposedly started in Glasgow in the 1880s as an alternative dining space to gin houses and taverns, especially aimed at women. Japanese-themed tearooms were opened in many urban hotels, featuring shoji screens, Japanese lanterns, hanging wisteria plants, and occasionally even Japanese servers. One such place was the elaborately appointed Japanese Tea Room in the Congress Hotel in Chicago, with a giant bronze tea urn, Oriental lanterns, and an elaborate inlaid ceiling. The 1908 menu offered "Japanese crystalized pineapple" and other candied fruits alongside a typical American menu. In 1917, the Ritz Carlton in New York advertised an outdoor restaurant with a Japanese tea garden designed and built by a team of artisans from Japan, including a running stream, stone bridges, and pagodas.[21] As the fashion spread to smaller cities, many Japanese tearooms in the 1910s and 1920s were founded by white middle-class women. Such venues were considered acceptable places for them to operate and patronize at the time.[22] An example is the Japanese Tea Room in San Antonio, Texas. It occupied an entire floor of the Wolff and Marx Company Department Store and was opened by Mrs. H. J. Trollinger in 1924. The owners invested USD 40,000 to convert the space into a faux Japanese garden. Patrons entered via one of two stone bridges that crossed a flowing stream with goldfish. Green and red tiles represented garden paths and grass. The space was adorned with murals and potted plants. The menu, however, contained American-style cakes and sandwiches, as few tearooms operated by white proprietors served Japanese cuisine (other than the ubiquitous Japanese tea).[23] A 1911 book, *Bright Ideas for Money Making,* suggested that a budding tearoom entrepreneur might adopt a Japanese theme with lanterns, paper parasols, and waitresses in kimonos. Rice could be served, opined the author, "but do not carry the idea of Japanese cookery any further, as there are very few Japanese dishes which are popular."[24] Thus, the Japanese tearoom was a celebration of *Japonisme* more than Japanese food.

The fashion for Japanese-themed tearooms spread in Europe as well. In 1908, in the cosmopolitan city of Prague, Josef "Joe" Hloucha, among the first Czech Japanophiles and a traveler, art collector, and writer, created a Japanese tearoom for the Industrial and Commercial Exposition held in the city. Like the California tearoom mentioned earlier, Hloucha's tearoom was

FIGURE 4.2 Villa Sakura, located in Roztoky near Prague, became known in the late 1920s and 1930s as a place to enjoy the "exotic tastes" of its Japanese-style hotel and tearoom, as well as cherry-blossom-viewing festivals held in its garden. ("Interior of Hotel Sakura," photo taken in 1928 by Eduard Hnilicka, Central Bohemian Museum in Roztoky near Prague, contributing organization)

turned into a permanent venue called Yokohama in the newly built Palace Lucerna, a cultural hub in the young Czechoslovakia. Among the kimono-clad waitresses, there were reportedly even one Japanese and one Chinese woman.[25] Hloucha, who had been to Japan twice, accumulated many Asian artifacts. In 1924, he bought a villa near Prague that he rebuilt in Japanese style, with a typical roof, outdoor animal ornaments, and cherry trees in the garden, and named it Villa Sakura.[26] In 1926, he sold the villa to the entrepreneur Josef Jiroušek, who built a similarly styled, larger venue next door as a "Japanese style hotel, tea-room and restaurant" that he named Big Sakura. Its interior featured Japanese paper walls, sliding doors, lampoon lanterns, and ink paintings. Next, Jan Marold, the owner of a famous Prague French restaurant and wine distributing company, bought Hotel Sakura, promoting it as a "place of exotic tastes." Its head chef was Tonio Horský, a Czech who had "worked for the King of Serbia, the Pasha Kemal, as well as in the restaurants in Istanbul or Cairo."[27] The hotel hosted frequent tea ceremonies, a *hanami* (cherry-blossom-viewing) festival, and other seasonal celebrations until shuttering with the Nazi invasion of Czechoslovakia in World War II.[28]

In neighboring Germany, tourists could also visit a Japanese tearoom with "original Japanese service" in Berlin's Potsdamer Platz. Opening in 1928, the six-floor urban amusement park Haus Vaterland housed twelve exotically themed restaurants with floor-to-ceiling dioramas and dance bands. Inspired by Coney Island, Haus Vaterland contained the largest café in Berlin, seating 2,500 guests and attracting a million visitors a year. It boasted the largest modern central kitchen in the world at the time. The complex promised the "world under one roof" and pioneered the "experiential gastronomy" of the early twentieth century, in which restaurants were a space of fantasy and travel. Originally, it housed Turkish, Spanish, Italian, Hungarian, and Wild West–themed restaurants. An Italian restaurant and Japanese tearoom were added in the 1930s to celebrate the establishment of the Axis alliance. It is unclear whether Japanese or other Asians worked in the tearoom and what Japanese dishes it served. In 1937, Kempinski, the Jewish family-run hospitality firm that owned it, was forced to sell the property by the Nazi government, its foreign staff were persecuted, and some were murdered. Haus Vaterland also was heavily damaged by aerial bombardments in 1943, though it briefly opened again after the war.[29]

The popularity of Japanese tearooms in the late nineteenth and early twentieth centuries could be regarded as the first global Japanese restaurant trend. It is remarkable because such places focused not on Japanese food but rather on Japanese aesthetics. Unlike many other eateries of the era, they often were run by women or hired women as staff, also creating spaces that were friendly to women as customers.[30] Although they faded as a fashion after World War II, they established basic details of design and staffing that appeared in subsequent Japanese restaurant booms, from the sukiyaki house to the sushi bar. Beginning with the tearoom, Japanese restaurants were endowed with an aura of aesthetic refinement that enabled them to command higher prices for the product and dining experience.

The "Butterfly Romanticism" of the Sukiyaki House

The sukiyaki house was the first global Japanese restaurant featuring a signature food item, rather than a beverage. Nevertheless, as with the tearoom, the fashion for sukiyaki from the 1920s to the 1960s was also about the décor and stylized service. And the sukiyaki house, like the tearoom, was a feminized space with waitresses embodying Japaneseness being the cultural intermediaries who introduced dishes to newcomers. As emphasized in Chapter 2, the pre–World War II sukiyaki houses featured eroticized accompaniment by female entertainers and servers. Even as working as a waitress in a sukiyaki house gradually lost its overt sexual expectations, the women still wore exotic kimonos and often provided table-side service preparing the signature dish.[31] Sliding shoji doors created intimate spaces festooned with Japanese prints, lanterns, and other Oriental paraphernalia. Another fresh experience for European and American consumers was food served in a sizzling brazier on the table. For some, soy sauce was a novel taste, although many knew it from Chinese chop suey restaurants. In addition to sukiyaki, the restaurants often served tempura, *tonkatsu* (Japanese-style fried pork cutlet), and teriyaki. Such savory, meat-based dishes appealed to Western palates. (Restaurants with many Japanese patrons also offered sashimi, sushi, and other items still unfamiliar to non-Japanese.)

The early sukiyaki craze was spurred by the rise of global culinary cities, where eating exotic foreign foods was an increasingly desirable experience. In these cities, a new coterie of professional culinary intermediaries cultivated an urban gourmet public by feeding them reviews and feature stories about dining options. A city of immigrants and the world's rising financial center, New York took the lead as a center of global culinary influence at the beginning of the twentieth century. The city was a unique culinary contact zone in which nearly all food providers—from pushcart vendors to chefs at top restaurants—were migrants, so its residents were used to "foreign" foods. It was also a city that celebrated diversity and novelty.[32] After World War II, the city became a nexus in global flows of culinary personnel, expertise, and media influence, solidifying its position as the apex culinary global city.

Japanese restaurants in New York, therefore, had an outsize influence on establishing Japanese food fashions. Between the two world wars, there were about thirteen Japanese restaurants in the city.[33] First and foremost was Miyako in Midtown near Columbus Circle, founded in 1914.[34] It was owned by Senzo Kuwayama, a merchant from Echigo Province (now Niigata Prefecture) who made a fortune as an importer of monosodium glutamate and manufacturer of his own patented *arare* (roasted sticky rice crackers). Miyako's manager was Kazuhei Tsukuda, a former Japanese navy man, also from Echigo. The first chef was another first-generation migrant, Kanjiro Matsuo, who had experience cooking Japanese and American dishes. By the 1930s, customers at Miyako included both Japanese corporate expatriates and a growing number of white New Yorkers. The interior featured Japanese paintings and a mirrored ceiling engraved with the Japanese character for Miyako (which means "capital"). Meals were served on fine porcelain on white tablecloths, and waiters wore white evening jackets and black bow ties, signaling to New Yorkers that this was a fine dining environment.[35] Though the Japanese-language menu was more expansive, Miyako's English menu appealed to white American tastes with meat and fried items. Offerings included sukiyaki, *tonkatsu, kushiyaki* (skewers), teriyaki, vegetable and seafood tempura, and stir-fried vegetables, including bamboo and Japanese mushrooms, that were familiar to patrons from Chinese restaurants. Miyako was best known for sukiyaki. Its popularity among white American diners was stoked by the early New York food journalists. One of them, Anne Lewis Pierce, wrote in 1924 of her visit to the restaurant for the leading New York daily *the Tribune*.[36] The restaurant received another boost by a glowing 1932 introduction to sukiyaki by Dorothy Marsh, a culinary authority for *Good Housekeeping* magazine, whose offices were around the corner.[37] Notably, both of these cultural intermediaries were pioneering women journalists, whose early work included writing about food.

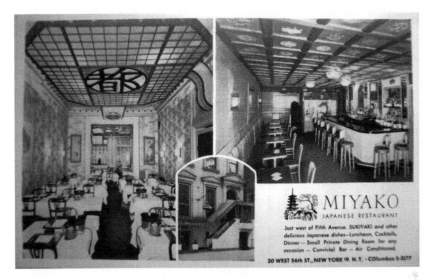

FIGURE 4.3 The Miyako restaurant was the preeminent Japanese dining spot in New York City before World War II. It was one of the first to popularize sukiyaki beyond the Japanese expatriate community. (Postcard postmarked January 1957, owned by James Farrer)

By the early 1930s, sukiyaki was established as a global food fashion. It evinced several dynamics seen in subsequent fashions. First, its center of gravity was New York. Second, it was popularized in mass media. Third, it featured a palatable dish made with ingredients familiar to Westerners. Fourth, its new flavoring, soy sauce, was increasingly manufactured in the United States. Most importantly, its service style was elaborate and aestheticized.[38] Otherwise, sukiyaki was flexible in terms of its other ingredients, and "American adaptations" appeared in newspaper recipes as early as the late 1930s.[39]

US media and elite white consumers played a key role. After dining at a New York sukiyaki restaurant, one critic proclaimed in 1934, "We recognize Japanese cooks as culinary artists and skilled craftsmen."[40] This declaration came after a lengthy description of an elaborately prepared sukiyaki meal. Sukiyaki was stylish. For example, it was the featured cuisine at a 1935 gathering of young women from leading families in a Japanese-themed "sub-debutante" party in Los Angeles, with guests arriving in kimonos.[41] The fact that sukiyaki could be cooked at home added to its popularity. A 1938 article in the *Los Angeles Times* urged readers to "experiment with this dish, capable of bringing so much romance to a meal."[42] Even the charcoal producers in Japan's Akita Prefecture noted that Americans were becoming "sukiyaki addicts," according to one 1936 report, and purchasing charcoal for their broilers.[43]

Emerging global transportation routes also played a role in popularizing sukiyaki. Passengers on the 1929 round-the-world flight of the *Graf Zeppelin* were treated to sukiyaki dinners as they floated out of Tokyo and across the Pacific. Sukiyaki dinner parties were also a popular event for American and British passengers on board Japanese-run ocean liners arriving in Yokohama.[44] In Asia, Shanghai was the leading transportation and trading hub and an early center of the global sukiyaki craze. The city had many sukiyaki restaurants serving the Japanese community, as described in Chapter 2. By the 1920s, interest spread to non-Japanese living in the city, and sukiyaki was mentioned with increasing frequency in Shanghai's English and Chinese newspapers.[45]

In the 1930s, sukiyaki restaurants began to open on fashionable Shanghai boulevards frequented by Westerners. One was Fuji House on Avenue Joffre, the fashionable main street in the French Concession.[46] A 1936 article described how the Shanghai Telephone Company hosted a "going away" party at Fuji House for Mrs. R. Streit and Mrs. E. Ling, female employees returning to their home countries.[47] A humor column in the *Shanghai Sunday Times* described the visit of several Western expatriates to a sukiyaki house on Avenue Joffre, most likely Fuji House. They marveled at the novel experiences, including taking off their shoes before climbing the wooden stairs to the private dining room. There, they found a "room which contained one table, the legs of which had been sawn off to the length of about nine inches, one electric hotplate which stood on the table, and a dozen flat cushions," which they struggled to sit on. "Then the knowing ones clapped their hands," the journalist wrote, "which I understand is the correct method of demanding attention and the mama-san entered carrying a sort of tray on which was piled the most extraordinary mixture of rice, onions, dismembered chicken, meat, etc., that I have ever seen, and it was all raw! This conglomeration was flung into a large pot which was placed on the hot-plate." A female member of the party was familiar with the rituals of eating sukiyaki. She attended to the pot, adding the soy sauce, while the newbie author of the article fumbled with his chopsticks.[48]

Shanghai's sukiyaki boom was associated with other entertainment fashions of the Jazz Age. In 1930, a sukiyaki restaurant opened at the Little Club, a central nightlife venue.[49] A newspaper gossip column described a

Japanese socialite who, after divorcing her husband, a Japanese count, came to Shanghai as a taxi dancer with a Russian musician and then announced she would open a sukiyaki house.[50] The restaurants were also places for sexual adventuring, as seen at the Japanese Kasen restaurant in Qingdao, another port city in Japan's imperial orbit in the 1930s. Its English-language menu featured sukiyaki for two dollars, Western and Japanese alcoholic beverages, and a notice that "geisha girls may be secured for $3 an hour or $5 for two hours." A further notice of private rooms and a "fee when a guest brings own friend" suggests that the restaurant normally served as a brothel.[51] As described in Chapter 2, sukiyaki also found a following among Chinese in the city that persisted even after the collapse of the Japanese empire in 1945.

While sukiyaki was still a leading, even edgy, urban fashion in the decade before World War II, its peak popularity (or massification) in Western countries occurred in the 1950s and 1960s. San Francisco's Yamato and Seattle's Bush Garden Restaurant exemplified the era's elaborate American sukiyaki restaurants. They featured well-stocked bars and Japanese-themed décor, including tatami rooms. In the immediate postwar years, many early non-Japanese patrons were former military personnel and their families who had resided in Japan. In addition, many Japanese waitresses were military brides of American soldiers recently stationed in Japan.[52]

Yamato was a family-owned restaurant opened in 1946 on Grant Avenue by Edward and Kikue Shigematsu.[53] By the 1950s, it was a culinary hot spot famous for its sukiyaki. The restaurant offered many novelties to the non-Japanese customers, including the taking off of shoes to sit on the tatami mats, and the "Japanese girls, attired in kimonos kneeling beside the diners and preparing, cooking, and serving the entire meal in front of the guests."[54] The Sukiyaki De Luxe menu offerings included beef, tofu, bamboo shoots, spinach, fresh mushrooms, celery, green onions, sweet onions, and *shirataki* (yam noodles).[55] This description shows how sukiyaki from this period used local ingredients, such as celery, rarely used in Japan. By the mid-1950s, Yamamoto had been selected by Japan Airlines to prepare meals for flights out of San Francisco. In 1997, the restaurant shuttered, but the family continued the lucrative airline meal business.[56]

Seattle's famous Bush Garden was opened in 1957 by Roy Seko. It sat five hundred diners and had forty private dining rooms with telephones. The restaurant employed five hostesses, four bartenders, twenty-three kimono-clad waitresses, and a roving photographer snapping polaroid portraits for sale.[57] Other upscale sukiyaki restaurants in San Francisco included Nikko Sukiyaki, known for its large piano bar, banquet hall, fireplaces, and tatami rooms, and Tokyo Sukiyaki, which could serve five hundred diners a day.[58]

The global sukiyaki fashion also reached European cities. As described in the previous chapter, adventurous diners could eat sukiyaki in Berlin before World War II. In postwar Germany, Japanese restaurants first re-emerged in the port of Hamburg, which had supported a Japanese business community and at least one Japanese restaurant in the prewar period. In 1962, a five-table sukiyaki restaurant named Kogetsu opened on Gurlitt-strasse, an upscale address near Hamburg's scenic Alster inland waterway. Its patrons included the four hundred Japanese nationals working in the city's thirty-five Japanese firms, as well as Germans curious about foreign foods. The restaurant was reviewed by Erik Verg, a journalist for the *Hamburger Abendblat*. "There is scarcely a small market town in which one can't find a Chinese restaurant with a Chinese cook," he wrote, "but in Hamburg one can eat Japanese! And that is something special. Other than in Hamburg, one can only find this in Paris and London."[59] Moreover, Verg was enamored with the feminine and attentive style of the waitresses, "butterfly romanticism" in his words. "The waitress in her silk kimono bows with a sweet smile to the guest. The guest then sits up and also bows. Only then does one talk about food." It was, Verg wrote, "a special pleasure" when she presented guests with tempura as an appetizer, requiring the use of chopsticks.[60] Sukiyaki also was the primary item served at two other Japanese restaurants in Hamburg in the 1960s.[61]

However, by the 1960s, the sukiyaki restaurant was a fading fashion in New York and Los Angeles, where it had started. In his 1961 review of New York's newly opened fine dining Kabuki restaurant, *New York Times* food critic Craig Claiborne not only noted that sukiyaki "is nearly as popular as pizza in this country" but also emphasized the newer items on the menu, including a nod to sashimi as "interesting."[62] Just as Marsh's 1932 statement that eating in a sukiyaki house was "something special" marked its establishment as an urban fashion, Claiborne's likening of the dish three decades later to the ubiquitous pizza pointed to its decline. At establishments famous for sukiyaki, chefs and owners began pushing other items on menus. For example, in 1968, the Imperial Gardens restaurant in Los Angeles steered customers away from the sukiyaki and tempura dishes to sushi, served up at its novel sushi bar. As explained by Lyle Nakano, the new owner of Imperial Gardens, "What we are attempting to do at Imperial Garden is to broaden the base of familiar selections so diners may be tempted to try something new the next time."[63]

The reinvention of San Francisco's venerable Nikko Sukiyaki also exemplified these shifting fashions. In the late 1960s, it was a high-end restaurant with a diverse, well-heeled customer base and stylish bar that attracted locals and tourists. However, by the early 1970s, the restaurant began losing customers to the newer, more fashionable sushi restaurants catering to the Japanese expatriate community. In 1974, Nikko Sukiyaki was purchased by Mitsuru "Mits" Akashi, a young Japanese bartender in San Francisco, and his friends. They transformed its piano bar into a high-profile sushi bar that attracted sports celebrities and other famous clientele.[64] However, sushi did not immediately displace sukiyaki. In between these two global Japanese food fashions lays another one—the teppanyaki steak house—that defined global Japanese restaurant culture for a decade and more in some places.

The "Samurai" Theatrics of the Japanese Steak House

In Craig Claiborne's 1966 review of "luxe" Japanese restaurants around New York,[65] the hottest trend was the Japanese teppanyaki steak house, sometimes called hibachi. Teppanyaki was, like sukiyaki, Japanese cooking with clear affinities to Western cuisines, but that was only one reason for its popularity. As with the Japanese tearoom and sukiyaki house, the Japanese steak house was a theatrical space arranged for dramatic performances by the staff.

From its inception in Japan immediately after World War II, the teppanyaki steak house was a transpacific hybrid. It seems to have been "invented," or at least popularized, by Shigeji Fujioka (1909–1999) at his restaurant Misono in Kobe. A café owner before the war, Fujioka recovered a metal sheet from a shipyard in 1945, repurposing it as a grill plate. Initially, he made *okonomiyaki* (savory pancake), but to satisfy the palate of a visiting US military officer in autumn of that year, he started grilling steak. It proved to be a hit.[66] Soon dance hall hostesses began bringing American soldiers to dine there. Foreign visitors were entranced by the skilled knife work of the chefs preparing the food on the metal sheet before their eyes. In 1960, a Tokyo branch opened, then a branch in Osaka two years later.[67]

In 1964, the teppanyaki concept was appropriated and embellished by another Japanese entrepreneur, Hiroaki "Rocky" Aoki, who opened Benihana steak house in New York.[68] Aoki was a larger-than-life character with a penchant for showmanship. His parents had run a successful restaurant in Tokyo, where he entered Keio University. He arrived in New York in 1959 on a wrestling scholarship but was expelled from school for brawling. For three years, he operated an ice cream truck in Harlem, selling otherwise ordinary ice cream in which he stuck Asian parasols. In reflecting on these early experiences, he reportedly said, "What I discovered is that Americans enjoy eating in exotic surroundings but are deeply mistrustful of exotic foods. People also very much enjoy watching their food being prepared."[69] Thus, Benihana's menu offered only shrimp, beef, and chicken seasoned mostly with salt and pepper. Other than the shrimp, which was familiar to Americans via the shrimp cocktail, no fish was served. To reassure American diners, the menu proclaimed, "No slithery, fishy things."[70]

At first, Aoki's Benihana, located on West Fifty-Sixth Street near several other popular Japanese restaurants, struggled to establish a reputation. An early lunch menu featured "sukiyaki steak," showing the need to explain the new style of cooking in terms of a familiar item.[71] Aoki credits a favorable review in the *Herald Tribune* by Clementine Paddleford, a leading food critic, with introducing the restaurant to New York diners. The promotion of this Japanese food fashion by mainstream (white) journalists repeated a pattern also seen in tearooms and sukiyaki houses.

Aoki's main innovation was to hype the performative aspects of the steak house. In contrast to the sukiyaki restaurant, the star at Benihana was not an attentive "geisha" but a knife-wielding chef,[72] dubbed a "samurai warrior" in restaurant advertisements.[73] The center stage was the teppanyaki grills alongside customers' tables in a Japanese-style setting built by carpenters from Japan. The main actors were skilled chefs hired from Japan who were given crash courses in English to turn them into wisecracking acrobatic performers while cooking at customers' tables. They juggled spatulas and knives, flipped eggs into shirt pockets and shrimp tails onto their red chef's hats, and stacked onion rings to make flaming volcanoes.[74]

The macho image of teppanyaki played well in a world becoming accustomed to an assertive Japanese economic presence. Aoki enjoyed the limelight and lived a public life as a playboy and socialite for decades,[75] making him one of the first Japanese restaurateurs to become a public figure outside the Japanese community. However, unlike most contemporary Japanese restaurateurs, he was less a spokesman for authenticity than for showmanship. This faux-Japanese experience was controversial. In 1979, a *Texas Monthly* restaurant critic lampooned the restaurant's theatrics as "the Japanese equivalent of the minstrel show." Aoki admitted that indigenizing his cuisine was key to his triumph. He told a *New York Times* reporter in 1974, "The minute I forgot I was Japanese, success began."[76] Despite criticism, Benihana was also a highly rationalized restaurant model. With just three entrées all cooked the same way, the minimal menu reduced wastage and food costs. The use of hibachi tables increased the consumer floor space by reducing the kitchen size. Local sourcing of meats and vegetables lowered food ingredient costs. The model was scalable and easily replicated, enabling the chain to expand by 2020 to almost seventy locations in the Americas, as well as in Europe, the Middle East, and India.[77]

Inspired by Benihana, the Japanese steak house became a wedge for Japanese restaurant corporations to enter new markets and appeal to consumers unfamiliar with Japanese foodways. The main imported ingredient for teppanyaki was soy sauce. In Europe the JFC group, a subsidiary of the Kikkoman soy sauce company, became a significant operator of Japanese steak houses, opening some of the earliest in Europe. In 1973 it founded the high-end Daitokai steak house in Germany, which expanded into several branches.[78] Following the success of teppanyaki in the United States and Europe in the 1970s, the Japanese steak house concept quickly spread throughout the world. Customers were especially receptive where there were few Japanese restaurants and most people still were unfamiliar with items such as sushi. For example, in Hong Kong, teppanyaki steak houses, such as the Osaka Restaurant in Kowloon, flourished in the 1980s, long before Chinese consumers developed a taste for sushi and sashimi.[79]

In the 1980s, a slew of cheaper Japanese steak houses opened in American regional markets. They used the basic service concept of Benihana, and often hired Asian migrant chefs. Most were run by Korean, Chinese, and other Asian migrants who had worked at Benihana and other teppanyaki chains, a development explored in Chapter 5. While the Japanese steak house faded as a food fashion in global culinary cities, it remained popular in their hinterlands. In the American Southeast, hibachi steak houses lured customers with showy chefs and voluminous portions of rice and meat smothered in savory mayonnaise-based sauces (generically labeled "white sauce," "yum yum sauce," or "shrimp sauce"). In this way, the edgy, urban Japanese steak house of the 1960s became a purveyor of a US regional comfort food a half century later.[80]

The Global Sushi Bar and the Masters of *Omakase*

Though ancient in its origins, sushi is surprisingly modern as a restaurant cuisine, even in Japan. The hand-formed and hand-pressed sushi that conquered the world's palate was not the fermented and preserved sushi made for centuries in Japan but rather a novel snack of fresh fish and vinegared rice popularized by takeout shops in nineteenth-century Tokyo. After World War II, sit-down sushi bars developed into expensive, high-status restaurants. Newly established ship-to-table cold chains distributed fresh fish to national and eventually global markets.[81] Still, since raw fish was not much eaten outside Japan, the texture and taste of sushi were challenging to consumers. Its global popularity from the 1970s rested on its striking aesthetics that extended from the glistening piece of fish on a white mound of rice to the social environment of the sushi bar, the sushi master, and the concept of the *omakase* (chef's choice) menu. Its "modern" image has as much to do with these blended imaginaries of exclusivity, craft, and expertise as with the taste itself.[82]

Well before the postwar sushi boom, some Westerners marveled at sushi for reasons that would characterize its later mass appeal. In 1934, a British columnist in *the North-China Daily News* gave a lighthearted account of a personal "adventure" with sushi, including a detailed appraisal of Japanese culinary aesthetics and hygiene. The author orders sushi delivered to his office, and it appears in a "delightful" package:

> There is a neat cloth, which is unwrapped to find another neat paper package. It is your duty to undo this. Within there is a boxed parcel, on top of chopsticks wrapped each in its own envelop. Within the box you will find first a clean palm leaf on which there is shredded ginger. Underneath this there is the sushi, which is a varied dish, all the way from raw fish or prawn on rice, to a roll of rice stuffed with egg and vegetable and wrapped in seaweed. Do not be put off by this description, for the true connoisseur of any nation has long since recognized the delight of these, to our palates, queer

forms of food. . . . But it is the final touch that makes one once again realize the thoroughness of the Japanese and their careful attention to the fitness of things. Sauce there must be, of course. In this case there is a tiny little individual bottle, clean as a whistle, with a fresh cork, which is included in each package, and there is no thought of collecting it again for the copper or two that it might bring.[83]

This anecdote shows how foreign encounters with sushi were already occurring in the culinary contact zones of globalizing cities such as Shanghai. Although the author equates this treat with "queer forms of food," his positive account also prefigures the global association of sushi with elegant presentation and notions of Japanese fastidiousness and cleanliness.

Decades later, restaurant critic Mimi Sheraton considered the rise of the sushi restaurant the most surprising development in her decades of writing about food in *the New York Times*. Described as "New York's greatest taste-maker," Sheraton helped define the role of a food critic while penning reviews that furthered the sushi boom after World War II.[84] It took root in Los Angeles' Little Tokyo, where a confluence of factors favored the opening of sushi restaurants. One was the preexisting culinary infrastructure in the Japanese migrant community. A key institution was the Mutual Trading Company, a consortium founded in Los Angeles in 1926 by migrant traders of Japanese foodstuffs. Another factor was the arrival in the 1960s of corporate expatriates from Japan willing to pay for expensive and refined Japanese meals. Finally, there was a novelty-seeking population of Angelenos attracted by new food fashions and with the star power to convey them to the world.

In the late 1960s, there were a handful of Los Angeles restaurants selling sushi, all in Little Tokyo and primarily to Japanese expatriates. Possibly the first sushi restaurant to open outside Little Tokyo was Osho, opened in 1968 in Century City, near the Twentieth Century Fox studios. It attracted movie stars, studio directors, and journalists who would transform sushi into a global fashion item.[85] Within two decades, sushi went from being an obscure culinary reference to a culinary trend that signified chicness, trendiness, and modernity around the world.[86]

Nothing represents global sushi culture better than the California roll, created in Los Angeles in the 1960s, perhaps by Japanese chefs at Tokyo Kaikan (described in Chapter 3).[87] It was a sushi roll with cooked king crab and avocado, neither previously used in sushi in Japan. Recipes using avocado in salads, including seafood salads, had long appeared in Japanese

American newspapers, so it seems likely that chefs happened upon this food combination in Japanese community restaurants or Japanese American homes.[88] Rolled sushi (*makizushi*) also had long been eaten in West Coast communities. Mayonnaise, sesame seeds, and cucumber were added to the recipe later. While the California roll may have originated to satisfy Japanese restaurant customers who missed fatty tuna when out of season, it also appealed to novice American palates. The use of cooked crab overcame some customers' squeamishness about eating raw fish, while the mayonnaise and avocado provided a satisfying fatty texture. Hirotaka Matsumoto, who operated New York's first sushi bar and wrote a history of the early Japanese food industry in the United States, views *kanikama* as the unsung hero in the success of the California roll. *Kanikama,* invented in the 1970s, is inexpensive, artificial crab meat made from Alaskan pollock. Introduced into the US market in 1977, it quickly became the mainstay of the California roll. Without this crab substitute, the rolls would have been too expensive for mass consumption.[89]

Many popular variations followed that used local ingredients. One of the most important was the Philadelphia roll. It used cream cheese to add a low-cost but fatty texture and became a staple on sushi menus worldwide. While appreciated by consumers, these rolls had a reputation as inauthentic, "dubious gastronomy," sushi created for white people lacking knowledge of the "real thing."[90] Elite food critics turned up their noses. In 1981, Sheraton cautioned *New York Times* readers about this "misbegotten invention" created solely for the American palate.[91] Sushi chefs would remain divided over the place of this innovation at the sushi counter, with purists panning it while a broader public embraced it.

In explaining sushi's popularity, journalists and academics have focused on the appeal of the food itself while overlooking the novelty of the sushi bar as a social space and cultural performance. The first sushi bar in Los Angeles might have been at the Tokyo Kaikan, a two-story restaurant with five hundred seats that was opened in 1964 by the Tokyo Eiwa group. Like other high-end Japanese restaurants in the city, it was supplied by Mutual Trading Company, which started the import of sushi-quality fish from Japan to Los Angeles. Its expatriate manager at that time, Noritoshi Kanai, claimed to have coined the term "sushi bar." He also set up other sushi bars, including one at Kawafuku, the most prestigious restaurant in Little Tokyo.[92] Sasha Issenberg credits Kawafuku with being the "first true sushi bar" in the United States that served sushi prepared by a trained sushi chef.[93]

Although the sushi bar was established as an American and global fashion in Los Angeles in the 1970s, it found its twenty-first-century home—and status as a symbol of crass extravagance—in the global financial capitals of New York, London, and Hong Kong. During the 1960s, the number of Japanese restaurants in New York grew from around ten to sixty (reaching five hundred by 1990). With the opening in 1963 of the luxury Nippon restaurant and an upscale branch of Saito (see Chapter 1 and later in this chapter), an era of Japanese fine dining began in New York that was more elaborate than at Miyako, established half a century earlier, as described previously. In a 1963 review of these restaurants, critic Craig Claiborne noted that "New Yorkers take to the raw fish dishes, sashimi and sushi, with almost the same enthusiasm they display for tempura and sukiyaki."[94] In Nippon, diners could order tempura and sushi at the counter.

New York's first stand-alone sushi bar was Take Sushi, opened by Hirotaka Matsumoto in 1975. Trained as a food science researcher, Matsumoto moved to New York in 1970 and began by driving Nippon's delivery truck to pick up fish daily from Fulton Market.[95] Based on this experience, he first started a seafood supply company and then the sushi bar. Take Sushi's second-floor space in Midtown had a fifteen-person sushi counter and tatami and table seating for forty-five customers.[96] Two sushi chefs from Japan made *nigiri* (hand pressed) sushi while catering to newbie Americans with a "beginner sushi" menu that included California rolls. His chefs even created a New York Maki that replaced the nori wrapping with crispy roasted salmon skins.[97]

Reports about the restaurant in the Japanese press, such as a 1976 article in the popular weekly magazine *Bungei Shunju,* spread the word of Take Sushi among Japanese business travelers. That year, *New York Magazine* introduced the restaurant to white New Yorkers. Until then, most customers were Japanese expatriates, but after that, both American and Japanese customers lined up outside the door. Matsumoto noted that early American sushi fans were "hippies" and "artists with long hair." The most important point of contact between the new customers and the restaurant were the two alternately taciturn and playful sushi chefs and kimono-clad waitresses who spoke good English (chefs rarely did). Matsumoto noted the critical role these waitresses played in explaining the foods to non-Japanese diners.[98] Though most staff were still Japanese in the 1970s, Matsumoto began hiring other Asian servers. He preferred Koreans because many could speak English and Japanese, both important since Japanese customers remained the big spenders. Take Sushi thrived and by the 1980s had branches in New York, Los Angeles, Brussels, and Tokyo.[99]

Matsumoto dates the beginning of the sushi bar boom in the United States to 1970 in Los Angeles and 1977 in New York. As with earlier Japanese food fashions, the first to embrace the dish were an adventurous cultural elite of artists, writers, musicians, and actors, but these were soon followed by high-flying executives and financiers. As food historian Eric Rath writes, "In less than twenty years, sushi went from hippy to yuppie food."[100]

The sushi chef as a star performer was a salient feature of the fashion for sushi bars. In contrast to the American expectation of consumer choice in their idea of a restaurant, Los Angeles gourmets in the 1980s began to celebrate sushi chefs for their control over the dining experience. For example, Kazunori Nozawa's Sushi Nozawa in Studio City became renowned for allowing no choices, even by famous guests. A sign reportedly said, "Special of the Day: Trust Me."[101] By the turn of the twenty-first century, the Japanese term "*omakase*" (leave it up to the chef) had become a keyword in fine dining culture (even beyond sushi). In abandoning choice, American gourmets gave these migrant sushi masters a degree of authority and autonomy in their work typically attributed to artists, thereby elevating sushi bars to the highest ranks of US fine dining. Even though reviewer Mimi Sheraton was dismayed at the diner's loss of control, the emergence of the *omakase* concept was a turning point, not only in Japanese cuisine but in American fine dining more generally.[102] At the same time, the sushi chef dealt intimately with customers, presenting pieces with their bare hands, a personalization of service wrapped in mystery that was unrivaled in other cuisines.

In the late 2010s, if you mentioned to a New York foodie that you were writing about Japanese food in the city, they would inevitably ask, "Have you eaten at Masa?" This Midtown restaurant, which opened in 2004, earned three Michelin stars in 2009, the first Japanese restaurant so awarded, followed by a four-star review from Frank Bruni at *the New York Times*. It was considered the city's most expensive restaurant, with a tasting menu starting at USD 595, not including drinks or extras. The rise of Masa (and sushi more generally) had dethroned European cuisine as the pinnacle of fine dining in the city.[103]

Like much of US sushi culture, Masa's American success began in Los Angeles. Its founder was chef Masayoshi "Masa" Takayama, who trained for eight years at the venerable Sushiko in Ginza. In 1980, he opened his first restaurant, Saba-ya, in Los Angeles, followed by a second restaurant, Ginza Sushiko. The latter was an exclusive sushi bar that did not advertise and had an unlisted number, much like upscale *sushiya* (sushi bars) in Tokyo. Takayama served all sushi *omakase* in meals that lasted two to three hours. He kept a record of each customer, including the date and what they ate, in order to offer something new on their next visit. Word spread to the Hollywood elite. Marlon Brando became a regular, and Ginza Sushiko became known as the most expensive restaurant in Los Angeles.[104] In 2004, Takayama sold the sushi bar to his sous chef and moved to New York to open Masa in the recently constructed Time Warner Center. It had a twenty-six-seat bar serving fish sourced from Tsukiji, the world's largest fish market in Tokyo. In a *New York Times* interview, Takayama exuded the air of a culinary purist by saying, "[Other] Japanese restaurants . . . mix in some other style of food and call it influence, right? I don't like that."[105] Yet even as Takayama was advocating purity and authenticity, he used expensive ingredients from European fine dining. One dish on his early menu was risotto with truffles, while another was foie gras cooked shabu-shabu style. These dishes, he maintained, were still prepared in a Japanese way.

Overall, high-end sushi restaurants in New York (and other global culinary cities) maintained a show of Japanese culinary authenticity, with a focus on chefs' Japanese pedigrees. In 2019, all the top ten sushi restaurants in New York ranked on Yelp offered an *omakase* sushi menu, with eight of them headed by an ethnic Japanese chef. Top chefs touted their restaurants directly to the public through interviews and media appearances. By 2019, Takayama headed a small fleet of restaurants and rarely served guests.[106] Like other celebrity chefs, his main job was representing his restaurant empire. Thus, while earlier food fashions were mediated by print journalists, in the twenty-first century, celebrity chefs like "Masa" became direct cultural intermediaries for the food fashions that they led.[107]

The high-end sushi bar in cities such as Hong Kong, London, and San Francisco was a fine dining form suited for a new social elite of venture capitalists and IT magnates who worked long hours despite burgeoning wealth. If tearooms and sukiyaki houses were a fashion for those who aspired to the slow-paced luxuries of the old-fashioned "leisure class," the USD 500 sushi course that could be finished in half an hour was a show of distinction for this new class of "working rich." Still, by the late 2010s, there were also signs the *omakase* sushi boom was peaking. On the one hand, the city was replete with these high-end options. As food journalist Adam Platt wrote in 2019, "Local sushi aesthetes we know are beginning to whisper that in terms of the variety of styles and even in terms of quality, New York might actually be beginning to rival Tokyo itself (which, to be fair, generally boasts only the traditional Edomae style)."[108] At the same time, Platt asserted, this surfeit of choices could be a sign that New York had reached a point of "peak omakase." There were too many chefs offering fine dining sushi. One response by restaurateurs was creative *kaiseki* (formal cuisine), a new fine dining fashion discussed in Chapter 8. Another was an explosion of low-end Japanese options, most notably the ramen craze discussed in the next section.

Global Ramen: A Food Fashion for the Internet Generation

By the 2010s, ramen had become the newest global Japanese food fashion, spreading through new cultural mediators working in manga, on food television, and on social media. It also was the first Japanese food fashion in which non-Japanese were not only influential cultural intermediaries, but also themselves producers, including celebrity chefs. Due to the influence of new media, ramen also was the first Japanese food fashion focused on young consumers rather than more affluent older ones. This was partly a result of price. A bowl of ramen cost less than sukiyaki, teppanyaki, or sushi due to its cheaper ingredients, simpler preparation, and quicker customer turnover.

Multiple culinary mobilities constituted the ramen bar. Originating in China, ramen became a quick meal for workers and students in Japanese cities in the early twentieth century. It was served by Chinese restaurants, Japanese pushcart vendors, and even Western-style cafés. By the 1990s, a new kind of ramen shop emerged in Japanese cities that embodied gourmet sensibilities.[109] Similar to "new craft" occupations, such as bartending and artisanal butchery in postindustrial countries, the ramen business attracted middle-class youths seeking an independent lifestyle in previously unglamorous working-class labor.[110] They elevated this working-class dish through attention to ingredients, preparation, and presentation. In an era of low economic growth, this trend spoke to young urban consumers looking for quality food and cultural distinction at a low price, the so-called B-grade gourmets. The imaginary of the ramen bar resembles that of the sushi bar in terms of its fetishization of artisanal labor performed for the diner by fastidious cooks behind the counter. However, while the ramen shops are celebrated in Japan for their independent operators and craft ethics, they are also sites of corporatization and deskilling, as described in Chapter 6.[111]

The eruption of ramen as a global fashion around 2010 occurred more rapidly than earlier booms, catching critics and reviewers off guard. As late as 2006, a Paris journalist was surprised that "Japanese pasta is replacing the sandwich" in Paris' Japanese Quarter, an area that would soon harbor the ramen boom.[112] Similarly, in the United States, though ramen had been served in Japantown restaurants for decades,[113] most Americans in the early 2000s only knew it as unfashionable instant Cup Noodles. Central to the repackaging of ramen to be a fashion trend were web-based cultural mediators.

No one embodied this new internet foodie role more than chef David Chang, who had an outsize role in making ramen mainstream. A former child golf prodigy with a liberal arts education, Chang spent his early twenties in Japan teaching English and working in ramen and soba shops. In his memoir, he writes that his most eye-opening eating experiences in Japan were "in homes, on the street and at McDonald's."[114] These experiences gave him an appreciation for Asian street food, and in his subsequent culinary career, he aimed to reduce barriers between high and low culinary cultures. His efforts made him one of the new hipster chefs who were transforming dishes considered lowbrow into trendy, fast, and relatively pricey cuisine.

Growing up between culinary cultures himself, Chang did not seek to create an "ethnic restaurant" hewing to conventional understandings of authenticity. He expressed his contrarian view as follows: "Everything can become Japanese, Korean or any other ethnic food if you present it as such, but at the same time, the same dishes can be purely American."[115] So instead of copying traditional ramen recipes, Chang developed his own recipes by drawing on his eclectic experiences. His iconoclasm proved a hit with food critics, ever eager to spot the "next big thing." This was seen in Peter Meehan's review in *the New York Times* of Chang's first ramen restaurant, Momofuku Noodle Bar, which opened in 2004. Meehan wrote that despite the open steel kitchen and long counter arrangement of a typical ramen shop, the menu was anything but conventional. The broth was made from roasted pork bones and shiitake mushrooms. Smoked bacon, instead of dried bonito flakes, provided umami, and toppings included green peas.[116] Chang's disruption of conventions gave him a "bad-boy" image that he playfully cultivated. For example, he selected "Momofuku" for the restaurant's name partly because it sounded like "mother-fucker" when pronounced quickly in English.[117] At the same time, he conformed to new industry values, such as the eco-friendly use of humanely slaughtered pork.

Meehan's review, published in 2005, brought Momofuku to the attention of New York diners. Slurping from a ramen bowl at a ramen bar counter became the newest trend. With an entrepreneur's eye for opportunity, Chang immediately built on his popularity to create new restaurants. In 2009, his restaurant Momofuku Ko, with a high-end tasting menu, won two Michelin stars. The same year, Chang wrote a recipe-based account of his restaurant in collaboration with Meehan, and between 2011 and 2017, they copublished a quarterly food magazine, *Lucky Peach.* The first issue devoted 174 pages to ramen, featuring an article about rising ramen chef-owner Ivan Orkin (discussed later) and a conversation about ramen and sushi between Chang, chef and food journalist Anthony Bourdain, and chef Wylie Dufresne.[118] In 2012, after guest appearances on culinary shows, he hosted a PBS food series produced by Anthony Bourdain, *The Mind of a Chef.* He then authored, produced, and hosted several popular culinary series for internet TV, including *Ugly Delicious,* which explored the cultural and sociological contexts of foods around the world.[119] While Chang's 2020 memoir presents him as a slacker stumbling into the restaurant trade, he is the poster-child cultural intermediary of the twenty-first century. He is a college-educated owner-chef who skillfully uses old and new media to bypass food critics and Michelin stars to directly tell people what is "delicious," all the while promoting his brand. His success as a non-Japanese ramen impresario proved inspirational to others.

One chef following Chang's playbook was Ivan Orkin, who graduated from culinary school in the 1990s to a job at Lutèce, a top French restaurant in New York. In 2003, Orkin went with his Japanese wife to Japan, where he had lived earlier. He was impressed with the fastidious approach to ramen by a new generation of ramen chefs. They were serving more refined soups than those he tasted in the 1980s, including ones that used two different broths (e.g., dashi and chicken) combined before serving to create a complex but cleaner flavor. Orkin learned the ramen trade mostly from observations as a customer and exhaustive experimentation with soups and noodles at home. In 2007, aided by his wife and Japanese in-laws, he opened his eponymous ramen shop in Setagaya in Tokyo. The Japanese media pounced on the unique story of an American bravely entering this fiercely competitive market. While his initial offerings were rather conventional, his second outlet, Ivan Ramen Plus, which opened in 2010, used new ingredients, producing his signature Four-Cheese Mazemen dish (ramen topped with mozzarella, Hokkaido white cheese, parmesan, and edam cheeses).[120] In 2011, after the Great Kanto earthquake, Orkin returned to New York and opened an Ivan outlet on the Lower East Side, an up-and-coming area adjacent to the trendy East Village. (He sold the Tokyo shops to a former employee in 2015.) He drew on his Tokyo success for self-promotion through writings and media appearances, including an episode on Netflix's *Chef's Table*. Following Chang's lead, Orkin designed his shop as a full-service restaurant, though still centered on a busy counter. He used rye-based noodles for his ramen bowls, including one that combined pork broth, shoyu-glazed pork (*chashu*), wood ear mushrooms, pickled mustard greens, a soft egg, and mayonnaise. Fusion side dishes included Japanese eggplant with tahini and charred garlic.[121]

The ramen shop became a global food trend through the image of fastidious culinary artisans in Japan and abroad. However, compared with other Japanese food booms, the ramen shop lent itself better to corporatization and popularization. As Orkin pointed out, creating a new style of ramen could be a complex process of trial and error, but reproducing it was relatively simple. Unlike sushi or *kaiseki,* which required years of training, ramen required minimal skills and could readily use local ingredients and adapt to local tastes. Moreover, at the price point at which ramen was sold, fastidious service and highly skilled staff were not possible. As Orkin writes, "When you are selling ramen for seven or eight bucks a bowl, it's impossible to pay veteran cooks twenty bucks an hour."[122] Recipes could be simplified and systematized for cooking by inexperienced staff. While Orkin's New York prices were considerably higher than those at his restaurant in Tokyo, the logic of deskilling he described would apply to the global ramen boom in general, despite its craft image. We can see this in the rapid spread of chain ramen shops in markets throughout the world, as described in Chapter 6.

All of the global Japanese culinary fashion booms began with the production of iconic dishes—sukiyaki, teppanyaki, sushi, and ramen—by highly skilled chefs in centers of culinary fashion such as New York City. These were then popularized—often with simpler recipes, cheaper ingredients, and lower prices—by imitators and corporations seeking efficiency to reach mass markets. Chapters 5 and 6 tell these stories.

Grassroots Culinary Emissaries and the Politics of Authenticity

Beyond professional food writers and celebrity opinion leaders, many restaurateurs saw themselves as on a mission to spread Japanese food culture. These owners, cooks, and managers acted as grassroots cultural intermediaries, spreading the food fashions just described and democratizing them. Many migrant restaurateurs from Japan represented themselves to non-Japanese as emissaries of an "authentic" Japanese cuisine, one grounded in the soil and traditions of Japan or in their own distinctly Japanese sensibilities. Others eschewed such claims of place-based and ethnic-based authenticity, explaining their cuisine as expressing their own inspirations and personal journeys. This tension between "authenticity" based on an essentialist ideal of Japanese cuisine, on the one hand, and, on the other, "originality" based on a romanticized notion of individual creativity and biography, motivates culinary politics in Japanese cuisine and drives new Japanese food fashions.

Finally, as noted earlier, popular accounts of the spread of Japanese cuisine have primarily focused on men, especially chefs. Our story of grassroots culinary emissaries highlights key female figures, including owners and front-of-house staff, as well as personnel managers and innovative chefs. We begin with an early female pioneer and end with those working on the current frontiers of Japanese culinary globalization.

From "Geisha Girl" to Culinary Avenger

The colorful life of restaurateur Moto Saito, touched on in Chapter 1, ties the prewar story of sukiyaki in Asia to its postwar revival in New York. In her autobiography, published in 1988, she presented her half-century involvement with Japanese restaurants as a cultural mission to bolster Japanese national pride. In many respects, including her gender, Saito was an unlikely emissary of Japanese cuisine. Born in 1906 in Shizuoka Prefecture, she was sold at the age of nine by her mother to a Nagoya geisha house. Despite her unhappiness as a geisha, the role introduced her to wealthy and powerful patrons. In 1930, she accompanied a patron and his wife (also a former geisha) on an around-the-world trip that generated worldwide press coverage, especially by Europeans fascinated by the sight of "geisha girls" wearing kimonos. In Paris, the party, eager for a Japanese meal, headed to the Ryokan Botan, a Japanese restaurant in the forest park by the Eiffel Tower. Despite the restaurant's good location, Saito was shocked at its bad food and shabby interior. For a "Meiji woman" like herself, the meal was not simply disappointing but rather a "national shame" for Japan. Avenging this shame became her lifelong motivation to open Japanese restaurants abroad that conveyed Japanese culinary excellence to foreigners.[123]

A brief marriage to a wealthy man gave Saito the financial means to pursue her dream of having a restaurant abroad. In 1938, as described in Chapter 1, she used her alimony to move to Shanghai and start a restaurant. Ignoring the advice of the Japanese business community, she sought a location in the glamorous International Settlement, eventually finding a prominent address on Nanjing Road. Unfortunately, the landlords, the fabulously wealthy Hardoon family, refused to rent to a Japanese national. So she prevailed upon the representative of the Nagoya Matsuzakaya company, a connection from her geisha years, to find a Chinese guarantor. In January 1939, she opened a two-story eatery adjacent to the Cathay Hotel, a Shanghai landmark. The first floor was a café, the second floor a fine dining restaurant, and Saito lived upstairs on the third floor.

Saito's Restaurant Queen became one of the largest Japanese eateries in Shanghai, seating over 150 diners. It had an open dining room and an English menu that targeted wealthy Westerners and Chinese. The featured dishes were tempura and sukiyaki, which Saito had observed Westerners enjoying on her around-the-world trip years earlier. They were served by waitresses on the staff of one hundred Chinese, ten Japanese, and ten Russians. The Chinese waitresses were migrants from rural villages trained by Saito, who was impressed by their work ethic. The first-floor café had a candy counter manned by a dapper Russian in a vested suit. Saito was the first Japanese to operate a restaurant in the British- and American-dominated International Settlement, and the Restaurant Queen received much coverage in the Japanese and English press. However, the defeat of the Empire of Japan brought an end to her run of fortune. In 1945, just before the end of hostilities, she sold the restaurant to a Russian proprietor and returned to Tokyo on one of the last civilian flights.[124]

In the immediate postwar period, Saito opened two successful restaurants in Tokyo. However, she still sought to erase the "shame of Paris"—her experience of bad Japanese food abroad. She was further motivated by a desire to "regain" her Shanghai restaurant that the Americans had "taken away" by defeating Japan.[125] In 1953, she flew to New York City. As in Shanghai, she sought a location for her restaurant on the most prestigious boulevard in the city. In New York this was Fifth Avenue. This time, Japanese bankers thwarted her ambition by refusing to loan money to a single woman. Additionally, the city's licensing requirements were obstacles, including permission to install gas stoves for sukiyaki on each table (first in the town, claimed Saito). It took her three years to open the eponymous restaurant Saito in a modest rented space on West Fifty-Fifth Street near Sixth Avenue. She hired thirty employees, about two-thirds Japanese and a third Korean and Chinese.

Restaurant Saito immediately became the most prominent of the handful of Japanese eateries in the city. Moto Saito bet that doing things the "Japanese way" would impress Americans. Guests ate using Japanese utensils, and ingredients were listed in the menu by romanization, such as *shirataki, take-no-ko* (bamboo shoots), and *tofu,* terms few American readers would have understood at the time. Customers could also eat at the wooden counter facing the tempura chef. The requirement for guests to remove their shoes to sit on the tatami mats earned Saito a degree of notoriety in the New York press. In the closing years of the sukiyaki boom, *New York Times* food critic Craig Claiborne gave Saito a positive review.[126] He described the sukiyaki as "Japanese cooking at its friendliest," prepared by the waitress at the table from "mysterious ingredients."[127]

As in Shanghai, Saito's restaurant thrived. In 1963, she moved to a larger, three-story venue on West Fifty-Second Street, near the venerable Miyako. Carpenters flown in from Japan built the exquisite redwood interior, shoji panels, and a large tatami room. The new venue employed 150 staff, half of whom were Japanese, including "war brides" working as waitresses, while the others were mainly Chinese and Korean migrants. Eighty percent of the customers were non-Japanese, and they could sit on chairs or tatami.[128] Saito described the restaurant as a stage for performing Japanese culinary culture—still primarily sukiyaki—for Americans: "We didn't serve any bread. Nor did we give knives and forks, because Japanese serving plates are made for chopsticks. My goal was to teach them about Japanese culture through cuisine, and until the very end I stuck to that. The way of cooking was Japanese too. In other shops sukiyaki is cooked in the kitchen and brought out on little plates. But that is nothing more than stewed meat. The original sukiyaki is always cooked in front of the customers, and you can eat it the way that you like."[129]

Saito wrote that many New Yorkers first experienced Japanese food, even soy sauce, in her restaurant. She held cultural events, such as mochi making, and flew a festive carp flag from the roof in the summer. Hirotaka Matsumoto, who worked at her nearby competitor Nippon, described "Madame Saito" as the doyenne of the New York Japanese food scene. She ran two branches of her restaurant in New York and another in Hong Kong.[130] In 1985, after thirty years in the city, she closed her New York restaurants and moved back to Tokyo. By then, there were hundreds of Japanese restaurants in town, and she wrote that she had succeeded in her mission to spread authentic Japanese cuisine to the United States.[131]

For contemporary readers saturated with the experiences of culinary hybridity and David Chang–style celebrations of "inauthentic" foods, it is easy to dismiss Saito's fixation with culinary authenticity as an affectation. Yet it was an attitude shared among many of her compatriots who saw Japanese cuisine as a point of national honor. Menus from some prominent New York restaurants were laden with texts laboriously explaining their devotion to Japanese culinary tradition. For example, the 1970 menu from Nippon included a page-long essay describing its mission as serving "uncompromisingly Japanese" dishes to a "small group of American and Japanese enthusiasts." It proclaimed the space "as a truly authentic corner of Japan," including furniture, dinnerware, decorative rocks, and the regional and seasonal styles of kimonos worn by waitresses.[132] While innovation, hybridity, and adaptation have characterized the global Japanese food fashions over the past century—from tearooms to ramen shops—the aspiration to authenticity was one of the key missions of many Japanese restaurateurs who served as both emissaries and boundary keepers of a globalizing Japanese culinary field.

Defending the Boundaries of Culinary Authenticity Today

Even in the twenty-first-century culinary global city, marketing authenticity remained important to many restaurateurs. But it became trickier. One problem was the globalized nature of the labor force, especially when Japanese culinary workers became very scarce and expensive. Continuing a process that began in Saito's era, Japanese restaurants abroad came to rely on multicultural workforces composed overwhelmingly of new non-Japanese migrants. In this context, restaurants struggled to maintain a distinctive "Japanese" taste and image when perhaps only one (and often none) of the staff was Japanese. One example of how restaurant companies manage this "authenticity" dilemma while still lowering costs through inexpensive migrant labor is the European chain Eat Tokyo.

Budget Japanese restaurant chain Eat Tokyo was founded in London in 2006 by Japanese entrepreneur Hiroshi Takayama. By 2020, the company had grown to eight Eat Tokyo outlets in London and three in Germany. In both the United Kingdom and Germany, the chain was popular among Japanese families, students, and local Europeans.[133] It featured set meals (*teishoku*) and bento boxes, including sushi, *karaage* (fried chicken), yakitori, and tempura. While the cuisine could not be described as fashionable or innovative, authenticity still was the selling point, including an emphasis on Japanese ownership, taste, and service style.

Japanese executive chefs produced the menus in both Düsseldorf and London, serving as guarantors of taste and also as the face of the restaurants in their marketing. Other than the executive chefs, the staff consisted of non-Japanese Asian migrants. Service staff, mostly Asian women, wore the restaurant's designer *yukata* (a summer kimono) to convey authentic "Japaneseness." In the kitchen, Eat Tokyo made extensive use of ethnic Chinese (and other non-Japanese) migrant labor. In London, the critical behind-the-scenes manager was Ms. Takayama, a native of China. According to our informants, her management of the predominantly Chinese workforce kept the enterprise running smoothly. In Düsseldorf, Takayama's son Shu oversaw operations, also serving as a public face of the restaurant.[134]

There was a distinct ethnic stratification in the kitchens of the Eat Tokyo outlets. East Asians, mostly Chinese and Koreans, usually did the cooking. Cooks from China and other Asian countries learned on the job by observing and imitating the experienced chefs (who were too busy to train new hires). Other Asians without an East Asian appearance and sufficient cooking skills cleaned floors, washed dishes, and performed other such jobs. According to one employee, non–East Asian people rarely worked in the visible front kitchen because they would present to customers an inauthentic experience.[135] In an interview with us in Düsseldorf, Shu Takayama emphasized the importance of training the service staff in Japanese service culture. We observed him giving a talk to Chinese staff about Japanese service ideals, with a Chinese chef translating from Japanese. The talk included words for greeting customers in Japanese and other service etiquette that was atypical in Germany.[136]

Eat Tokyo aggressively sought to establish its authenticity by creating its own certification system. Hiroshi Takayama founded an organization called the Nihon Nintei Restaurant Association to award badges of "authentic Japanese restaurant" to restaurants around the world. The judging was done mainly by Takayama family members. Awardees received a certificate and a sticker to post in their restaurant windows. Additionally, they were listed in a self-published guidebook, *Authentic Japanese Restaurants*, prominently displayed in Eat Tokyo branches.[137] Eat Tokyo's unique approach to asserting its authenticity by establishing its certifying organization attested to the ongoing importance of authenticity in the global Japanese restaurant industry. At the same time, Eat Tokyo evinced the growing multiculturalism of restaurant staff, and the role of non-Japanese owners, such as Ms. Takayama, in managing them. Authenticity claims by such organizations were always subject to counterclaims that they were not "Japanese" enough. The transition to non-Japanese ownership of restaurants, which is explored in the next chapter, makes such claims even more contentious.

Emissaries to the Culinary Borderlands

The spread of Japanese food fashion far beyond urban Japantowns and outside major culinary global cities was facilitated by chefs and restaurateurs serving as grassroots cultural intermediaries. As in decades past, some of these culinary migrants were lifestyle migrants for whom opening a Japanese restaurant was a pathway toward independence. Others were marriage migrants who tied the knot with a non-Japanese person and then opened a restaurant in their spouse's home country. In these latter cases, the non-Japanese spouses were often key cultural intermediaries interpreting ideas of Japanese cuisine to local customers.

We came across one typical situation of a migration and marriage leading to culinary entrepreneurship in Mozambique. Even though the country was poor and had fewer than one hundred Japanese expatriates,[138] there were ten Japanese restaurants in the capital, Maputo, in 2018. They catered to a diverse foreign community of diplomats, aid workers, and businesspeople, underscoring how Japanese restaurants had become accoutrements of cosmopolitan communities everywhere. In addition, some outlying cities that attracted foreigners had Japanese restaurants, such as Sumi, located in the scuba-diving center Tofo by the Indian Ocean. Sumi was founded in 2017 by Nobie from Japan and her South African husband. Nobie was a multiple migrant, having grown up in Singapore, studied marine biology in Australia, worked in Brazil, and then moved to Mozambique for research. To finance her academic career, the couple opened a Japanese restaurant, even though Nobie lacked experience as a chef. Their path was similar to that of other expats who ran bed-and-breakfasts, restaurants, and diving schools in the area. However, Nobie saw restaurants as the best option because the business was year-round rather than seasonal, and she could rely upon her Japanese cultural capital.[139]

Before opening, Nobie flew her mother to Mozambique to teach her the basics of Japanese cooking. This family influence was visible in the home-style dishes on the menu, such as *nikujaga* (meat-and-potato stew), *shōgayaki* (pork ginger sauté), and *buta no kakuni* (stewed pork belly). These were much appreciated by Japanese aid workers for the Japanese International Cooperation Agency, who gathered monthly at Sumi. Patrons at Sumi dined on an outside patio surrounded by tropical plants or perched indoors on high stools at the sushi counter. For Nobie, her mother's recipes were a touchstone of authenticity. Nevertheless, her menu included American-style sushi rolls to meet the expectations of the majority of (non-Japanese) customers.[140] Such compromises were necessary for most migrant restaurateurs to remain in business, even those who aspired to serve "authentic" Japanese cuisine.

A different type of marriage migration involves culinary professionals who marry locals. For example, Yoshihiro Fujiwara, started as a culinary migrant and then became a marriage migrant in the undeveloped Japanese restaurant market of Ukraine. Fujiwara was the son of a fish market owner in Shikanoshima, Fukuoka Prefecture, who started working in a sushi restaurant at age fifteen. Five years later, he accompanied his boss to New York to open a sushi restaurant during the Japanese food boom of the 1980s.[141] Fujiwara started and ran a range of Japanese restaurants—*kaiseki*, tempura, sushi, and udon—across the United States, helping to popularize multiple Japanese food fashions. Then, in 1999, he got an offer to assist the business development of the Benihana chain in Europe in the Ukrainian capital, Kyiv. In 2000, he met his future wife, Oksana, a college student with a part-time job in the same restaurant. Having worked her way up from waitress to sushi chef, she dreamed of having her own Japanese restaurant. They married, becoming life and work partners. She attributed much of her knowledge of Japanese cuisine to working with Fujiwara. She said in our 2019 interview, "The opportunity to grow while working with Yoshi-san on multiple projects was the best school I could hope for."[142] In 2002, they accepted jobs in Moscow when oil money was driving the market for high-end sushi in Russia.[143] When the 2008 global financial crisis ended the boom, and after their son was born in 2010, the couple returned to Ukraine. They opened their first restaurant, called simply Fujiwara Yoshi, in Oksana's hometown of Cherkasy in central Ukraine, then later two venues in Kyiv. In this way Oksana became the key cultural intermediary explaining Japanese cuisine to a provincial customer base lacking knowledge of Japanese cuisine. She worked mainly as the hostess and front-of-house manager, leading the female front-hall staff, while Yoshihiro worked in the kitchen with a male team of locally hired cooks.

The couple said their mission was to "introduce Ukrainians to sushi and other Japanese dishes that were the same as in Japan."[144] The interior of their second Kyiv branch on Dragomyrova Street was crafted from natural materials in a "modern Japanese design." It offered multiple Japanese dining experiences, including a tatami room, counter seating in front of the sushi master, and chairs by the *robata* (open charcoal) grill or tempura bar. "We serve Japanese culture," said Yoshihiro.[145] The female wait staff wore colorful *yukata* and regaled guests with shouts of "*irasshaimase*" (welcome) and "*arigatō gozaimasu*" (thank you). Such details as a displayed photo of the Japanese imperial couple, Japanese vases, sculptures and dolls, and even Japanese Toto Washlet toilets in the restroom created an ambiance of "a small Japan within Ukraine."[146] The omnibus menu reflected Yoshihiro's experience in multiple Japanese restaurant forms, including sashimi and sushi, rice bowls, tempura, noodles (udon, soba, and ramen), and *robata* grill dishes. Live seafood aquariums and a Japanese garden conveyed luxury as well as Japaneseness. A special monthly show for the guests was the decapitation and slicing of a whole tuna (*maguro kaitai*), in which Yoshihiro displayed his knife techniques.[147]

The Fujiwara family business faced the dual challenges of pandemic and war in 2021 and 2022. They survived the pandemic by promoting home delivery, especially the sushi sets. They also frequently updated their social media channels, and Fujiwara even started sharing live videos where he taught some of his favorite Japanese home recipes. Their resilience was tested further after Russia's attack on Ukraine in February 2022. After closing their restaurants during the initial phase of the conflict, Fujiwara provided work and housing to their employees who stayed in Ukraine, firstly in the city of Cherkasy. At the end of May, they reopened the Kyiv venues, and in summer they restarted the tuna slicing performances for customers. In November 2022, the situation worsened as Russia began bombing the infrastructure in Kyiv. The family evacuated to Japan, but as of late November 2022, the restaurant Fujiwara Yoshi still was being operated by its staff. They hoped to continue even during scheduled electricity outages by using gas stoves and candles.[148]

Reclaiming Dubious Japanese Gastronomy

Other migrant restaurateurs grounded their culinary authority in personal stories of migration or experiences of immigrant foodways, bucking the dominant tendency to claim Japan-centered authenticity. This type of personal culinary storytelling is exemplified by Shalom Japan, a kosher Japanese Jewish supper club that opened in 1980 on Wooster Street in New York's artsy Soho district. It was operated by Miriam Mizakura, who also gave an evening vaudeville performance of song, dance, impressions, and jokes. She was born in Japan to Japanese parents who converted to Judaism after World War II and immigrated to the United States.[149] Shalom Japan served fusion kosher dishes with humorous Japanese Yiddish names, such as Mount Fuji Matzo Ball Soup, Nippon Borscht, and Kamikaze-Gefilte Fish.[150] However, the restaurant soon closed, possibly proving too peculiar even for New Yorkers.

While Shalom Japan was clearly a bit tongue-in-cheek, such personalized menus also can be thought of as culinary narratives representing the culturally mixed foodways of ordinary migrants. This notion of migration-based authenticity was seen in an updated form in the "Japanese-American" restaurant Bessou, operated by second-generation Japanese American Maiko Kyogoku. Her father ran Sushi Rikyu on Columbus Avenue in the Upper West Side in the 1970s and 1980s. Kyogoku told us that her father was one of the first chefs to serve California rolls in New York, even appearing on television to show how to make them. Like most children of restaurateurs growing up with their parents' grinding schedules, Kyogoku initially avoided the family business, working in publishing and then as a personal assistant to pop artist Murakami Takashi. However, after her mother's death, she sought a means of connecting with her Japanese American heritage. So she opened her restaurant Bessou on Bleecker Street in 2016.[151]

Kyogoku's description of Bessou's menu as "Japanese American comfort food" distinguished it from food in Japan while still claiming to be Japanese. For her, the touchstone of her Japaneseness was not distant Japan but rather her immigrant family meals in New York. "There was definitely curry on rotation, Japanese curry," she said. "There was definitely *damako nabe* [rice cake and chicken hot pot] which we are doing this week, which is pounded rice ball, it is a cousin of *kiritanpo nabe* [rice dumpling hot pot] from Akita Prefecture. I would have *tororo gohan,* which is Japanese yam grated, with miso soup, and rice. But I would also have stew or [spaghetti] *Napolitan.*" Kyogoku resisted the idea that her menu was fusion food. Echoing David Chang, she explained, "I think of Japanese food in America, like I think most Americans think of spicy tuna rolls as Japanese food, like California rolls. That doesn't exist in Japan, and it is not really authentically Japanese, but it is definitely Japanese food here. And I don't think that is blasphemous or inauthentic. I think that is authentic American Japanese. And I think of myself, too. I am very comfortable being in this middle ground of being Japanese and American. And I don't call myself a fusion person. Why would I consider the food fusion?"[152]

She designed most dishes at Bessou with Canadian head chef Emily Yuen, a classically French-trained cook with no prior Japanese cuisine experience. Kyogoku said she avoided hiring an expatriate Japanese chef. "I was so terrified to work with a Japanese chef," she said. "Because I know my dad! There is no way we would get along." She was concerned that a Japanese chef would insist on offering dishes as they are made in Japan rather than following her lead. Nevertheless, her father helped out, instructing Yuen in Japanese techniques, such as slicing fish. The dishes created by Yuen and Kyogoku ranged from ones based on personal preferences, such as grilled romaine lettuce (with soy-marinated quail eggs and sesame dressing) and crispy rice (a rice "tater tot" topped with spicy tuna) to such home-style comfort foods as tempura udon or *karaage,* all with creative fine dining frills expertly applied by Yuen. The restaurant received good reviews, including from *the New York Times,* but some customers were confused by the cuisine, especially those coming from Japan. Kyogoku remarked that some customers had fixed notions of authenticity that she could not satisfy.[153]

To further complicate authenticity claims, many customers had turned into self-appointed defenders of Japanese cuisine. As Chang warned Orkin when he opened his first ramen restaurant in New York City, "Get ready for criticism from the whole Asian demographic. Half the food bloggers in the world are Asian women. You are going to be their bread and butter. They are going to laugh at you and yell at you. They will be upset that your food isn't 'authentic' or that it's not Japanese enough." Chang opined that many of these arbiters of authenticity were not even Asian, but maybe "just someone who had an Asian girlfriend."[154]

According to Kyogoku, celebrity chefs such as Chang and Orkin have indeed pushed the boundaries of acceptable "Japanese" cuisine. Ironically, however, ethnic Japanese restaurateurs such as herself are often still held to a narrower standard, she said. As sociologist Krishnendu Ray writes, "ethnic" restaurants are meant to offer a taste of the ancestral homeland, providing a role for the "ethnic restaurateur" while also trapping them in an "ethnic restaurant" niche.[155] To use the phrase of Asian American studies scholar Robert Ji-Song Ku, anything new created by migrants is often regarded as "dubious gastronomy," translated (lost-in-translation) foods that are not as good as the "original."[156] This struggle over authenticity remains central to the consumer culture surrounding Japanese cuisine, even as producers and consumers contest the bases for authenticity claims.[157]

The Dynamics of Global Japanese Food Fashions

The restaurant fashions described in this chapter not only popularized Japanese cuisine far beyond Japanese urban enclaves but, especially in the case of the sushi bar, propelled it to the pinnacle of culinary status (and price) in cities from New York to Shanghai. The reasons for this outward and upward mobility are complex. One common explanation focuses on the visibility of corporate Japan and Japanese corporate expatriates in the world's global cities from the 1970s. The association of Japan with wealth and cutting-edge technology made Japanese cuisine classy, especially in Western countries with legacies of negative images of Asian countries and Asian migrants.[158] Our narrative partially supports this thesis while showing it also to be incomplete. We point out that several global Japanese restaurant fashions predate the 1970s economic boom by decades, whereas others continued long after Japan's economic luster faded. We emphasize complex interactions among multiple actors who drove restaurant fashions, including the Japanese state, corporations, consumers, culinary migrants, and most importantly cultural intermediaries inside and outside the restaurant business.

First, the Japanese state, beginning with the teahouse expositions in the nineteenth century, promoted Japanese culinary culture. This continues into the present era with projects such as the Cool Japan initiative and Japan House (see Chapter 8). Second, on the consumer side, bohemian intellectuals and artists and other adventurous urban gourmets acted as fashion leaders, supporting the emergence of Japanese food fashions in Western cities in the early and mid-twentieth century. Japanese corporate expatriates with expense accounts only played a major role in the 1970s and 1980s, when Japanese corporations were expanding abroad. Third, professional cultural intermediaries, mostly non-Japanese, fostered these fashions in print and electronic media. Their interest in Japanese restaurant forms usually centered on their peculiar aesthetics and the performative features of service. Fourth, Japanese corporations directly sponsored high-end Japanese restaurants, such as Kikkoman's Daitokai chain and the Suntory corporation's restaurants in various countries. Even Japanese industry groups with no connection to the food and beverage industry bankrolled luxury restaurant projects, including the Nippon-Kan in Düsseldorf in 1964 and Inagiku in New York's Waldorf Astoria Hotel in 1974. These projected national pride and impressed business partners.[159] Finally, migrant restaurateurs and culinary workers have always been the grassroots intermediaries introducing Japanese food fashions to new audiences. They defined the actual consumer experience. The numerous non-Japanese migrants working in these restaurants were also key interpreters of the cuisine. These diverse actors interacted differently in each Japanese restaurant boom, depending on the period.

Our narrative thus complicates the story of the steady rise of Japanese cuisine, a story often centered on sushi as a unique type of food. The popularization of Japanese restaurants actually involved multiple restaurant fashions, each with its own arc—discovery by urban trendsetters, rising status among urban elites, and popularization to a broad public. As Simmel predicts, the status of a particular restaurant fashion rises but then trends downward as it becomes democratized and commonplace. If there is something unusual about Japanese cuisine, it may be less its steadily increasing popularity than the variety of restaurant forms that Japan has exported. There has been a continual production of new restaurant fashions in the context of Japanese cuisine, requiring further study. This is an issue we come back to in the concluding chapter.

Finally, each Japanese food fashion involves a tension between values of Japan-based authenticity and creative adaptation. As described in this chapter, creativity involves both personal expression and adaptation to consumers. Additionally, these creative adaptations are driven by the diversity of the producers themselves. As the case of Eat Tokyo illustrates, even a restaurateur intent on policing the boundaries of "authentic" Japanese cuisine relies heavily on non-Japanese chefs and servers. These non-Japanese employees, in turn, become among the most important actors bringing Japanese cuisine to the world, founding restaurants far beyond the global cities highlighted in this chapter. This wave of non-Japanese migrant culinary entrepreneurs is the story of the next chapter.

Notes

1. Georg Simmel, "Fashion," *American Journal of Sociology* 62, no. 6 (1957): 541–558.
2. "As fashion spreads, it gradually goes to its doom." Simmel, 547.
3. We found this phrase in several online posts during the 2010s, including Satsuki Yamashita, "Imagine Little Tokyo Short Story Contest: Mr. K," Discover Nikkei, November 3, 2014, http://www.discovernikkei.org/en/journal/2014/11/3/mr-k/.
4. The concept was initially used by Pierre Bourdieu in *Distinction: A Social Critique of the Judgement of Taste* (Cambridge, MA: Harvard University Press, 1984). The term has been broadly picked up in social sciences. See Jennifer Smith Maguire and Julian Matthews, "Are We All Cultural Intermediaries Now? An Introduction to Cultural Intermediaries in Context," *European Journal of Cultural Studies* 15 (2012): 551–562.
5. For a discussion of celebrity chefs as cultural intermediaries, see Nick Piper, "Jamie Oliver and Cultural Intermediation," *Food, Culture and Society* 18, no. 2 (2015): 245–264.
6. For another example of the grassroots cultural intermediary, see Richard E. Ocejo, "At Your Service: The Meanings and Practices of Contemporary Bartenders," *European Journal of Cultural Studies* 15, no. 5 (2012): 642–658.
7. "The Round of the Restaurants at the Paris Exhibition," *Pall Mall Gazette*, August 14, 1867, 10, British Library Newspapers, Part I: 1800–1900, cited in Masaki Morisawa, "The Paris International Exposition of 1867," The Gale Review (blog), April 13, 2017, https://review.gale.com/2017/04/13/the-paris-international-exposition-of-1867/.
8. Katie Rawson and Elliott Shore, *Dining Out: A Global History of Restaurants* (London: Reaktion Books, 2019), 280.
9. "Round of the Restaurants," 10.
10. The founding members were historian of art Léonce Bénédite; art critics Zacharie Astruc and Philippe Burty; engraver Jules Jacquemart; painters Henri Fantin-Latour, Carolus-Duran, and Alphonse Hirsch; and painter-ceramists Félix Bracquemond and Marc-Louis Solon. For more details, see Angélique Saadoun, "Japonisme et collection-

neurs: Reseaux d'amateurs dans le Paris de la seconde moitié du XIXe siècle" [*Japonisme* and collectors: Networks of amateurs in Paris of the second half of the 19th century], *Hypotheses: Carnet de l'Ecole Doctorale d'Historie de l'Art et Archeologie,* Sorbonne University, April 5, 2020, https://124revue.hypotheses.org/4592.

11. Yvonne Thirion, "Le japonisme en France dans la seconde moitié du XIXe siècle à la faveur de la diffusion de l'estampe japonaise" [*Japonisme* in France in the second half of the 19th century thanks to the spread of the Japanese prints], *Cahiers de l'Association internationale des études françaises,* no. 13 (1961): 122.

12. Ernest Chesneau, "Le Japon à Paris" [Japan in Paris], *Gazette des Beaux-Arts,* July 1, 1878, 387; "Le Japonisme, Felix Bracquemond," Centre culturel franco-japonais de Toulouse, June 6, 2018, http://ccfjt.com/meiji150eme/japonisme-felix-bracquemond/.

13. Morris Low, *Japan on Display: Photography and the Emperor* (Abingdon, UK: Routledge, 2006), 17.

14. Kurokawa Naoki (黒川直樹), "1893 Nen shikago sekai hakurankai ni okeru nihonkan 'Hōōden' no shikichi kyōyo ni tsuite" (1893年シカゴ世界博覧会における日本館「鳳凰殿」の敷地供与について) [Regarding the sharing of space at the Japanese Phoenix Pavilion at the 1893 Chicago World Exposition], *Gakujutsu koen kogaishu* 9 (1999): 295–296.

15. Christian Tagsold, *Spaces in Translation: Japanese Gardens and the West* (Philadelphia: University of Pennsylvania Press, 2017), 60.

16. Katherine Wilson, *Golden Gate: The Park of a Thousand Vistas* (Caldwell, ID: Caxton Printers, 1950), 70–71.

17. Shelley C. Berg, "Sada Yacco in London and Paris, 1900: Le rêve réalisé," *Dance Chronicle* 18, no. 3 (1995): 343–404.

18. Tagsold, *Spaces in Translation,* 36–37.

19. Takako Day, "The Chicago Shoyu Story—Shinsaku Nagano and the Japanese Entrepreneurs," pt. 1, Discover Nikkei, February 17, 2020, http://www.discovernikkei.org/en/journal/2020/2/17/chicago-shoyu-1/.

20. Takako Day, "The Chicago Shoyu Story—Shinsaku Nagano and the Japanese Entrepreneurs," pt. 3, Discover Nikkei, March 2, 2020, http://www.discovernikkei.org/en/journal/2020/3/2/chicago-shoyu-3/.

21. Jan Whitaker, *Tea at the Blue Lantern Inn: A Social History of the Tea Room Craze in America* (New York: St. Martin's, 2015), Kindle loc. 291–311.

22. Cynthia A. Brandimarte, "'To Make the Whole World Homelike': Gender, Space, and America's Tea Room Movement," *Winterthur Portfolio* 30, no. 1 (1995): 1–19.

23. Brandimarte.

24. Quoted in Whitaker, *Tea at the Blue Lantern Inn,* Kindle loc. 1695.

25. Eduard Burget, "Čajovna Yokohama, villa Sakura a Joe Hloucha" [Tearoom Yokohama, villa Sakura and Joe Hloucha], *Dějiny a Současnost* 7 (2006): 12–14.

26. Petr Holý, "Cheko kyōwakoku ni okeru Tōkaidō Yotsuya kaidan" (チェコ共和国に於ける 東海道四谷怪談) [Tokaido Yotsuya Kaidan in the Czech Republic], departmental bulletin of the International Institute for Education and Research in Theatre and Film Arts, Waseda University, 2004, 123–138.

27. Marcela Šášinková, "Vznik přípražských letovisek" [Emergence of Prague residence suburbs], online archive of the Museum of Central Bohemia in Roztoky, accessed May 20, 2020, https://www.muzeum-roztoky.cz/sites/default/files/attachments/2018/06/11/vily_roztoky_44.pdf.

28. Burget, "Čajovna Yokohama," 14.

2

29. Maren Möhring, "Von Schwalbennestern und neuen Fingerfertigkeiten: Globalisierung und esskulturelle Transfers am Beispiel asiatischer Küchen in Deutschland" [Globalization and food culture transfers using the example of Asian kitchens in Germany], *Jahrbuch für Kulinaristik* 2 (2018): 31–51; Linus Geschke, "Berlins 'Haus Vaterland': Mutter der Erlebnisgastronomie," *Der Spiegel,* March 22, 2013, https://www.spiegel.de/geschichte/erlebnisgastronomie-haus-vaterland-in-berlin-a-951068.html; Rawson and Shore, *Dining Out,* 283–289.

30. Whitaker, *Tea at the Blue Lantern Inn,* Kindle loc. 2325–2338.

31. New York restaurateur Moto Saito describes how some Japanese male customers in the 1950s still expected sexual "service" from the restaurant, which she refused to provide. Saitō Moto (斎藤もと), *Nyūyōku no koinobori* (ニューヨークの鯉のぼり) [A carp flag in New York], (Tokyo: PHP Press, 1988), 177–179.

32. Paul Freedman, *Ten Restaurants That Changed America* (New York: Liveright, 2016); Krishnendu Ray, "The Immigrant Restaurateur and the American City: Taste, Toil, and the Politics of Inhabitation," *Social Research* 81, no. 2 (2014): 373–396; Audrey Russek, "Appetites Without Prejudice: U.S. Foreign Restaurants and the Globalization of American Food Between the Wars," *Food and Foodways* 19, no. 1–2 (2011): 34–55.

33. Daniel H. Inouye, *Distant Islands: The Japanese American Community in New York City, 1876–1930s* (Boulder: University Press of Colorado, 2018), 154–156.

34. The restaurant was located on West Fifty-Sixth Street. It remained well known in postwar Japanese circles, although it seems to have lost its leading culinary reputation by the 1950s. See also Matsumoto Hirotaka (松本紘宇), *Nyūyōku Take Sushi monogatari* (ニューヨーク竹寿司物語) [New York Take Sushi tale] (Tokyo: Asahi shinbunsha, 1995), 28.

35. Inouye, *Distant Islands,* 99–104.

36. This report thrilled the reporters from the local Japanese-language paper. "Beijin ga mita Nihonryōri: Toribyun kisha shishokuki" (米人が観た日本料理：トリビュン記者試食記) [An American view of Japanese cuisine: A Tribune reporter's report on her meal], *Japanese Times,* June 25, 1924, 3.

37. Dorothy B. Marsh, "Chopsticks for the Adventurer, Forks for the Timid," *Good Housekeeping,* March 1932, 88, cited in Robert Hegwood, "Sukiyaki and the Prewar Japanese Community in New York" (paper presented at the Columbia Graduate Student Conference on East Asia, Columbia University, New York, 2014).

38. Day, "Chicago Shoyu Story," pt. 1.

39. "These Foreign Dishes Are Practical," *Los Angeles Times,* September 17, 1939.

40. "Kitchen Door of Japan Opens Wide, Discloses Culinary Artists at Work," *Washington Post,* June 14, 1934.

41. "Sub-deb Hostess at Nippon Party on Anniversary," *Los Angeles Times,* October 20, 1935.

42. "Sukiyaki Recipes Show Variety," *Los Angeles Times,* May 23, 1938.

43. "Sukiyaki Popular with Americans," *North China Daily News,* January 14, 1936, 15.

44. Hegwood, "Sukiyaki."

45. "Japanese at the Table: Flesh Pots of the West: The Origins of Sukiyaki," *North China Daily News,* December 21, 1920, 5.

46. In that neighborhood, it is likely that many of these were Russian owned, perhaps with Japanese backing, since the major landlords in these areas would not lease businesses to Japanese.

47. "Sukiyaki Party," *Shanghai Times,* April 2, 1936, 6.

48. "Sukiyaki," *Shanghai Sunday Times,* May 27, 1934, 5.

49. "Sukiyaki at the Little Club," *North China Daily News,* May 7, 1930; Andrew Field, "The Opening of Shanghai's Toniest Nightclub, the Little Club, in 1926," *Shanghai Sojourns* (blog), June 19, 2018, http://shanghaisojourns.net/shanghais-dancing-world/2018/6/19/the-opening-of-the-little-club-shanghais-toniest-club-in-1926.

50. "Countess to Run Sukiyaki House Here," *China Press,* December 2, 1936, 13. Taxi dancers, or paid dance companions, were another global fashion in the 1930s; see James Farrer and Andrew David Field, *Shanghai Nightscapes: A Nocturnal Biography of a Global City* (Chicago: University of Chicago Press, 2015), 27–28.

51. Kasen menu from the private collection of William Savadove. The currency is likely the widely circulated "Mexican" silver dollar.

52. Saitō, *Nyūyōku no koinobori,* 149–217.

53. "Our Story," Yamato Flight Kitchen, accessed March 20, 2020, https://www.yamatoflightkitchen.com/about.

54. "Frisco Serves Native Food from Many Lands," *Chicago Tribune,* January 31, 1954.

55. "Yamato Menu," Culinary Institute of America Menu Collection, Bruce P. Jeffer Menu Collection, menu 41-682, http://ciadigitalcollections.culinary.edu/digital/collection/p16940coll1/id/13338/rec/2.

56. "Our Story," Yamato Flight Kitchen.

57. Hugo Kugiya, "Once-Swanky Bush Garden: A Symbol of a Bygone Era," Crosscut, February 17, 2011, https://crosscut.com/2011/02/onceswanky-bush-garden-symbol-bygone-era.

58. Katarzyna Joanna Cwiertka, *Modern Japanese Cuisine: Food, Power and National Identity* (London: Reaktion Books, 2006), 184.

59. Erik Verg, "In Hamburg ist die ganze Welt zu Hause: Japanische Mondnacht auf der Alster" [In Hamburg the whole world is at home: A Japanese moonlit night on the Alster], *Hamburger Abendblatt,* July 11, 1962, 9.

60. Verg, 9.

61. Uly Foerster, "Tenno—Der Sushi-Kaiser von Hamburg" [Tenno—the sushi emperor of Hamburg], *Hamburger Abendblatt,* October 27, 2001, https://www.abendblatt.de/archiv/2001/article204945329/Tenno-Der-Sushi-Kaiser-von-Hamburg.html.

62. Craig Claiborne, "Restaurant on Review: Kabuki Is Japanese and One of the Best," *New York Times,* April 4, 1961, 40.

63. "East Meets West at Imperial Gardens," *Los Angeles Times,* June 14, 1968.

64. "About," Moshimoshi, accessed October 2020, https://moshimoshisf.com/about/.

65. Craig Claiborne, "New Yorkers Take to Tempura and Chopsticks with Gusto," *New York Times,* March 10, 1966, 22.

66. Nancy Snow, "Teppanyaki: A Japanese Cooking Tradition Made in America," *Japan Today,* May 17, 2019, https://japantoday.com/category/features/food/teppanyaki-a-japanese-cooking-tradition-made-in-america.

67. "Our History," Misono, accessed October 10, 2020, https://misono.org/en/concept/.

68. While Benihana is often described as New York's first teppanyaki steak house, another claimant is restaurateur Sal Cucinotta's Japanese Steak House. This pagoda-style restaurant on West Broadway also featured hibachi tables, where staff prepared

steak in front of customers. "Japanese Steak House Menu," Culinary Institute of America Menu Collection, Bruce P. Jeffer Menu Collection, menu 41-963, http://ciadigitalcollections .culinary.edu/digital/collection/p16940coll1/id/13327/rec/50; "Obituary for Salvatore Cucinotta," *New York Times*, June 14, 2010, https://www.legacy.com/obituaries/nytimes /obituary.aspx?n=salvatore-cucinotta&pid=143574651&fhid=2058.

69. W. Earl Sasser, "Benihana of Tokyo," Harvard Business School case study, 1972, rev. 2004.

70. Sasser, 18.

71. "Benihana Menu," Culinary Institute of America Menu Collection, George Lang Menu Collection, menu 2-3192, http://ciadigitalcollections.culinary.edu/digital /collection/p16940coll1/id/7435/rec/3.

72. Elaborate knife work in front of diners had long been part of Japanese dining culture and was associated with the samurai class. See Eric Rath, *Oishii: The History of Sushi* (London: Reaktion Books, 2021), 63–67.

73. Sasser, *"Benihana of Tokyo,"* 16.

74. For more, tricks see the video posted by a food culture website, First We Feast, called "All of the Benihana Teppanyaki Tricks," YouTube video, 1:33, posted November 14, 2016, https://www.youtube.com/watch?v=mG1-jULNHoA.

75. Mayukh Sen, "A Flower in the Debris: The Legacy of Benihana, Rocky Aoki's All-American Empire," *The Ringer*, July 24, 2018, https://www.theringer.com/2018/7/24 /17606204/benihana-rocky-aoki-feature.

76. Sen.

77. A. K. Dey et al., *Benihana: Operations Management Case Study Report*, Birla Institute of Management Technology, accessed October 20, 2022, https://www.academia .edu/6251953/Operations_Management_Case_Study_Report_Case_Benihana_of _Tokyo_UNDER_THE_GUIDANCE_OF_Contents.

78. The last outlet, in central Berlin, closed in 2019. "History," JFC Europe, accessed December 1, 2020, https://www.jfc.eu/en/profile/history/; "Geschichte" [History], Daitokai, accessed September 1, 2019 (no longer online) www.daitokai.de/index.php?jp _geschichte.

79. Fieldwork by James Farrer, March 2019.

80. Hanna Raskin, "Popularity of Japanese Steakhouse a Cultural Phenomenon in South Carolina," *Post and Courier*, May 30, 2018, updated September 14, 2020, https:// www.postandcourier.com/food/popularity-of-japanese-steakhouse-a-cultural -phenomenon-in-south-carolina/article_20eb97e2-3d89-11e8-9c61-9f1cdce083ad.html.

81. Rath, *Oishii*, 97–131.

82. Theodore C. Bestor, "Supply-Side Sushi: Commodity, Market, and the Global City," *American Anthropologist* 103, no. 1 (2001): 76–95; Irmela Hijiya-Kirschnereit, "Das Sushi-Sakrileg: Zur Verbreitung von Sushi in Mitteleuropa" [The sushi sacrilege: The spread of sushi in Central Europe], *Jahrbuch für Kulinaristik* 2 (2018): 134–165.

83. Akabo, "Shanghai by Night and Day: The Adventure of Japan's Sushi," *North-China Daily News*, November 22, 1934, 3. In the essay, the author emphasizes the positive impression of Japanese food delivery service and hygiene in comparison to Chinese purveyors.

84. Wendell Steavenson, "Meet New York's Greatest Taste-Maker," *Prospect*, May 15, 2018, https://www.prospectmagazine.co.uk/magazine/new-york-mimi-sheraton-1970s -food-cookbooks-history.

85. Sasha Issenberg, *The Sushi Economy: Globalization and the Making of a Modern Delicacy* (New York: Gotham Books, 2007), 87–91.

86. Hijiya-Kirschnereit, "Das Sushi-Sakrileg," 148.

87. There are competing claims to this invention. See Issenberg, *Sushi Economy*, 87–91; and Rath, *Oishii*, 151–152.

88. For example, "Avocado Half-Shell with Seafood," *Rafu shinpō*, May 11, 1941, 20.

89. Matsumoto, *Nyūyōku Take Sushi monogatari*, 164. See also Becky Mansfield, "'Imitation Crab' and the Material Culture of Commodity Production," *Cultural Geographies* 10, no. 2 (2003): 176–195.

90. Robert Ji-Song Ku, *Dubious Gastronomy: The Cultural Politics of Eating Asian in the USA* (Honolulu: University of Hawai'i Press, 2013), 7.

91. Mimi Sheraton, "East Side Steak and Side Dishes of Japan," *New York Times*, March 20, 1981, 16.

92. "YuYu Interview Noritoshi Kanai," *San Diego YuYu*, April 30, 2007, https://sandiegoyuyu.com/index.php/features-2/interviews-en/666-yuyu-interview-noritoshi-kanai.

93. Issenberg, *Sushi Economy*, 87–91.

94. Craig Claiborne, "Variety of Japanese Dishes Offered, but Raw Fish Is Specialty on Menu," *New York Times*, November 11, 1963, 37.

95. Matsumoto, *Nyūyōku Take Sushi monogatari*, 82.

96. Matsumoto, 84.

97. Matsumoto, 165–166.

98. Matsumoto, 84–95.

99. Matsumoto, 169–171.

100. Rath, *Oishii*, 145.

101. Issenberg, *Sushi Economy*, 101.

102. Steavenson, "Meet New York's Greatest."

103. Adam Platt, "Ichimura Raises Its Prices and Loses Some of Its Charm after Declaring Independence from Brushstroke," *Grub Street*, May 7, 2017, https://www.grubstreet.com/2017/05/ichimura-nyc-restaurant-review.html.

104. Michael Neill and Nancy Matsumoto, "Any Way You Slice It, Masayoshi Takayama's Sushi Eatery Is L.A.'s Priciest Restaurant," *People*, November 19, 1990.

105. Alex Witchel, "Food from a Perfectionist Does Not Come Cheap, or Easy," *New York Times*, March 17, 2004.

106. Platt, "Ichimura Raises Its Prices."

107. For a discussion of how celebrity chefs became media figures in the West, see Signe Rousseau, *Food Media: Celebrity Chefs and the Politics of Everyday Interference* (London: Berg, 2013).

108. Adam Platt, "The Absolute Best Sushi in New York," *Grub Street*, February 6, 2019, https://www.grubstreet.com/bestofnewyork/best-sushi-omakase-nyc.html#_ga=2.149850611.430499996.1589342000-182375031.1589342000. See also Rachel Tepper Paley, "The Omakase Chasers: Among New York City's Dining Elite, High-End Omakase Is the New Top Prize," *Bon Appetit*, March 19, 2019, https://www.bonappetit.com/story/omakase-chasers.

109. George Solt, *The Untold History of Ramen: How Political Crisis in Japan Spawned a Global Food Craze* (Berkeley: University of California Press, 2014), 136–137.

110. See Richard E. Ocejo, *Masters of Craft: Old Jobs in the New Urban Economy* (Princeton, NJ: Princeton University Press, 2017).

111. Solt, *Untold Story of Ramen,* 181.

112. "Les pâtes japonaises supplantent le sandwich" [Japanese pasta supplants the sandwich], *Le Parisien,* October 26, 2006, https://www.leparisien.fr/essonne-91/les-pates-japonaises-supplantent-le-sandwich-26-10-2006-2007449580.php.

113. See the 1969 menu for the San Francisco restaurant Osome, Culinary Institute of America Menu Collection, Lois Westfall Menu Collection, menu 51-320a, http://ciadigitalcollections.culinary.edu/digital/collection/p16940coll1/id/11156/rec/10.

114. David Chang, *Eat a Peach* (New York: Clarkson Potter, 2020), 37.

115. Chang, 77.

116. Peter Meehan, "At a Noodle Bar, the Noodles Play Catch-Up," *New York Times,* April 13, 2005, https://www.nytimes.com/2005/04/13/dining/reviews/at-a-noodle-bar-the-noodles-play-catchup.html.

117. Other reasons were the auspicious meaning in Japanese of "lucky peach" and as a nod to Ando Momofuku, the inventor of instant noodles. David Chang and Peter Meehan, *Momofuku* (New York: Clarkson Potter, 2009), 28.

118. David Chang and Chris Ying, eds., *Lucky Peach,* no. 1, July 12, 2011, https://luckypeacharchive.wordpress.com/2020/02/21/lucky-peach-archived-web-pages/.

119. *Breakfast, Lunch & Dinner,* Netflix, 2019, https://www.netflix.com/ua/title/81038022; *Ugly Delicious,* Netflix, 2018 (season 1) and 2020 (season 2), https://www.netflix.com/title/80170368.

120. Ivan Orkin and Chris Ying, *Ivan Ramen: Love, Obsession, and Recipes from Tokyo's Most Unlikely Noodle Joint* (Berkeley: Ten Speed, 2013), 185–186.

121. A bowl of ramen was USD 18; fieldwork by James Farrer, April 2019.

122. Orkin and Ying, *Ivan Ramen,* 54.

123. Saitō, *Nyūyōku no koinobori,* 55–56.

124. Saitō, 87–148.

125. Saitō, 150.

126. Claiborne, "Variety of Japanese Dishes," 37.

127. "Saito Menu," Culinary Institute of America Menu Collection, Bruce P. Jeffer Menu Collection, menu 41-1743, http://ciadigitalcollections.culinary.edu/digital/collection/p16940coll1/id/13362/rec/6.

128. Saitō, *Nyūyōku no koinobori,* 149–217.

129. Saitō, 191.

130. Matsumoto, *Nyūyōku Take Sushi monogatari,* 70–71.

131. Saitō, *Nyūyōku no koinobori,* 217.

132. "Nippon Menu," Culinary Institute of America Menu Collection, Roy Andries de Groot Menu Collection, menu 3-350, http://ciadigitalcollections.culinary.edu/digital/collection/p16940coll1/id/13346/rec/8.

133. Fieldwork in London by Chuanfei Wang in August 2017; fieldwork in Düsseldorf by James Farrer in August 2017, December 2018, and January 2019.

134. Fieldwork in London by Chuanfei Wang in August 2017.

135. Fieldwork in London by Chuanfei Wang in August 2017.

136. Shu Takayama, interview by James Farrer, August 21, 2017.

137. Shu Takayama, interview.

138. "Poverty and Well-Being in Mozambique," United Nations University, October 2016, https://www.wider.unu.edu/event/conference-poverty-and-well-being-mozambique.

139. Nobie, interview by Hina Nakamura, March 2018.

140. Nobie, interview by Hina Nakamura, March 2018.

141. Yoshihiro Fujiwara, interview by Lenka Vyletalova, October 28, 2017.

142. Oksana Fujiwara, interview by Lenka Vyletalova, March 27, 2019.

143. Yoshihiro Fujiwara, interview by Lenka Vyletalova, October 28, 2017.

144. Yoshihiro Fujiwara and Oksana Fujiwara, interview by Lenka Vyletalova, March 27, 2019.

145. Yoshihiro Fujiwara, interview by Lenka Vyletalova, October 28, 2017.

146. Fieldwork by Lenka Vyletalova, October 2017, March 2018, and March 2019.

147. Fieldwork by Lenka Vyletalova, January and February 2019.

148. Oksana Fujiwara, interview by Lenka Vyletalova, November 20, 2022.

149. Yukie Ohta, "Shalom, Japan!," SoHo Memory Project, November 5, 2011, https://sohomemory.org/shalom-japan-0.

150. "Shalom Japan Menu," Culinary Institute of America Menu Collection, George Lang Menu Collection, menu 2-1575, http://ciadigitalcollections.culinary.edu/digital/collection/p16940coll1/id/12817/rec/15.

151. Kazuhiko Kyogoku, conversation with James Farrer, August 23, 2019; Maiko Kyogoku, interview by James Farrer, September 17, 2019; fieldwork by James Farrer, April 2019 and September 2019.

152. Maiko Kyogoku, interview by James Farrer, September 17, 2019.

153. Maiko Kyogoku, interview by James Farrer, September 17, 2019; fieldwork by James Farrer, April 2019 and September 2019.

154. David Chang, foreword to Orkin and Ying, *Ivan Ramen*, ix–xi.

155. Krishnendu Ray, *The Ethnic Restaurateur* (New York: Bloomsbury, 2016).

156. Ku, *Dubious Gastronomy*, 6–7.

157. James Farrer and Chuanfei Wang, "Who Owns a Cuisine? The Grassroots Politics of Japanese Food in Europe," *Asian Anthropology* 20, no. 1 (2021): 12–29.

158. Ray, *Ethnic Restaurateur*, 82–83, 108; Maren Möhring, *Fremdes Essen: Die Geschichte der ausländischen Gastronomie in der Bundesrepublik Deutschland* [Strange foods: The history of foreign gastronomy in the Federal Republic of Germany] (Berlin: Walter de Gruyter, 2012), 115.

159. Matsumoto, *Nyūyōku Take Sushi monogatari*, 79.

5 | Global Migrations and the Mass Market Japanese Restaurant

David L. Wank, James Farrer,
and Chuanfei Wang

I n the last decades of the twentieth century, Japanese cuisine rapidly spread
outside metropolitan city centers through independent restaurants run
by non-Japanese chef-owners. Most were migrants operating restaurants
in the midmarket range, priced below restaurants owned by Japanese but
higher than fast-food and takeaway eateries. Their large numbers, far-flung
mobilities, and entrepreneurship created a global mass market for Japanese
cuisine. This process began first in the United States in the 1980s, then in
Europe, China, and Brazil in the 1990s, Oceania and Southeast Asia in the
2000s, and South Asia, the Middle East, and Africa in the 2010s.[1] According to Japanese government statistics, the number of Japanese restaurants
globally quintupled from 2006 to 2017.[2] This spread was influenced by the
Japanese food fashions described in the previous chapter and also by regional patterns of migrant entrepreneurship.

The rise of non-Japanese chef-owners reflected two factors. One was the
relatively high value of Japanese cuisine in the eyes of consumers. A cycle of
Japanese restaurant fashions, as described in Chapter 4, established the
popularity of Japanese cuisine in leading urban centers around the world,
with media outlets and individual restaurateurs promoting these trends
outside Japanese immigrant communities. According to a multicountry
survey in 2012 by the Japanese government, Japanese cuisine was the foreign food consumers most wanted to eat in a restaurant because they saw
it as healthy and tasty.[3] The enhanced status of and demand for the cuisine

elevated its market value. This is evident in the changing average costs of restaurant meals in New York and other US cities. In 1985, a meal at a Japanese restaurant was the fifth most expensive among fourteen cuisines, after French, Italian, Continental, and Southern, but by 2013, its cost was virtually tied for first place with French cuisine.[4] A similar pattern occurred in China in the 2010s as Japanese restaurants began dominating lists of the most expensive restaurants in cities such as Shanghai and Tianjin.[5]

The other factor has been changing immigration patterns in the latter twentieth century. Japan's rising wealth reduced the outmigration of poorer Japanese seeking their livelihoods in the service sector (as described in Chapter 3). Since the 1960s, Japanese going abroad increasingly were better-off sojourners—corporate salarymen, students, and tourists—who eschewed the backbreaking work of founding and operating restaurants. While Japanese chefs and entrepreneurial restaurateurs did not disappear from the global Japanese restaurant scene, they concentrated in higher-end dining (see Chapter 8). At the same time, changing conditions stimulated new large-scale migrations of non-Japanese to various places around the world. These new migrants—especially those from Asia—capitalized on the rising status of Japanese cuisine by opening mass-market restaurants. Their entrepreneurship greatly expanded the market for Japanese cuisine, stimulating the emergence of fast-food chains, a phenomenon discussed in the next chapter.

This chapter focuses on the patterns of culinary migration that have conveyed Japanese restaurants deeper into societies around the world. Due to low barriers to entry, the restaurant industry is associated with transnational and domestic migration of owners and staff.[6] From 1980 to 2020, non-Japanese migrant chef-owners started Japanese restaurants on all continents. The first section of this chapter examines the social organization of transnational chain migration and the culinary imaginaries regarding Japanese restaurants founded by migrants in the United States. The second section shifts to Europe, where, in the context of migration patterns resembling those in the United States, we focus more on the culinary politics of race, ethnicity, and class, and their intersections with gender in the Japanese restaurant ethnoscape.[7] The third section considers transnational and rural-to-urban migration in Japan's nearby Asian neighbors, the world region least influenced by US-inflected Japanese cuisine trends. The fourth section views migration and Japanese restaurants in developing countries in Africa and South Asia.

Ethnic Succession and Mass Market Japanese Cuisine in the United States

The phenomenon of non-Japanese operating Japanese restaurants in the United States generally conforms to a pattern of ethnic succession seen throughout the migrant-dominated hospitality industry.[8] Running a restaurant offers a livelihood for newly arrived immigrants lacking English ability and other resources. However, the cuisine of a new immigrant group may not be known to American consumers, so they move into an existing ethnic cuisine niche established by an earlier immigrant group. Such movement occurs between two groups originating from nearby regions and whose members may be regarded as culturally or racially similar by US consumers. Thus, when dining at these restaurants operated by the newer immigrants, many consumers assume they are eating "authentic ethnic" dishes made by people from an appropriate ethnic background.[9] Some examples over the past century are Japanese running Chinese restaurants (see Chapter 3), Greeks operating Italian restaurants, and Bangladeshis and Nepalis running Indian curry houses. Furthermore, the newly arrived immigrant group serves as "ethnic capital" for their entrepreneurial compatriots to access funds, cheap labor, and business information within the group.[10]

Key spurs to ethnic succession in Japanese restaurants were the 1965 repeal of immigration policies that discriminated against Asians and other non–northwest European groups and the influx after 1975 of Vietnamese refugees following the Vietnam War. These events brought many new immigrants from Asia to the United States. Some found work in Japanese-owned restaurants facing labor shortages due to upward mobility among second- and third-generation Japanese Americans. These restaurants were mostly in major cities, as described in Chapters 3 and 4. The recent Asian immigrants, especially those from Japan's former colonies of Korea and Taiwan, were already familiar with Japanese cuisine, and some spoke Japanese due to colonial education policies. They learned Japanese cooking skills in their new jobs by working under Japanese chefs.[11] Further opportunities for the new Asian immigrants opened in 1984 with the sudden jump in the value of the Japanese currency against the US dollar. This erased the economic incentives for chefs from Japan to ply their craft in the United States, thus curtailing the ability of the Japanese restaurateurs in the United States to recruit them. Additionally, US work visas for Japanese chefs were difficult to obtain, while other Asians arriving on immigration visas were allowed to work. As some Japanese chefs returned to Japan, the Asian assistants they had trained were promoted to chefs. Soon, some non-Japanese Asian chefs bought restaurants from Japanese owners who lacked successors or established their own restaurants that served teppanyaki, sushi, and other Japanese dishes. During the 1990s, some non-Japanese restaurateurs began moving to smaller cities and towns with lower business costs, creating new markets for Japanese cuisine.

Underlying all this movement was the fact that Japanese cuisine was more profitable than other Asian cuisines in the US market. This is suggested in Table 5.1, displaying relative changes in restaurant meal prices for four Asian cuisines from the 1980s to the 2010s.

Krishnendu Ray links the prestige of a cuisine in the United States, as seen in its menu price, to the social status of the group associated with the cuisine.[12] Thus, the higher price of Japanese cuisine could be linked to the favorable image of Japanese Americans relative to Koreans, Vietnamese, and Chinese, who, at that time, had more poor immigrants, including refugees, and came from countries with lower international status than Japan. While testing Ray's hypothesis is beyond our scope, it does highlight that the relative popularity of cuisines alone cannot account for the price differences in Table 5.1. (In fact, Chinese food was popular in the United States long before Japanese food, enticing many early Japanese migrants to run Chinese restaurants as described in Chapter 3.)

Based on fieldwork, we see three waves of ethnic succession in ownership of Japanese restaurants. The first began in the 1980s as Korean, Taiwanese, and Vietnamese migrants and a smaller number of ethnic Chinese

TABLE 5.1 Increase in Average Meal Price of Asian Cuisines

Cuisine category	Average meal price (USD) in 1985	Average meal price (USD) in 2013	Percentage increase
Japanese	31.88	62.73	97
Korean	21.00	42.10	100
Vietnamese	24.50	31.72	29
Chinese	24.20	32.78	35

Source: Zagat price data reported by Krishnendu Ray in Ana Swanson (2016), "Why So Many of America's Sushi Restaurants Are Owned by Chinese," *Washington Post,* September 29, 2016, https://www.washingtonpost.com/news/wonk/wp/2016/09/29/the-fascinating-story-behind -who-opens-sushi-restaurants-and-why/.

from Southeast Asia opened Japanese restaurants in urban areas, including smaller cities. The second wave began in the 1990s when many Chinese migrants to New York City began running Japanese restaurants. As competition intensified, they began relocating outside the city, first to the greater New York region and then farther afield, conveying Japanese restaurants more broadly and deeply into US society. A third wave in the 2010s was more multicultural, including many Asian restaurateurs who do not come from East Asia and a small but noticeable number of white chef-owners. These waves are not strictly exclusive. While many owners and chefs from earlier waves leave the industry as they age out and their families experience upward mobility, others stay, competing with those from subsequent waves.

An example of a first-wave Asian migrant restaurateur is Billy Truong, who was born in 1964 in Saigon, Vietnam. Ten years later, his family fled Vietnam and spent four years as refugees in Hong Kong and Japan before arriving at a refugee camp near Pensacola, Florida.[13] Truong graduated from high school and went to work in a Benihana Steakhouse near Florida's Disneyland under Japanese chefs who taught him to cut fish and cook Japanese dishes. In 1985, he was promoted to a chef position when a Japanese chef returned to Japan because of the appreciating Japanese yen. In 1993, he opened a steakhouse in Jacksonville, Florida, but went bankrupt during the 2007 financial crisis. Seeking a new start, he opened a teppanyaki and sushi restaurant in 2010 in Lancaster, Pennsylvania, where his son was attending college. During our interview in 2013, Truong expressed pride in his *nigiri* (hand pressed) sushi made to the exacting standards of his Japanese teacher. He opined that Chinese chefs who now dominated the market lacked the skill to make such authentic sushi. Even though he hired a Chinese chef, he only permitted him to make rolls, but not to add the colorful and decorative sauces that Chinese chefs specialized in. However, Truong's business faltered, possibly because his concern for authenticity failed to meet consumer expectations for colorful, sauce-doused sushi rolls, and he closed in 2015.

Many other first-wave restaurateurs had more flexible ideas of Japanese cuisine than Truong, and they created hybrid menus of dishes from Japanese and other Asian cuisines. Japanese dishes included *nigiri* sushi and California-style rolls featuring fatty, non-fishy-tasting ingredients, such as avocado, tuna, and king crab, as well as fried dishes, such as tempura, that appealed to mass-market consumers. While influences from other cuisines varied according to the background of the owners and chefs, many menus included such Chinese American standards as General Tso's chicken and chow mein (sometimes written as "yakisoba"). These seemingly pastiche-like menus were a pan-Asian business strategy to broaden market appeal. A family dining there could find dishes to satisfy all tastes, with younger members going for the sushi, older members sticking to familiar Chinese dishes, and others trying the Thai, Korean, and even Indian dishes when offered.

Predictably, the innovations in the taste and presentation of Japanese cuisine at these non-Japanese-owned restaurants were criticized by culinary purists. Internet bloggers derided their Japanese food for not being the same as in Japan. For example, in 2003, a Japanese blogger living in New York accused Korean- and Chinese-owned Japanese restaurants of "cultural exploitation," not for selling Japanese food, but for selling *bad* Japanese food. "They simply mimic the way Japanese food looks, and nothing more. They put a piece of raw fish on a ball of rice and call it 'sushi,' not realizing that sushi rice is made quite differently from ordinary rice. They deep-fry breaded pieces of vegetables and call them 'tempura,' not realizing that tempura batter and sauce are nothing like what you use for chicken cutlet."[14] These attacks from the blogosphere did little to halt the expansion of mass-market Japanese restaurants, but they did help create a distinction for the high-end restaurants discussed in later chapters.

Fuzhou Chinese Restaurateurs Spread Japanese Cuisine in the US Hinterlands

The influx of Chinese immigrants from the People's Republic of China beginning in the 1980s carried Japanese restaurants deeper into American society. This process was driven by a large number of immigrants, including undocumented ones, and their innovative use of communication technology.[15] The migrants were from rural areas around Fuzhou City, a coastal region in southeast China's Fujian Province with a long tradition of out-migration. With the relaxation of emigration controls in China after the Cultural Revolution (1966–1976), Fuzhou Chinese began coming to New York to seek their fortunes, as China was still a poor country. Although many early migrants were undocumented, they received amnesty after the violent suppression of protests in China in 1989. Subsequent migrants congregated through chain migration in New York City's Chinatown, which acquired the moniker Little Fuzhou. By 1994, about one hundred thousand Fuzhou Chinese immigrants lived there, with thousands arriving each year, tripling its population over the next two decades.[16] Many immigrants went into the textile industry as owners and workers. Others opened Chinese-cuisine restaurants to prepare meals for female textile workers too busy to cook for their families. Soon, the restaurants became popular beyond the Chinese community and reoriented their menus toward US consumers. The restaurateurs quickly realized that US consumers would pay a premium for food labeled "Japanese," which had a better image than Chinese food, as the latter had become stigmatized by the 1990s as laden with MSG and calories.[17] Therefore, restaurateurs began including sushi and other Japanese dishes on their menus and installing sushi bars. By 2000, increasing competition in the New York restaurant industry impelled Fuzhou Chinese restaurateurs to move to local markets increasingly far from the city.[18]

Their restaurants had several characteristics. Most notably, the chef-owners called them "sushi restaurants" and put US-style sushi rolls at the center of the menu. For taste and aesthetics, they garnished the rolls with colorful sauces made from spicy mayonnaise, ponzu, soy sauce, Japanese eel sauce, and Vietnamese hot sauce. To lower labor and ingredients costs, they simplified food preparation, such as eliminating dashi—seaweed and bonito soup stock—from the miso soup and reducing the vinegar in the sushi rice (thereby extending its time before souring). The service included takeout and delivery, which had long been widespread in Chinese restaurants. The restaurants' names conveyed Japaneseness by incorporating a handful of Japanese words familiar to Americans, such as "samurai," "zen," "arigato," and "wasabi," as well as Japanese place-names, usually Kyoto, Osaka, or Tokyo.

The independent restaurants of the Fuzhou Chinese relied on the labor of the family and coethnics in the migrant communities. Typically, the husband served as the chef and the wife as the front-of-house manager and cashier. Other relatives could be employed as well; however, a full-service restaurant required labor beyond the family. According to one owner we interviewed, the staff requirement for a typical Japanese restaurant was fifteen people, including sushi chefs, hot cooks, and servers.[19] These labor needs for both Chinese- and Japanese-cuisine restaurants operated by Fuzhou Chinese were met by a half dozen private Chinese employment agencies concentrated on East Broadway in Little Fuzhou. A restaurateur hundreds of miles from New York City could fax or text an order for staff to one of these agencies, which dispatched them immediately. In this way, just-arrived immigrants could find work throughout the eastern United States. The employees traveled to their jobs on Chinese-owned bus lines that started in 1998 to transport new migrants at lower prices than established carriers. The first buses ran from New York to Boston, Philadelphia, and Washington, DC, but soon expanded to more than twenty states.[20] At their new jobs, Fuzhou Chinese staff lived in housing provided by restaurateurs, returning to New York from time to time to visit their families. Migrant servers and entry-level cooking staff were the most economically vulnerable participants in this industry. Some employers forced servers to share tips, an illegal practice that could push their real wages below the legal minimum.[21] Such low-wage labor also was a key factor in the profitability of these businesses.

The 2007 global financial crisis created opportunities for restaurateurs by opening up inexpensive real estate, especially in suburban shopping malls. This led to a sharp increase of Fuzhou Chinese–run restaurants in small markets in the eastern half of the United States. Cities with a few Japanese restaurants now had two or three times as many, while even rural hamlets acquired one. The Little Fuzhou labor network, held together by fax machines and mobile phones, ensured a supply of hardworking chefs, kitchen staff, and servers. The tight link of far-flung restaurants to coethnic labor in the New York migrant enclave enabled many Fuzhou Chinese restaurateurs to open multiple outlets, spreading Japanese cuisine farther into American society. Here, we describe this process in two locales.

Fuzhou Chinese Restaurateurs on the Northeast Megalopolis Fringe. Lancaster is a small city in Pennsylvania of sixty thousand people, an exurb of Philadelphia and a three-hour drive from New York, 170 miles away. It is a tourist destination and the hub of Lancaster County with a thriving agricultural sector of family farms, many owned by the Amish people. Around 2005, the first Japanese restaurant run by a Fuzhou Chinese chef-owner opened, with the number multiplying over the next few years. By 2010, when we began our fieldwork, there were over a dozen Fuzhou Chinese restaurants, more than double the number established earlier by first-wave Asian restaurateurs.

One chef-owner we met was Qiankai Li. He was born in 1972 to a fishing family in Lianjiang County, Fuzhou City. In 1990, he immigrated to New York and labored in several restaurants, learning to cook Chinese and Japanese food by watching the chefs. He then worked in Chinese restaurants in the Midwest and Pennsylvania owned by his friends. In 1997, he started a Chinese eatery in downtown Lancaster that served stir-fried noodles, egg foo young, and other Chinese dishes familiar to Americans. Then, in 2005, he started a Japanese restaurant called Sakura serving Japanese, Chinese, and Thai dishes next door to his Chinese restaurant. The two restaurants had separate storefronts and dining areas but overlapping kitchens. The Chinese restaurant had a fast-food format with counter service and a functional interior, while the Japanese one had table service that met customer expectations of more upmarket Japanese cuisine.[22]

The Japanese dishes centered on sushi rolls, including the Lancaster roll with seaweed and eel and the Philadelphia roll with salmon and cream cheese. Refrigerator trucks from Samuels & Sons, a Philadelphia seafood company, delivered fish several times a week. Li sourced fresh vegetables and basic supplies in farmers' markets and supermarkets, and Asian ingredients on his trips to New York. His wife was the cashier in the Japanese restaurant, and his three brothers worked as hot cooks and managers; his sushi chefs and servers were hired through his personal ties. Business was good, and he opened a Chinese eatery in a Hispanic neighborhood, serving spicy and deep-fried foods that appealed to the community. Then, in 2015, in an upmarket move, he opened Oka, a Japanese-Asian fusion restaurant next to Franklin & Marshall College, whose students were a key clientele.[23]

Experienced sushi chefs were critical to these restaurants. An example is Jason, the head sushi chef at Sakura and Oka. He was born in 1976 in Changle County, Fujian, to a large family. His father owned a small factory that made umbrellas for export. He went to culinary school and worked as a Chinese and Western cook in a hotel restaurant in Fuzhou. But he wanted to earn more money and came to New York in 1995 at age nineteen. He worked at Chinese, Japanese, French, and Mexican restaurants in New York and then in the Midwest at jobs given to him by relatives and friends. In 2009, a friend who had just opened a restaurant in Lancaster invited him to be a sushi chef. In our interview, Jason expressed pride in the many sauces he had concocted to flavor his rolls. He lived around the corner from the restaurant in housing provided by the restaurant owner. Once a month, he traveled to New York to visit his son and wife, who was a waitress in a Chinese restaurant. Jason's mother looked after their son. He also traveled to casinos near Philadelphia some evenings, hoping for a big win to bankroll his dream of opening his own restaurant.[24]

Servers were next in importance. We spoke to Amy, a server in her mid-twenties working at a sushi restaurant in a suburban shopping mall in Lancaster. Her entire family—parents, three brothers, and sister—emigrated from Changle County to New York beginning in the 1990s. They all worked in the catering industry while their mother cared for their children. While waitressing in New York, she tired of daily urban commutes and found a job in Lancaster through an employment agency in Little Fuzhou. There, she lived in a house near the restaurant owned by the restaurateur. To save money for her daughter's education, she spent her free time in the apartment watching Chinese television and talking on the phone with friends. Once or twice a month, she visited her family in New York. Her situation underscored the movement of Fuzhou Chinese migrants within the United States, traveling back and forth between Little Fuzhou and often-distant jobs. Yet despite living far from Little Fuzhou, Amy worked for a Fuzhou Chinese boss alongside compatriots, talked daily by phone and text with her kin around the United States, and regularly traveled to Little Fuzhou to see family.[25]

As successful restaurateurs expanded, they had to find managers outside their networks of family and friends. They often hired immigrant Chinese from Taiwan or overseas Chinese from Southeast Asia who typically spoke better English and had more managerial experience than Fuzhou Chinese. One such manager was Jan Teng, an overseas Chinese woman from Ipoh, Malaysia. She had immigrated to the United States at age twenty-eight and spoke Mandarin and English. When we met her in Lancaster, she had decades of restaurant experience. She first worked in restaurants in New York, including as a server in a Japanese restaurant and then as a manager in a Thai-Indian-Myanmarese restaurant. Saving her money, she moved to a medium-sized city in Florida, using her network from her membership in a Buddhist sect to buy a Chinese restaurant that she converted to Malaysian cuisine. In 2005, after a hurricane tore off the roof of her restaurant, Teng once again returned to managing restaurants owned by others. In 2009, she got a managerial position in a Japanese restaurant in Lancaster by responding to an advertisement in a Chinese-language newspaper.[26]

During our fieldwork in the 2010s, we noticed growing numbers of local white employees in the Fuzhou Chinese restaurants. This was due to slowing immigration from China and the upward mobility of restaurateurs' offspring who had little interest in restaurant work. In 2015, one of the restaurants that we had patronized for several years hired its first local, a white woman in her twenties who had been a frequent customer. She told us that she jokingly told the owner that her dream was to work in a sushi restaurant, and he hired her on the spot. Within two years, she became trusted enough to serve as the cashier, replacing the owner's wife, who wanted to stay home to raise her children.[27]

A white server who was a local hire in one restaurant gave us insight into the impact of these Japanese-cuisine restaurants on the area's eating habits. Michael Frey worked at Wasabi, a restaurant in the small town of Willow Street, a few miles outside Lancaster. The restaurant, which opened in 2009, was owned by a Fuzhou Chinese couple and managed by the wife, who drove in every day from the couple's other restaurant closer to Philadelphia. The restaurant sat between a Pizza Hut and GNC vitamin store in a shopping mall amid rural fields, near an old gun shop said to have crafted the first long rifles in colonial America. Frey, who lived in the neighborhood with his family, was the restaurant's first local hire. He told us that many local people started coming out of curiosity. On their first visit, they typically ordered vegetable rolls containing familiar avocado and cucumber. On subsequent visits, they tried the cooked fish, then rolls with raw fish, and eventually *nigiri* sushi and sashimi. Soon they were stopping to buy takeout dinner on their way home from work. Frey said, "Takeout is big. Manager Li runs back and forth carrying bags of takeout like a train. Dude, it is amazing. I would not expect to have these people . . . they are rednecks . . . my people . . . driving pickup trucks that get four miles to the gallon. They come and eat sushi like it is popcorn. I think to myself, 'What turned a switch on in you that made you want to eat this stuff?'"[28] He observed that locals considered sushi to be healthier than pizza or hamburgers. It was also more convenient, as an order could be placed online, the turnaround time was quick, and the package was compact. Takeout orders spiked just before the Super Bowl and other major television events.

Frey noted that local patrons had no idea that Wasabi was owned and operated by Chinese people. He described this in terms of his own experience.

It took me a week to realize that the people who worked here were all Chinese. It wasn't even they who told me. I was standing outside [the rear entrance] smoking a cigarette. An [Asian] truck driver was there from Philadelphia unloading tuna tenderloins . . . who spoke perfect English. He . . . looks at me and . . . said, "I never saw a white guy standing here before." I said, "How hard is it to learn Japanese?" And he said, "There aren't any Japanese in there." And

I said, "What do you mean?" And he said, "Well, it's a Japanese restaurant, but they are all Chinese." And I thought, "Thanks for telling me." They must not have liked it when I said "Konnichiwa" to them.[29]

Similarly, many local diners apparently had no idea that those cooking and serving their food were Chinese rather than Japanese. This deliberate ambiguity or blurring of ethnic categories is one way that restaurants convey "authenticity" to consumers.[30] Of course, concerns about authenticity vary among customers. When we told diners eating sushi at restaurants in Lancaster that the restaurants were owned and operated by Chinese, they expressed momentary surprise. But this information did not seem to diminish their enjoyment of the meal, and they continued to patronize the restaurants. These observations, while selective, suggest that in the midmarket range, consumers were less concerned about whether Japanese chefs prepared their food. The low price and portion size attracted them. This was even more apparent during our fieldwork in southern Appalachia.

Fuzhou Chinese Restaurateurs in Appalachia. Our fieldwork in the Appalachian regions of North Carolina and Tennessee encompassed small urban centers and mountain villages lying about 750 miles southwest of New York. In the 2000s, the region's Japanese restaurant scene became dominated by Fuzhou Chinese, who adapted to local tastes by serving both sushi and grilled meats.

Wasabi (unrelated to the Wasabi in the previous section) was located in Asheville, a touristy city and economic hub of the western North Carolina region of Appalachia. It was owned by two Fuzhou Chinese brothers who had worked in a Japanese restaurant in New York, with one preparing sushi and the other managing the hibachi grill. They came to Asheville in the 1990s, starting a teppanyaki steak house called Ichiban, and then opened Wasabi in 2005, the first sushi bar downtown. Wasabi was repeatedly named the best sushi restaurant in local newspapers and on culinary websites.[31] Its shellfish offerings, which distinguished its menu from those of other local restaurants, included conch, sea abalone, clam, and live lobster. These high-quality ingredients made Wasabi's prices, at about USD 30 per meal, among the highest in the region, although reasonable given the high rents in the heavily touristed downtown. Other Japanese restaurants appealed to the locavore and dietary concerns of young professionals and hipsters by sourcing vegetables from area farms and offering vegan and vegetarian sushi.[32]

Fuzhou Chinese restaurateurs quickly picked up on teppanyaki, a craze in the 1960s and 1970s, described in the previous chapter, that found a lasting home in the American South. Some of the earliest teppanyaki restaurants had been founded by Japanese migrants who marketed them as hibachi, copying the service and aesthetics of the Benihana steak house chain (see Chapter 4).[33] In 2019, we visited Fuji Steak and Sushi in Chattanooga, Tennessee, part of a small restaurant chain owned by Fuzhou Chinese migrants. The menu included hibachi with various fish and meats and roll and *nigiri* sushi. The dining room layout was dominated by several teppanyaki grills, each surrounded by a three-sided counter seating ten customers who could watch their meats being grilled. Food critic Hanna Raskin notes that this arrangement encouraged an unusual degree of sociability in the American South among randomly seated Black and white diners.[34] Our chef was a Chinese Indonesian who commented that hibachi was simpler to learn than sushi, and it was easy to master the cooking performance tricks, such as juggling raw eggs on a spatula. The Chattanoogans at our grill clearly enjoyed the performative chef, as they dumped mayonnaise-based white sauce onto glistening mounds of fried rice and meats. The emphasis on volume, with leftovers filling a take-home box, signified hibachi as a hearty working-class meal in the region.

In small mountain towns, some hibachi restaurants skipped the sushi altogether. This was the case in New Tokyo Restaurant, owned by a Fuzhou Chinese couple, in the town of Burnsville, an hour from Asheville. It was a fast-food restaurant in a strip mall alongside a Dollar General Store, a Mexican restaurant, and a bargain supermarket. Several Japanese fans, lanterns, and other generic Asian decorations added color to the functional interior with booth-style seating. The dishes were prepared on a plate grill in the kitchen, not in front of customers as at the aforementioned Fuji Steak and Sushi. The most popular dishes were hibachi chicken and teriyaki chicken, while many dishes with Japanese names were indistinguishable from such Chinese fast foods as fried noodles and dumplings. Locals came for cheap eats rather than "authentic" Japanese food. The restaurant's original deep-fried wontons, stuffed with cream cheese and vegetables, appealed to Southern customers. The owner said this suited the tastes of locals who were not well traveled. "If you were in a big city, you could have the roast ducks hanging from the ceiling." When we asked if this was simply a Chinese restaurant with a Japanese name, the Chinese waitress noted several Japanese-named items on the menu.[35]

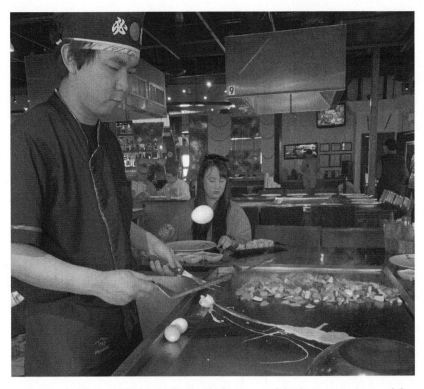

FIGURE 5.1 Acrobatic performances by the chefs are part of the dining experience at hibachi restaurants, such as Fuji Steak and Sushi in Chattanooga, Tennessee. The chef is a migrant from Indonesia. (Photo by James Farrer, April 13, 2019)

The relationship of Fuzhou Chinese in Appalachia to Little Fuzhou was tempered by distance: Asheville was four times farther from New York than Lancaster, at least a twelve-hour drive. Our conversations with Jennifer Li, co-owner (with her husband) of Zen Sushi, illuminated the personal situation of a Fuzhou Chinese restaurateur family in the region. Li moved to the United States in 1993 to join her brother, who had a green card. After living in New York for several years, she and her husband decided to come to Asheville to run a Chinese restaurant to give their children a better environment. She felt that New York was convenient for adult immigrants but that children were left unsupervised in its Chinese community and did not learn proper study habits or English. Li appreciated the easygoing ways and friendliness of Asheville residents and described herself as part of its community. She rarely visited New York, and when interviewed in 2019, she said

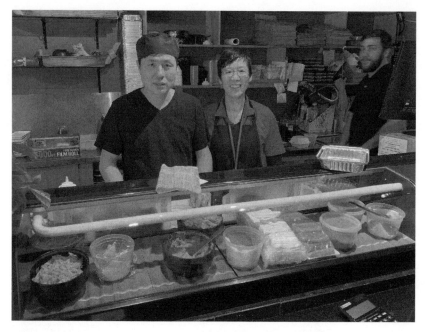

FIGURE 5.2 Jennifer Li poses with her husband and a waiter at their restaurant in Asheville, North Carolina. Li manages the front of the house and relations with customers and suppliers, while her husband mans the busy sushi bar. Both the husband and wife originally are from Fuzhou, China. (Photo by James Farrer, April 24, 2019)

she had not been there in several years.[36] Her relationship with Little Fuzhou was very different from that of her compatriots in Lancaster, who regularly visited New York to see relatives and obtain supplies.

The distance from New York was disadvantageous for tapping into the Little Fuzhou labor market. The head chef at Asheville's Wasabi told us in 2019 that it was increasingly difficult to hire Chinese sushi chefs: "Everyone still lands in New York and is recruited from New York. Most of them want to stay closer to New York, like New Jersey, or such. So, the further away you are, the harder it is to recruit them."[37] This helped explain the more multicultural staff that we saw in Asheville restaurants compared with Lancaster. But hiring locals was not a cure-all. At Asheville's Zen Sushi in 2019, the front-of-house staff were all local white residents working part time. But Li had been unsuccessful in hiring Americans as cooks, she said, as they soon quit, sometimes before finishing their training. Fortunately, Zen Sushi still had two Chinese cooks, but Li saw no long-term solution to the labor problem. Some restaurateurs responded by shifting from table service to less labor-intensive fast-food-style counter service, takeout, and buffet. One innovation was the mega-buffet, which, while marketed as a Japanese restaurant, served a huge array of mostly Chinese foods alongside inexpensive sushi and rolls made from low-cost vegetables, *tamagoyaki* (Japanese omelet), king crab, and cheap cuts of fish. Such down-market strategies threatened to devalue the "Japan brand" of high quality, taste, and healthiness. Therefore, some Fuzhou Chinese restaurateurs began moving into trendier cuisines, such as Vietnamese-Cajun.[38]

By the 2010s, the number of Fuzhou Chinese–owned restaurants seemed to be declining. This is suggested by a *New York Times* analysis of Yelp on the changing composition of restaurants from 2014 to 2019 in the top twenty metropolitan regions. They show the number of Chinese restaurants falling by 1,200 establishments even as all restaurants increased by 15,000 establishments, including upticks in Korean, Indian, and other ethnic restaurants. In other words, the Chinese restaurant share of all restaurants declined from 7.3 percent to 6.5 percent. According to the reporters, the key reason was the upward mobility of the second generation, who were spurning restaurant work in favor of university or less backbreaking jobs.[39] While the statistics do not distinguish Chinese-owned Japanese-cuisine restaurants in the sample, the restaurants are owned by the same ethnic group (Chinese) that is the focus in the Yelp study, and so the trend fits the stories we heard in our fieldwork. At Zen Sushi in Asheville, Jennifer Li told us that her eldest two children were college students with no interest in the restaurant or even helping out. She and her husband planned to keep running the restaurant until her youngest child finished university. "The kids will do their own thing," she said.[40]

Multicultural Trends

The decline of Chinese immigration created opportunities for restaurateurs and chefs of other ethnicities. By the 2010s, we saw third-wave restaurateurs, including immigrants from Asian countries more distant from Japan, such as Cambodia, Thailand, and Nepal, as well as white chef-owners, in our field sites. This growing multiculturalism adds another dimension to the process of ethnic succession. The South and Southeast Asian entrepreneurs can be considered a continuation of ethnic succession, as they possess the requisite physical capital—namely, an "Asian" face—to convey cultural authenticity to the consumers. However, this is not the case with white chef-owners. We have already noted their emergence in Chapter 4 with a description of Ivan Orkin, who established a ramen shop in New York in 2013 after running a popular one in Tokyo for a decade. Even more noteworthy was the growing number of white chefs far removed from New York in the small markets where we conducted fieldwork.

One such chef-owner in Lancaster County was Tim Klunk, a professionally trained chef like Orkin. In 2017, he opened Julienne Sushi Bar in Elizabethtown, a borough of twelve thousand people. The moderately priced restaurant served Japanese dishes reflecting local tastes in a light blue café-like interior devoid of Asian décor. In his late thirties, Klunk had graduated from the Pennsylvania School of Culinary Arts and then worked in restaurants in nearby Hershey, a resort and tourist city. He got the idea to start a Japanese restaurant when he noticed that Elizabethtown had sixteen sub and pizza shops but only one sushi restaurant (opened in 2014 by a Chinese restaurateur), which did roaring business. Julienne Sushi Bar served Japanese dishes that Klunk learned via the internet. His signature rolls were stuffed with smoked fish, including trout, salmon, and shrimp, that he made in the meat smoker in his backyard. This, he said, reflected the region's German heritage and the popularity of fishing and hunting there. Additionally, he served poke bowls and such comfort dishes as barbecue sandwiches and miso mac and cheese. He made Japanese desserts, including green tea fudge brownies and banana sushi sliced to resemble a sushi roll and covered in peanut butter, granola, strawberries, and caramel drizzle.[41]

This "whitening" of Japanese restaurants also occurred among people with little culinary experience. In Lancaster City, Nate Abel, a white local, opened Chop Sushi in 2016, a counter-style restaurant specializing in poke bowls of raw fish and vegetables over rice. He had previously worked as an auditor and decided to open a poke bowl restaurant after eating the dish in California. Customers ordered from the counter, choosing from a dozen sauces, four kinds of fish (tuna, salmon, spicy tuna, or lump crab), vegetables (avocado, edamame, etc.), and toppings that included pickled ginger, masago, and cilantro.[42] The raw or precooked ingredients required only cutting and mixing skills. Costs were further reduced by the lack of table service and a hot kitchen, making a poke bowl restaurant a viable business for a young entrepreneur with modest financial and culinary capital (see Chapter 6).

While the emergence of white chef-owners is noteworthy, it did not sig-nify the "de-ethnicization" of Japanese-cuisine restaurants.[43] After all, the premium value of Japanese cuisine was due to its Japaneseness, or at least its perception as such by customers. Therefore, generally speaking, an "Asian face" served to validate the authenticity of the cuisine. This was especially so for the most visible position in the restaurant—namely, the chef behind the sushi counter. In practice, the "openness" to non-Asian-appearing chefs was limited mainly to white males, usually with professional culinary train-ing. White people could be chefs in Japanese restaurants, even fine dining ones (see Chapter 8) if they proved themselves professionally, but those from other ethnicities and races were regarded with suspicion unless they could "pass" as Japanese. For example, a Hispanic chef we interviewed in New York City said it was tough for a Hispanic man to be accepted as a sushi chef. It took him years to become a head chef because Hispanics were not associated with Asian cuisines.[44] Also, Black chefs were rare, even in regions with large Black populations, and faced racial stereotyping from employ-ers and customers.[45] This situation is consistent with academic research in-dicating that ethnic stereotyping plays a role in the reception of chefs.[46]

Significantly, we also encountered very few female sushi chefs. For ex-ample, Samantha was a multiracial half-Filipino woman who had been an assistant sushi chef for five years in a Japanese-owned restaurant in an Ap-palachian city when we met her in 2019. She said, "There is a lot of preju-dice against women in this business. Then, I am not fully Asian, so it is a double mark against me."[47] She described herself as the apprentice of a Japa-nese chef who was open-minded enough to teach her the craft of sushi making. But she noted that there were very few female head sushi chefs, and she was unlikely to advance to head chef when her master retired. There-fore, she saw no alternative but to eventually quit the profession and do something else. Of course, some women, including non-Asian minority women, persisted in this career, but customers challenge their knowledge more than they do for Asian or male chefs. As one Black woman sushi chef told an interviewer, "There tend to be tests—oral pop quizzes of sorts—that present things that any properly trained sushi chef always knows."[48]

In sum, the Japanese restaurant industry has become quite multicul-tural, but ethnicity, race, and gender still matter, especially in the highly visible position of the sushi chef. Therefore, we see the growing multicul-turalism in the Japanese restaurant industry as the increasing penetration of racial, ethnic, and gender discourses from the broader society into Japanese restaurants. Customers still appear to associate a visible "face" with authenticity, or at least restaurant owners who hire the staff are convinced that they do. This complex issue is considered further in the following section regarding Europe.

The Cultural Politics of Ethnic Succession in Europe's Japanese Restaurants

In Europe, which has been quick to pick up on trends across the Atlantic, we see broadly similar migration and ethnic succession processes. We focus on different groups and their interactions in Japanese restaurants to examine the cultural politics of the variegated ethnoscapes of Japanese restaurant scenes in Europe.[49]

Ethnic Succession in a Japanese Culinary Street in Paris

From the 1980s to 2009, the number of Japanese restaurants in Paris shot up from fifty to seven hundred, run mainly by immigrants from China and, increasingly, other Asian countries.[50] Chinese entered the Japanese food sector for similar reasons as in the United States, including chasing profits from higher-margin Japanese food and negative media publicity about the safety and healthiness of Chinese food.[51] Among the earliest were Japanese restaurants opened in the 1970s on the Rue Monsieur-le-Prince. Located near Sorbonne University and government ministries, they attracted trend-setting young intellectuals and bureaucrats. Within a decade, ten Japanese restaurants lined the street, most owned by refugees from Southeast Asia, part of a family network of overseas Chinese tracing its lineage to Chaozhou City, Guangdong Province. By the time of our fieldwork in the late 2010s, most of the original owners had sold their establishments to more recent migrants. They mainly came from China's Chaozhou and Wenzhou regions, with Wenzhou Chinese being the most extensive Chinese migrant group in Western Europe.

One such restaurant was Royal Sushi, founded in 1989 by a Chaozhou Chinese restaurateur. By the time we visited in 2018, the owner was a Chinese woman from Shanghai in her early fifties. She came to Paris in 1993 and started working at Royal Sushi as a waitress, becoming its owner in

2008. She manned the sushi counter and hired two Chinese chefs to cook hot dishes in the kitchen. She took up sushi making because it was an easier skill to acquire than cooking Chinese dishes and reduced labor costs. She managed the restaurant by herself because her husband, also Chinese, ran a textile business. She noted to us that women sushi chefs were uncommon in Japanese restaurants.[52] (They remain rare in Paris and our other field-work sites.) The dishwashers were Sri Lankan and African, a racialized division of labor we also saw in other Japanese restaurants in Europe. Invariably, whites and East Asians held front-of-house positions to engage with customers while African and South Asian migrants labored behind the scenes.

Most Chinese owners we interviewed ordered all fish and other ingredients from local Chinese suppliers. Unlike the Japanese, they seldom sourced ingredients in the fresh market. Many placed their orders of mostly frozen items via WeChat for delivery. At Royal Sushi, for instance, suppliers had a restaurant key to put deliveries directly in the refrigerator every morning.[53] During our interviews, we observed such deliveries. The thin-skinned *gyōza* (dumplings) and sushi rolls were machine-made, while the salad, skewers, and soups were prepared by wholesalers. The fish was frozen, with the most popular being salmon, followed by tuna. The only fresh delivery was the avocados used in the sushi and salads. In interviews, owners admitted that the food preparation required little skill. But they were proud of the food at their restaurants, and their regular customers seemed satisfied. The use of frozen and pre-prepared ingredients cut labor costs and food spoilage, enabling the family businesses to survive ups and downs in demand.[54]

These non-Japanese-owned restaurants were viewed with a mix of frustration and resignation by the Japanese restaurateurs whose establishments predated them.[55] One Paris-based Japanese manager of a Japanese-owned restaurant whom we interviewed in 2017 expressed a feeling of a loss of control over defining the standards of Japanese cuisine. He said,

It is really the Chinese who have popularized Japanese cuisine here, not Japanese. And from that point of view, it is a good thing. [Customers] first will learn about Japanese cuisine and then come to my place. The only problem is if they come here and say that the way we Japanese are making Japanese food is wrong, and ask us to do it another way. That is difficult for us to accept. For example, someone comes in and says, "Why don't you have a spoon with the miso soup?" Or if you serve sashimi, they say, "Why is the soy sauce not sweet?" That sort of thing.[56]

The criticism by Japanese chef-owners that Chinese-owned restaurants did not serve "authentic" Japanese food echoed what we heard from restaurateurs in the United States. They attributed inauthenticity to the Chinese chefs' lack of fish-cutting skills, use of inferior-quality fish, and reliance on labor-saving practices, such as not adding dashi to the soup stock or vinegaring the sushi rice.

By the late 2010s, Rue Monsieur-le-Prince was waning as a Japanese food street. The flow of working-class Chinese migrants that had driven its expansion had dried up, and new immigrant groups from Southeast Asia were now the driving force, as in the United States. They bought Japanese restaurants from the earlier immigrants, and some changed the menus to feature other ethnic cuisines. According to our informants, the number of Japanese restaurants on Rue Monsieur-le-Prince dropped from ten in the 1980s to six by the

FIGURE 5.3 All-you-can-eat Japanese-cuisine buffets like this one were a popular lunch option in Paris. Most were owned by Chinese migrants from Zhejiang Province. (Photo by James Farrer, February 22, 2017)

time of our fieldwork in 2018. The four former Japanese restaurants were replaced by a Thai restaurant, a Vietnamese restaurant, and boutique shops.

Wenzhou Chinese Restaurateurs Spread Japanese Restaurants in Italy

As in France, the earliest Japanese restaurants in Italy were opened by Japanese migrants in a few major cities, including Rome and Milan. By the 2010s, however, the Japanese restaurant sector was dominated by Chinese from Wenzhou Prefecture, Zhejiang Province, a Chinese dialect group with an entrepreneurial tradition of operating small factories. They began coming to Italy and other European countries in the 1980s. In Italy, many opened small factories producing Italian-branded consumer goods. They have since played an outsize role in the Italian economy, including restaurants. Their entry into the Japanese restaurant sector began in the early 2000s, when, facing increasing competition and a SARS-related food safety panic regarding Chinese restaurants, they started Italian café bars and Japanese restaurants. They created a market for low-cost US-style sushi rolls and all-you-can-eat Asian fare that became influential throughout Europe.[57] By then, these restaurant-owning families included members who came to Europe as young children and a second generation born in Italy. These gave the family businesses the advantages of younger members with fluent Italian, a keen business acumen honed in family firms, and ethnic networks providing capital and cheap labor.[58]

The creation of all-you-can-eat Asian buffets offering Chinese and Japanese foods at low prices is often credited to restaurateur Marco Hu, who came to Italy from China in the early 1980s. In 2006, he founded the Wok Sushi buffet restaurant in Padua, which quickly grew into a local chain that inspired hundreds of imitators across northern Italy. The term "wok sushi" became a generic term for these Chinese-Japanese fusion buffet restaurants.[59] The menu consisted of quick-service sushi rolls stuffed with salmon and vegetables, stir-fried dishes, and foods prepared in small factories. By around 2010, with the saturation of large urban markets, restaurateurs moved into smaller, less competitive regional ones. While they initially relied on the national Wenzhou Chinese network for labor, declining migration from China in the 2010s pushed them to hire workers from other immigrant groups, as occurred in France and the United States.

An example of one such restaurant is Osaka in Verona, famous as the setting of William Shakespeare's drama *Romeo and Juliet*.[60] Verona had a sophisticated fine dining Italian cuisine scene serving affluent tourists, but its Asian fare was aimed at locals seeking an affordable meal. Located near the central train station, Osaka's entrance featured a large picture of an Asian woman in traditional Chinese garb. The interior decorations were Chinese, including the twelve Chinese zodiac animals, traditional Chinese paintings, calligraphy brushes hanging in a wooden stand, and a Chinese wooden screen. When we visited in 2017, songs by Hong Kong crooner Jackie Cheung were playing.[61] Osaka was owned by Liu, born in Wenzhou in 1981.[62] He came to Verona in 2004, sponsored by his uncle, living in Italy for decades. He said that he left Wenzhou not because of economic hardship but rather because of his belief that a young man had to travel abroad to make his fortune. This widely shared expectation drove the chain migration that created the Wenzhou diaspora in Europe. For his start in business, Liu drew on his uncle's extensive ties among local Wenzhou Chinese and understanding of the local market. He opened a hair salon but then switched to a Japanese restaurant when he saw them thriving in large cities. In 2015, he started Osaka, the second Japanese restaurant in Verona. In two years, the number of Wenzhou Chinese–owned Japanese restaurants in the city grew tenfold.

Liu learned the basics of Japanese cooking by working for two months alongside a Chinese chef in Verona, following a common pattern of kitchen-based transmission of simple Japanese cooking skills. Liu only needed to know the basics, such as making sushi rolls and some fish dishes, because most of his dishes, including egg rolls, were bought ready-made from Chinese suppliers. The only fish for the sushi was salmon, which he said Italian consumers viewed as the quintessential fish for Japanese cuisine. The menu included spicy salmon, teppanyaki salmon, thin and fat salmon rolls, and salmon bowls. Osaka had six cooks, including Liu. He and two other Chinese chefs made the sushi and Chinese dishes, while three Pakistani migrant cooks made the salads and assisted the Chinese chefs. The two waitresses were Wenzhou Chinese.

When we interviewed Liu in 2017, competition among Japanese restaurants was skyrocketing. He said that the all-you-can-eat buffet was the most profitable model because there was little food waste, but that it was only possible in smaller markets where local people could not distinguish between Chinese and Japanese food. Despite growing competition, he was happy to run a Japanese restaurant because he felt the fashionable image of "cool" Japanese food complemented his chic clothes and copious tattoos. He swore he would never run a Chinese restaurant because this would make him appear a restaurateur of necessity who could only cook his native cuisine. In contrast, running a Japanese restaurant conveyed status, showing his money, networks, and sophistication. The situation of Osaka illustrates how Wenzhou Chinese chef-owners spread Japanese cuisine deep into Italian regional towns while creating perceptions for consumers of what constituted Japanese cuisine.

Vietnamese Restaurateurs Create Hipster Japanese Cuisine in Berlin

The Japanese-cuisine industry in Germany is ethnically segmented, unlike in France and Italy, where Chinese predominated. Certain Asian ethnic groups were ascendant in specific cities, such as Koreans and Nepalese in Hamburg, Vietnamese in Berlin, and Wenzhou Chinese in cities along the Rhine River. Only in the Japanese expatriate enclave of Düsseldorf do the Japanese remain dominant (see Chapter 3). Here we examine Berlin, which, in the three decades since the reunification of Germany, has transformed from a politically divided, poor, and isolated city during the Cold War to Germany's rising culinary global city. The change was fueled by young expatriates, designers and architects, and immigrant entrepreneurs attracted to the city by its low cost of living. Due to the relative lack of free-spending financial professionals compared with other global cities, Berlin's culinary scene has focused on high-concept, low-budget restaurants. These are places to be enjoyed as much by the eyes as the mouth. This sector had many innovative fusion eateries owned by migrants, including Japanese restaurants run by non-Japanese Asians, most prominently Vietnamese.

This boom started in the 2000s as Vietnamese migrants founded Japanese restaurants serving US-style sushi rolls. The Vietnamese in Germany were centered in the eastern regions, especially Berlin. They included dispatched workers stranded after the collapse of the (East) German Democratic Republic in 1990 and refugee "boat people" who had come to West Germany in the 1970s and 1980s. Most began in the restaurant business by opening pan-Asian restaurants, but in the 2000s, some switched to more profitable Japanese cuisine. Some operated Japanese restaurants next to their Vietnamese restaurants (similar to Fuzhou Chinese in the United

States running Chinese and Japanese restaurants with the same kitchen), which were also increasing in the capital.[63] These Vietnamese-run restaurants drew on a culinary infrastructure of a Vietnamese-run food market, migrant labor from Vietnam typically arriving in Germany on family reunification visas, and capital investments from successful pioneers.

A few of these Vietnamese pioneers in Japanese gastronomy learned sushi making in Berlin's first sushi shop, Sushi Berlin, founded in the 1990s by American migrant Tilmann Zorn. He had learned sushi making in Kobe, married a German woman, and then moved to Berlin. His second venture was Sushi Sachiko, Germany's earliest revolving sushi bar, featuring sushi plates on small wooden junks floating past customers on a circular stream of blue water. When we visited in 2017, Zorn's son ran the business, and the sushi chefs were all Vietnamese, by then common in the city. The young Zorn still made his father's traditional *nigiri* sushi even though he said customers were bored with it. "They want these fancy rolls piled high with different things and a jalapeno pepper on top," he said dismissively. However, newer Vietnamese-run sushi shops pushing US-style sushi rolls were driving the market.[64]

The most visible Vietnamese purveyor of Japanese cuisine was The Duc Ngo. Dubbed the "Duke of Kantstrasse" by the media, Ngo initiated fashionable Japanese cuisine for young hipsters.[65] He was born in Hanoi in 1974 to an ethnic Chinese father and a Vietnamese mother who fled persecution during the 1979 Sino-Vietnamese War. Eventually, they came to Germany. Ngo went to a local high school and majored in Japanese studies at Berlin's Freie University while working part time at Zorn's Sushi Berlin in the 1990s.[66] After learning sushi craft, he got a lucrative job as a sushi chef in Moscow. In 1999, he returned to Berlin and opened Kuchi, a Japanese restaurant serving US-style sushi rolls on Kant Street, an upscale avenue long known for Japanese and Chinese restaurants. "We were the first hipster-Asians," Ngo told the *Berliner Zeitung.*[67] Not content with purveying cheap eats, Ngo tried his hand at fine dining restaurants, partnering with leading chefs and restaurateurs, and appeared on the German television series *Kitchen Impossible.*[68] Ngo's success points to the increasing presence of second-generation Asian migrant entrepreneurs in Europe's Japanese restaurant scene.

Ngo attributed his success to three factors.[69] First was his constant travel to spot new culinary trends.[70] Upon seeing sushi rolls, ramen, and *izakaya* (pubs) on a trip to the United States, he introduced them to Berlin. Kuchi became the first Japanese eatery to offer US-style Philadelphia and California rolls, served alongside Ngo's inventions, such as Mr. Miyagi's Pizza Sushi, made with fried sushi rice, salmon, chili mayo, cucumber, salmon, and masago. The second factor was his eye for design. "The ambiance of a restaurant is always the opener," Ngo told a reporter. "The feel-good factor is just as important as the food."[71] His avant-garde interiors, created by the Korean Berliner designer Huanjing Kim, featured bold colors and eye-catching artworks that departed from the familiar (and tired) Japanese wood and bamboo interiors. The third was his local knowledge. He explained to a reporter, "As an Asian, you are either cigarette-mafia, Chinese restaurant owner, or nail salon operator, and I didn't want to be any of them. I grew up in Spandau, and always closely observed what motivates the people here, because that also motivates me. So I know Berlin better than restaurateurs from elsewhere."[72] Yet despite Ngo's desire to counter Asian stereotypes, he arguably created a new one—namely, the Vietnamese chef-owner of Japanese restaurants—and spawned many imitators selling roll sushi alongside Vietnamese dishes.

Other Japanese restaurants in Berlin have developed along this hipster line to produce unique dishes. Papa Nô, located in the trendy Friedrichshain district, proclaimed "Creative Eating" on its signboard. One menu item was "Nô-Ritto," a sushi burrito inspired by the manager's trip to the United States. It consisted of a sizable deep-fried sushi roll stuffed with vegetables and meats. The Vietnamese orthography notwithstanding, Papa Nô was named for Japanese Nōh theater and decorated with painted images of Nōh theater masks. Its website extolled the invented legend of Papa Nô, described as a chef for a traveling Nōh troupe who cooked delicious dishes from locally available ingredients for the performers. Another hipster innovation was a Japanese-cum–Southeast Asian cuisine for the growing vegan market. Veganz, a Vietnamese chain, specialized in vegan sushi under its English slogan in blunt Berlin style, "Who the f—k needs fish." Its outlets served Southeast Asian fusion vegan offerings with "Vietnamese" dishes that included coconut curry and other Thai flavors.[73] These reasonably priced restaurants appealed to young Berliners through their offbeat, edgy marketing.

By the late 2010s, however, successful Berliner Vietnamese restaurateurs were upscaling to appeal to the wealthier young professionals moving into the rapidly gentrifying central city. One strategy emphasized the Japanese authenticity of their dishes by hiring Japanese cooks and managers. These Japanese were often lifestyle migrants who had come to Berlin for a change

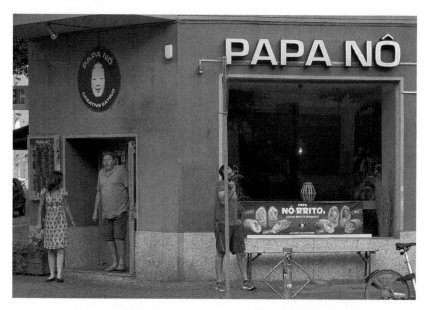

FIGURE 5.4 Owned by a second-generation Vietnamese German entrepreneur, Papa Nô in Berlin featured the fusion Nô-Ritto, a sushi burrito filled with beef, fish, or vegetables, on its menu. (Photo by James Farrer, July 28, 2019)

of pace or to pursue personal interests.[74] One such establishment was Iro Izakaya, also in Friedrichshain. Its Japanese manager, who came to Europe to pursue artistic interests, had worked in Western and Japanese restaurants in Paris and Berlin for twenty years. He was disdainful of the Vietnamese-run restaurants, noting that their vegan sushi lacked basic Japanese ingredients. Iro Izakaya offered standard Japanese *izakaya* fare, such as yakitori and *agedashi tofu* (fried tofu in broth), alongside imported *sake*. Still, it embraced the offbeat and colorful design typical of the hip restaurants that other younger second-generation Vietnamese were opening in Berlin.[75]

Ethnicized Practices of Hiring and Competition in Restaurant Ethnoscapes

By the 2010s, Japanese restaurants in Europe had become multicultural ethnoscapes of Asian and non-Asian owners, chefs, and staff. During our fieldwork, people often made such comments as, "Chinese work harder than Bangladeshis," and "Filipinos tend to argue with the boss."[76] Such ethnic and racial stereotyping highlights the racialized employment practices in the Japanese restaurant industry based on race, ethnicity, or putative ancestry.[77] During visits to dozens of restaurants in Europe (as in the United States), we observed that people with specific attributes seen as indicating a certain ethnicity or race typically worked in particular jobs. Jamal, a Palestinian Danish owner of a sushi restaurant in Copenhagen, explained how these racialized hiring practices reflected customer expectations. Jamal started his business with a Japanese partner, whose presence behind the sushi counter was meant to convey authenticity, but they parted ways when Jamal discovered the partner was incompetent and a "pot head." Henceforth, Jamal ensured that an Asian man was always the sushi chef standing behind the counter. "People don't like to eat at a restaurant and see an Albanian or a Turkish guy making the pizza," he told us. "They want the Italian guy making the pizza. Even if the Turkish guy is better than the Italian, but you know, you have this thing. Yeah, and people also want to see an Asian guy behind the counter making the sushi." The actual Asian ethnicity or nationality did not seem to matter as long as the man fit customer expectations for a Japanese (or East Asian) appearance. When we visited his restaurant in 2012, the sushi chef was a Mongolian man, who had learned to make sushi from a Japanese woman at another restaurant. White employees served as front-of-house staff, such as the attractive blond Armenian female host who greeted customers. As for himself, Jamal commented that no one wanted to see a Palestinian owner because "they think we should be selling kebabs."[78] A similar example of racial profiling involved hiring Nepalis to work in Japanese restaurants in Hamburg because employers saw them as more Asian in appearance than some other migrants.[79]

Another ethnicized practice was "putting a face" on the competition. This could be seen in Copenhagen, with a sizable Japanese dining scene and multicultural chef-owners. In 2014, we spoke to Lucas, a white sushi chef working at a moderately priced sushi restaurant near the city center. When asked about ownership of local restaurants, he said that there were about 180 Japanese restaurants in the city, with Danes (white) and Chinese each owning a third, and the rest run by Cambodians and other groups.[80] He opined that white Danish chefs made the best sushi in town. To back up this claim, he noted that one such chef, Pepi Anevski, a chef at Umami, a French-Japanese fine dining eatery in Copenhagen, had won the top prize for the most creative chef at the World Sushi Cup two years in a row (2013 and 2014).[81] This had inspired Lucas to upgrade his skills to qualify for the competition. He then said that Chinese chefs offered low-quality sushi, which he attributed to their lack of commitment to the craft of sushi. "If they suddenly found that they could make more money in the construction business, they would go there," he said.[82] His concern was that their low-quality sushi, which undersold his, lowered customers' expectations of sushi in Copenhagen. This stereotyped view of Chinese restaurateurs also expressed the concern of high-end sushi chefs to preserve the economic "value" of their Japanese food against inexpensive pan-Asian buffets and US-style sushi rolls.

In southern Europe, we encountered similar discourses of competition. We spoke to a Japanese chef in Rome who had observed the transformation of the Japanese restaurant scene in the city over twenty years. It had become dominated by Wenzhou Chinese running all-you-can-eat buffets of pan-Asian factory-made food represented as Japanese cuisine. He said, "When I came to Rome [in the 1990s], there were only three or four Japanese restaurants. This was before everyone came in and started opening up the all-you-can-eat restaurants like crazy. They are destroying the image of Japanese food."[83] His comments reflected the fear of Japanese chefs and restaurateurs that they had lost the advantage of their culinary skills and ethnic capital because customer expectations of Japanese cuisine were increasingly shaped by Wenzhou Chinese restaurateurs.

Race, ethnicity, and gender are complex issues manifested differently in each region described in this book. However, there are some patterns in racial and ethnic boundary making in Japanese restaurant ethnoscapes in Europe and North America. The dominant theme is defending the value of the "Japan brand" and a fear of its being cheapened by low-status entrants. In particular, early Japanese entrants into the market complained of the cheapening of the brand by competing ethnic entrepreneurs, often Asians from poorer countries, such as Vietnam, Nepal, or Afghanistan. White chefs, particularly those with fine dining credentials working in pricey restaurants, were seen as keeping the Japan brand valuable because they were part of the ethnic majority and not associated with the poor migrants with low social status. These high-end chefs, in turn, performed their own "boundary work," drawing a new line—one based less on ethnicity and more on cultural capital—between themselves and those who did not take Japanese cuisine seriously. In both types of boundary work, migrant ethnic "intruders" were often blamed for cheapening the image of Japanese food.[84]

Japan-Centered Culinary Mobilities in East Asia

The Japanese restaurant boom that started in Japan's neighbors—China, Korea, and more recently Vietnam—in the late 1990s took a different course from that in the United States and Europe. These Asian countries have their own historical interactions with Japan and cultural closeness in cuisine, as described in Chapter 2. Many chef-owners of Japanese restaurants in these countries had lived in Japan, where they acquired food skills and then became restaurateurs or chefs after returning to their countries. Their circular (or return) migration differs from the more indirect patterns of culinary knowledge transmission common in Europe and North America.[85] As a result of circular migration, Japanese-cuisine restaurants in East Asia more closely resembled those in Japan, with fewer US-style sushi rolls and knife-twirling teppanyaki chefs and a greater focus on how things were done in Japan.

There were two modes of circular migration. The most common involved young people, first Chinese and Koreans and then Vietnamese, acquiring Japanese food skills by working part time in restaurants in Japan. They mainly came to Japan to study in language schools or colleges and worked part time in restaurants to earn money. From the 1990s, the number of international students in Japanese universities and vocational schools increased dramatically. The Japanese student visa allowing up to twenty-eight hours of weekly part-time work made them a cheap labor supply for the service industry (though, in practice, many students worked many more hours than allowed).[86] In particular, large chain restaurants in Tokyo and other cities increasingly depended on these students for low-cost labor. Despite mainly doing menial tasks, the students acquired enough food knowledge to prepare passable Japanese cuisine back in their home countries.

For these young people, another channel for learning Japanese culinary skills was enrolling in culinary schools. These schools started in 2002 to bypass the traditional system of lengthy apprenticeships in restaurants. Among the first was the Tokyo Sushi Academy, offering three-to-four-month courses that focused on specific dishes. While this approach rankled the sushi restaurant industry in Japan, it met the need to quickly train sushi chefs for the rapidly growing chain sushi restaurants in Japan. Soon, some schools started four-to-eight-week English-taught courses to meet the rising demand from non-Japanese due to the growth of Japanese restaurants around the world. As of 2018, there were 136 culinary schools, with

20 offering courses in English for international students. The number of students, while relatively small, grew quickly from 178 in 2010 to 424 in 2017. They came almost entirely from Asia, with Chinese accounting for 31.6 percent, South Koreans for 24.3 percent, Vietnamese for 15.6 percent, and Taiwanese for 14.6 percent.[87] Upon completing their studies, some stayed in Japan to help fill the domestic labor shortage, while others took their skills back to their countries.[88]

Another migration mode in developing Japanese cuisine in East Asia was the rural-to-urban migration of culinary workers (also common in Africa and South Asia). This mode is not unique to Japanese cuisine but rather characterizes most restaurant work in developing countries, in which rural people move to cities and get service jobs with low barriers to entry. In some cases, they acquired culinary skills in Japanese cuisine and then moved to smaller urban markets to establish Japanese restaurants. Thus, this mode of return migration furthered the spread of Japanese restaurants to second- and third-tier cities.[89] We discuss these patterns in the Chinese context, though similar patterns also can be found in Korea, Vietnam, and other countries in the region.

Circular Migration between Japan and Top-Tier Chinese Cities

The reintroduction of Japanese restaurants into China in the 1990s described in Chapter 2 was led by Japanese chefs and restaurateurs. However, by the 2000s, Chinese chefs and restaurateurs were ascendant in all but the highest-end sector. Given the greater familiarity of Chinese with Japanese cuisine, midmarket Japanese restaurants in China were much more varied than in other countries. Top-tier markets, such as Shanghai and Tianjin, discussed in this section, replicated the specialty restaurants in Japan—from yakitori stalls to high-end *yakiniku* (grilled meat) restaurants. At the same time, they innovated in ways that echoed Chinese restaurant practices in other markets, most notably the all-you-can-eat format that had proved successful in North America and Europe, albeit with table service rather than buffet-style self-service. And while *nigiri* sushi was more popular in China, midmarket restaurants also offered US-style sushi rolls with creative ingredients and designs.

In the 2010s, these midmarket restaurants spread rapidly in Chinese cities. One impetus was Japan's Great Kanto earthquake on March 11, 2011. According to Naoki Inoue chief editor of *Jin,* a lifestyle magazine for Japanese expatriates in Tianjin, the earthquake and associated danger of nuclear radiation spurred many Chinese studying in Japan to return to China. However, back in China, they could not find suitable work, so some started Japanese restaurants, capitalizing on their experience of part-time restaurant work in Japan.[90] We observed this circular migration during our fieldwork in Tianjin, a port city and second-tier market in Northeast China (see Chapter 2). After 2011, the pre–World War II Japanese concession area became a vibrant district of Japanese restaurants. The small street-level fronts of the surviving two-story Japanese colonial buildings were atmospheric settings for Japanese restaurants, and rents were relatively affordable. In 2012, the *izakaya* Okachimachi opened on Wuchang Road, the heart of the historic concession, with many restaurants soon following.

An example of one such restaurant is Yilu Yixian Jujiuwu (One Stove and Fresh Food Izakaya), opened in 2015 by the Zhangs, a couple in their thirties, who studied Japanese literature at university. Mr. Zhang, a Tianjin native, went to Japan in 2000 to study finance at a university in Fukuoka City, Kyushu, and worked part time for six years at a restaurant. Upon graduating, he worked in a Japanese company in Tokyo for four years and then returned to Tianjin as a team manager for Toyota's Tianjin branch. Mrs. Zhang, from Xinjiang Province, often visited Mr. Zhang in Japan, married him when he returned to Tianjin, and started an event planning company. She never lived in Japan but appreciated its culture, often visiting with her friends and children. Even though the husband and wife both had full-time jobs, they started the restaurant to supplement their income. Mrs. Zhang's mother oversaw the business during the daytime, and the husband and wife came every evening after work, staying until closing time shortly before midnight.

The Zhangs' establishment imitated the cozy *izakaya* they had known in Japan. The staff wore T-shirts with the restaurant logo printed in Japanese and greeted customers with shouts of "*irasshaimase*" (welcome). There was seating for seventeen diners, either at tables for two or at the counter by the open kitchen. After diners were seated, a waitress served cups of tea and *teshibori* (hot towels) in transparent plastic bags while Japanese songs on MTV emanated from a wall television. The menu featured fresh seafood while including such familiar dishes as sashimi, yakitori, sukiyaki, *gobo maki* (burdock rolls), *yaki onigiri* (grilled rice balls), and *tamago yaki* (omelets). A hired chef prepared fish dishes at the counter while Mr. Zhang made chicken dishes in the hot kitchen. He was proud of the Fukuoka-style dipping sauce (*tare*) that he learned at the restaurant in Fukuoka. Despite using the same recipe as in Japan, he admitted that the Chinese-sourced ingredients imparted a slightly different flavor (an oft-voiced complaint of Japanese chefs in China). He also cooked other Japanese dishes that he learned from instructional videos on the internet and the Japanese cookbooks his wife bought on her frequent visits to Japan.[91] Yilu Yixian Jujiuwu became one of the top-rated Japanese restaurants in Tianjin, encouraging the Zhangs to open a Japanese bar (*sakaba*) at a different location.

Other returnees found work as chefs, such as Chef Liu at Tianjin's higher-end Jiuxi Japanese Restaurant.[92] His story illustrates the rising status of work in Japanese restaurants as returned migrants with university degrees became chefs. Chef Liu spent six years in Japan studying at a language school and then graduated from Tsukuba University. While there, he worked part time in restaurants, learning the basics of Japanese seafood preparation and cooking. Upon returning to China, he became a chef because it paid more than working at a Japanese company branch. At Jiuxi Japanese Restaurant, he was one of several cooks cutting the sashimi. The restaurant was started as an investment by a businessperson who had never been to Japan, had no familiarity with Japanese culture, and rarely visited the establishment. However, it employed two Japanese, the general manager and the head chef, who was a middle-aged Japanese woman with a decade of experience in the city's high-end Japanese restaurants. Five Chinese chefs, including Liu, were from Tianjin, and one came from Qingdao. Large numbers of returned migrants, as illustrated by Liu and the Zhang couple, ensured familiarity with the norms of Japanese food preparation.

Rural-to-Urban Migration and the Spread of Japanese Restaurants in China

Rural-to-urban migrants, far more numerous than the returned migrants just discussed, provide the low-cost labor that is the backbone of the restaurant industry in major Chinese cities. In all restaurants we studied in Shanghai, upward of 90 percent of employees at independently owned restaurants were rural-to-urban migrants.[93] A 2015 survey of twenty-four Japanese sushi restaurants in Shanghai found that all their head chefs were rural-to-urban migrants, mainly from Anhui Province, a less affluent region to the west of Shanghai. Most had acquired Japanese culinary skills by working under Japanese chefs in the city.[94] These patterns are replicated in other large Chinese cities, including Tianjin.

An example of such migrants was Lin, head chef at the Qianhe Japanese Restaurant, a popular restaurant in Tianjin.[95] When we interviewed him in 2016, he was thirty-four years old. A decade earlier, he had left his town in Hebei Province, North China, for a restaurant job in Shanghai arranged by a hometown compatriot. He learned to cook Chinese food there but switched to Japanese cuisine because of the higher demand. While working in Shanghai and Beijing, he learned to cook types of Japanese food, including sushi, tempura, and ramen, that were the requisite knowledge for a chef to be hired. Even though his time working under a Japanese chef was relatively short, it gave him credibility as a chef of Japanese cuisine to find work. The restaurant's five chefs and other staff came from poorer areas in Anhui, Henan, Hebei, and Shandong Provinces. He said that the growing number of Japanese restaurants in Tianjin made chef jobs easy to find, and salaries were rising. Lin noted proudly that he earned over CNY 8,000 a month, about the average wage of an office employee.[96] Due to the shortage of trained chefs, Lin was often asked by chef friends at other Japanese restaurants to assist at large events or cover for a chef who suddenly quit. This extra work augmented his salary and industry ties. He noted that the circulation of chefs through Tianjin restaurants was homogenizing the taste and appearance of their dishes.

Due to China's low birthrate, it was becoming increasingly difficult to find workers in the 2010s. One large all-you-can-eat Japanese restaurant in Shanghai that we visited recruited its workers from the far western province of Yunnan, a region that had supplied little labor to the city's restaurants only a few years earlier. One young waitress we spoke with said that her mountain village in Yunnan had no restaurants at all and that despite Shanghai's high cost of living, working in the city was the adventure of a lifetime.[97] Some young rural-to-urban migrant chefs dreamed of opening their restaurants. Their career strategy was to work in first-tier cities with the highest-paid service sectors and the best kitchens for culinary training. However, it was extremely difficult for migrant restaurant workers to obtain the urban household registration in first-tier cities for access to social services, including schooling for children.[98] Therefore, after working in first-tier cities for a few years, many chefs took their newly acquired culinary skills to second-tier cities, such as Tianjin (still a large, prosperous city), or even third-tier cities. It was easier in these lower-ranking cities to obtain urban household registration to bring their families, and business costs were lower.

By the end of the 2010s, these culinary migrants had carried Japanese restaurants into smaller Chinese cities around the country. An example of one such restaurant is Hanakitsune (Flower Fox) in Kunshan, a city forty-four miles from Shanghai, which we visited in 2016. It was cofounded by an energetic twenty-one-year-old female migrant from Shenzhen and staffed by migrant cooks from various Chinese cities, all of whom had learned to cook Japanese food in Shanghai. Its dishes resembled those of Japanese restaurants in Shanghai, focusing on sushi, sashimi, and US-style rolls, with several Western-style cooked dishes for those less inclined to raw food (the most popular dish was roast beef, said the owner). Strictly speaking, this migration pattern was not circular, as migrant cooks often moved to lower-tier cities rather than returning to their rural hometowns. Nevertheless, the mobilities of the culinary migrants spread Japanese restaurants and culinary skills more broadly in society.[99] We have only documented these patterns in China; however, our preliminary fieldwork in Vietnam, which also sends many students to Japan, suggests similar patterns. These culinary mobilities in East Asia of circular migration through Japan are distinct from the ethnic succession pattern in North America and Europe and the rural-to-urban migration in developing economies further from Japan.

Japanese Culinary Migrations in South Asia and Africa

In the early twenty-first century, developing economies in Africa and South Asia became new frontiers of global expansion for Japanese restaurants, even though most people in these lower-income regions could not afford to dine in one. The 2010s saw a growing number of Japanese restaurants opening to serve urban elites, expatriate professionals, and tourists, as well as some cheaper eateries for the small but growing middle class. Japanese restaurant sectors began in capital cities, with subsequent expansion to resort areas (as seen in Tofo, Mozambique, in Chapter 4). This section views this process in Colombo and Nairobi, the capitals of Sri Lanka and Kenya. Both countries were considered middle-income countries by the World Bank, with Sri Lanka being more prosperous.[100]

The patterns of culinary migration bringing Japanese cuisine to South Asia and Africa show similarities to those in China, as well as differences. As in China, the earliest Japanese restaurants typically were opened in major cities in the 1980s by Japanese companies (or by restaurateurs with close corporate ties) to serve Japanese corporate expatriates. They were few and pricey until the global boom in Japanese cuisine came to these regions. The principal culinary intermediaries who popularized the cuisine in these markets were non-Japanese entrepreneurial migrants. In countries with extensive outbound educational and labor migration, such as Sri Lanka, many return migrants became Japanese restaurateurs. In other places, such as Kenya, the intermediaries have been non-Japanese Asian entrepreneurs, primarily Chinese or Koreans. Also, rural to urban migrants were the main culinary labor force, just as in China. However, a key difference from China is that, while earlier migrants had acquired their culinary knowledge in Japan, by the 2010s, subsequent ones acquired it in other markets, from the Middle East to Australia.

Culinary Mobilities in Colombo, Sri Lanka

Colombo, in 2019, was the largest metro region in Sri Lanka, with a multiethnic population consisting of the country's main ethnic groups (Sinhalese, Tamils, and Muslims), a European community, a rapidly growing Chinese community, and a small Japanese community of 365 people and offices of eighty-nine Japanese firms.[101] The foreign-cuisine restaurant scene reflected the confluence of colonialism, geopolitics, tourism, business, and diplomacy that has shaped the city. Chinese was the most popular foreign cuisine, and there were high-end European, Indian, and Thai restaurants; German beer halls; American fast-food outlets; and Japanese restaurants. Our fieldwork (in 2019) found thirty-eight Japanese restaurants.

The earliest Japanese restaurants were started in the 1980s by Sri Lankans who had culinary experience in Japan and were encouraged by the Japanese government and financially supported by Japanese businesses to open upscale dining establishments. This situation echoes the cooperation among Japanese business and government elites described in Chapter 4 to open elegant Japanese restaurants overseas to serve Japan's economic expansion from the 1960s to the early 1990s. At that time, Japan was Sri Lanka's largest provider of development assistance for building infrastructure. The restaurants gave Japanese expats in trading and construction companies and

Japanese officials from the embassy and overseas development agencies a place to eat familiar foods, hold events, and entertain Sri Lankan counterparts. At the same time, the restaurants introduced Sri Lankan elites to Japanese cuisine as a refined dining experience.

The first restaurant was Sakura, an *izakaya* that opened in 1983. Its founder was Jayantha Kumara, a chef who graduated from the RKC Culinary School in Kochi, Japan. He invited Japanese teachers from the school to come train the staff at Sakura and 80 percent of the clientele were initially Japanese expatriates and tourists.[102] The second restaurant was the more upscale Ginza Hohsen, founded in 1987 at the five star Hilton Colombo hotel by Richard Balasuriya, who was conversant in Japanese. He was a Sri Lankan Ministry of Agriculture official who had studied in Japan as part of its development aid to Sri Lanka. In the early 1980s, with the backing of a Japanese restaurant company, he founded a Sri Lankan restaurant in Tokyo's upscale Ginza shopping district to promote Sri Lankan cuisine and *arrack* (distilled coconut spirits). He then returned to Sri Lanka to open Ginza Hohsen with the collaboration of the same company, eventually becoming the restaurant's sole owner.[103] Ginza Hohsen was patronized by the Japanese embassy, which commended Balasuriya (in 2015) for "his dedication to promote fine Japanese cuisine in Sri Lanka."[104] Eventually Sakura and Ginza Hohsen relocated to more central locations in Colombo and still operated in 2022.

After the Sri Lankan civil war (1983–2009), foreign investment began flowing back into the country and dozens of new Japanese restaurants opened. They were concentrated in the mid-market and fine dining sectors and increasingly attracted local diners and Chinese tourists and business people who were now flocking to the country. Their ownership was diverse, including Sri Lankans, Chinese and Filipino owners, Singapore-based private equity firms, and Japanese investors and franchisers. The Sri Lankan owners and chefs were mostly circular migrants who gained exposure to Japanese cuisine in countries other than Japan and then returned to Sri Lanka to open restaurants. Their restaurant offerings reflected global trends, such as ramen, conveyor-belt sushi, and Japanese–Southeast Asian fusion menus, as well as *kaiseki* (formal cuisine) fine dining.

Some of the upmarket new establishments were opened or staffed by Sri Lankan professional chefs, who trained in Sri Lanka and then left during the civil war to work abroad. Their British-style service training in Sri Lankan culinary and hostelry schools and fluent English enabled them to find chef positions in top Japanese and other restaurants in the Middle East. After the war ended, they returned to Sri Lanka to work as chefs in new upmarket Japanese cuisine restaurants. They introduced menus that followed the global trend of menus featuring US-style rolls and fusion dishes with fanciful names. While such fare was characteristic of midmarket eateries in the United States and Europe, the restaurants targeted Colombo's growing number of upper-middle-class professionals, businesspeople, and foreign tourists. After all, a sushi roll costing LKR 850 (USD 5) was still an extravagance in a country where the median monthly salary was LKR 142,000 (USD 800), and a filling meal at a local curry and rice shop cost only LKR 250 (USD 1.4).[105]

One returnee chef was Chamila Lakshitha Perera, a 1996 graduate of the Ceylon Hotel School who had worked abroad in the Maldives, Abu Dhabi, and Dubai in the kitchens of Nobu (discussed in Chapter 8) and other acclaimed Japanese restaurants. His extensive experience working under chefs from Japan taught him how to prepare traditional Japanese and fusion dishes, the aesthetics of presentation, and the importance of hygiene. In an interview with us, he recalled his strict training under Japanese chefs. At his first job in the Maldives, the chef was "very traditional and had learned to make Japanese dishes from his father and grandfather at home."[106] Another chef made Perera write down all the recipes he had taught him over five years. Perera returned to Sri Lanka in 2013 to be the head chef at the newly opened upscale Mizu, located in the Ramada Hotel, where he supervised several Sri Lankan chefs and a Japanese sous-chef. His sushi rolls used local ingredients, examples being Dragon Roll, made from deep-fried prawns and avocado topped by a cocktail sauce flavored with Thai spices, and Cheese Maki, which used cream cheese, mango, and pineapple. The spectacular Japanese High Tea was a three-tiered serving of sushi, tempura, *karaage* (fried chicken), fried shrimp, and sweet and spicy chocolates served with Japanese green tea.

Other circular migrants founded mid market restaurants, an example being Bowl'd, which opened in 2018 and featured poke bowl. It was founded by two young Sri Lankans who first ate Japanese cuisine while attending university in Australia. They decided to open a poke bowl restaurant in Sri Lanka for health-conscious young people. Lacking culinary training, they pursued self-teaching through the internet (a phenomenon we saw among chef-owners in other countries). The partners watched YouTube videos to learn how to make bowls, develop a menu, and train their workers in cutting and mixing. They tested the market by doing pop-up restaurants before opening Bowl'd in the center of Colombo. The restaurant was in an old house refurbished as a hostel for foreign guests. It was airy and open, with an outside deck and reggae music playing in the background during our visit in 2019. The menu featured Sri Lankan tastes in fusion bowls. A popular bowl was Tangy Tuna, consisting of mango, green chilies, and passion fruit–drizzled tuna served on a choice of white or red rice, mixed greens, or zoodles (zucchini noodles). The restaurant catered to special diets, including vegan, low-carb, vegetarian, gluten-free, and halal. Dessert bowls had bases of local fruit or granola covered with ice cream or yogurt, while drinks were sweetened with *khitul* (palm tree sap). According to its owners, the clientele was mainly Sri Lankans and young international travelers, but no Japanese.[107]

Many restaurateurs mentioned the opportunities and challenges of running a Japanese restaurant in multicultural Sri Lanka. A key opportunity lay in the abundant low-cost labor from rural migrants coming to Colombo. One of the biggest challenges was obtaining a liquor license in a predominantly Buddhist country where public drinking of alcohol is seen as threatening Buddhist values. Therefore, many restaurants in Sri Lanka had a BYOB policy, although the existence of several *izakaya* and *sake* bars showed that liquor licenses could be obtained.

Transnational and Domestic Migrants in Nairobi

The Japanese restaurant sector in Nairobi reflected the smaller size of Kenya's middle class and lower levels of investment capital compared with Sri Lanka. In 2019, Nairobi had an ethnically diverse population of 4.4 million people, including Indians, Western expatriates, a growing number of Chinese investors, and 783 Japanese nationals (in 2016), many of them foreign aid workers.[108] Restaurants serving Asian foods were relatively novel, aside from long-established Indian and Chinese restaurants. During the 2010s, there was a small boom in fine dining restaurants, especially Italian, catering to wealthy Kenyans and expatriates, and an emerging mid-market restaurant segment.[109] By the time of our fieldwork in 2018, there were about thirty Japanese restaurants in the city—from expensive establishments in guarded expatriate compounds to moderately priced chain outlets in urban shopping malls. Dining in a Japanese restaurant in Nairobi was even more of a luxury for most local people than in wealthier Colombo. A meal at an expensive Japanese restaurant could cost KES 2,000

(USD 18) per person and a set meal in a modest teriyaki chain restaurant about KES 250 (USD 2), while a meal in a small Kenyan eatery cost only about KES 50 (USD 0.50). Still, it was becoming a bragging point among young Nairobians to have eaten sushi.[110]

The best-known and most expensive Japanese restaurants were owned mostly by non-Japanese foreigners, while newer and cheaper ones were run by Kenyans, including chains (see Chapter 6). Many owners were Koreans, including some who came as Christian missionaries, while others were Chinese and Lebanese. Only two restaurants were Japanese owned and managed, Cheka Izakaya and Cheka Ramen (see Chapter 7). Interviewees told us that early Japanese restaurateurs had been scared off by crime, unlike Koreans, who settled down and coped. Customers were primarily non-Japanese expatriates, underscoring how international migration drives the globalization of restaurant cuisine in both production and consumption.

The oldest and most prestigious restaurant in Nairobi was Misono, founded in 1996. Its owner was sixty-year-old Chef Song, originally from Korea and a naturalized Kenyan citizen who spoke fluent Swahili. Misono was located in Ngong, a district with houses of former British colonial settlers, and offered a range of Japanese dishes. The downstairs had three teppanyaki tables, while the more elegant upstairs was for à la carte dining and served sushi, including American-style sushi rolls and sashimi, such as local lobster. Local Kenyan customers favored the outdoor seating area, and there was also a tatami room. The president of Kenya was an occasional patron, which perhaps explained why Misono was the only high-end Japanese restaurant where many patrons were Kenyan. In contrast, the Misono branch at the Mombasa resort area had fewer than 10 percent Kenyan customers.

Song had trained as a French chef and worked in Tokyo. He learned to cook Japanese food as a trainee in Misono, a pioneering teppanyaki steakhouse chain in Japan. In 1986, he came to Kenya to work at a safari park hotel as a French chef, cooking Japanese, Korean, and Chinese cuisine, while teaching cooking at Kenya Utalii College, a leading hospitality and tourism school. Japanese cuisine was unknown when he opened Misono (borrowing his former employer's name), so he served teppanyaki, which newbie Kenyan consumers could readily accept, and later added sushi. He said that the key to success in the local market was serving large portions of grilled meat, an emphasis on volume that we saw in other developing economies and less expensive market segments in Europe and the United States. It was daunting to run a Japanese restaurant in Kenya due to the lack of a sizable fishing industry and Japanese suppliers. Song imported salmon from Norway and eel and fish roe from India.[111]

However, one problem that Song did not face when we interviewed him was a labor shortage. Unlike in North America and Europe, and increasingly China, in Kenya there were many applicants for every job. Song preferred to train workers with no previous experience and spurned university graduates he felt lacked the humility for work in the service industry. He had twenty-eight employees in Nairobi and twenty-four in Mombasa. His head chef had been with him for twenty years. Some chefs had left for other restaurants, which Song saw as the natural flow of the industry. He claimed to have trained over one thousand chefs, who found jobs at restaurants in Kenya and neighboring countries. As the longest-serving Japanese chef in East Africa, he had much status, with many seeking to work at Misono.[112]

One chef trained by Song was David Mureithi from Meru County, over one hundred miles from Nairobi, who worked at a Misono competitor named Ginza. It was owned by Chinese investors and located in an elite neighborhood near the Chinese embassy in a building that housed a Thai-invested casino and Brazilian barbeque restaurant. Ginza featured Japanese and Chinese foods, including teppanyaki, and could serve two hundred diners on its three floors. About half the customers were Chinese, with others being Japanese and Western expatriates and a few Africans. A security guard stood at the restaurant door, typical of eateries patronized by expatriates. David's hero was Chef Jiro, featured in *Jiro Dreams of Sushi,* a documentary about a perfectionist Tokyo sushi master. David proudly told us that Jack Ma, founder of the Chinese internet giant Alibaba, had dined at Ginza and praised his sushi.[113]

The situation of Chef David is typical of restaurant staff in developing countries. While transnational migrant workers staffed kitchens in Berlin and New York, the staff in Nairobi, as in Colombo, were ethnically diverse migrants from poorer, rural regions. In Nairobi, the starting monthly earnings for restaurant workers was about KES 15,000 (USD 150), twice the national average, although still low compared with white-collar salaries. Restaurant work also conferred status to the workers because of the luxurious environments. Chef Song and other foreign restaurateurs focused on training Kenyans since visa difficulties, relatively low wages, and security concerns deterred transnational culinary migrants from coming.[114]

The menus of Japanese restaurants in Colombo and Nairobi would be familiar to diners with experience in New York, Paris, or Berlin. They would note the prominence of sushi rolls featuring salmon farmed in Norway and Chile, and some Chinese dishes. More expensive establishments served fusion dishes, including steaks with Japanese-style sauces. These menus reflected the global Japanese restaurant cuisine that began on the US West Coast in the 1970s, was subsequently popularized by non-Japanese Asian transnational migrants, and conveyed to developing countries through the culinary mobilities described earlier.

The New Migrant Faces of Global Japanese Cuisine

This chapter has examined the mobilities of non-Japanese migrant restaurateurs that have increasingly driven the global expansion of Japanese restaurants from the late twentieth century. In some places, these newer migrants replaced Japanese restaurateurs and chefs (also migrants) who were aging out of the industry. In others, non-Japanese migrants introduced Japanese restaurants into new markets, starting in capital cities and key business centers. To a great extent, the transfer and reproduction of culinary skills happened in the contact zones of kitchens, with exchanges of ideas and techniques among different ethnic and migrant groups. While training under a Japanese chef conferred status and credibility, migrant chefs increasingly were trained by other migrant chefs from their own ethnic groups or of other ethnicities. The workforce thus became more diverse in terms of ethnic background and, to a lesser extent, gender.

In the early years of the global Japanese restaurant boom, most migrant chefs were of East Asian backgrounds, but we also see increasing diversification in this regard. In Hamburg, for example, we found Nepali migrant chefs learning from Korean chefs, and Afghanis learning from Nepalis.[115] In the southern United States, we saw an increasing number of Hispanic chefs manning hibachi tables. And in China, South Asia, and Africa, there was a rapid diffusion of skills to migrants from rural areas in these regions. The growing diversification of the labor force producing Japanese cuisine thus became a major driver of its global popularity.

This diversity of the Japanese restaurant labor force does not mean that ethnic networks were becoming inconsequential, nor that restaurant labor became "de-ethnicized." Ethnic marketing, such as hiring people for their Asian appearance, remained common in many markets. Compatriot ties and personal networks continued to be used for recruiting labor. For these reasons, East Asian migrants retained an advantage as owners and operators of independent midmarket Japanese-cuisine restaurants around the world. At the same time, culinary migrants from East Asia were decreasing in many regions, while more migrants from Central Asia, Latin America, Africa, and other regions began working in Japanese-cuisine restaurants. Finally, a new force for diversification was the routinization of work through corporatization, as described in the next chapter.

Notes

1. Tomomi Endo, *Special Report: Serving Japanese Food to the World, Aided by Health Consciousness Boom* (Japan External Trade Organization, November 2013), https://www.jetro.go.jp/ext_images/en/reports/survey/pdf/2013_11_other.pdf.

2. The statistics were collected by the Japanese Ministry of Agriculture, Forestry, and Fisheries. According to the ministry, there were 117,568 Japanese restaurants in October 2017, a 30 percent increase from 2015, and a fivefold increase from 2006. The number grew most rapidly in Asian countries, which, by 2017, accounted for 69,000 restaurants, or 60 percent of all Japanese restaurants worldwide, even as the increase in Japanese restaurants was leveling off. "Number of Overseas Japanese Restaurants Tops 100,000," Nippon.com, June 15, 2018, https://www.nippon.com/en/features/h00218/.

3. The other cuisines were, in order of popularity, Chinese, Italian, Thai, Korean, French, American, Mexican, Indian, Spanish, Mideast/Arabian, and African. The sample was 2,800 consumers in China, Hong Kong, Taiwan, South Korea, the United States, France, and Italy. See Endo, *Special Report*.

4. Krishnendu Ray, *The Ethnic Restaurateur* (New York: Bloomsbury, 2016), 76–86; Krishnendu Ray, cited in Ana Swanson, "Why So Many of America's Sushi Restaurants Are Owned by Chinese," *Washington Post*, September 29, 2016, https://www.washington post.com/news/wonk/wp/2016/09/29/the-fascinating-story-behind-who-opens-sushi -restaurants-and-why/.

5. In 2020, six out of ten restaurants on the "most expensive" lists in Shanghai and four out of ten in Tianjin were Japanese. James Farrer and Chuanfei Wang, "Japanese Cuisine in Urban Chinese Foodways" (paper presented at the Modern Chinese Foodways Conference, Emory University, April 23–24, 2021).

6. Krishnendu Ray, *The Ethnic Restaurateur* (New York: Bloomsbury, 2016), 62–70; Wilbur Zelinsky, "The Roving Palate: North America's Ethnic Restaurant Cuisines," *Geoforum* 16, no. 1 (1985): 51–72.

7. "Intersectionality" refers to how multiple aspects of a person's identity pattern the discrimination and advantages they experience in society.

8. Krishnendu Ray "Ethnic Succession: A Review Essay," *Food, Culture & Society* 8, no. 1 (2005): 124–131.

9. Consumers may be confusing ethnic backgrounds, such as assuming Chinese employees of a Japanese restaurant are Japanese, or assuming a similarity in the respective cuisines of, for example, China and Japan. We saw both patterns in our fieldwork.

10. See Donna R. Gabaccia, *We are What We Eat: Ethnic Food and the Making of Americans* (Cambridge, MA: Harvard University Press, 1998); Roger Waldinger, Howard Aldrich, and Robin Ward, *Ethnic Entrepreneurs: Immigrant Business in Industrial Societies* (Newbury Park, CA: Sage, 1990).

11. Ujita Norihiko (宇治田憲彦), *Amerika ni nihon shoku bunka wo kaika saseta samuraitachi* (アメリカに日本食文化を開花させたサムライたち) [The samurai who popularized Japanese food culture to the United States] (Tokyo: Sanyo shuppansha, 2008), 185.

12. Ray, *The Ethnic Restaurateur*, 83.

13. Billy Truong (pseudonym), interview by David Wank, August 29, 2011.

14. Dyske Suematsu, "How to Tell a Real Japanese Restaurant," Dyske Suematsu's blog, September 24, 2003, https://dyske.com/paper/786.

15. Chinese migration to the United States increased after the loosening of emigration controls in the People's Republic of China in 1978 and normalization of US-China relations the following year. The Chinese migrant population in the United States grew sevenfold, from 299,000 in 1980 to 2.1 million in 2016. Jie Zong and Jeanne Batalova, "Chinese Immigrants in the United States," Migration Policy Institute, September 29, 2017, https://www.migrationpolicy.org/article/chinese-immigrants-united-states-2016.

16. Kenneth J. Guest, "From Mott Street to East Broadway: Fuzhounese Immigrants and the Revitalization of New York's Chinatown," *Journal of Chinese Overseas* 7 (2011): 24–44; "Fuzhounese in the New York Metro Area," All People's Initiative, December 2009, http://unreachednewyork.com/wp-content/uploads/2012/11/Fuzhounese-Profile-Final.pdf.

17. Robert Ji-Song Ku, *Dubious Gastronomy: The Cultural Politics of Eating Asian in the USA* (Honolulu: University of Hawai'i Press, 2013), 187; Yong Chen, *Chop Suey, USA: The Story of Chinese Food in America* (New York: Columbia University Press, 2014), 150.

18. This section is based on research first reported in David L. Wank and James Farrer, "Chinese Immigrants and Japanese Cuisine in the United States: A Case of Culinary Glocalization," in *The Globalization of Asian Cuisines: Transnational Networks and Culinary Contact Zones,* ed. James Farrer (New York: Palgrave Macmillan, 2015), 79–99.

19. Jennifer Li, interview by James Farrer, July 22, 2012.

20. New York Department of City Planning, *Chinatown Bus Study* (New York: Department of City Planning, October 2009), http://www.nyc.gov/html/mancb3/downloads/cb3docs/chinatown_final_report.pdf.

21. Nelson Oliveira, "Restaurant That Took Share of Waiters' Tips—While Paying Them $3 an Hour—Must Return Money: Labor Department," *New York Daily News,* August 31, 2021, https://www.yahoo.com/news/restaurant-took-share-waiters-tips-174600195.html.

22. Qiankai Li, interview by David L. Wank, February 20 and 22, 2013.

23. Qiankai Li, interview by David L. Wank, February 20 and 22, 2013.

24. Jason (surname unknown), interview by David L. Wank, February 8, 2013.

25. Amy (pseudonym), interview by David Wank, February 6, 2013.

26. Jan Teng, interview by David L. Wank, February 15, 2012.

27. Fieldwork by David L. Wank, February 2013 and February 2017.

28. Michael Frey, interview by David L. Wank, February 10, 2013.

29. Michael Frey, interview by David L. Wank, February 10, 2013.

30. For the historical roots of this practice of hiring ethnically coded staff in the United States see Audrey Russek, "Appetites Without Prejudice: U.S. Foreign Restaurants

and the Globalization of American Food Between the Wars," *Food and Foodways* 19, no. 1–2 (2011): 34–55.

31. "Awards," Wasabi, accessed December 23, 2020, https://wasabiasheville.com/awards/.

32. Fieldwork by James Farrer, July 2012.

33. Hanna Raskin, "Popularity of Japanese Steakhouse a Cultural Phenomenon in South Carolina," *Post and Courier,* May 30, 2018, updated September 14, 2020, https://www.postandcourier.com/food/popularity-of-japanese-steakhouse-a-cultural-phenomenon-in-south-carolina/article_20eb97e2-3d89-11e8-9c61-9f1cdce083ad.html.

34. Hanna Raskin, "Popularity of Japanese Steakhouse;" fieldwork by James Farrer, April 2019.

35. Fieldwork by James Farrer, July 2012.

36. Jennifer Li, interview by James Farrer, July 22, 2012, and April 23, 2019.

37. Fieldwork by James Farrer, April 2019.

38. Matthew Korfhage, "Spicy, Claw-Cracking Chinese Viet-Cajun Boil Is Taking Over Hampton Roads. Here's Why," *Virginian-Pilot,* October 23, 2020, https://www.pilotonline.com/food-drink/vp-db-viet-cajun-boils-20201023-mj4ninxhizdyxonrwir4acqlbe-story.html.

39. Amelia Nierenberg and Quoctrung Bui, "Chinese Restaurants Are Closing. That's a Good Thing, the Owners Say," *New York Times,* December 24, 2019, https://www.nytimes.com/2019/12/24/upshot/chinese-restaurants-closing-upward-mobility-second-generation.html.

40. Jennifer Li, interview by James Farrer, April 23, 2019.

41. Fieldwork by David L. Wank, March 2018.

42. Jennifer Kopf, "Poke Bowls' Prep Puts Lancaster's Chop Sushi on the Cutting Edge," Lancaster Online, August 23, 2017, https://lancasteronline.com/features/food/poke-bowls-prep-puts-lancaster-s-chop-sushi-on-the/article_9466710a-8746-11e7-9ac5-57070d76d49f.html.

43. De-ethnicization is the antithesis of ethnicization, which is drawing organizational and discursive boundaries between people based on such ethnic or racial characteristics as language, skin color, customs, and ancestry. See Marisca Milikowski, "Exploring a Model of De-ethnicization: The Case of Turkish Television in the Netherlands," *European Journal of Communication* 15, no. 4 (2000): 443–468.

44. Marc (surname withheld), interview by James Farrer, September 27, 2019.

45. For a discussion of racism faced by Black sushi chefs in North America, see Urban Diplomat, "Dear Urban Diplomat: How Can I Convince My Racist Boss to Hire a Black Sushi Chef?," *Toronto Life,* April 8, 2015, https://torontolife.com/city/urban-diplomat-hire-ground/.

46. Akihiko Hirose and Kay Kei-Ho Pih, "'No Asians Working Here': Racialized Otherness and Authenticity in Gastronomical Orientalism," *Ethnic and Racial Studies* 34, no. 9 (2011): 1482–1501.

47. Samantha (pseudonym), interview by James Farrer, April 9, 2019.

48. Marisa Baggett, "The Changing Face of the American Sushi Chef," Marisa Baggett's website, October 23, 2008, http://www.marisabaggett.com/2008/10/23/the-changing-face-of-the-american-sushi-chef/.

49. This section is based on research first reported in James Farrer and Chuanfei Wang, "Who Owns a Cuisine? The Grassroots Politics of Japanese Food in Europe," *Asian Anthropology* 20, no. 1 (2021): 12–29.

50. Eriko Arita, "Making the Cut at Sushi Academy," *Japan Times,* October 17, 2010, https://www.japantimes.co.jp/life/2010/10/17/general/making-the-cut-at-sushi -academy. However, restaurant review sites show greater increases of Japanese restaurants, probably reflecting looser criteria in defining a Japanese restaurant.

51. Kato Toshinobu (加藤亨延), "Nihonryōri no mirai wo shisa suru pari no washoku jijō" (日本料理の未来を示唆するパリの和食事情) [Japanese food in Paris suggests the future of Japanese cuisine], Diamond Online, January 30, 2015, http://diamond .jp/articles/-/65913?page=1.

52. Fieldwork by Chuanfei Wang, August 2018.

53. Fieldwork by Chuanfei Wang, August 2018.

54. Fieldwork by Chuanfei Wang, August 2018.

55. Farrer and Wang, "Who Owns a Cuisine?"

56. Chef Kazuki (surname withheld), interview by James Farrer and Chuanfei Wang, February 2, 2017.

57. Antonella Ceccagno, "The Chinese in Italy at a Crossroads: The Economic Crisis," in *Beyond Chinatown: New Chinese Migration and the Global Expansion of China,* ed. Mette Thunø (Copenhagen: NIAS Press, 2007), 115–136. According to government statistics, in 2011 there were 3,955 Chinese-run restaurants in Italy, constituting about 10 percent of all Chinese businesses. Anna Marsden, "Second-Generation Chinese and New Processes of Social Integration in Italy," in *Chinese Migration to Europe: Prato, Italy and Beyond,* ed. Loretta Baldassar et al. (London: Palgrave Macmillan, 2015), 101–118.

58. Gabi Dei Ottati and Daniele Brigadoi Cologna, "The Chinese in Prato and the Current Outlook on the Chinese-Italian Experience," in Baldassar et al., *Chinese Migration to Europe,* 32–34.

59. Francesco Wu, "Marco Hu e l'idea geniale del wok (che dà lavoro anche agli italiani)" [Marco Hu and the brilliant idea of the wok (which also gives work to Italians)], *Milano Corriere,* December 27, 2012, http://lacittanuova.milano.corriere.it/2012/12/27 /marco-hu-e-lidea-geniale-del-wok-che-da-lavoro-anche-agli-italiani/.

60. The restaurant name Osaka is a pseudonym.

61. Fieldwork by Chuanfei Wang, November 2017.

62. The surname Liu is a pseudonym.

63. For Vietnamese chefs, a family reunification visa was easier to obtain in Germany than a work visa, which helps explain the increase of Vietnamese restaurants in Berlin. Ann-Julia Schaland, *The Vietnamese Diaspora in Germany* (Berlin: Deutsche Gesellschaft für Internationale Zusammenarbeit, 2015), 10.

64. Fieldwork by James Farrer, November 2017.

65. Franz Michael Rohm, "Vom Flüchtling zum Gastrom: Der Herzog von Der Kantstrasse" [From refugee to restaurateur: The Duke of Kantstrasse], *Berliner Morgenpost,* March 28, 2016, https://www.morgenpost.de/bezirke/charlottenburg-wilmersdorf /article207304605/Vom-Fluechtling-zum-Gastronom-Der-Herzog-von-der-Kantstr asse.html.

66. Fieldwork by James Farrer, November 2017.

67. Tina Hüttl, "Koch über Gastro-Ideen, Als Asiate bist du Zigarettenmafia, Imbiss oder Nagelstudio" [A cook talks about Gastro ideas: As an Asian you are either dealing cigarettes, or running a snack bar or a nail studio], *Berliner Zeitung,* November 2, 2018, https://www.berliner-zeitung.de/berlin/koch-ueber-gastro-ideen---als -asiate-bist-du-zigarettenmafia--imbiss-oder-nagelstudio--29648196.

68. Kai Röger, "Der Kiez-King," *Der Tagespiegel,* August 14, 2017, https://www
.tagesspiegel.de/berlin/gastronomie-an-der-kantstrasse-der-kiez-king/20174856.html.

69. Fieldwork by James Farrer, July 2019.

70. Röger, "Der Kiez-King."

71. Rohm, "Vom Flüchtling zum Gastrom."

72. Hüttl, "Koch über Gastro-Ideen."

73. Fieldwork by James Farrer, July 2019.

74. See Cornelia Reiher, "Negotiating Authenticity: Berlin's Japanese Food Producers and the Vegan/vegetarian Consumer," *Food, Culture & Society* (2022), DOI:10.1080/
15528014.2022.2076028.

75. Chef-manager Nobu, interview by James Farrer, July 18, 2019; fieldwork by James
Farrer, July 18, 2019.

76. Chef Murata, interview by James Farrer and Chuanfei Wang, October 29,
2017.

77. Racialization is the process by which racial attributes are projected onto social
situations. See Michael Omi and Howard Winant, *Racial Formation in the United
States,* 3rd ed. (New York: Routledge, 2015); and Edna Bonacich, Sabrina Alimahomed,
and Jake B. Wilson, "The Racialization of Global Labor," *American Behavioral Scientists* 52, no. 3 (2008): 342–355.

78. Jamal (pseudonym), interview by James Farrer; fieldwork in Copenhagen by
James Farrer, April 1, 2012.

79. Fieldwork by James Farrer, August 2016. Similarly, informants explained that in
New York City, Nepalis of the Tamang ethnicity were favored in Japanese restaurants
because of their supposedly closer physical resemblance to East Asians than other Nepalis. Fieldwork by James Farrer, September 2019.

80. Lucas (pseudonym), interview by David Wank, June 23, 2014.

81. This event was held by the Japanese food industry and Chiba prefectural government beginning in 2012.

82. Lucas (pseudonym), interview by David Wank, June 23, 2014.

83. Chef Murata, interview by James Farrer and Chuanfei Wang, October 29, 2017.

84. For the concept of "boundary work" in the racialization of social life, see Douglas S. Massey, "Racial Formation in Theory and Practice: The Case of Mexicans in the
United States," *Race and Social Problems* 1, no. 1 (2009): 12–26.

85. George Gmelch, "Return Migration," *Annual Review of Anthropology* 9, no. 1
(1980): 135–159.

86. For the general phenomenon of Chinese student labor, see Gracia Liu-Farrer,
Labor Migration from China to Japan: International Students, Transnational Migrants
(Abingdon, UK: Routledge, 2011).

87. Kyodo News Service, "Foreign Cooks Flocking to Japanese Culinary Schools
amid Boom in Cuisine's Global Popularity," *Japan Times,* June 14, 2018, https://www
.japantimes.co.jp/life/2018/06/14/food/foreign-cooks-flocking-japanese-culinary
-schools-amid-boom-cuisines-global-popularity/.

88. Voltaire Cang, "Sushi Leaves Home: Japanese Food and Identity Abroad," in *Food
Identities at Home and on the Move: Explorations at the Intersection of Food, Belonging
and Dwelling,* ed. Raul Matta, Charles-Edouard de Suremain, and Chantal Crenn
(Abingdon, UK: Routledge, 2020), 19–33.

89. The term "tier" refers to informal rankings of economy and population, not official administrative classification of cities.

90. Naoki Inoue, interview by Chuanfei Wang, March 2017.

91. Fieldwork by Chuanfei Wang, March 2017.

92. Fieldwork by Chuanfei Wang, March 2017.

93. For a discussion of migrant laborers in Shanghai fine dining restaurants, see James Farrer, "Shanghai's Western Restaurants as Culinary Contact Zones in a Transnational Culinary Field," in Farrer, *Globalization of Asian Cuisines*, 103–124.

94. Wang Haofan (王昊凡), "Shanghai no taishū sushiten ni okeru rōkaruka to 'sushishokunin' no seiritu oyobi sono yakuwari" (上海の大衆寿司店におけるローカル化と'寿司職人'の成立及びその役割) [Localization in Shanghai's popular sushi restaurants and the establishment of "sushi chefs" and their roles], *Nihon rōdō shakai gakkai nenpō* 27 (2016): 138.

95. The surname Lin is a pseudonym.

96. Fieldwork by Chuanfei Wang, September 2016 and March 2019.

97. Fieldwork by James Farrer, April 2016.

98. Nalini Mohabir, Yenpeng Jiang, and Renfeng Ma, "Chinese Floating Migrants:Rural-Urban Migrant Labourer's Intentions to Stay or Return," *Habitat International* 60 (2017); 101–110.

99. Fieldwork by James Farrer, September 21, 2016.

100. In 2019, the World Bank classified Sri Lanka as an upper-middle-income country (USD 3,995–USD 12,375), and Kenya as a lower-middle-income country (USD 1,260–USD 3,995); "World Bank Country and Lending Groups," World Bank, accessed January 14, 2020, https://datahelpdesk.worldbank.org/knowledgebase/articles/906519 -world-bank-country-and-lending-groups.

101. "One Japanese National Killed, Four Others Injured as Sri Lanka Attacks Rock Expat Community," *Japan Times,* April 22, 2019, https://www.japantimes.co.jp /news/2019/04/22/national/taro-kono-sends-sympathy-sri-lanka-terror-attacks -amid-report-japanese-among-fatalities/#.XeBg0OnVKZ0.

102. "Sakura Celebrates Two Decades of Authentic Japanese Food," *Sunday Times,* January 18, 2004, https://www.sundaytimes.lk/040118/tv/6.html.

103. Fieldwork by Shayani Jayasinghe, November 2022; "Japanese Ambassador Commends 'Ginza On Edge' Chairman," *Daily FT,* January 30, 2015, https://www.ft.lk /article/385838/Japanese-Ambassador-commends--Ginza-on-the-Edge--Chairman.

104. "Japanese Ambassador Commends 'Ginza On Edge' Chairman," *Daily FT.*

105. Fieldwork by Shayani Jayasinghe, November and December 2019.

106. Chamila Lakshitha Perera, interview by Shayani Jayashinghe, August 3, 2019.

107. Rahaal Balasuriya, interview by Shayani Jayashinghe, July 20, 2019, and April 21, 2020.

108. "Japan-Kenya Relations (Basic Data)," Ministry of Foreign Affairs of Japan, accessed November 29, 2019, https://www.mofa.go.jp/region/africa/kenya/data.html.

109. "Restaurants Thrive as Kenyan's Appetite for Foreign Dishes Grows," *Business Daily,* February 25, 2010, https://www.businessdailyafrica.com/bd/lifestyle/society/restau rants-thrive-as-kenyans-appetite-for-foreign-dishes-grows-1957176.

110. Fieldwork by Purity Mahugu, April 2018.

111. Chef Song, interview by Purity Mahugu, July 13, 2018.

112. Chef Song, interview by Purity Mahugu, July 13, 2018.

113. David Mureithi, interview by Purity Mahugu, April 20, 2018.

114. Chef Song, interview by Purity Mahugu, July 13, 2018.

115. Fieldwork by James Farrer, August 2016.

6 | Fast and Japanese

Corporatizing Japanese Restaurants

DAVID L. WANK, MÔNICA R. DE CARVALHO,
JAMES FARRER, LENKA VYLETALOVA,
AND CHUANFEI WANG

A wave of corporatization that began in the 1970s swept through the global Japanese restaurant industry in the twenty-first century. It was manifested in expanding fast-food chains purveying Japanese dishes—grilled meats, noodles, and sushi—already popularized by individual migrant-owned restaurants, as described in previous chapters. Corporatization further simplified and standardized the dishes and atmosphere of Japanese restaurants, even as "Japaneseness" remained part of the appeal. In North America and Europe, corporatization has reflected the decline of low-cost migrant labor and industry consolidation, with profits increasingly derived from cost efficiencies. In newer markets in Southeast Asia and Eastern Europe, as well as Africa and South Asia, corporatization has been expanding the number of restaurants. And in cities all over the world, corporate systems of Japanese food production and marketing have been increasingly shaping Japanese restaurant scenes.

In contrast to individual-owned restaurants, corporate chains are designed for expansion. They have transferable shareholding, management detached from ownership, and limited investment liability. They expand through chains linked by contractual relationships, with the franchise being the most common. In a franchise, a corporation sells the right to build and operate outlets to franchisees. This shifts expansion risks onto the franchisee while letting the corporation profit from ongoing royalties and fees. In return, the franchisee gets an established brand and business know-how that reduces the risk of business failure. This restaurant form was popularized from 1955 by the US-based McDonald's Corporation, which merged American cafeteria and roadside food culture to change the image of fast food from meals for men on the move to family dining for the suburban middle classes.[1] McDonald's created a scalable business model operating through four principles that the sociologist George Ritzer dubbed "McDonaldization." First, "efficiency" is the speed of food delivery to the customer from a limited menu. Second, "calculability" refers to offering large servings at a low cost. Third, "predictability" is standardizing the product across multiple outlets. Fourth, "control" deskills food preparation into simple steps.[2] Yet despite their McDonaldized operations, Japanese fast-food chains have emphasized the Japaneseness of the taste, quality, and healthiness of their products.

Most Japanese fast-food dishes are Western and Chinese dishes reinvented in Japan and dishes from Japan reinvented abroad beginning in the late nineteenth century. The most popular noodle dish is ramen, the wheat-based "pulled" noodles introduced from China to Japan in the nineteenth century. Popular meat dishes are beef bowl (*gyūdon*), basically sukiyaki over rice that became a fashion in Japan in the Meiji period, and teriyaki beef and chicken popularized in Hawaiian and West Coast Japanese communities. The sushi is primarily versions of the California roll created in the United States after World War II, as well as Hawaiian poke and *temaki* (cone-shaped sushi) created in Brazil. By marketing their dishes as Japanese, the chains came to occupy the "ethnic" fast-food niche of Asian fast-casual, offering better quality than McDonald's but at lower prices than full-service restaurants.

The global Japanese fast-food industry contains both Japan-based chains and indigenous ones, defined as chains originating outside Japan. 1970 was the "year zero" of Japan's modern food service industry, according to Japanese food historian and restaurateur Hirotaka Matsumoto.[3] The first Kentucky Fried Chicken in Japan opened at the 1970 Osaka World Expo, with McDonald's opening next year in Tokyo's Ginza, an upscale shopping area. New chains in Japan emulated the McDonald's model to reach a growing middle class with rising incomes. Soon, cash-rich chains ventured overseas, starting with the United States.[4] Then, from the 1990s, overseas expansion became a survival strategy for corporate chains due to the bursting of Japan's bubble economy and population decline.[5] China became the top overseas market for expansion because of its vast consumer base that valued Japanese products as high quality.[6] When expanding abroad, fast-food corporations from Japan focused on key cities like New York, Shanghai, and Singapore to establish brand recognition. Meanwhile, indigenous chains were started in the 1980s by locally based entrepreneurs creating their Japanese brands. Some were started by Japanese migrants, while others were opened by non-Japanese restaurateurs who had little knowledge of Japan and its cuisine, similar to the independent restaurants described in Chapter 5. The sometimes highly inventive branding by indigenous chains has helped shape the image of Japanese cuisine around the world.

This chapter examines how corporations create chains that embody the seeming conundrum of "fast" and "Japanese."[7] On the one hand, their operations embrace the standardizing principles of McDonaldization. On the other hand, their marketing emphasizes the particular values associated with Japanese food. The first section of this chapter examines the corporate imaginaries of pioneering Japanese and indigenous chains that merged "fast" and "Japanese."[8] The second section focuses on corporate efforts to make their multiple deterritorialized and reterritorialized dishes legible to consumers through simple origin stories. The third section describes strategies of Japan-based corporations to manage their brands across their transnational chains. The fourth section explores how indigenous corporations draw on local knowledge to create brands. The fifth section examines how corporate consolidation and chain expansion in the global Japanese restaurant industry is increasingly driven by holding companies. Among the many chains, we have selected cases that illustrate key processes of culinary mobilities, imaginaries, and politics.

Corporate Imaginaries of Japaneseness

When dining at a restaurant, patrons consume not only food but the experience of the restaurant through its décor, ambiance, and service style.[9] To create this consumer experience, fast-food chains use a total design philosophy that coordinates the architecture, menu, service, and pricing under a distinct logo—what historian John Jakle terms the "place-product-package."[10] This section describes how place-product packages serve as imaginaries of "fast" and "Japanese" cuisine. The following five cases highlight distinct modalities of these corporate imaginaries.

Authenticity: Marketing Original Tasting Ramen at Dosanko

One of Japan's first fast-food chains to expand abroad was Dosanko Ramen, a miso-ramen chain from Hokkaido founded in 1967. In a few years, it had over 1,200 outlets in Japan, and it opened in New York in 1974.[11] Its flagship was in Midtown Manhattan, near the North American offices of Japanese corporations, whose employees were a natural clientele.[12] The timing was auspicious, as cup noodle ramen, recently invented in Japan, had just been introduced to the American market. Dosanko's US operations were managed by Dosanko Foods, Inc. (DFI), a joint venture by three Japanese companies: Nisshin Flour Milling, noodle manufacturer Hokkoku Shoji, and the trading firm Mitsubishi International Corporation. One of DFI's missions was to promote Japanese culture abroad. At the opening of the flagship shop, a Mitsubishi manager explained this mission: "Dosanko contributes to Mitsubishi's image as a marketer of Japanese culture in this country."[13] Cultural promotion extended to the chain's name—Dosanko Larmen. The word "larmen" was a spelling of the word "ramen" intended to make Americans pronounce it the Japanese way.[14]

Reviews of the ramen outlet were generally favorable. In 1974, *New York Magazine* deemed its four ramen dishes—miso paste, soy sauce, spicy curry, and salty butter—to be "terrific" and the "next big thing since cheese Danish." However, the dining experience befuddled the reviewers. They noted that the salty butter ramen "tasted neither salty nor buttery," the interior was "functional," the counter seating was "not the most comfortable," and the service was "friendly, energetic, and sometimes jumbled, but the staff always seems anxious to please."[15] They also observed that American customers did not know how to eat ramen, twirling their noodles around the chopsticks like spaghetti.

The chain's expansion fell short of corporate expectations. DFI managers attributed its difficulties to the lack of localization. In a 1981 interview with a *New York Times* reporter, the only American manager at DFI said, "'Our major problem so far—and it's not being resolved—is that we're not Americanizing. . . . Some of the cashiers can't even communicate in English.' Repetition and misunderstanding may slow takeout and delivery service. 'Answers may seem rude because of lack of English-speaking ability,' explained Mr. McDermott, who is campaigning for more American workers or better trained Japanese."[16] A DFI vice president noted the failure to explain the concept of a ramen restaurant to American consumers. He said that 85 percent of Dosanko's business was during weekday lunch because Americans did not see a ramen shop as a place for dinner and weekend dining.[17] The chain grew to only twenty-seven outlets before shutting down in 1995.

In 2014, the chain again ventured abroad, opening in Melbourne, Los Angeles, and Paris. This time, Dosanko's survival was at stake, having shrunk to three hundred shops in Japan. Its website equated "growth strategy" with "overseas expansion," calling its outlets in Japan a "symbolic" presence in its homeland. A spokesperson attributed the earlier New York failure to Americans' lack of "understanding [of] the essential appeal of ramen." But now, he said, Dosanko's time had come because Westerners saw Japanese culture as "cool." His use of the word "cool" was not happenstance; The chain's overseas foray was helped by the Cool Japan Fund, a Japanese public-private partnership created in 2013 to promote Japanese culture abroad.[18] The noodles were imported from Japan, and its US website proclaimed, "Dosanko's miso ramen strives to retain its authenticity to give homage to Japanese cuisine."[19] The spokesperson noted, "Our Paris shop competes with nearby Japanese eateries run by ethnic Chinese and Koreans. But those places don't compare in regard to quality." The Paris outlet was also very profitable, with customers spending twice what they spent at Dosanko outlets in Japan, and with turnover four times greater.[20]

Glocalization: From Beef Bowl to Anything in a Bowl at Yoshinoya

The beef bowl chain Yoshinoya was a pioneer in localizing its place-product package for overseas markets, now common among Japanese-owned chains. Yoshinoya opened its first shop in 1899 at Tokyo's Nihonbashi fish market, spread after World War II through owner-operated shops, and began franchising in 1968 to spur growth. In 1973, Yoshinoya established a firm in the United States for purchasing beef to supply its rapidly expanding chain in Japan. However, that year the Japanese government suspended beef imports to protect domestic producers hit by rising feed costs. So Yoshinoya USA, unable to ship US beef to Japan, repurposed itself to operate a beef bowl chain. The first shop opened in 1975 in Denver, Colorado, starting a path of overseas expansion resulting in 994 restaurants by 2019, mainly in Asia.[21]

Yoshinoya quickly learned to create dishes adapted to local tastes in overseas markets. In 1982, it made a teriyaki chicken bowl for US consumers who were coming to see chicken as healthier than red meat.[22] Yoshinoya Philippines served a beef stew bowl containing chunks of beef that resembled *adobo,* the national dish, while in Hong Kong diners could order beef and noodles over rice. Yoshinoya Indonesia served dishes with salty and sweet tastes made from halal foodstuffs and beef slaughtered according to Islamic law.[23] Outlets in India featured chicken-oriented rice bowls to accommodate the Hindu proscription against eating beef.[24] Yoshinoya touted its adaptation to local tastes. The chain's US website proclaimed in 2020, "As our customers' tastes have evolved, so have we."[25] The corporation used market surveys to guide menu development and continuously introduced new dishes and seasonal menus.[26]

Localization had to surmount Japanese management practices, as seen in Yoshinoya's Indonesia outlets. The chain first came to the country via a partnership with Hero Supermarket in 1994 but withdrew four years later. According to one study, the failure was due to a lack of menu localization, managers from Japan who did not understand Indonesian culture, burdensome rules from the Japan headquarters, and high overhead costs (due presumably to foods imported from Japan).[27] Then, in 2010, Yoshinoya returned to Indonesia with a new local partner (Wings Group), having learned from its earlier mistake. The management was localized by putting Indonesians in all key positions and reducing communication with the Japan headquarters. The new menu had dishes with Indonesian tastes, such as the Red Hot Chili Beef Bowl, made with locally sourced ingredients, and it catered to local religious sensibilities with halal certification and vegetarian bowls.

Localization extended to the entire place-product package. Overseas outlets replaced the ticket machines and counter seating typical in shops in Japan with walk-up ordering and table service in markets where Yoshinoya was pricey relative to local options. The chain's distinctive orange, black, and white color theme was also localized. Black was replaced by white-gray accents in US outlets for a more modern look. In China, the chain's signature orange color, signifying high rank and spirituality in Japan, became redder, an auspicious color in Chinese culture. The chain also rethought its target customers and physical location. In Japan, most outlets lay on transportation arteries to cater to men. However, in some Asian markets, fast foods were not seen as inexpensive, so Yoshinoya opened in malls for middle-class families. In China, where young people were a core clientele, Yoshinoya concentrated on university, business, and fashion districts in Beijing, Shanghai, and other major cities on the wealthier east coast.[28]

Indigenization: Japanese Fast Food becoming Indonesian at HokBen

HokBen, which opened in 1985, The chain's Japanese cuisine for Indonesia's growing middle class, helping to make it the second most popular restaurant cuisine after Chinese-Indonesian food.[29] It was founded by Hendra

Arifin, an employee of an Indonesian automotive group that partnered with Japanese car manufacturers. Spotting a business opportunity in the lack of Japanese restaurants in Indonesia, he went to Japan to buy licensing rights for Hoka Bento, a takeout lunch box chain. He then developed his company independently from the Japanese firm, which went out of business in 2008.[30] In 2013, the corporation changed its name to HokBen, reflecting the Indonesian habit of shortening names to enhance feelings of familiarity.[31] As of 2019, there were 153 HokBen restaurants in urban areas across the country, all corporately owned and operated. The chain's dishes and signature blended rice were prepared in a central factory kitchen in Jakarta and distributed to outlets via transit stations.[32] Its canary-yellow and red theme, plastic tables, and poster-size wall menus have been likened to McDonald's, although its founding preceded the US chain's first outlet in Indonesia by six years.

HokBen's place-product package was extensively adapted to Indonesian lifestyles and tastes. The chain logo and mascot were two children portrayed in Japanese anime style and wearing *kopiah* (round brimless hat often worn by Muslim males). The food was served in bento boxes but consumed on the premises at tables, fitting Indonesians' expectations of restaurants as places to socialize. Customers ordered food cafeteria-style by moving along stainless-steel sideboards to select dishes, drinks, soups, and desserts, while HokBen's food court outlets served bento boxes. The chain attracted families by having playgrounds and special lunches for children with toys called Kidzu Bento and by catering birthday parties. Many menu items had Japanese names, such as Takoyaki Mentai and Ebi Furai, but strong Indonesian tastes. Local ingredients were used to make the food halal while also deepening the local taste. For example, mirin and soy sauce, which contain alcohol due to the fermentation process, were replaced by sambal chili sauce and other flavors.[33] One blogger even described the dishes as "Indonesian *gorengam,* which are fried snacks coated in flour batter and served in sweet or savory flavors that can be eaten alone or as a main meal. The names of the food sound Japanese enough, but the foods are not recognizable in Japanese cuisine. They are completely different."[34] HokBen's signature dish was Ekkado. The menu described it as "delicious petite quail eggs coated with processed shrimp meat and wrapped with tofu skin, cooked with deep frying methods." The Japanese sounding name "ekkado" combined the English word "egg" with the Indonesian word "*kado,*" meaning "gift." Although the chain patented Ekkado as its creation, it was similar to the Chinese dish money bag wonton (*zha huangjin fudai*).[35] Some menu items were, in fact, Chinese-Indonesian, such as Shumay Steam and Shrimp Roll.

As the first mover of Japanese food in the country, HokBen occupied a distinct niche for consumers as comfort food. Indonesian students we interviewed who were studying abroad expressed a longing for HokBen dishes. One student studying in Japan said that eating at HokBen was among the first things she and her friends did upon returning to Indonesia.[36] The indigenization of HokBen's fare was also reflected in the decision in 2018 by Garuda, the national airline, to provide inflight HokBen meals. However, this provoked a backlash among business-class customers who saw the meals as down-market. Quite possibly, these travelers had developed a taste for sushi and other more "authentically" Japanese dishes that became widely available in Jakarta and other Southeast Asian cities in the 2010s.[37]

Postmodernism: Doing *Kaizen* at Wagamama

Another pioneering indigenous chain was Wagamama, founded in London in 1992, which helped make Japanese fast food hip for the youth market. The restaurant was the brainchild of Alan Yau, son of Chinese immigrants from Hong Kong who ran a Chinese takeout shop in Norfolk. Wagamama's menu exposed young non-Asian UK diners to ramen, as well as Japanese curry. Of particular note, Wagamama introduced innovative cost-cutting measures that it called *kaizen,* the Japanese management philosophy, even as its menu broke with established Japanese culinary principles. In a 1994 interview, Wagamama's chief interior designer called the chain "the creation of a postmodern culture in eating." "'It was quite obvious to us,' he says, ('us' being the four bright twentysomethings—two English and two Japanese—who formed Wagamama Ltd in 1992) 'that there was a gap in the British market. Anybody who had lived in Japan would have recognized it instantly. Apart from a need for good, cheap, healthy fast food, the British had not yet developed the concept of commercial design. Wagamama is supposed to be more subliminal than McDonald's—the concept is far more complex than the red-and-gold arches.'"[38] By 2020, Wagamama had 212 restaurants, including 151 company-operated outlets in the United Kingdom, 6 joint ventures in the United States, and 55 franchised outlets in Europe and the Middle East.[39]

The décor was upscaled from McDonald's-like Formica tables and loud colors to a stylish modernism of wood furniture and brick walls with black and gray accents, illuminated by overhead spotlights. Wagamama helped change the perception of eating ramen from a quick, solitary meal to social dining. Customers sat facing each other at long tables. Yau called his restaurant a "noodle canteen" rather than using the standard term "noodle bar." Dishes were touted for their healthiness to counter the view of fast food as starchy and oily (although some were, in fact, deep-fried). They were prepared by unorthodox mixes of Japanese cooking techniques, including deep-frying, simmering, vinegaring, grilling, sautéing, steaming, and dressing. "This may not be the most authentic Japanese cuisine, but we have never claimed to provide that kind of food," declared *The Wagamama Cookbook* in 2004.[40] As the chain's reputation grew, it began selling pan-Asian dishes. Regarding a curry dish, a reviewer wrote, "Called firecracker prawn ($15), it proved to be a stir fry of bell peppers, onions, and crustaceans, like something from a Chinese carryout menu. Though pleasantly spicy, it bore no resemblance to curry—Japanese, India, or otherwise. Which made us think that eating at Wagamama requires a certain level of culinary cluelessness to be enjoyed."[41]

Wagamama shrewdly integrated its innovative operations into its Japanese imaginary by playing on stereotypes about the sublimeness of Japanese technology and traditional culture. The operations brought together several innovations in the fast-food sector. First, service people took orders on handheld computers that transmitted them directly to the kitchen (point-of-sales technology).[42] Second, the menu replaced the concept of the "appetizer" with "sides," thereby destabilizing the meal sequence so that dishes could be served to customers when ready, irrespective of any particular order. Third, each dish was prepared at its own station in the kitchen to be served when ready. Fourth, ingredients for cooking a dish were pre-prepared so that the skill of cooks was probably only that of a short-order cook in a diner. The chain referred to these operations by the Japanese word "*kaizen*," a term used by the Toyota Corporation in the mid-twentieth century to refer to continuous small improvements by front-line production personnel to reduce costs and improve quality. It described its operational analytics, which integrated surveys, assessments, interviews, and text mining, using the Japanese verb "*satoru*"—"to know"[43]—a word connoting the Zen Buddhist concept of sudden enlightenment (*satori*).[44]

A Failed Imaginary: Fast Steak Hits a Cultural Wall

However, not all "fast" and "Japanese" novelties were a hit, as illustrated by Ikinari Steak. The chain invented the "fast steak" restaurant using innovative cost-cutting measures, including stand-up dining, to offer high-quality steak at lower prices than mainline steak houses. Started in 2013, the chain grew in a few years to forty-six shops in Tokyo and three hundred nationwide, reportedly due to repeat patronage of "big-eating men."[45] In 2017, the chain opened its first overseas outlet in New York's East Village. It named its signature dish "J-Steak," a sign of corporate confidence in its place-product package of Wagyu steak, low prices, and a casual setting. However, in 2019, the chain shuttered its by then eleven US outlets. Its failure overseas provides a perspective on the conundrum of "fast" and "Japanese."

Fast steak was the brainchild of Kunio Ichinose, who started a teppan-yaki restaurant in suburban Tokyo in the 1970s. Upset that his chefs did not follow instructions, he replaced them with an electromagnetic cooker that rapidly heated an iron plate to 500 degrees and retained the heat. The meat was served almost raw on these hot iron slabs for customers to cook to their satisfaction. In 1994, he launched the Pepper Lunch chain, touted as the "original Japanese Do-It-Yourself Teppan restaurant." Its signature dish was a mound of rice surrounded by the customer's choice of meat in a heated iron bowl. Customers cooked it while mixing in the chain's trademark pepper paste. Over time, menu offerings expanded to steak, pasta, curry, and sukiyaki, while the chain grew to two hundred outlets in fifteen countries, mostly in Asia, by 2020. Ichinose capitalized on his meat know-how by founding Ikinari Steak in 2013. The word "Ikinari" means "suddenly," signifying a customer's joy at the swift appearance of a steak in front of them. The menu was a pared-down selection of steaks served with a side of corn and a choice of salads. Customers specified the weight of the steak, and it was served raw on a sizzling iron plate. Service was minimal as the standing counters held the silverware and sauces. The main skill required of cooks was cutting, enabling the chain to hire retired or part-time cooks at lower wages.

Initial reviews of the New York outlet praised the meat quality while highlighting a cultural disconnect that was the chain's undoing:

> If you love steakhouse quality steaks but hate—uh—sitting, America's latest
> Japanese restaurant import, Ikinari Steak, may prove to be your new favorite

eatery. . . . Overall, the concept certainly sounds good for a novel experience, but whether it will appeal to an American audience over the long haul may be more interesting to follow. Pricewise, Ikinari Steak offers a significant discount over a traditional steakhouse . . . but [that] also doesn't make Ikinari Steak a suitable replacement for, say, grabbing a burrito bowl. Not that it is supposed to, but when meals sometimes only last about 30 minutes, a different sort of cost-benefit analysis kicks in.[46]

Business stagnated. The chain adapted to American food culture by replacing standing solitary dining with group seating, but the layout remained unsuitable for social dining. A senior executive acknowledged that Ikinari Steak did not fit American food culture. He said, "The American way to eat steak is buying it at a supermarket to eat at home, or going to a high-end restaurant."[47] Nor did Japanese fast steak suit East Village diners' view of Japanese food as healthy, trendy, and artisanal.[48] In short, the wrapping of a familiar food in a fast Japanese culinary imaginary did not always work, especially for an item like steak, which US consumers thought of as neither particularly fast nor Japanese. The failure of Ikinari Steak raises the issue explored in the following section—namely, how Japanese-cuisine fast-food chains represent their dishes outside Japan.

Representing Deterritorialized and Reterritorialized Dishes

The fast-food chains serve deterritorialized and reterritorialized dishes that accrue the meanings of the cultures and cuisines of various places. Most corporations make their signature dishes "legible" to patrons by eliding some aspects of their entangled travels to fashion a streamlined story of their link to Japan. First, we examine how chains from Japan represent their dishes in markets outside Japan. Next we discuss how indigenous chains represent the links to Japan of dishes "invented abroad."

Japanese Corporate Reterritorializations of Fast-Food Dishes

Most corporations based in Japan simplify the non-Japanese origins of dishes connected to multiple places. One way is to represent a dish as Japanese. This was done by Gyu-Kaku, a *yakiniku* (grilled meat) chain founded in 1996 that grew over the next two decades to seven hundred shops in Japan and outlets in over a dozen countries. *Yakiniku* was invented in Japan in the 1940s to cook offal. The dish was often considered Korean in Japan because it resembled *kalbi* (grilled ribs) and *bulgogi* (barbecue), it was served with kimchi, and Zainichi Koreans typically ran restaurants serving the dish.[49] However, the corporation calls its product "Japanese BBQ" in the overseas markets where it has expanded since 2007. For example, the chain's US website touts its "authentic Japanese *yakiniku* (grilled meat) dining experience where customers share premium cooked meats over a flaming charcoal grill, while sipping on Japanese sake, *shōchū* (distilled spirits), and frosty cold beers."[50] Gyu-Kaku websites in some countries claim the meat comes from Japan.[51]

Many corporations represent their signature dishes as East-West hybrids. For example, Mos Burger imparted Japanese flavors to the American hamburger, such as teriyaki sauce and rice buns, introduced in Japan in 1973 and 1987, respectively. Outside Japan, the company chose product names that highlighted connections between its hamburgers and Japan, including Wasabi Beef Burger, Tokyo Chicken Burger, and Sushi Burger.[52] Hybridized Japanese-Western pastries also became increasingly popular around the world. Beard Papa's was founded in 1997 to sell matcha cream puffs and other hybrids. By 2020, it had six hundred shops, two-thirds of them abroad. Its Canadian website told the chain's origin story of a friendly bearded pastry chef near Osaka who created cream puffs for neighborhood children that he then brought to the world.[53] Its Chinese site touted the "delicious puffs brought from Japan by Papa Beard."[54] Its US website said, "We began in Japan . . . and are committed to bringing you a pastry that is super *oishi!* (delicious!)."[55]

A further style of representation is emphasizing a country of origin other than Japan. This could be seen at Saizeriya, an Italian diner chain founded in 1967 in Chiba Prefecture, which expanded to over 1,000 outlets in Japan by 2013 and 411 overseas shops, mainly in Asia, by 2020. The corporation used an Italian-themed place-product package in all of its domestic and international outlets, including a logo with a red, green, and white European coat-of-arms and the words "Ristorante e Caffè." Its overseas websites touted its "authentic Italian cuisine" (Australia) and "long tradition . . . of Italian food culture" (Singapore) even though menus contained some hybrid dishes, such as Mentaiko Flavour Shrimp & Broccoli and pizzas with corn and mayonnaise toppings.[56] Such an origin story was rare among Japanese corporations, possibly because it did not capitalize on the value of the "Japan brand."

Also less common is representing the complexities of a dish's transnational entanglements. Go! Go! Curry depicted the multiple origins of its curry dish with a raconteur's delight. The chain was founded in 1997 in Kanazawa, Ichikawa Prefecture, expanding overseas to New York in 2007. The first shop, near Times Square, featured the chain's characteristic bright yellow and red colors and gorilla logo, *noren* (curtains) with the chain's name in Japanese, wall clocks set to New York and Tokyo times, and menu items in English and Japanese. The chain's US website recounted the complexities of its "authentic Japanese curry," including its British and Indian origins and status as a comfort food for Japanese people. Additionally, it explained the chain's name: "Go Go" is the number five in Japanese pronounced twice, which represents the number fifty-five on the baseball uniform of New York Yankees superstar Hideki Matsui, who hails from Kanazawa, which is why the dish is called "Kanazawa curry" in Japan.[57] While such a jumbled origin story more accurately depicts the entanglements of the chain's curry, it makes it difficult tell a story of its "Japaneseness" that consumers can easily understand. Therefore, corporations rarely represent the cultural complexities of their dishes.

Localized Branding of Teriyaki in the United States

The case of teriyaki on the US West Coast illustrates how indigenous chains reterritorialize dishes by representing them as products of locales outside Japan. Such representations may have begun in the 1960s when Japanese soy sauce giant Kikkoman marketed its Hawaiian Teriyaki Sauce to Americans as the product of Japanese migrants in Hawai'i who sweetened the traditional soy-based sauce with pineapple juice.[58] While its origins in Hawaiian pineapple plantations may be apocryphal, teriyaki in Seattle had a characteristic syrupy sweetness. According to Seattle food critics, the city's first teriyaki shop was Toshi's Teriyaki, opened in 1976 by Japanese migrant Toshihiro Kasahara. Seattle writer Naomi Tomky described the dish: "The meat, traditionally chicken thighs slippery and brown from marinade, gets slapped on a hot grill. The high heat caramelizes the sugars, crisping the meat and leaving it with a crunch of barely burnt soy on the outside. Sliced into bite-size pieces, it's served fanned out across a molded mound of white-as-snow rice, the sauce seeping down between the grains. The salad, like the meat, is sweet and crunchy, the iceberg lettuce and slivers of carrot and cabbage reminiscent of coleslaw, with only the rice vinaigrette separating it from old-school American picnic fare."[59] Another food writer noted that the dish's taste differed from teriyaki's "subtle sweetness" in Japan. "In Seattle, subtlety gets short shrift. Cooks sweeten with white sugar and pineapple juice. They thicken with cornstarch and peanut butter."[60]

The rise and fall of the dish's popularity traced Seattle's transformation from a blue-collar to a high-tech city. It began as a cheap meal for workers, migrants, and students served in utilitarian shops "with fluorescent lights overhead and neon signs glaring from smudged storefront windows."[61] Soon, there were teriyaki burgers and teriyaki corn dogs, with migrant shop owners adding Korean garlic and ginger, and Vietnamese lemongrass flavors. By the early 2000s, about one hundred independently owned shops sold teriyaki, and it was served in sports arenas, Hawaiian restaurants, and steak houses. From this peak, the number declined to about sixty shops in the 2010s as gentrification drove up rents and displaced working-class patrons. The new tech professionals flocking to the city spurned teriyaki. Tomky observed, "The simple dish doesn't fit the narrative of the shiny, new city. Teriyaki shops—dirty and run-down—aren't listed on any hot lists of where to eat in Seattle."[62] Instead, the professionals wanted the "authentic" Japanese restaurants seen in other West Coast cities. Seattle pundit Knute Berger suggested that the dish had become so absorbed into the city's foodways that it was no longer considered Asian. "Seattle likes to talk about local foods, about ridiculous things like fiddlehead coulis," Berger said. "Seattle yuppies love the idea of going to some obscure Chinese place for dim sum but won't dare tell you that they eat chicken teriyaki. Those places are so much a part of the streetscape that we can't even see them."[63]

Yet even as it declined in its namesake city, Seattle teriyaki was gaining popularity elsewhere. We will examine two chains that variously represented the dish. One chain was Teriyaki Madness, which opened in 2003. It represented teriyaki as an iconic dish of Seattle, similar to the Philly cheesesteak and Chicago deep-dish pizza, which also began as high-calorie, tasty meals for working people. Its website proclaimed, "Some people say you can take the sea out of Seattle, but you can't take out the teriyaki. Well, we proved them wrong."[64] The chain first opened in Las Vegas to gain national exposure to tourists from around the country and expanded by franchising. The outlets had an industrial theme, perhaps evoking Seattle's industrial past, with red and gray colors, concrete floors, and high-top tables for socializing. By 2018, there were 150 outlets, mostly in malls in third-tier cities. Another representation was the upscale Glaze Teriyaki, founded in

2010 as a "fine casual" restaurant. The website declared its teriyaki to be "efficient Japanese-influenced fare . . . [from the] culinary scene of the Pacific Northwest," made with artisanal principles, such as "small batch teriyaki-sauce."[65] The chain expanded to trendy districts in New York, Chicago, and San Francisco. Its outlets conveyed the environmental ethos of the Pacific Northwest through interiors containing recycled wood and green plants. Thus, at Glaze Teriyaki, Seattle-style teriyaki became a stylish regional cuisine for urban professionals and hipsters, the very consumers spurning it in its city of origin.

Making *Temaki* a National Dish in Brazil

Some deterritorialized dishes are represented in national images other than Japan's. An example is *temaki* in Brazil. *Temaki* is cone-shaped sushi regarded as home cooking in Japan but considered a Brazilian dish in Brazil. In the 1980s, the dish moved from the dining tables of Nikkei Brazilian families to restaurants. This movement occurred with the arrival of the US sushi bar fashion in Brazil, creating a broader demand for sushi. Nikkei Brazilian chefs began to open sushi bars and included *temaki* on the menus. Their adaptations to Brazilian tastes by using such local ingredients as chives, bacon, fried kale, leek, *biquinho* pepper, mango, and even Doritos made the *temaki* very successful. One popular and inventive version was the *temaki de coxinha* that mimicked the beloved Brazilian *coxinha* snack of chopped chicken meat coated in batter and deep-fried. In the 1990s, the growing vogue for *temaki* merged with the US fast-food model in a new type of chain restaurant specializing in *temaki* called *temakeria*. The first *temakeria* was said to be Temaki Bar, which opened in São Paulo in 1992.[66] In the 2000s, the emergence of chain *temakeria* spread *temaki* widely in Brazil. This reflected demand from young diners and the growing middle class, who wanted to eat trendy Japanese food by dining out but on modest budgets. By 2020, there were over a dozen national *temakeria* chains and many regional chains with outlets in storefronts and shopping malls. The largest chain was Makis Place, which opened in São Paulo in 2006 and grew to 140 outlets nationally in a decade, including several in the United States.[67] Furthermore, *temaki* became so popular that it was even sold in bakeries and stores at gas stations.

Chefs and media outlets have made various claims about the "Brazilianness" of *temaki*. One claim concerns the dish's localization. Chef-owner

Ricardo Yoshikawa (see Chapter 8) said, "The types of *temaki* found here are a Brazilian creation, fit to the Brazilian taste, and even to the Brazilian market. On average, cheaper but still carrying an aura of an original Japanese dish. . . . A date at a *temakeria* is a dream for many young people from the outskirts of São Paulo."[68] Another claim emphasized the difference between *temaki* in Brazil and Japan. Cecilia Nagayama, the owner of Japanese restaurants in the Nagayama Group, explained, "*Temaki,* as offered here, is a Brazilian dish. There is no similar product in Japan, and here it is consumed as fast food, something like the conveyor-belt sushi in Japan. Young people, with lesser means, consume it as a Japanese dish, even though what is offered here has no resemblance to the *temaki* found in Japan. In Japan, it is a homemade dish. . . . Brazilians recreated *temaki,* giving it local colors and flavors. It is almost a national dish that doesn't have much to do with what is consumed elsewhere." While acknowledging that Brazilian diners may be unaware of *temaki*'s history, Nagayama said they considered it Japanese cuisine in Brazil. "*Temaki* has become a must-have menu item, and Brazilians would find it very odd not to find them in any Japanese food menu; it is a Brazilian creation."[69] Yet another claim for *temaki* as Brazilian is based on the local origins of the *temakeria* restaurant form. For instance, an article in the mass-circulation newspaper *Otempo* described the *temakeria* as "a genuinely Brazilian invention, which follows the contemporary trend of healthy fast food."[70]

By the 2010s, *temaki* had spread to all market levels. Chain *temakeria* used inexpensive ingredients and deskilled labor to offer large portions cheaply. Some served up to forty types, including barbecued meat, cheddar cheese, Nutella, and strawberry with hazelnut cream. (US-style sushi rolls used similar production methods, offering varied options through substitutable ingredients.) The fish mainly was salmon, appearing in many styles, including cubed with mayo and scallions, and seared with a blowtorch. *Temaki* also appeared on the menus of mass-market Japanese restaurant chains, such as Makis Place. Its menu offered one hundred *temaki* options, along with US-style sushi rolls, ceviche, and poke bowls. A single *temaki* was large enough to be a meal, such as the Big Makis wrapped in an entire sheet of nori.[71] The flavors were strong to ensure tastiness. "Imagine how bland it would be to eat a roll of rice, seaweed and salmon," opined *Otempo*.[72] The *temaki* offered in higher-end Japanese restaurants, such as those of the Nagayama Group, were modestly sized and used a greater variety of seafood, including tuna, shrimp, eel, scallops, and *ikura* (salmon roe).[73]

While temaki appeared with Japanese names on menus in Brazil, in Brazilian restaurants abroad, names were often written in Portuguese to emphasize a connection to Brazil. An example is Temakinho, specializing in Japanese-Brazilian and Peruvian cuisine, including *temaki,* ceviche, and Nikkei poke. Founded in Milan in 2012 as a partnership between two Brazilians and an Italian, it grew to nineteen tropically themed outlets in Italy, France, Monaco, and the United Kingdom.[74] The menu's two top *temaki* specials had Brazilian place-names: Noite Paulista (Night in São Paulo) mixed seared amberjack, breaded shrimp, mango, cucumber, sesame seeds, flying fish roe, and teriyaki sauce, while Foz do Iguazu (Iguazu Falls) contained raw amberjack, breaded shrimp, avocado, guacamole, crushed nachos, and salsa ceviche. However, the manager of the Rome outlet told us that the best sellers were US-style rolls, including the Philadelphia roll with cream cheese and the Mexican roll with protruding nachos.[75]

The Politics of Authenticity in Poke

Corporate representations of dishes can precipitate culinary politics of authenticity. An example is poke, a dish from Hawai'i that became a global fad in the mid-2010s. Food scholars have described it as a precolonial dish of cubed raw fish, salt, and seaweed that merged with rice, fish, and flavorings brought by Asian migrants, especially Japanese laborers, who began coming in the late nineteenth century.[76] In Hawai'i in the 1970s, this marinated fish and rice dish moved from homes and ethnic Japanese food stores (delis) to supermarkets and restaurants. From 2010, it became a food fashion on the US mainland, probably starting in Los Angeles. Many of the new poke bowl restaurants used the production method popularized in the 1990s by the Chipotle Mexican Grill, a pioneer fast casual chain. This entailed using higher-quality ingredients and organizing dishes on the menu by categories, such as base (starch), proteins, toppings, and sauces that customers selected according to their tastes and dietary needs. Like McDonaldization, Chipotlization involved deskilled labor (mostly chopping and mixing) and a limited menu that gave the appearance of many choices, but did not require a hot kitchen, further reducing costs. Restaurateurs jumped into the market, from entrepreneurs with no culinary training to corporations seeking scalability. According to Yelp, poke restaurants in the United States grew from 67 in 2012 to 1,811 six years later.[77] By the mid-2010s, poke bowl restaurants could be found in the Japanese food scenes of many cities worldwide, and the dish entered the menus of existing Japanese-cuisine restaurants. The food fashion was built on a novel combination of Chipotlicized production (although some delis in Hawai'i had done this) and blended Japanese-Hawaiian culinary representation.

While acknowledging poke's Hawaiian origins, mainland chefs and restaurateurs often suggested its "Japaneseness" in representing it to consumers. For example, Sweetfin, a chain started in San Diego in 2013, described poke on its website in 2020 as follows: "Each culture does it differently: Japan has sushi and sashimi, Latin America has ceviche, Italy has crudo and Scandinavia has gravlax. Hawaii has poké. We fell in love with poké after visiting the Hawaiian Islands. Fresh, healthy and delicious, poké took all of the best components of sushi and put them in an easy to eat container."[78] Even as this statement acknowledged poke's Hawaiian origins, it assured customers that it was just a deconstructed version of the familiar sushi. Sweetfin's celebrity chef Dakota Weiss dubbed it "the next generation of sushi" in an interview with the mass-circulation *People* magazine.[79] Chefs, food writers, and menus usually described it in terms of other Japanese dishes (e.g., *chirashizushi* [scattered sushi], *donburi* [rice bowl dish]) and tastes (e.g., umami, yuzu). Mainland chefs also changed the dish to make it more Instagrammable. Whereas in Hawai'i the fish pieces were darkened by marinating and mixed with rice when served, mainland chefs arrayed sashimi-grade fish and raw vegetables on top of the white rice to make a strikingly colorful dish. In these ways, corporations emphasized Japaneseness to make poke legible to US diners. This representation accords with the logic of fashions, discussed in Chapter 4: a trendy "new" product is acceptable to consumers because it resembles the existing "old" one.

The absorption of poke into the mass market engendered authenticity claims. One concerned changes to the spelling of "poke" so that mainland Americans would pronounce it the Hawaiian way as "POH-keh." Hawaiian food blogger and chef-owner Mark Noguchi explained, "Poke is a word—poké and poki are not. It would be like if I didn't know how to pronounce your last name and said, screw it, and changed it around. You don't just change a word to sell it better."[80] Such discussion in the media pushed some chains to change their names to avoid the bad publicity of cultural appropriation (thus, Sweetfin Poké, mentioned earlier, changed its name to Sweetfin). Another authenticity claim was linked to concerns about the sustainability of fish stocks, an issue that has increasingly embroiled sushi in the twenty-first century. The claim was that whereas poke traditionally used near-shore fish, poke restaurants influenced by global sushi culture served endangered deep-sea fish, such as ahi tuna. Noguchi wrote, "If these franchises take on Chipotle proportions, they run a risk of disrupting the [food] chain even more so."[81]

The case of the poke bowl also provides a window into authenticity claims for dishes that are acknowledged as hybrids. The claims did not invoke purity with Japan as the touchstone (see Chapter 5) but rather centered on the appropriate acknowledgment of the dish's transnational entanglements. Yet the claims still hewed to the general logic of authenticity claims: debasement of the dish was attributed to the failure of outsiders (non-Hawaiians) to use traditional ingredients and preparations. As examined next, the representation of signature dishes is intertwined with a chain's management strategy and capitals.

Brand Management in Japanese-Owned Chains

From a business perspective, culinary imaginaries are a brand and the primary repository of a firm's economic value. For Japan-based chains, maintaining consistency in the brand may become more difficult as brands spread to other countries. This section shows there is no singular or most efficient way to maintain a brand. Instead, corporations take diverse approaches toward ownership and management, reflecting their imaginary of Japaneseness and how they value consistency.[82]

Flexible Management at Ajisen

Ajisen Ramen, one of the most prolific ramen chains, shows how corporations may pursue different control strategies, each tailored to specific overseas markets. The chain's founder, Tanxiang Liu, was born in rural Taiwan in 1925, when the island was a Japanese colony. He arrived in Japan in the 1940s, became a Japanese citizen named Takaharu Shigemitsu, and worked in ramen shops. In the 1950s, he helped create Kumamoto ramen, featuring a whitish pork-based broth, called *tonkotsu*, that included fried garlic and black sesame oil, topped with wood ear mushrooms and boiled egg.[83] In 1968, he opened an eight-seat noodle shop in Kumamoto, adding beef and chicken to the broth to reduce the pork odor. The lighter taste attracted female diners, who typically spurned ramen joints as places for men to grab a high-calorie meal. In the early 1970s, he set up Shigemitsu Industry to run a noodle factory for his growing chain that began operating under the Ajisen name. The chain spread nationally, with its logo of a smiling cartoon girl holding a red and white bowl of ramen, and ventured abroad in 1994.[84] Over the next twenty-five years, the chain expanded to 75 outlets in Japan and 787 shops in fifteen countries.[85]

The global expansion of Ajisen has relied on Chinese people as both partners and consumers. The most important country is China, where Ajisen began in 1996. The country's 716 outlets constituted 86 percent of all Ajisen outlets in the world in 2019.[86] Shigemitsu Industry held a minority share in Ajisen China, giving it a stake in this valuable market. In the United States, the first Ajisen restaurant opened in Chinatown, New York, in 2001, as franchises owned by locally based Chinese, a pattern seen in most outlets in Western countries. As a result, Ajisen's customers in Western countries were predominantly Chinese. Similarly, patrons were mainly of Chinese descent in Southeast Asian countries, including places with religious restrictions on pork eating.[87] To ensure brand standards, Shigemitsu Industry screened potential franchisees through a fourteen-stage process that required them to tour the corporate facilities in Japan.[88] Additionally, the corporation asked franchisees to monitor the quality of dishes in their outlets by cooking and serving in them.

The head of Ajisen Ramen China was Daisy Poon, who possessed the local knowledge and connections for the competitive Chinese market. She had worked as a food trader in the 1980s and 1990s, buying foodstuffs in China, processing them in Shenzhen, and exporting them through Hong Kong. As competition increased, she looked for new opportunities and learned about Ajisen Ramen. At the time, there were no Japanese ramen shops in China, and she felt that the white pork broth, reminiscent of Chinese-style noodle soups, and the shops' clean style would appeal to Chinese consumers. So she negotiated an exclusive franchise for China, Hong Kong, and Macau and the right to subfranchise in China due to the large size of the market. Before opening outlets, she established a supply network of factories and kitchens, drawing on her knowledge of food processing and access to cheap labor and raw materials. By 2019, Ajisen China had four factories making noodles and soup ingredients, a pig farm, six central kitchens, and smaller satellite kitchens for delivery service. Additionally, Poon's franchise contract let her develop new products for the China market, such as packaged noodles. These products were created in two Ajisen research

centers that included staff sent from Japan by Shigemitsu Industry to ensure the "Japanese taste."[89] In 2019, Poon bought franchise rights to open
Ajisen ramen shops in international airports worldwide, starting in Rome
and Helsinki. A bowl of familiar Ajisen ramen may have been welcome for
many Chinese and other travelers transiting these airports.

In other countries, Ajisen franchisees were holding companies, a business form discussed later. An example is Singapore-based Japan Food Holdings Corporation, founded in 1997. It held the Singapore franchise for
Ajisen Ramen and other Japanese fast-food eateries, including Menya
Musashi, discussed shortly, and subfranchise rights in Southeast Asian
countries. In Singapore, it operated twenty Ajisen outlets and more than
thirty outlets of other brands. They were all supplied by a central kitchen in
Kampong Ampat (also called KA Foodlink), a dedicated food factory
built by the Singapore government for the food packaging, catering, and
manufacturing companies.[90] Ajisen's large size gave it clout with real estate developers to get lucrative sites in shopping malls, highlighting the need
for fast-food chains from Japan to find well-connected local partners.[91] Thus,
Shigemitsu Industry, Ajisen's parent company in Japan, maintained standards by a variegated ownership structure. For Singapore, it sold franchise
rights to a local franchisee, which developed its manufacturing and distribution centers for the noodles. In China, Shigemitsu Industry took a minority stakeholder position to ensure brand consistency in its most
important market.

Central Command at Ippudo

Ippudo exerted centralized control of brand consistency through outreach
from headquarters, supervision by globally mobile managers, and directly
owned flagship outlets, while permitting some localization. It was founded
in Fukuoka in 1985 by Shigemi Kawahara, whose fame in televised ramen
competitions in the 1980s and 1990s drove the popularity of pork soup ramen in Japan. In 2008, Ippudo established its first foreign outlet in New
York's Little Tokyo, the trendy culinary district described in Chapter 3. This
flagship outlet pioneered Ippudo's trademark ramen restaurant concept.
While the typical Japanese noodle bar had a counter and functional interior
for a quick meal by solo diners, East Village Ippudo encouraged customers
to linger over *sake* drinks on dates and family birthdays.[92] Upon entering
the restaurant, customers could enjoy Japanese alcohol and fusion appetiz-

ers at a bar and then move to the dining room with table seating and expensive wood furnishings under a high ceiling with spotlighting. The menu had far more alcohol options than a typical ramen shop. This upscale dining was reflected in the prices, with ramen bowls costing twice that in Japan. The outlet was a big hit, receiving a Michelin star the following year, the first ramen eatery so awarded. By 2017, there were 130 Ippudo outlets in Japan and 65 in Asia, Australia, Europe, and North America, with a target of 300 overseas outlets by 2025.[93]

The New York outlets, with the deepest international experience, were the center of Ippudo's global operations. Their managers were Japanese expatriates who provided links to Japan and traveled to help launch new outlets worldwide.[94] Ippudo expanded to a country by establishing a corporate-owned flagship restaurant there to maintain standards and supervise franchisees. However, despite the company's tight control over operations, franchising was necessary, as there were not enough Japanese managers locally, and those sent from Japan and New York were unfamiliar with local food regulations and suppliers. For example, Ippudo Australia ran corporate-owned outlets in Sydney and Melbourne, while its outlets in Perth and Auckland were run by the franchisee Papparich, a Malaysian food and beverage corporation operating fast-food chains in the Asia-Pacific region. In Ippudo Australia, four Japanese expatriates managed operations, while other employees were locally hired. In Sydney, Japanese on working holiday and student visas were a large share of the employees.[95] However, the staff were all locals in lower-income markets, such as the Filipino staff at Manila Ippudo.[96]

Ippudo's corporate headquarters sought consistency across the chain while permitting some localization in specific markets. This approach was expressed in its motto, "Expand to the 'global' and take root in the 'local.'"[97] Noodles were made in central kitchens in each country. Preparation required minimal cooking experience, making it easy to hire local kitchen staff. Chefs prepared the ramen according to a manual specifying the ratio of soup stock to water, water temperature, and minutes of boiling. The restaurant manager was the gatekeeper for food quality and consistency.[98] The ramen menu was the same in all outlets, with traditional pork-based broth and vegan sesame broth. The *bao,* a Chinese-style steamed bun, was a popular side item in all outlets, but other side dishes reflected local palates. The general manager of Ippudo Australia explained to us that all ingredients except soy sauce were locally sourced, reflecting both lower costs and legal restrictions on food imports. The taste was also localized.[99] For example, Ippudo China served less salty and fatty food, New York Ippudo featured sides of Ippudo Wings, and Manila Ippudo offered *teppan tonkatsu* (grilled pork cutlet) curry rice.

At the same time, the Tokyo headquarters ensured consistency in staff training and décor to create the chain's trademark Japanese atmosphere. Locally hired staff called out "*irasshaimase*" (welcome) and "*arigatō gozaimasu*" (thank you) to customers. This audible Japaneseness featured in all Ippudo outlets we visited in Manila, New York, Shanghai, and Melbourne. The consistency of this Japanese-style service was established by training materials created at Ippudo headquarters and translated into local languages. New hires received a three-hour lecture on the concept of Japanese service—*omotenashi* (hospitality) and *kizukai* (considerateness)—and a two-hour class on the menu, followed by a week of on-the-job training.[100] The program appeared effective. During our visit to the New York flagship in 2019, the staff kept up a spirited chorus in Japanese of welcomes and orders. Even busy Hispanic cooks in the open kitchen punctuated their Spanish banter with shouts of "*irasshaimase*." The white American woman who served us remarked, "It is part of the performance of the place."[101] Additionally, the Tokyo headquarters ensured consistency of the physical space of all Ippudo outlets. It worked with local companies to design interiors combining local elements with the chain's brand colors and themes, including the red and white chairs that symbolized its ramen dishes—Akamaru (spicy ramen in red bowls) and Shiromaru (plain ramen in white bowls).[102] This centralized control replicated Ippudo's corporate imaginary in new markets while allowing localization for side dishes and ingredient sourcing.

Hands-Off at Menya Musashi

Menya Musashi pursued a very different branding strategy from Ajisen and Ippudo by giving its franchisees a large amount of freedom, enabling rapid chain expansion. It was founded in 1996 by apparel industry veterans Yu Yamada and Yoshiharu Sato, who were credited with upscaling the ramen shop from a greasy spoon to a more sophisticated dining experience. The company name referred to Miyamoto Musashi (1584–1645), a famous samurai with a two-sword fighting technique. His portrait hung in chain outlets, and the franchise holding company was named Five Rings after his war strategy treatise *Book of Five Rings* (small businesses in Japan often used historical figures as brand icons based on fanciful connections).[103] By 2021, after twenty-five years, the chain had fifteen directly owned outlets in Japan and about one thousand franchised outlets in Asia, Europe, and North America.[104]

Through an interview with chain founder Sato, we learned that the corporation viewed the ramen business as branding rather than food. He considered ramen to be a dish made with low-skill labor using products available in supermarkets (even though customers like to hear about the chefs' skills and secret ingredients). Therefore, to differentiate Menya Musashi's product from that of other ramen chains, the corporation emphasized the dining experience. Modern wooden interiors and jazz background music gave the outlets a "cool" atmosphere.[105] The chain also broke from the prevailing *tonkotsu* ramen broth craze by developing a broth with fish-based dashi, first using pike (*sanma*), and then bonito (after the 2011 Tohoku earthquake destroyed the dried pike factory in Ishinomaki). However, outlet managers could adjust the taste, so it differed by outlet. This reflected Sato's belief that ramen eaters were fickle, so it was better to make changes to attract new customers rather than maintain a specific taste.[106]

The Singapore-based Five Rings company pursued this hands-off strategy with all outlets outside Japan. Potential franchisees contacted the headquarters via the internet. Upon completing the contract and paying the franchising fee, they became franchisees, with no requirement to visit restaurants in Tokyo or corporate headquarters in Singapore. Sato then sent them the operating plans for a chain outlet in digital format. He emphasized in our interview that the plans were only guidelines. He said, "If your budget is not sufficient, you can make the interior design cheaper. As for the taste, it is 'no touch' from me. If you ask, I will send recipes. Some [franchisees] want them, but others make their own." We asked him, if franchisees could do as they pleased, why would they want to purchase a costly franchise? He answered, "When you arrive in a new town and are hungry, it is difficult to go to a place you don't know. So [you see] there is a Hidakaya . . . a McDonalds . . . people are like that. Therefore, the brand should be recognized quickly. . . . 'Aaaah, I know this brand, so let's go there.' People rely on brands to act." In other words, franchisees paid for the Menya Musashi name and connection with Japan to distinguish themselves in competition with less known and esteemed ramen brands.[107]

However, franchisees could send staff to Menya Musashi outlets in Tokyo for on-the-job training if they wished. Such training, said Sato, was only requested by franchisees in Western countries. An example is Menya Musashi in Ukraine.[108] The franchisees were young gastro-entrepreneurs from Luhansk who had operated burger restaurants in eastern Ukraine until forced to close by the 2014 Russian invasion. Moving to the capital Kyiv, they searched for a food trend in the United States and Europe not yet in the city. They hit upon ramen and found a partner online to provide necessary know-how, which led them to Menya Musashi.[109] In 2015, the Ukrainian chain sent their brand chef Artem Syvochub for training at Menya Musashi in Japan. He spoke no Japanese and only limited English, and had no experience cooking Japanese food. In Tokyo, he spent several weeks "learning by doing and working" in multiple outlets and shot videos of staff cooking in the open kitchens. Upon returning to Kyiv, he assumed responsibility for the ramen taste, ingredient procurement, and staff training in all five local outlets. He sought to impart a "samurai-like" atmosphere by urging staff members to strive for mastery of their work in the Japanese spirit of *kaizen*. His videos shot in Tokyo continuously played on monitors in the dining rooms of the Ukrainian outlets to emphasize their link to Menya Musashi in Japan and the Japanese artisanship of the dish.[110]

Thus, Menya Musashi delegated the maintenance of standards in its place-product package to franchisees. This reflected the parent company's view that it was selling a brand name conveying associations of Japan and that local franchisees best understood these associations. This hands-off approach contrasted with Ippudo's emphasis on consistency in its signature ramen dish and Japanese-style service while permitting localization of side dishes. Ippudo achieved this balance by relying on directly owned flagship restaurants and franchised outlets. Lying somewhere between the approaches of Menya Musashi and Ippudo, Ajisen Ramen permitted some localization in the taste of its ramen. It used diverse ownership arrangements that reflected the parent company's variable relations to specific national markets. The following section looks at how locally based entrepreneurs have used their local knowledge and ties to create their own Japan brands with a flexible approach toward cultural authenticity.

Establishing Brands in Indigenous Chains

While chains from Japan could draw on the resources of Japan-based headquarters, indigenous chains relied on their founders' cultural and social capitals. They come from diverse backgrounds and pursue various strategies to create brands and gain resources for chain expansion. This section illustrates some patterns we observed through brief sketches of founders and their chains. These cases are only a cursory sampling as all the indigenous restaurants described elsewhere in this chapter, and indeed throughout this book, were established through utilizing their founders' cultural and social capitals.

Cultural Capital and Brand Creation

Founders of indigenous chains draw on their cultural capitals to create distinct brands. One of their advantages, especially for those born or raised in the country, is an understanding of what foods appeal to local customers. In developing markets, where upmarket Japanese restaurants served teppanyaki using expensive beef and shrimp, restaurateurs seized on teriyaki made with chicken as a gateway dish to Japanese cuisine for the new middle classes. This choice reflected their knowledge of the meats that could be locally sourced at lower cost and that grilling was common in many countries. An example is Teriyaki Boy, a popularizer of chicken teriyaki in the Philippines. It was the brainchild of Bryan Tiu, who was exposed to Japanese food and culture through his parents' business relations with Japanese firms. At age eighteen, he started a Japanese restaurant under his brand to avoid franchise fees.[111] Opened in 2001, Teriyaki Boy was among the first Japanese restaurants in Manila priced for the mass market. The chain's signature teriyaki bento box meal was both familiar and exotic, as grilled chicken was already popular in the country. Tiu opened nine more outlets in the metro region and expanded the menu to ramen, sushi, and curry. His local knowledge helped Teriyaki Boy to avoid the costly stumbles faced by Japan-based corporations (such as Dosanko and Yoshinoya) in new markets.

Other founders, even those with little to no experience regarding Japan, had knowledge of local cultural values that could be advantageous in conceiving brands. This can be seen in sustainability ethics for seafood, such as the overfishing of ahi tuna and the environmental impact of salmon farming. Kristofor Lofgren, based on the US West Coast, switched from pursuing a career in environmental law to the sustainable restaurant business.[112] In 2008, he founded Bamboo Sushi, the self-declared "world's first certified sustainable sushi restaurant," in Portland, Oregon, a city known

for its environmentally concerned population.[113] The menu and verbal pat-
ter of the service staff described the origins of each of its wild-caught fish,
and the restaurant's website listed eight sustainability certifications from
various organizations.[114] In about a decade, the chain grew to ten outlets,
including ones in Denver and San Francisco, cities with similar consumer
profiles to Portland. Bamboo Sushi was more expensive than the sushi restaurants run by Asian immigrants (see Chapter 5) because of the higher
costs for wild-caught fish and obtaining sustainability certification. Therefore, sustainability branding was a niche for higher-end sushi restaurants,
although, during the 2010s, it became more widespread.

Other founders drew on their understanding of the local sense of humor in creating brands that were not easy for competitors to imitate. Mosch
was a Frankfurt-based ramen chain that tickled the funny bone of Germans.[115] The founders were two friends, Matthias Schönberger and Tobias
Jäkel, who had studied hotel management. Jäkel saw the popularity of Japanese restaurants in the United States, where he lived in the 1990s, and decided to open a sushi eatery in Frankfurt. However, fresh fish proved hard
to obtain, so the partners switched to ramen. Neither had been to Japan,
so they learned to make it from the internet and a Japanese friend. In 2002,
they opened their first ramen bar, expanding to twelve outlets in several
German cities by 2019. The partners playfully created a mythical founder,
Heidi Tama Goshi, the reputed Japanese granddaughter of a Tokyo ramen
shop owner living in a Tyrolian hut in the Alps.[116] This myth was woven
into the restaurant décor, such as the cartoons of Heidi on the menu page,
to claim Japaneseness through corny humor that created familiarity with
German customers. The décor of the outlets featured Scandinavian mini-
malism with oak accents, typical of trendy but inexpensive restaurants in
Europe appealing to young people.

Many restaurateurs draw on their ethnic backgrounds to create brands.
An example was the Dubai-based chain Sumo Sushi & Bento in the multicultural (and sports-mad) United Arab Emirates (UAE). It was founded in
2000 by two married couples consisting of one Lebanese and three Hawai-
ians (with some Japanese descent). Seeing the lack of Japanese and casual
restaurants, they decided to open a "family friendly" restaurant serving
the "authentically fun Japanese cuisine" they knew in Hawaii, including
poke bowls, sushi rolls, *temaki*, and *yakisoba* (fried noodles).[117] Its marketing invoked "Japaneseness" in Dubai, a multicultural context similar to
Hawaii in terms of ethnic diversity. The "About Us" section on its website

stated: "Rooted in their Japanese and multi-cultural backgrounds, where they grew up surrounded by diverse cultures with rich histories that valued family, food and the bonds made around the dining experience." An accompanying video, "The Many Faces of Sumo," featured the faces of the chain's ethnically diverse employees.[118] Notably, the first face shown was that of a Japanese (seemingly) knife-flashing sushi chef; this may have reflected the "samurai chef" image popularized by Benihana (see Chapter 4), and the importance of a Japanese (or East Asian) "face" in the front (see Chapter 5). The brand caught on. By 2020 there were fourteen franchised outlets in the UAE and Bahrain, with more planned for Saudi Arabia, India, South Africa, Turkey, and Mexico.[119]

Some indigenous restaurants create a distinct Japanese brand that not only drives the chain's expansion but is used for other businesses connected to its Japan imaginary. Yo! Sushi opened by Simon Woodroffe in 1997 is a notable example. The restaurant helped make sushi hip to young British consumers by playing to their limited knowledge of Japan. Woodroffe drew on his background as a stage designer for rock concerts to create a dining venue that played up the consumer experience of an exciting and entertaining physical space. It served sushi on a very long orange conveyor belt and featured robots taking drink orders, Japanese anime playing on large-screen TVs, and pop music blaring over a sound system.[120] One reviewer acutely observed, "Yo! It's meant to feel new and vibrant, to feel the way the British *expect* Japan to feel—young, modern and an itsy bit wacky, but with a hint of a historical connection."[121] In 2008, Woodroffe sold his stake to a corporation that expanded the chain to over one hundred outlets in Europe and the Middle East (and the United States, briefly). He then used the brand's imaginary of Japanese high-tech hipness to launch micro-apartment developer Yo! Homes and Yotel, which made and operated capsule hotels inspired by those in Japan.[122]

Social Capital and Resource Access

Through their social capital Japanese brand entrepreneurs gain access to various resources for operating a restaurant, including financial capital, labor, influencers, and political support. An example is the brothers Alessio, Dennis, and Daniele Tesciuba, who, inspired by Japanese restaurants in Paris, started Daruma Sushi in Rome in 2003. Within five years, they had thirteen outlets featuring takeout US-style sushi rolls and ramen.[123] The partners pursued strategies that differentiated their menus from lower-cost all-you-can-eat buffets run by Chinese migrants offering similar items. One was upscaling. In 2018, the brothers collaborated with the Italian celebrity chef Bruno Barbieri to create seasonal dishes combining Italian and Japanese ingredients. One dish was *spaghetti alla chitarra*, a crunchy, flavored spaghetti served with dried seaweed powder, lobster, algae, capers, and herbs.[124] Another strategy was micro-localization, such as offering certified kosher dishes in the chain's Roman Ghetto outlet. These strategies established the simultaneous Italianness and Japaneseness of the brand while appealing to customers with religious dietary restrictions. They were more readily pursued by restaurateurs like the Tesciuba brothers, whose deeper local roots (relative to those of migrants) made it more likely to collaborate with a celebrity chef and get a site in a popular tourist area.

Entrepreneurs with ties to corporate Japan have the transnational social capital to liaise with labor and product markets in Japan. An example is Haruhiko Saeki, a former corporate manager from Hokkaido who opened an *izakaya* (pub) in 1995 in Düsseldorf's Little Tokyo, the largest Japantown in Europe (see Chapter 3). Looking to New York for trends, typical of restaurateurs in Europe, he entered the ramen business in 2007 by opening Takumi Ramen in Little Tokyo.[125] The chain grew by directly owned shops in Berlin, Frankfurt, and Hamburg and franchisees in Amsterdam, Rotterdam, and Barcelona. Saeki used his ties to Japan for business advantage. He recruited chefs and managers directly from Japan[126] and hired Japanese youths on student and working holiday visas as servers.[127] (Such young transient workers from Japan were generally more willing to work for longer hours and at lower wages than native hires.)[128] Additionally, Saeki leveraged his import of noodles from Japanese manufacturer Nishiyama Seimen to become a noodle reseller in Europe.

However, founders who draw on migrant networks to develop their business may need linking social capital with local corporate and financial institutions for subsequent chain expansion.[129] This can be seen in Edo Japan, a teppanyaki restaurant opened in 1972 in Calgary, Canada, by Susumu Ikuta. A Buddhist monk from Japan, he started the restaurant to create income for a Buddhist temple he founded in Calgary.[130] In 1981 he began franchising outlets in mall food courts to family members. In 1999, Ikuta, busy with his new appointment as bishop of the Buddhist Churches of Canada, hired a (white) Canadian with executive experience in Pizza Hut to manage the chain. The new manager transformed the chain's "mom and pop" operation by modernizing the franchise system, opening table-service restaurants, and introducing an omnibus menu that included sushi.[131] This tie to Canada's corporate sector helped propel Edo Japan to over 140 outlets by 2020.[132] While Ikuta was no longer with the chain, his immigrant experience adapted to multicultural Canada remained its brand narrative. The chain's website said, "We are a blend of taste, culture and community. Our founder, Reverend Susumu Ikuta, came from Japan to Canada..[and].. opened Edo Japan over 40 years ago as a means for both nourishing and providing for the community . . . It's why we blend the words Welcome and Konnichiwa (good day) together and say . . . Welcomichiwa."[133]

In addition to corporate resources, linking social capital could include ties to government officials in countries with challenging business environments. An example is Russia, where Japanese cuisine became extremely popular in major Russian cities starting in the 1990s. By 2009, there were over one thousand sushi bars in Moscow and three hundred in Saint Petersburg, and Japanese restaurants were among the most profitable.[134] They belonged to indigenous chains that were much larger than elsewhere in Europe. The absence of chains from Japan was explained to us by an official from the Japan External Trade Organization. He said that Japan-based corporations viewed Russia as a difficult market due to opaque regulations and the importance of business-government connections.[135] Thus, the Russian market appeared to favor entrepreneurs with locally grounded social and cultural capitals. The largest of these indigenous chains, Eurasia, was founded by Alexy Fursov in 2001. He had studied economics and management at top-ranked Russian universities, including one for training civil servants, and then worked as a manager in the banking and telecommunications sectors. In 2001, he started a Japanese restaurant chain that grew via franchising to 133 outlets in Russia, Belarus, and Ukraine by 2018.[136] The restaurant served Japanese, pan-Asian, and European dishes in dining halls accompanied by television screens showing bungee jumping, snowboarding, and other sports to the pounding beat of workout music.[137] This sports theme was presumably a tie-in to the parent company's fitness club chain and may even have been a play on the healthy image of Japanese cuisine. These indigenous chains only operated in the successor countries of the former Soviet Union, possibly showing the geographic limits of the social capital they enjoyed in these home markets.[138]

Some entrepreneurial restaurateurs gained the support of the Japanese state in creating indigenous chains, especially in new markets that lack

FIGURE 6.1 Eurasia, starting in 2001 in St. Petersburg Russia, became the largest sushi chain in Russia, Belarus, and Ukraine, with over 130 shops at its peak. The Ukraine operation is now independent. According to the Eurasia Ukraine corporate website, in November 2022 there were 19 Eurasia branches in Kyiv, including the one pictured here on Liuteranska Street. (Photo by Lenka Vyletalova, August 31, 2017)

awareness of Japanese cuisine. An example is Sushi and More, a small chain in India that catered to a young middle-class clientele. Its founder was Harry Kosato, a multiple migrant from Kobe who attended university in the United Kingdom. In 1995 he went to India for a friend's wedding and spotted a business opportunity in the country's lack of Japanese restaurants.[139] In 2006, he founded La Ditta Company to trade in Japanese food ingredients and, in 2011, opened Sushi and More in Mumbai. He drew on his ties to the Japanese government cultivated during his trading career to promote the chain. In particular, he helped organize Cool Japan festivals in Mumbai, introducing Japanese food and pop culture to a vast market.[140] By 2022 he had nine outlets in Mumbai, Delhi, and Gurugram specializing in delivery and takeaway with a menu centered on *makizushi* (rolled sushi), including vegetarian versions.[141] Of course, large food corporations from

Japan, such as Ippudo, were also supported by the Cool Japan Fund in their overseas business activities.

These brief case studies illustrate how founders of indigenous restaurant companies can build on their cultural backgrounds and social networks while playing to local food tastes and values to create imaginaries of Japan that enlarge the idea of Japanese cuisine and how to eat it. Local and transnational forms of social and cultural capital play a key role in entrepreneurial success, but not all capitals are equally valuable. The case studies show the importance of ties to mainstream corporate institutions, governments, and funding sources, the use of which also entails specialized forms of cultural capital such as knowledge of finance and regulations. New migrants are not likely to have such resources, which is why many of these cases of successful corporatization involve native entrepreneurs or migrants with a corporate background. Also, the cases of Sumo Bento & Sushi and Yo! Sushi highlight the growing role of global holding companies in the industry, as explored next.

Deepening Corporatization

In the twenty-first century, the expansion of Japanese fast-food chains has been increasingly driven by holding companies in the hospitality, food and beverage, and lifestyle industries that have acquired numerous chains in their asset portfolios. These companies are organized to reduce the costs of management, taxes, and acquiring capital while enhancing asset protection.[142] Many fast-food chains, including most mentioned in this chapter, have either reincorporated as holding companies or been bought up by them.

Both Japan-based and indigenous holding companies compete in the Japanese fast-food industry. Among the biggest Japan-based ones was Zensho. It began in 1982 as the bento chain Lunchbox, which then became Sukiya, Japan's largest beef bowl chain.[143] By 2020, the company had 105 firms with ten thousand retail locations employing 142,000 people worldwide. It owned nineteen Japanese and Western food chains, supermarket chains, food services, food and business service operations, and a rice brokerage.[144] Among the largest holding companies started outside Japan was Yo! Sushi, mentioned earlier, which used mergers and acquisitions to become a global vendor of Japanese food. In the 2010s, it bought up Bento Sushi, with nine hundred US locations; Taiko Foods, a British manufacturer of Japanese products for supermarkets; and Snowfox, with seven hundred sushi counters across all fifty US states.[145]

Our research also shows how holding companies based in regions with few Japanese restaurants use their local knowledge to introduce chains to these new markets. An example in Southeast Asia is Japan Foods Holding, the Singapore-based Ajisen franchisee mentioned earlier, which held franchise rights in Southeast Asian countries for a dozen chains from Japan, including Ajisen and Menya Musashi, also mentioned earlier. The corporation used its local knowledge to introduce ramen to the Singapore market, which already had extensive noodle soup dishes, such as *wantan mee* (wonton noodles) and *mee pok tah* (fishball noodles). It created acceptance of ramen at its first Ajisen outlet in 1997 by letting customers not pay if they did not like the dish (everyone paid).[146] Another example was the Dubai-based Apparel Group, a global fashion and lifestyle retail conglomerate that held franchise rights for over seventy-five brands, mainly in the Middle East, including Dubai-based Sumo Sushi & Bento, mentioned earlier.[147] This latter example shows how corporatization has become so variegated in the Japanese global restaurant industry that transactions can proceed entirely among multiple food corporations, all originating outside Japan.

The deep pockets of holding companies propelled their chains into newer markets in Africa, the Middle East, and South and Southeast Asia.[148] The Tokyo-based Toridoll Corporation illustrates this expansion of the global Japanese fast-food chains. It began as a yakitori shop in 1985 in Kakogawa, Hyogo Prefecture, opened by Awata Takaya, a former truck driver. In 2000, he started Marugame Seimen, a self-service udon chain that grew to hundreds of outlets across Japan.[149] In 2015, Awata reincorporated the firm as a holding company to better operate its by-then nineteen chains, including eight overseas chains. The holding company appeared to use franchise, subsidiary, or joint venture contracting with its chains depending on the market.[150] This flexibility has helped Toridoll to expand in both mature and newer markets. In one of these newer markets, it partnered in 2015 with a Kenyan importer of Japanese printing ink to open Teriyaki Japan. Toridoll owned 90 percent of the chain, while the Kenyan partner provided local knowledge, including scouting locations in Nairobi.[151] In Russia, a large market avoided by Japanese firms (see earlier discussion), Toridoll introduced Marugame Seimen to Moscow in 2013, which grew to seven outlets. (It pulled out in 2022 due to Russia's invasion of Ukraine.) Toridoll

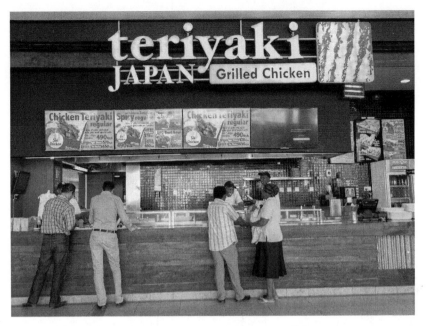

FIGURE 6.2 Teriyaki Japan is a Nairobi-based fast-food chain aimed at the rising Kenyan urban middle class that was founded by capital from a Japan-based restaurant corporation. It serves grilled meats, which are more familiar to Kenyans than seafood-based Japanese dishes. (Photo by Purity Muhagu, May 30, 2018)

was active in older markets. In 2018, it invested in Pokéwork, a US poke bowl chain with almost one hundred outlets. Toridoll used its experience in multiple countries to advise Pokéwork on multinational operations and international sustainability standards for fish.[152]

Corporatization in the twenty-first century, increasingly spearheaded by holding companies, was transforming the global Japanese restaurant. One way was through acceleration. This was visible in the life cycle of restaurants, such as Toridoll's investment in Pokéworks, which helped move it from startup to international chain in three years. The chain's hastened life cycle, accompanied by social media, also accelerated food fashions. Thus, the boom in poke bowl restaurants, beginning in Los Angeles around 2012, spread globally in 2015 via transnational franchising by US chains and the founding of indigenous chains.[153] By 2018, US food pundits were declaring poke bowl passé and the dish began appearing on omnibus menus alongside other has-been fashions, such as sukiyaki.[154] Another effect of corporatization was increasing homogeneity. This was most visible in the omnibus menus increasingly found in fast-food chains that enabled dishes to be swapped in and out according to trends and tastes. Homogenization could also be seen in place-product packaging as holding companies instituted best practices and design elements across their multiple chains. Additionally, the deepening of corporatization suggested a flattening of the growth in Japanese cuisine in developed countries. With the saturation of North American and Western European markets, holding companies invested in riskier markets and more upmarket establishments with higher profit margins.

Yet despite their place-product packaging and McDonaldized fast operations, chains have continued to draw on the value of the "Japan" brand. In sometimes fanciful ways, corporations have merged fast-food dishes prepared through deskilled labor and industrialized foodstuffs with the reputation of Japanese cuisine for artisanal techniques and healthy ingredients. Such corporate balancing of seemingly contradictory values of standardization and cultural particularity in a nationally defined cuisine is explored in the following chapters through global Japanese restaurant forms in higher-end markets.

Notes

1. John A. Jakle and Keith A. Sculle, *Fast Food: Roadside Restaurants in the Age of the Automobile* (Baltimore, MD: Johns Hopkins University Press, 1999), 29.

2. Ritzer sees McDonald's as a metaphor for modern culture. George Ritzer, *The McDonaldization of Society: An Investigation into the Changing Character of Contemporary Social Life* (Newbury Park, CA: Pine Forge, 1993), 13–14.

3. Matsumoto Hirotaka (松本紘宇), *Nyūyōku Take Sushi monogatari* (ニューヨーク竹寿司物語) [New York Take Sushi tale] (Tokyo: Asahi shinbunsha, 1995), 148–149.

4. See Matsumoto.

5. "When It Comes to Foreign Hires, Restaurant Chains in Japan's Chubu Region Are Taking a Long View," *Japan Times,* August 30, 2019, https://www.japantimes.co.jp/news/2019/08/30/business/corporate-business/restaurants-in-japans-chubu-long-view-foreigners/#.XWkktZNKh1N.

6. Himeda Konatsu (姫田小夏), "Shanhai ni mikiri wo tsukeru nihonjin inshokuten keieisha ga ato wo tatanai riyū" (上海に見切りをつける日本人飲食店経営者が後を絶たない理由) [The endless reasons why Japanese restaurants owners give up on Shanghai], Diamond Online, August 23, 2019, https://diamond.jp/articles/-/212569?utm_source=daily&utm_medium=email&utm_campaign=doleditor&utm_content=free.

7. For a related argument, see Guojun Zeng, Henk J. De Vries, and Frank M. Go, *Restaurant Chains in China: The Dilemma of Standardisation versus Authenticity* (Singapore: Palgrave Macmillan, 2017).

8. For the term "corporate imaginaries," see Sheila Jasanoff and Sang Hyun Kim, *Dreamscape of Modernity: Sociotechnical Imaginaries and the Fabrication of Power* (Chicago: University of Chicago Press, 2015), 273.

9. See the essays in David Beriss and David Sutton, eds., *The Restaurants Book: Ethnographies of Where We Eat* (Oxford: Berg, 2007).

10. John A. Jakle, "Roadside Restaurants and Place-Product-Packaging," *Journal of Cultural Geography* 3, no. 1 (1982): 76–93.

11. Dosanko, accessed on May 23, 2021, https://dskgroup.co.jp/company/; "'Dosanko ramen' wa ima . . . kyū seicho kara suitai made no kei'i to fukkatsu no shinario ni semaru" ('どさん子ラーメン' は今 . . . 急成長から衰退までの経緯と復活のシナリオに迫る) ["Dosanko Ramen" is now . . . approaching the history of its rapid growth to decline and the scenario of revival], IT Media ビジネス Online, May 28, 2019, https://www.itmedia.co.jp/business/articles/1905/28/news037.html; Masato Iishi, "Japanese Ramen Firms Dig into International Market," Nippon.com, August 5, 2015, https://www.nippon.com/en/features/c02202/.

12. There are competing claims for the title of "first ramen shop" in the United States. Dosanko's New York outlet predates one contender, the Koraku Japanese Restaurant, which opened in 1976 in Los Angeles' Little Tokyo. Alexander LaRose, "America's First Ramen Noodle Restaurant Is Los Angeles' Best Midnight Snack," Discover Nikkei, May 31, 2010, http://www.discovernikkei.org/en/journal/2010/5/31/koraku/. To be clear, ramen was on the menu of Japanese-immigrant-run restaurants long before the emergence of shops specializing in ramen. See, for example, the Osome Restaurant menu from San Francisco in 1969, CIA Digital Collections, Culinary Institute of America, accessed October 25, 2020, http://ciadigitalcollections.culinary.edu/digital/collection/p16940coll1/id/11156/.

13. "Japanese Noodles as Fast Food," *New York Times*, June 13, 1981, section 2, p. 31.

14. According to an ex-DFI general manager, the company changed the *r* in "ramen" to an *l* to reflect Japanese vocalization of the *r* sound, while an additional *r* was added to the end of the first syllable, resulting in the word "larmen." This was intended to make English speakers say "lah-men" rather than the Americanized "lay-men." Kazuhiko Sato, Official Ramen Home Page, accessed June 25, 2020, http://www.umich.edu/~wewantas/brooke/pics/Picturesfood/ramen.html.

15. Milton Glaser and Jerome Snyder, "The Underground Gourmet," *New York Magazine*, April 22, 1974, 93, http://ciadigitalcollections.culinary.edu/digital/collection/p16940coll1/id/11156/rec/1.

16. "Japanese Noodles as Fast Food."

17. "Japanese Noodles as Fast Food."

18. Iishi, "Japanese Ramen Firms."

19. Dosanko Ramen, accessed June 25, 2020, http://dosankoramenla.com.

20. Iishi, "Japanese Ramen Firms."

21. "History of Overseas Expansion," Yoshinoya, accessed June 15, 2020, https://www.yoshinoya-holdings.com/english/company/oversea/date.html.

22. One factor was the 1977 McGovern Report, a US Senate study highlighting excessive fat consumption by Americans, which helped create growing interest in Japanese food. See Matsumoto, *Nyūyōku Take Sushi*, 122–126.

23. Ministry of Economy, Trade and Industry, *White Paper on International Economy and Trade 2012*, December 18, 2012, chap. 3, sec. 3, p. 559, https://www.meti.go.jp/english/report/downloadfiles/2012WhitePaper/3-3.pdf.

24. Atul Ranjan, "Japan's Beef Bowl Chain Yoshinoya Enters Indian Market," Kyodo News Service, April 17, 2018, https://english.kyodonews.net/news/2018/04/82ab4751f2b8-japans-beef-bowl-restaurant-chain-enters-indian-market.html.

25. "Our Company," Yoshinoya, accessed June 15, 2020, https://www.yoshinoya america.com/our-story.

26. Ministry of Economy, Trade and Industry, *White Paper,* 559.

27. James Yaury, "How to Win in the Indonesian Market: Case Analyses on the Pair of Competitors" (MBA thesis, Waseda Business School, 2019).

28. Xiang Zhang, "Spatial Patterns and Social/Cultural Implications of Japanese Fast-Food Chains in China," *Asian Geographer* 35, no. 1 (2018): 28.

29. An Indonesian food critic attributes the popularity of Japanese food to the centrality of umami in Japanese and Indonesian cuisines. Ian Lloyd Neubauer, "Japanese Cuisine on a Roll in Indonesia," *Nikkei Asia,* April 1, 2020, https://asia.nikkei.com/Life-Arts/Life/Japanese-cuisine-on-a-roll-in-Indonesia.

30. "Hotto motto, tenposū de gyōkai shui ni 'hokaben' ridatsu de hajimatta shiretsuna jintori gassen" (ほっともっと, 店舗数で業界首位に'ほか弁'離脱で始まった熾烈な陣取り合戦) [Hotomoto's Hokaben has the greatest number of outlets in the industry in a fierce battle that began with retreat], *MONEYzine,* August 15, 2009 (last accessed Jan. 27, 2018, no longer accessible) https://www.livedoor.com/?utm_source=news&utm_medium=rd.

31. Rinda Gusvita, "7 Fakta Hokben: Hati-hati, fakta nomor 6 bisa menyeretmu ke penjara" [7 Hokben facts: Beware fact number 6 that can get you imprisoned], Vitarinda, October 25, 2018, https://www.rindagusvita.com/2018/10/7-fakta-hokben-hati-hati-fakta-nomor-6.html.

32. "Hokben's Brand Strategy: Thoroughly Localize the Japanese Food That Is Part of Japanese Culture," Bahtera Hisistem, October 18, 2020, https://bahtera.jp/en/hokben/.

33. Yaury, "How to Win."

34. Highly Classified, "There Is Nothing Japanese about Hoka Bento . . . ," review on Trip Advisor, January 13, 2013, https://www.tripadvisor.com/ShowUserReviews-g294229-d1108114-r149619358-Hoka_Hoka_Bento-Jakarta_Java.html.

35. "Hokben's Brand Strategy."

36. Karisa Djohan, interview by David Wank, July 26, 2020.

37. "Garuda Indonesia Serving Japanese Fast Food HokBen in Business Class Sparks Debate Online," Coconuts Jakarta, July 5, 2019, https://coconuts.co/jakarta/news/garuda-indonesia-serving-japanese-fast-food-hokben-in-business-class-sparks-debate-online/.

38. Vicky War, "Noodles and a Long Wait: Post Modern Dining," *Independent,* February 20, 1994, https://www.independent.co.uk/news/uk/home-news/noodles-and-a-long-wait-post-modern-dining-1395354.html.

39. "Interim Report for the 13-Week Period to March 29, 2020," Wagamama no longer accessible), www.wagamama.com/investors/quarterly-reports.

40. Hugo Arnold, *The Wagamama Cookbook* (2004; New York: Metro Books, 2010), 11.

41. Robert Sietsma, "Slurping the Anglo-Japanese Ramen at Wagamama NYC," Eater New York, November 22, 2010, https://ny.eater.com/2016/11/22/13714114/wagamama-nyc-food.

42. "Wagamama's Use of Technology Delivers Healthy Returns," The Caterer, April 28, 2005, https://www.thecaterer.com/news/restaurant/wagamamas-use-of-technology-delivers-healthy-returns.

43. "Wagamama: The New Home of the Happy Meal," Savanta, accessed August 15, 2020, https://savanta.com/case-studies/wagamama-2/; "Wagamama: Working in Partnership to Develop the Hub," HGEM, accessed August 15, 2020, https://www.hgem .com/our-clients/wagamama.

44. *Satori* is translated into English as "looking into one's nature" by the Buddhist scholar D. T. Suzuki, who popularized Japanese Zen Buddhism in North America and Europe (D. T. Suzuki, *Essays in Zen Buddhism*. New York: Grove Press [1994], 259).

45. Shizuka Tanabe, "Ikinari Steak Wants to Reduce Reliance on Big-Eating Men," *Nikkei Asia*, February 14, 2020, https://asia.nikkei.com/Business/Food-Beverage /Ikinari-Steak-wants-to-reduce-reliance-on-big-eating-men.

46. Mike Pomranz, "Japan's Standing Room Only Steakhouse, Ikinari Steak, Is Coming to America," *Food and Wine*, February 21, 2017 (last accessed August 20, 2020, no longer accessible) https://www.foodandwine.com/news/ikinari-steak-nyc.

47. "Buatsui Amerika sutēki ichiba no kabe, 'ikinari!' ichibu tettai" (分厚い米ステーキ市場の壁、'いきなり！' 一部撤退) [The thick American steak market wall: "Ikinari!" partially withdraws] *Nihon Keizai Shinbun*, February 15, 2019, https://www.nikkei .com/article/DGXMZO41308150150220190000000/.

48. One New York resident noted that fast-food steak in the United States was a suburban phenomenon of chain restaurants (such as Sizzler) that lacked appeal for diners in the gentrified East Village. Fieldwork by James Farrer, September 2019.

49. John Lie, *Multi-ethnic Japan* (Cambridge, MA: Harvard University Press, 1972), 77.

50. "What Is Japanese BBQ?," Gyu-Kaku, accessed July 18, 2020, https://www.gyu -kaku.com.

51. For example, see Gyu-Kaku's Singapore website at https://www.gyu-kaku.com.sg.

52. "Menu," Mos Burger, accessed July 20, 2020, https://www.mosburger.com.au /menu/burgers/.

53. "The Beard Papa's Story," Beard Papa's, accessed July 3, 2020, http:// beardpapascanada.com/story.html.

54. "Bei'erduo babade pinpai qiyuan" (贝儿多爸爸的品牌起源) [Origin of the Beard Papa's brand], Shanghai Maohaosui Shipin Youxian Gongsi, accessed July 3, 2020, http://www.maihaosui.com/portal/list/index/id/15.html.

55. "About Us," Beard Papa's, accessed July 3, 2020, https://beardpapas.com.

56. "Concept," Saizeriya Singapore, accessed July 3, 2021, https://www.saizeriya.com .sg/concept.

57. "Japanese Comfort Food at Go! Go! Curry! America," Go! Go! Curry!, accessed July 20, 2020, https://gogocurryamerica.com/about/.

58. Kikkoman no longer markets this product. See Melissa Kaman, "It's Actually Hawaiian: Teriyaki Chicken Is Classic Fusion," *East Bay Times*, August, 8, 2004, https:// www.eastbaytimes.com/2004/08/25/its-actually-hawaiian-teriyaki-chicken-is-classic -fusion/.

59. Naomi Tomky, "The Slow and Sad Death of Seattle's Iconic Teriyaki Scene," Thrillist, August 23, 2016, https://www.thrillist.com/eat/seattle/seattle-teriyaki -japanese-restaurants-disappearing.

60. John T. Edge, "A City's Specialty: Japanese in Name Only," *New York Times*, January 5, 2010, section D, p. 1.

61. Tomky, "Slow and Sad Death."

62. Tomky.

63. Quoted in Edge, "City's Specialty."

64. "Manifesto," Teriyaki Madness, accessed August 20, 2020, https://teriyakimad ness.com/manifesto/.

65. Glaze Teriyaki, accessed August 20, 2020, https://www.glaze.com.

66. "A Makis," Temakeria Makis Place, accessed September 2, 2021, https://www .makisplace.com.br/a-makis. Makis Place bought the Temaki Bar brand in 2009.

67. "A Makis."

68. Ricardo Yoshikawa, interview by Monica Carvalho, December 12, 2016.

69. Cecilia Nagayama, interview by Monica Carvalho, August 20, 2021.

70. "Temakeria: Uma invenção brasileira" [Temakeria: A Brazilian invention], *Otempo*, February 18, 2010, https://www.otempo.com.br/diversao/magazine/temakeria -uma-invencao-brasileira-1.580196.

71. "Cardápio," Temakeria Makis Place, accessed August 27, 2021, https://www .makisplace.com.br/cardapio.

72. "Temakeria: Uma invenção brasileira."

73. Fieldwork by Monica Carvalho, August 20, 2021.

74. The cities were Bologna, Brescia, Florence, Lyon, London (2), Milan (5), Monte Carlo, Rome (4), Trieste, Turin, and Verona. "Restaurants," Temakinho, accessed August 27, 2021, https://www.temakinho.com/pages/japanese-brazilian-history#.

75. Fieldwork by James Farrer, October 2017.

76. Rachel Laudan, *The Food of Paradise: Exploring Hawaii's Culinary Heritage* (Honolulu: University of Hawai'i Press, 1996), 37; "Poke Bowl," Takeaway.com, accessed August 4, 2021, https://www.takeaway.com/foodwiki/japan/poke-bowl.

77. Maura Judkis, "Poke's Popularity Surges Even as Argument about Authenticity Heats Up," *Washington Post*, August 24, 2018, https://www.washingtonpost.com/news /voraciously/wp/2018/08/23/pokes-popularity-surges-even-as-arguments-about -authenticity-heat-up/.

78. "Our Story," Sweetfin, accessed August 10, 2021, https://www.sweetfin.com/our -story/.

79. Stephanie Emma Pfeffer, "What Is a Poke Bowl? A Chef Breaks Down the Food Trend," People.com, June 5, 2017, https://people.com/food/poke-bowl-food-trend-recipe/.

80. Mark Noguchi, "A Conflicted Chef from Hawaii Reacts to the Mainland Poke Bowl Trend," *First We Feast*, March 1, 2016, https://firstwefeast.com/eat/2016/03/hawaii -chef-has-problems-with-poke-trend.

81. Noguchi.

82. For a general argument about franchising strategies, see Jeffrey L. Bradach, *Franchise Organizations* (Boston: Harvard Business School Press, 1998).

83. Shigemitsu Katsuaki (重光克昭), *Chūgoku de ichiban seikō shite iru Nihon no gaishoku chēn wa Kumamoto no chīsana rāmenya datte shittemasuka?* (中国で一番成功している日本の外食チェーンは熊本の小さなラーメン屋だって知ってますか?) [Do you know that the most successful Japanese chain restaurant in China is a small ramen shop from Kumamoto?] (Tokyo: Daiyamondosha, 2010), 19–23.

84. PricewaterhouseCoopers, *Franchising Opportunities in China, Japan and Singapore* (Singapore: Asia-Pacific Economic Cooperation Secretariat, 2006), 197, https:// www.apec.org/docs/default-source/publications/2006/4/franchising-opportunities-in -china-japan-and-singapore-april-2006/06_tp_franchising.pdf?sfvrsn=3ceb288a_1.

85. "Chūgoku eria ichiran" (中国エリア一覧) [China area list], Ajisen, accessed March 1, 2019, http://www.aji1000.co.jp/wp/wp-content/uploads/2019/02/165402f5b9 80d6b6139a9f6e2f52da79.pdf; "Takaigai eria ichiran" (他海外エリア一覧) [Other over-

seas area list], Ajisen, accessed March 1, 2019, http://www.aji1000.co.jp/wp-content /uploads/2019/02/44d778377bd7be6403fcce4f5ecfd3b8.pdf.

86. Ajisen, "Chūgoku eria ichiran."

87. Shigemitsu, *Chūgoku de ichiban,* 172–174.

88. "Sekai hinshitsu wo anata no moto ni" (世界品質をあなたの元に) [World quality for you], Ajisen, accessed March 1, 2019, http://www.aji1000.co.jp/assets/media /quality.pdf.

89. Shane Cubis, "Using Her Noodle: Daisy Poon," *CEO Magazine,* August 22, 2019, https://www.theceomagazine.com/executive-interviews/food-beverage/daisy-poon/; Yasuo Awai, "Ajisen (China) Plans Delivery-Only Sites for Japanese Restaurant Chains," *Nikkei Asia,* March 24, 2016, https://asia.nikkei.com/Business/Ajisen-China-plans-deli very-only-sites-for-Japanese-restaurant-chain.

90. "Corporate Profile," Japan Foods Holding, accessed October 28, 2020, https:// www.jfh.com.sg/html/about.php. For Kampong Ampat see Mapletree, accessed December 6, 2022, https://mapletree.com.sg/All-Properties/MIT/Singapore/Kampong -Ampat.aspx.

91. The importance of local partners is illustrated in the case of Japanese chain Hachiban Ramen, based in Ishikawa Prefecture. The chain has 135 stores abroad, mostly in Thailand, where it opened in 1992. The local partner Thai Hachiban did not have to search for sites because mall developers included Hachiban outlets in their blueprints and then made overtures to the firm. Noboru Toyoshima, "Japanese Restaurants in Thailand: Dining in the Ambience of Japanese Culture," *Journal of Asia-Pacific Studies* 19 (2013): 279–296.

92. Elizabeth Rosen, "Japanese Restaurants Feed Their Global Ambitions with New York Branches," *Nikkei Weekly,* September 22, 2016, https://asia.nikkei.com /NAR/Articles/Japanese-restaurants-feed-their-global-ambitions-with-New-York -branches.

93. "Japanese Ramen Chain Takes on the U.S. Foodie Scene for Overseas Growth," *Japan Times,* May 20, 2017, https://www.japantimes.co.jp/life/2017/05/20/food/japan -ramen-chain-takes-u-s-foodie-scene-overseas-growth/.

94. Fieldwork by James Farrer, September 2019.

95. Yoshimura Shō, interview by Chuanfei Wang, February 24, 2018.

96. Fieldwork by James Farrer, February 2018.

97. The phrase in Japanese is "Global ni tenkai, Local ni nezuku" (Global に展開, Local に根く) [Expand globally, take root locally]. See "Glocal," Ippudo, accessed December 6, 2018, https://ippudo-outside.net/tag/glocal/.

98. Yoshimura Shō, interview by Chuanfei Wang, February 24, 2018.

99. Yoshimura Shō, interview by Chuanfei Wang, February 24, 2018.

100. Yoshimura Shō, interview by Chuanfei Wang, February 24, 2018.

101. Fieldwork by James Farrer, September 8, 2019.

102. Yoshimura Shō, interview by Chuanfei Wang, February 24, 2018.

103. Katarzyna Joanna Cwiertka and Yasuhara Miho, *Branding Japanese Food: From Meibutsu to Washoku* (Honolulu: University of Hawai'i Press, 2020), 74.

104. "The Chain of Restaurants Menya Musashi," OSA, accessed September 19, 2020, https://osa.com.ua/en/portfolio-item/the-chain-of-restaurants-menya-musashi/.

105. Kotajima Daisuke (古田島大介), "Rāmenkai no kakumeiji ga 'ishoku no ko-rabo' ni chikara wo ireru riyū. 2-daime shachō ni kiku" (ラーメン界の革命児が '異色のコラボ' に力を入れる理由. 2代目社長に聞く) [The reason why revolutionary children in

the ramen world are focusing on "unique collaboration." Ask the second president Daisuke Kotajima], bizSPA!, April 16, 2020, https://bizspa.jp/post-298202/.

106. Sato Yoshiharu, interview by James Farrer and Kimura Fumiko, April 2, 2021.

107. Sato Yoshiharu, interview by James Farrer and Kimura Fumiko, April 2, 2021.

108. Fieldwork by Lenka Vyletalova, September 25 and November 14, 2017.

109. Artem Syvochub, interview by Lenka Vyletalova, November 14, 2017.

110. Artem Syvochub, interview by Lenka Vyletalova, November 14, 2017.

111. "Brian Tiu of iFoods Group, Inc.," Primer, July 4, 2017, https://primer.com.ph/business/2017/07/04/bryan-tiu-of-ifoods-group-inc/.

112. Gretchen Kurtz, "Kristofor Lofgren on Sustainable Seafood and Bringing Bamboo Sushi to Denver," Westword, July 20, 2006, https://www.westword.com/restaurants/kristofor-lofgren-on-sustainable-seafood-and-bringing-bamboo-sushi-to-denver-8111386.

113. Bamboo Sushi, accessed December 6, 2020, https://bamboosushi.com/page/sustainability.

114. Bamboo Sushi, accessed April 29, 2017, https://bamboosushi.com/; fieldwork by James Farrer, April 31, 2017.

115. Mona Jaeger, "Nudelsuppe auf dem Tisch, Flugzeuge im Blick" [Soup noodles on the table, a view on the airplanes], *Frankfurter Allgemeine Zeitung,* August 20, 2010, https://www.faz.net/aktuell/rhein-main/wirtschaft/moschmosch-nudelsuppe-auf-dem-tisch-flugzeuge-im-blick-1593843.html?printPagedArticle=true#pageIndex_0; fieldwork by James Farrer, January 2018.

116. "Über uns: Glück ist eine Nudel" [About us: Happiness is a noodle], Mosch-Mosch, accessed October 31, 2020, https://www.moschmosch.com/ueber-uns.php.

117. "The Sumo Way," Sumo Sushi & Bento, accessed July 18, 2020, https://sumosushibento.com/sumoway/thesumoway/.

118. Sumo Sushi & Bento, accessed December 4, 2022, https://sumosushibento.com/sumoway/ourteam/.

119. Amit Singh, "Sumo Sushi Shares Its Big India Plans," *Entrepreneur India,* November 5, 2019, https://www.entrepreneur.com/article/341866.

120. Will Smale, "Simon Woodroffe: The Yo! Sushi Boss Who Beat Depression," BBC, June 25, 2014, https://www.bbc.com/news/business-27938824.

121. Kate Crockett, "Sushi: What Goes Around Comes Around," cited in Katarzyna Joanna Cwiertka, *Modern Japanese Cuisine: Food, Power and National Identity* (London: Reaktion Books, 2006), 197, emphasis in the original.

122. Sophie Witts, "No! Sushi: What Yo! Is Doing Next," BigHospitality, February 4, 2020, https://www.bighospitality.co.uk/Article/2020/02/04/How-YO!-Sushi-became-a-global-restaurant-group.

123. Fieldwork by James Farrer, October 2017; ANSA, "Un po giappo un po' emiliana, la cucina Seasons di Barbieri" [A little Japanese, a little Emilian, the cuisine of Seasons of Barbieri], *Terra e Gusto,* May 15, 2018, https://www.ansa.it/canale_terraegusto/notizie/dolce_e_salato/2018/05/15/un-po-giappo-un-po-emiliana-la-cucina-seasons-di-barbieri_5c6a8ed0-8dff-4558-866c-5cb1384d0b73.html.

124. "Daruma Seasons by Chef Bruno Barbieri," Daruma, accessed May 15, 2018, http://www.darumasushi.com/daruma-seasons/.

125. "Alles im Ramen: Zu Besuch bei Saeki Haruhiko von Takumi" [Everything in ramen: A visit with Takumi's Saeki Haruhiko], RP Online, November 8, 2018, https://rp

-online.de/nrw/staedte/duesseldorf/alles-im-ramen_aid-24311915; Haruhiko Saeki, interview by James Farrer, August 28, 2017.

126. According to Japanese restaurant managers and government officials we interviewed, Japanese culinary workers could obtain work visas in North Rhine-Westphalia more easily than elsewhere in Europe due to the region's ties to Japanese businesses. Fieldwork by James Farrer, August 2017; Japan External Trade Organization Düsseldorf office officials, interview by James Farrer, August 28, 2017.

127. Fieldwork by James Farrer, August 2018.

128. We observed similar labor exploitation in other countries, including Australia, where young Japanese were also on working holiday visas. See Jock Collins, "Australia's New Guest Workers: Opportunity or Exploitation?," in *Critical Reflections on Migration, "Race" and Multiculturalism,* ed. Martina Boese and Vince Marotta (Abingdon, UK: Routledge, 2017), 71–87.

129. Robert W. Fairlie, "Immigrant Entrepreneurs and Small Business Owners, and Their Access to Financial Capital," *Small Business Administration* 396 (2012): 1–46.

130. *Calgary Herald,* April 28–30, 2014, https://www.legacy.com/obituaries/cal garyherald/obituary.aspx?pid=170830894.

131. Brenda Bouw, "Edo Japan Owner Fixed the Company, Then He Bought It," *Globe and Mail,* July 15, 2014, https://www.theglobeandmail.com/report-on-business /small-business/sb-growth/edo-japan-owner-fixed-the-company-then-bought-it /article19759845/#skip-link-target.

132. "Edo Japan Strengthens Presence in Winnipeg with Addition of Two Street Locations: Canadian-Made Franchise Continues Cross-Country Expansion," Intrado Global News Wire, January 22, 2020, https://www.globenewswire.com/en/news-release /2020/01/22/1973722/0/en/Edo-Japan-Strengthens-Presence-in-Winnipeg-With -Addition-of-Two-Street-Front-Locations.html.

133. "Overview," Edo, accessed July 25, 2021, https://www.edojapan.com/about-us.

134. Andrei Panibratov, "Russian Restaurant with Japanese Cuisine Makes Foreign Markets' Selection: The Case of Two Sticks," *Asian Case Research Journal* 16, no. 2 (2012): 335–346.

135. Japan External Trade Organization Tokyo office official, interview by James Farrer, Tokyo, March 30, 2018. See also Jordan Gans-Morse, "Demand for Law and the Security of Property Rights: The Case of Post-Soviet Russia," *American Political Science Review* 111, no. 2 (2017): 338–359.

136. Eurasia, accessed June 10, 2021, https://evrasia.spb.ru/about/ceo/.

137. Fieldwork by Lenka Vyletalova, November 2017.

138. Panibratov, "Russian Restaurant," 345–346. Panibratov describes how a Russian owner of a Saint Petersburg-based chain, after exploring expansion in Western Europe and China, saw greater possibilities in the latter. The owner felt that his idea of a Japanese restaurant would be more appealing to Chinese consumers because of the "similar histories of national development" in Russia and China.

139. Harry Kosato, interview by James Farrer, January 24, 2012.

140. Shotaro Kumagai, "Japan-India Human Exchange Research Series 2: Japan Visit Promotion through 'Cool Japan,'" Japan Research Institute, July 2017, https://www .jri.co.jp/MediaLibrary/file/english/periodical/occasional/2017/02.pdf.

141. Sushi and More, accessed December 4 2022, https://www.sushiandmore.com /about.

142. Kawabata Motoo (川端基夫), *Gaishoku kokusaika no dainamizumu: Atarashī "ekkyō no katachi"* (外食国際化のダイナミズム: 新しい '越境のかたち') [The dynamism of the internationalization of the restaurant industry: The new "pattern of transnationalism"] (Tokyo: Shinhyoron, 2016), 138–148.

143. "History," Zensho Holdings, accessed September 12, 2020, https://www.zensho.co.jp/en/company/outline/history/2011.html.

144. "Group Organization and Four Priority Areas," Zensho Holdings, accessed September 1, 2020, https://www.zensho.co.jp/en/company/outline/priority_areas/.

145. Witts, "No! Sushi."

146. "Japan Foods Engineer Myriad Tastes of Home," *Business Times,* January 28, 2019, https://www.businesstimes.com.sg/companies-markets/japan-foods-engineers-myriad-tastes-of-home.

147. "Company," Apparel Group, accessed August 17, 2020, https://www.apparel uae.com/company/.

148. See Kawabata, *Gaishoku kokusaika no dainamizumu,* 138–148.

149. Kanda Hiroharu (神田啓晴), "Marugameseimen, Awata Takuya shi (2) yōgashiten de no baito ga tenki, gamushara ni kigyō e" (丸亀製麺, 粟田貴也氏(2)洋菓子店でのバイトが転機, がむしゃらに起業へ) [Marugame Seimen's Takaya Awata (2) a part-time job at a pastry shop was a turning point, and he started his own business], Nikkeibijinesu, February 7, 2020, https://business.nikkei.com/atcl/NBD/19/00129/020300010/.

150. Toridoll Holdings, accessed December 7, 2022, https://www.toridoll.com/en/company/history.php.

151. "Japanese Fast-Food Chain to Open Nairobi Outlet in February," Food Business Africa, January 25, 2015, https://www.foodbusinessafrica.com/japanese-fast-food-chain-to-open-nairobi-outlet-in-february-2/.

152. "Nation's Leading Poke Brand Signs Agreement with Japanese Holding Company to Propel Global Expansion and Further Quality Standards," Cision PR Newswire, August 6, 2018, https://www.prnewswire.com/news-releases/pokeworks-partners-with-global-restaurant-investment-powerhouse-toridoll-300692389.html.

153. From 2014 to 2015, the number of shops in the United States more than doubled from 342 to 700, while Google searches for "poke bowl" increased almost fourfold. Vince Dixon, "Data Dive: Tracking the Poke Trend," Eater, September 14, 2016, https://www.eater.com/2016/9/14/12839882/poke-trend-hawaiian-food-growth.

154. Brenna Houck, "Has the Poke Trend Peaked?," Eater, November 6, 2018, https://www.eater.com/2018/11/6/18057316/poke-bowl-trend-fast-casual-restaurant-closures.

7 | The *Izakaya* as Global Imaginary

James Farrer, David L. Wank, Chuanfei
Wang, and Mônica R. de Carvalho

aking off in cities around the world in the 2000s, the *izakaya* is one
of the most recent global Japanese food fashions (see Chapter 4 for
earlier ones). It is also the global Japanese restaurant form that best
illustrates the significance of the restaurant as a social environment, or the
priority of space over taste in defining restaurant fashions. The *izakaya* is
an immersive social experience in which food, though served in great variety, is clearly not the defining element. While there are typical *izakaya*
menu items, it has no signature dish. Instead, the menu is capable of great
flexibility, allowing restaurateurs to constantly update offerings. The most
salient aspect of the *izakaya* is a convivial atmosphere of sharing food and
drinks that is often enhanced through edgy design and loud music. Thus,
this latest Japanese restaurant fashion shares with the oldest—the Japanese
teahouse (see Chapter 4)—an emphasis on style and fantasy over gastronomy. In some ways, the *izakaya* brings culinary japonaiserie full circle with
the restaurant as a space of imagined cultural differences that can be appropriated by restaurateurs serving almost anything, as with the Japanese
teahouse a century earlier.

The *izakaya* is a space of imagined sociability. It can be regarded as an
Asian relative of the global Irish pub that has traveled the world as a simulacrum of Gaelic sociability and fun only loosely associated with actual venues in Ireland or Irish people.[1] Like the imaginary of the Irish pub, the
global *izakaya* is a cultural form that borrows eclectically from the original
Japanese drinking culture while accruing new associations outside Japan.
Broadly translatable as "tavern," in the West, the *izakaya* is frequently described as a "Japanese tapas restaurant" or "Japanese gastropub." These

comparisons reveal two core innovations of this globalized Japanese restaurant concept: an emphasis on shared small plates (much like Spanish tapas) and alcohol, often Japanese *sake* (promoted with limited success in earlier Japanese food booms).[2] Another element of the *izakaya* is deliberate auditory and visual "noisiness" that fuels sociability over drinks and shared foods. In contrast to the sushi bar—which represents a minimalist and restrained Japanese aesthetic—the *izakaya* is a global culinary imaginary associated with a different register of Japanese culture: urban, rowdy, disorderly, and even grungy.

The *izakaya* is not just a malleable fantasy space but also a flexible, profit-focused business model. Due to its scalability and adaptability, the *izakaya* lends itself to corporate-led globalization, like the Japanese fast-food chains discussed in the previous chapter. Corporate *izakayas* thus represent an upmarket "McDonaldization," with kitchens resembling fast-service chain restaurants serving precooked dishes rather than the made-from-scratch offerings of fine dining. Moreover, the *izakaya* experience, while still a performance of "Japaneseness," shifts the burden of performing away from restaurant staff onto the consumer. In general, there is no elaborate knife work or fastidious table-side service work, reducing the need for highly trained staff. Instead, the consumers are exhorted to entertain themselves through drinking games and other forms of sociability. Alcohol sales drive this business model, creating new profit streams.

This chapter describes this flexible global imaginary through examples from ethnographic fieldwork. We first explain its urban origins and global spread. Subsequent sections focus on its key elements: flexible cuisine, cultures of alcohol consumption, and spaces of sociability. We conclude by reflecting on the implications of this trend for the ongoing global spread of Japanese cuisine.

Inventing the Global *Izakaya*

There is no single model of the global *izakaya*. Instead, it has emerged from the multiple mobilities of chefs, ideas, customers, and, above all, restaurateurs, moving among global cities of various scales. Similarly, there is no single birthplace of the global *izakaya*. Nevertheless, we consider two spots to be seminal—postwar Tokyo and early 2000s New York—with each making a distinct contribution to the global imaginary of the *izakaya*.

Tokyo Noir and the *Yokochō* Aesthetic

The term *izakaya* in Japan refers to any establishment that serves casual food to accompany drinks. An *izakaya* in Japan can be rural or urban, small or large, run by a person who is simultaneously owner, chef, and service person, or a big chain operating in every major city in Japan. While there are a few typical menu items, such as yakitori (grilled skewered chicken), *yakizakana* (grilled fish), or *agedashi tofu* (deep-fried tofu in broth), *izakaya*s may serve nearly any food—from pizza to sashimi. There are even Thai and Chinese *izakaya*s. In recent years, urban chain *izakaya*s have increasingly employed international students as a cheap and flexible labor force. Thus, the domestic *izakaya* in Japan is already a globalized culinary form, with a menu of items from around the world served by a staff of diverse, casualized workers.[3] This has made this space both easily comprehensible and adaptable for commercialization abroad.

The global imaginary of the *izakaya* is inspired by establishments in the narrow and dense parallel alleyways (*yokochō*) of postwar Tokyo. This alleyway style of *izakaya* is grimy and intimate and associated with nightlife districts near Tokyo's main commuter stations. In the bombed-out postwar cities of the late 1940s, small *izakaya* in ramshackle black markets served cheap cooked foods (e.g., grilled innards) paired with illegal *kasutori shōchu* (essentially moonshine).[4] Patches of the old black market *yokochō* still cohere around Shinjuku, Shibuya, and Shinbashi stations in central Tokyo, as well as suburban Kichijōji, allowing international tourists an immersive experience in the imagined nostalgia of postwar Tokyo. This image of the urban *izakaya* has also been celebrated in transnational media representations of Japan. For example, the popular television series *Late Night Diner* (*Shinya Shokudo*), debuting on TBS in 2009 and on Netflix in 2016, unfolds in an *izakaya* in Shinjuku's Golden Gai, one of Tokyo's largest surviving *yokochō*.[5] In these representations, the *izakaya* is a space where individuals can liberate themselves from daytime social roles and enjoy the relative democracy of nocturnal sociability.[6] This iconic image of the *izakaya* has inspired the *izakaya* imaginary in New York, Hong Kong, and other global cities.

The "Wildly Authentic" *Izakaya*s of New York's East Village

Like the Irish pub, the US simulacrum of an "authentic" Japanese *izakaya* may be as influential worldwide as the Tokyo originals. While the first *izakaya* in the United States was probably in Hawai'i or on the West Coast, the most fertile ground for their global boom was New York's East Village. It was here that the *izakaya* became a broader urban cultural phenomenon rather than a Japanese expatriate institution. As described in Chapter 3, the East Village developed a Little Tokyo oriented less toward a resident Japanese community than toward feeding a growing interest in Japanese cuisine and culture among Manhattan's cultural avant-garde. Some culinary pioneers in Little Tokyo also helped create the *izakaya* boom. Village Yokocho, founded by entrepreneur Tony Yoshida in 1995, was one of the first *izakaya*s to appeal beyond Japanese expatriates. As its name indicates, it was modeled on the shabby commuter *izakaya*s in urban Japan. When we visited in 2019, its menu was the standard *izakaya* fare found in Tokyo, emphasizing yakitori prepared by chefs behind the wooden counter. The bar was festooned with red lanterns emblazoned with the logo of Orion Beer (a regional brand from Okinawa). Customers mostly drank beer and *sake*. Village Yokocho represented the burgeoning *izakaya* image associated with the East Village. It was an informal and fun space that evoked both Tokyo's grimy postwar *yokochō* and Prohibition-era New York drinking spots, with the latter represented in the speakeasy-style Angel Share bar, also owned by Yoshida and accessed through an unmarked door inside the *izakaya* (see Chapter 3). (Village Yokocho and Angel Share closed in 2022, victims of rising rents in post-pandemic New York.)

While "authenticity" (meaning Japaneseness) was a constant theme in conversations about East Village *izakaya*s, Kenka, the area's most popular *izakaya*, seemed more like a caricature than a replica of a Tokyo *izakaya*. A 2013 review for the *Village Voice* described it as "a wildly authentic *izakaya* that might be the most high-functioning example of a Japanese themed restaurant around, an edible amusement park of the fermented, fried, and freaky."[7] "Wildly authentic" seemed apropos for this *izakaya*, or maybe *Japonisme* with a punk sensibility. Kenka was opened in 2004 by immigrant Yuji Umeki in St. Mark's Place, beneath Umeki's punk-rock clothing store. The *izakaya* quickly became popular. A human-sized statue of a drunken *tanuki* (raccoon dog) with flashing red eyes and a rolled-back head greeted customers lined up waiting to enter. A figure of a uniformed Japanese traffic cop advertised Kenka as the "cheapest in the world." A surly Japanese doorman beckoned customers from the waiting list in seemingly random order. On several visits in 2018 and 2019, we waited in lines of college-age customers for an hour to enter. They included long-term New Yorkers who

FIGURE 7.1 The Kenka *izakaya*, created by Yuji Umeki, is one of the more colorful venues in Little Tokyo between St. Mark's Place and Tenth Street in New York's East Village. (Photo by James Farrer, April 2, 2017)

were Kenka regulars and accustomed to the wait, and tourists, such as a young South African woman, in town for a church conference, who was skittish of the panhandlers working the queue. There were even Japanese chefs from another *izakaya* checking out the competition. All were attracted by the low prices and provocative vibe.

Upon entering Kenka, a hallucinogenic vision of a Tokyo *izakaya* assaulted the senses. Customers entered an exotic and erotic caricature of a postwar Japanese urban space accompanied by World War II Japanese martial music. On the walls, they could see posters from Japanese bondage movies, mannequins wearing Japanese long-nosed *tengu* masks, and World War II imperial Japanese flags. The menu offered classic *izakaya* dishes, including *yakisoba* (fried noodles), *gyōza* (dumplings), *karaage* (fried chicken), sashimi, kimchi fried pork, and ramen, as well as gimmicks, such as bull's penis, "maggot fried rice," and a jumbo curry rice plate that was free if eaten within twenty minutes. In addition, the menu was overloaded with pictures of food interspersed with bizarre comments, such as "Taste speed violation!!" (*Aji no speedo ihan*!!). This décor played on the image of Japan as an untranslatable land of perversity and nonsense to spur drinking and fun.

In contrast to the erotic-grotesque-nonsense aesthetic of Kenka,[8] other East Village *izakaya*s aimed for the intimate human scale of the Tokyo alleyway *izakaya*. One of these was simply called The Izakaya. It was opened in 2015 by Yudai Kanayama, a twenty-four-year-old from Hokkaido who studied fashion at a university in New York. Upon graduating, he began peddling secondhand clothing in Brooklyn. Since his roommate, Dai Watanabe, was a chef with experience cooking Italian cuisine (in both Italy and Japan), they decided to open a restaurant. Echoing the early Japanese cultural intermediaries described in Chapter 4, Kanayama described his goal of communicating authentic Japanese culinary culture to Americans: "There were many places here calling themselves *izakaya*, but no one really knew what this was, so I opened this place called 'The Izakaya' in order to share this culture."[9] Most menu items were similar to those in an *izakaya* in Tokyo, including *karaage* and *agedashi tofu*, but there were also such creative flourishes as basil-pesto mayonnaise on the French fries. The menu did not include ramen or sushi because, said Kanayama, "we are not a sushi restaurant!" Instead, he and his cooks decided the tastes of dishes based on their own perceptions of authentic *izakaya* cuisine: "If you try to make something for a customer who really doesn't understand the food, then you will end up making something that you don't want. So, we make something that we like that we believe in and give it to the customer. If they don't want it, then there's nothing you can do about it. . . . I don't want to localize. I really don't like that. I want to do everything I can to explain what my dishes are and have them accepted as they are."[10] The staff was all Japanese because, as Kanayama explained, American employees did not understand the flexible character of work at an *izakaya,* where staff members work together by doing whatever job is necessary.

Kanayama aimed to shape "Japanese" sociability and style at The Izakaya while celebrating elements of regional American culture. From the Japanese side, he wanted Americans to learn to share dishes as Japanese typically did at an *izakaya,* because, in his words, they were "not good at all at sharing."[11] The alcohol was imported from Japan, including Sapporo beer from his home region of Hokkaido and his own house-branded *sake* from Yamagata Prefecture. The *sake* bottle labels replaced the technical Japanese labeling system (based on the degree of milling of *sake* rice) with labels reflecting moods, including "Sake for a relaxing day," "Sake for a sunny day," and "Sake for a rainy day." Additionally, each label featured a cartoon image of Kanayama and his wife. On the locavore side, he engaged with various aspects of regional American culture. His dishes used products from upstate New York, where he had studied as an undergraduate, and the walls displayed Amish hats acquired during his frequent visits to Lancaster County. The Izakaya thus represented a dual-track place-based authenticity grounded in regional Japan and the New York region.

Little Tokyo restaurateurs in the East Village, such as Tony Yoshida, Bon Yagi, Yuji Umeki, and Yudai Kanayama, were cultural intermediaries introducing the idea of the Japanese urban *izakaya* to a largely non-Japanese clientele. The global *izakaya*s created by these migrant Japanese restaurateurs did not adhere to a single model but were a collection of distinct yet interlinked restaurant concepts, running the gamut from Kenka's noisy partying space to The Izakaya's intimate drinking nook. All, however, included elements of drinking culture and sociability. These takes on the *izakaya* imaginary in New York were quickly adopted in other global cities, transforming the *izakaya* into a global restaurant form and food fashion that was refined, enlarged, and corporatized.

Propagating the Global *Izakaya*

Even as it spread quickly in the 2000s into smaller cities, the *izakaya* constituted a translation problem. Few customers knew what it was, so both individuals (owners and chefs) and corporations acted as grassroots cultural intermediaries. They explained it with analogies that non-Japanese customers could grasp, such as Japanese gastropub, tavern, tapas bar, casual dining, *sake* bar, bistro, and lounge. Despite these efforts, as late as 2013, an article on *izakaya*s from *the New York Times* fretted that ". . . most Americans haven't figured them out yet. Where's the sushi bar? What's with the tiny portions? Is this Asian fusion tapas or what? That's the izakaya: easy to love, but hard to nail down. It's friendlier than a French bar à vin, has more food choices than a Spanish tapeo, and takes itself less seriously than a British gastropub. But it makes the same point: drinking is primary; food is secondary; and if you're doing it right, there will be hangovers."[12] Despite this ambiguity, the *izakaya* imaginary quickly filtered from central global cities down to second- and third-tier cities.

This spread was enabled by three kinds of cultural intermediaries—individual migrant restaurateurs (primarily Japanese), midsize restaurant groups, and large-scale chain *izakaya*s. Each drew on their distinct backgrounds and capitals to reinterpret and render the *izakaya* for non-Japanese consumer markets outside Japan. The earliest reinterpretations were among long-term Japanese migrant communities, where Japanese restaurateurs were instrumental in translating the *izakaya* to new customers. Outside these communities, the larger trend was upscaling and forming chains by restaurant groups and holding corporations. These have transformed the *izakaya* into an easily replicable restaurant form.

Pioneers in Translating *Izakaya* Style

The oldest overseas *izakaya*s were Japanese community spaces. Relatively cheap and serving familiar Japanese comfort foods, these *izakaya*s were an everyday "third place" for expatriate Japanese men commuting between their offices and expatriate living compounds and for taking their families for weekend meals. For example, in the 1980s, roughly a dozen such establishments in Los Angeles served Japanese corporate expats stationed there by Japanese companies. One such *izakaya* was Daruma, described in a 1989 review in the *Los Angeles Times* as a place where Japanese expatriates on two-to-five-year assignments could relax and feel comfortable. The reviewer noted the lack of "Western faces" among clientele and that the non-English-speaking waitresses discouraged him from ordering the "more Japanese dishes."[13] Even a decade and a half later, a review of Hagi, a small basement *izakaya* in New York, noted its all-Japanese clientele.[14] However, as seen in Chapter 3, with the slower growth of the Japanese economy in the 1990s, Japanese expatriate communities began shrinking and losing purchasing power. This occurred as the market for Japanese cuisine was expanding among non-Japanese, so *izakaya* owners refocused on these new customers. They were among the first to "translate" the space of the *izakaya* for new consumers.

As home to the largest Japantown in Western Europe, Düsseldorf had several *izakaya*s serving the Japanese community. Among the most popular was Kushi-tei, founded in 1995 by Hokkaido native Haruhiko Saeki (see Chapter 6), owner of the Brickny Europe group, which grew to nine restaurants in the city.[15] Kushi-tei began as an *izakaya* specializing in yakitori with a customer base that was 90 percent Japanese at the time when the local Japanese population peaked at ten thousand people. Saeki grilled chicken at the counter for Japanese expatriate regulars in their forties and fifties, who chatted with him and each other, just as in an *izakaya* in Japan. When we visited in 2017, he said that his Japanese customer base had shrunk and that the newer, younger expats came along and ate in solitude. He attributed this change in Japanese customers to their socialization into the recent "convenience-store-ization" (*konbini-ka*) of eating culture in Japan: an after-work pattern of eating alone quickly rather than socializing with workmates over drinks. So, in Saeki's view, the expatriate community had declined in numbers, spending power, and even conviviality. The new growth market was among non-Japanese.[16]

In the mid-2000s, when visiting New York, Saeki saw the *izakaya* concept catching on. He returned to Düsseldorf, inspired to refashion Kushi-tei into a more globalized *izakaya* with an expanded and eclectic menu, including California rolls, ramen, tempura, and other items already becoming familiar to Germans. Nevertheless, transitioning to a German clientele proved difficult. "Germans are conservative about new foods," Saeki said. "If you open up something in America, they will immediately try it, but with Germans, it takes time." It took ten years to convert locals to the *izakaya* idea. By the latter 2010s, Germans had become the primary clientele, along with Chinese and other Asian customers (echoing the pattern in New York). Germans have also taken to *sake*, he said, not only the familiar *atsukan* (warmed sake) but also chilled *sake* served in a wine glass.[17]

Saeki was keenly aware of his role as a cultural intermediary. "The keyword *izakaya* has come here, but the culture of sharing has not taken deep root," he said. "Germans will still walk in and order a *katsudon* [pork cutlet on rice] udon, and sushi, one for each person. . . . I am trying to get them to order things slowly, one at a time."[18] He explained "*izakaya* style" on a sign in front of the entrance and in manga-like frames on the menu, each with a German-language injunction:

(1) *Prost!* [Cheers]
(2) *Teilen! Essen!* [Share! Eat!)
(3) *Sprechen! Lachen!* [Speak! Laugh!)
(4) *Manchmal weinen* [Sometimes cry)
(5) *Das ist izakaya style!* [This is *izakaya* style)

The restaurant was popular and always packed during our visits in the late 2010s. On one evening visit, a lone Japanese man sat at the bar reading a German newspaper and sipping a draft beer while eating a set meal dinner (*teishoku*). Around him was a mixed-gender group of noisy young Germans. Most were drinking Kirin draft lager, presumably because it was much cheaper than *sake* but still "Japanese." However, the German diners approached the meal in European fashion by dividing their order into appetizers for sharing and entrées for eating individually. We asked the Japanese waitress if German customers commonly ignored the injunction to share, the basic etiquette in an *izakaya* in Japan. She nodded in affirmation. However, the noisy soundscape and interior remained very "Japanese." Smoke wafted up from the grill, manned by a Japanese grill master. Guests were greeted with cascades of "*irasshaimase*" (welcome), and orders were shouted in Japanese across the room.[19]

The waitstaff were all Japanese, mostly women in their twenties. Each wore a loose blue *happi* (traditional jacket worn during festivals), with their name pinned on the lapel, and a thick black headband to contain their hair. In our visits, we observed staff struggling to communicate with German customers in English and German. However, this did not deter German patrons; on the contrary, their comments on social media showed that they saw these young migrant servers speaking basic German as bearers of culinary authenticity. Saeki said that the Japanese staff ensured "a Japanese atmosphere." Some cooks were hired directly from Japan on Saeki's trips to Hokkaido, while the young service workers were students and holders of German working holiday visas, often employed for only a few months. Thus, Kushi-tei's business model depended on cheap and casual Japanese labor, a pattern we also saw in Japanese-managed *izakaya*s in the United States and Australia, staffed with Japanese students and travelers, some with working holiday visas and some working illegally.[20]

Saeki's Kushi-tei represents an expatriate community restaurant adapted to German tastes and organized for expansion. However, it was not easy to localize the *izakaya* concept for Europeans. One issue was the cost. Restaurants targeting Japanese expatriates used expensive imported ingredients; hence, their prices were much higher and portions considerably smaller than what Europeans were used to. Localizing ingredients, however, could disappoint existing Japanese clients (still important in Düsseldorf) while failing to attract new customers. Another issue was staffing, as hiring Japanese could be expensive and difficult. While hiring students and holders of working holiday visas helped contain costs, their greater exploitation was difficult due to national and European Union laws regarding overtime, holidays, and minimum wages.

In some cases, Japanese owners of early *izakaya*s sold out to local owners who then effected the transition to new localized markets. For example, Izakaya Isse, on Rue de Richelieu in the heart of Paris' Japantown, billed itself as the oldest *izakaya* in Paris. It was established in 2003 by Toshiro Kuroda, who came to Paris in the 1980s as a translator at the Japan External Trade Organization and other Japanese agencies. Suffering from an illness in the 2010s, Kuroda sold the *izakaya* to Patrick Duval, a Japanese-speaking journalist and *sake* lover who was a regular. Duval kept the *izakaya*-style interior, with its wooden tables, a tatami alcove, walls covered with posters and Japanese papers, and *sake* barrels (supplied as décor by Dassai, the aggressively expanding brewery from Yamaguchi Prefecture). However, he overhauled Kuroda's sushi-centered menu, which Duval saw as a losing strategy in a market saturated with Chinese-run sushi buffets. A more "authentic" *izakaya* menu created by the head chef from Nagoya featured regional Nagoya dishes, such as miso-glazed eggplant and cod, that were prized by Parisian customers.

However, even in cosmopolitan Paris in the late 2010s, the *izakaya*'s service model and dining style still puzzled local diners.[21] Duval said that he had to explain the dining style to each customer at the beginning of the meal because most assumed it was organized like a French meal, with an entrée (appetizer) followed by the main dish and then dessert. Just as at Kushi-tei, Duval's staff repeatedly explained to European customers that *izakaya* food was served in no fixed order and in small quantities for sharing. Such "translation" was needed, said Duval, to convey "the spirit of *izakaya*."[22]

Upscaling and Supersizing the *Izakaya*

According to industry observers, 2005 was an inflection point in the *izakaya* fashion, with the launching in New York of two *izakaya* restaurants, both with novel approaches to drinking and décor. One was Kenka, described earlier as defining the rowdy style of *izakaya* that attracted students and tourists looking to party in the East Village. The other was En Japanese Brasserie, which introduced an upgraded and upscaled chain *izakaya* concept founded in Japan in the 1990s, partly to revive interest in *sake* among young Japanese. It was created by Taiwanese Japanese Reika Yo Alexander, whose family-owned BYO restaurant group in Japan operated several up-scale *izakaya*s called En. Drawing on her experience at En, Alexander helped pioneer the upscale *izakaya* concept in New York.[23] In a media inter-view, she highlighted the importance of her link to the family restaurant group in Japan. "En in Japan and En in New York are sister establishments that inspire each other. A monthly telephone conference also serves the pur-pose of quickly understanding the trends in Japan. She said, 'Food, interior decoration, and plate selection change with the times, so I think it's an important management aspect to catch trends in real time.'"[24]

New York Times reviewer Frank Bruni noted how this transnational res-taurant import fit seamlessly into gentrifying New York:

> Find a location in a putatively hip or genuinely desirable downtown neigh-borhood. (En goes for the West Village instead of TriBeCa or the meatpack-ing district.) Arrange the tables and sushi counters in a vast, visually arresting space that looks as much like a stage set as a place to eat. (The main dining room at En has a celestially high ceiling, a central column covered in tin tiles, a two-story wall of enormous windows and an entirely open kitchen with cooks rushing to and fro.) Garnish with theatrical flourishes. (. . . The staff at En screeches a greeting as newcomers enter the main dining room; upon hearing it, I never failed to flinch.) Construct an extremely long, confusing menu that suggests boundlessness, emphasizes small plates, encour-ages sharing and, most important of all, accommodates rampant carbohy-drate phobias.[25]

After raving about the sesame tofu and *shōchū* (distilled spirits), Bruni noted that En Japanese Brasserie combined the healthful allure of Japanese cuisine with the timelessness of a bustling drinking place. Although not as kooky as Kenka, it still created a rowdy *izakaya* atmosphere. Customers were greeted by animated shouts of "*irasshaimase*" from the cooks and serv-ers wearing cotton headscarves. There were communal dining counters to foster commensality and a long dining bar made of blond Japanese pine that held stacks of Japanese crockery and a big, steaming tofu cooker.[26] The res-taurant's signature dish was housemade tofu. By 2019, En Japanese Bras-serie had shifted to a more exclusive *omakase* (chef's choice) menu that featured familiar *izakaya* foods as well as high-end fusion dishes designed by Akiko Thurnauer, the executive chef. Thurnauer, a Tokyo native, had learned to cook in innovative New York restaurants, starting at Nobu, a fine dining restaurant described in Chapter 8, with stints in Ivan Ramen and

Mission Chinese, as well as her own restaurant Family Recipe (which closed in 2014). Her boundary-crossing résumé helped explain the Chinese touches as well as the blackened cod and other Nobu-style dishes on the menu. (In 2021 Thurnauer opened an equally eclectic Chinese restaurant, Cha Kee, in Chinatown, showing how high-end chefs migrate among national cuisines, as described in Chapter 8.)[27]

En Japanese Brasserie pioneered various revenue-enhancing strategies. One was the fixed-price *omakase,* a practice adopted from high-end sushi restaurants. While this business model may seem anathema to the casual atmosphere of the *izakaya,* other upscale *izakaya*s use it. These include Zenkichi, which opened in Brooklyn in 2014, and Chateau Hanare in Los Angeles, the latter also by Reika Yo Alexander. Another strategy was pairings with expensive craft *sake* and *shōchū.* A third strategy was emphasizing creative adaptations of Japanese cuisine, often using luxury ingredients.

The corporate *izakaya* was easily copied. Even restaurant groups with no experience in Japanese cuisine jumped into the market. An example is the Blue Ribbon group, owned by Bruce and Eric Bromberg, which operated a chain of restaurants known for fried chicken.[28] In 2012, they founded Blue Ribbon Sushi Izakaya, which combined *izakaya* service with a sushi bar while functioning as an in-house restaurant for a busy Lower East Side hotel. The seating in its spacious interior ranged from intimate booths to large tables for parties of thirty people. When we visited, the head sushi chef was a Nepali sushi master who had worked for over two decades in the business. While sushi was popular, the menu included Western dishes cooked in the hot kitchen by a team of mostly Hispanic cooks. Blue Ribbon Sushi created the *izakaya* atmosphere through shouts of "*irasshai!*" (welcome). On weekends, groups of young employees from the city's Financial District engaged in noisy rounds of *sake* bombs.[29] In this ritual (which might have originated among American soldiers in Japan), a shot of hot *sake* is perched on chopsticks atop a glass of beer, and the table is pounded to chants of "*Sake!* Bomb! *Sake!* Bomb!" until the shot plunges into the beer. The fizzy cocktail is then downed in one gulp.[30] In 2019, Blue Ribbon had nine Japanese-themed restaurants across the United States, combining sushi, *izakaya* dishes, alcohol, and conviviality.

London restaurant operators may have bested New York–based ones in developing the corporate *izakaya* chain. With its dynamic restaurant industry and extensive ties to second-tier global cities throughout Europe and the former British Empire, London has become a top-tier culinary global city for spreading restaurant concepts—including the *izakaya*. The exemplar of the transnational corporate *izakaya* trend is Zuma, cofounded in London in 2002 by Rainer Becker and Arjun Waney. Described on its website as a "sophisticated twist on the traditional Japanese *Izakaya* style of informal eating and drinking," Zuma was the first high-end *izakaya* restaurant in Europe to become a transnational restaurant brand.[31] The non-Japanese partners brought considerable experience to support the venture. German head chef Becker had trained in top restaurants in Germany and worked at Tokyo's Park Hyatt in Shinjuku, where he was exposed to *izakaya* culture. "And when I returned to London," he explained, "my goal was to open a Japanese restaurant that would appeal to a more Western palate, whilst still respecting the ingredients and traditions I had learnt."[32]

Time Out magazine described Zuma as follows: "Dangerously seductive and relentlessly fashionable, this high-gloss Knightsbridge rendezvous is a slinky honeypot for A-list celebrities, swanky bankers and sporting superstars." Its interior resembled a high-end nightclub or art space, while its noise and crowds sustained the casual *izakaya* ambiance.[33] The high prices enabled fastidiousness in presentation and ingredients, and a personalized service that few smaller *izakaya* could match. Many dishes were elegantly plated versions of such *izakaya* favorites as grilled miso cod, grilled scallops topped with black cod roe, and spinach with sesame paste. Chef creations included a yellowtail *maki* (rolled sushi) with pepper, avocado, and wasabi mayo. There were luxury splurges, such as wagyu sushi with Osetra caviar, to give big spenders a way to show off. Thus, Zuma was a corporate *izakaya* with a nightclub-style atmosphere and pricing.

Becker's innovative dishes were designed to be easily replicable in Zuma locations around the world. By 2020, Zuma operated sixteen locations, including Hong Kong (2007), Dubai (2008), Istanbul (2008), Miami (2010), Bangkok (2011), Turkey (2013), and Abu Dhabi (2014). All the managers and chefs in the global chain were trained in London because few had previous experience in Japanese cuisine. The chain's standard design featured a main hot kitchen, sushi counter, and *robata* (open charcoal) grill. Zuma was very profitable, with revenue for the Dubai outlet alone being USD 30 million in 2018.[34] Though corporate restaurants are often snubbed by critics, Zuma branches have won critical acclaim from international media and received prestigious restaurant awards. Both Zuma London and Hong Kong made it onto the "Top 100" listing of World's 50 Best Restaurants. At the same time, Becker has received industry recognition, including Harpers and Moët

Chef of the Year award in 2004.[35] Much as Nobu remade the image of the high-end sushi restaurant (see Chapter 8), London's restaurant industry has spearheaded the global remaking of the *izakaya* as a scalable high-end dining model.

Japanese Chain *Izakaya*s Venture Abroad

The first chain *izakaya*s in Japan were founded in the 1970s and began expanding abroad around 2000. Their operations and expansion accord with the operating procedures of chain restaurants described in the previous chapter, especially their McDonaldized menus of prepared foods that only required heating. They headed abroad due to Japan's shrinking population and domestic market, first to Asia, and then to North America and Europe. In these countries, they entered growing markets for *izakaya*s pioneered by individual restaurateurs, as described earlier.

The first Japanese *izakaya* chain to venture abroad, and probably the most prolific, was Watami. Its founder, Miki Watanabe, said that he was inspired to open overseas outlets while visiting a live music club in New York in 1984. There, he observed how "happy people look when they are with people they like in a place with good food, good service and good atmosphere." This gave him the idea for the restaurant as a "[social] space provider business" (*kūkan teikyō-gyō*) with a goal of "providing as many customers as possible with a place of encounter, contact, and a space of tranquility."[36] From its first outlet in Hong Kong, the chain has marketed itself globally as "fashionable Japanese dining where you can easily enjoy Japanese food style."[37] By 2021, of the chain's 743 outlets, 97 were overseas, mainly in Asia.[38]

Izakaya chains have localized in various ways. In Asia, they have been successfully represented as somewhat high-end family restaurants with "authentic" Japanese food and dining styles. This emphasis as an eating space let the *izakaya* restaurant form overcome its identification as a masculine and rowdy drinking space to broaden its appeal to Asian consumers. The shift from a drinking to eating space was captured in the new term "*ishokuya*," which had been embraced by Watami for marketing in Japan in the early 1990s. In this term, "*zaka*," meaning "alcohol," was replaced by "*shoku*," meaning "food." "*Ishokuya*" thus translates into English as a "dining-oriented bar" that provides "a comfortable and sophisticated dining experience at reasonable prices with friendly service."[39] As Watami headed into Asian markets, it became an *"izakaya* where no alcohol is ordered," according to one industry analyst.[40] The Watami concept has shaped the understanding among overseas customers, especially in Asia, that the *izakaya* is a food-oriented space. Japanese chain corporations have represented their *izakaya*s as trendy midrange restaurants providing many Japanese dishes that people of all ages can enjoy.[41] Thus, the *ishokuya* concept has made the chain *izakaya* in Asian countries outside Japan a space for sociability over food rather than alcohol (though alcohol is still served).

In the West, chain *izakaya*s have also upscaled, although for a different reason from in Asia. This can be seen in Ootoya, an *izakaya* chain that has established three outlets in New York since 2012. Adjusting to the New York market required the company to emphasize classier décor and presentation. America Ootoya CEO Tomonori Takada explained in an interview, "Design-wise, Ootoya in Japan is very casual, but we designed the New York restaurants to be modern and Japanese to meet the expectations of the customers here."[42] For example, it replaced the extensive laminated menus filled with colorful photos of foods used in its hundreds of Asian outlets with pictureless menus using austere fonts on simulated rice paper. It also met US customers' image of Japanese cuisine by putting sushi and sashimi on the menu, a global first for the chain.[43] While such localized chains may use the McDonaldized operation of their Japan outlets, they have moved beyond the low-margin market to seek a position in the upper-middle range of dining options in markets outside Japan.

Authenticity and Innovation in *"Izakaya* Cuisine"

The flexible menu of the *izakaya* is both an opportunity and conundrum for restaurateurs. How do they represent the authenticity—or *izakaya*-ness—of the restaurant to non-Japanese diners if there are no easily recognized and frequently repeated dishes on the menu? In looking at these practices, we see how culinary authenticity is socially constructed, contested, and negotiated between diners and producers.[44] It is most often associated with particular places and origin stories, but it can also be attributed to a chef's culinary pedigree, reputation for creativity, or even a transnational story of multiple migrations. In practice, the varied approaches to *izakaya* cuisine often depended on the chefs' backgrounds and involved the dialectic between "Japaneseness" and innovation explored in previous chapters. On the one hand, the Japanese origin story of the *izakaya* permitted ethnic Japanese restaurateurs to emphasize Japanese roots, authentic tastes, and service style. On the other, the flexibility of the *izakaya* imaginary provided a point of entry for restaurateurs and chefs whose experience lay outside Japanese cuisine, allowing them to introduce other culinary standards and narratives to legitimate their offerings. In both approaches, however, the authenticity of the restaurant was established as much through design elements and the small-plate format as through a particular set of dishes.

"Authentic" Japaneseness as Market Distinction

In twenty-first-century global cities in which most Japanese restaurants are now owned by other types of migrants, the *izakaya* could be marketed as a new and authentic Japanese culinary experience. This strategy was particularly appealing to ethnic Japanese migrant restaurateurs, who could emphasize the Japaneseness of the menu, service style, and taste (even if they lacked culinary training themselves). For example, the Japanese owners of Izakaya Hachibeh, founded in 2009 in downtown Melbourne, Australia, grounded their claims to culinary authenticity in their own biography, tastes, and habitus. The owners, a couple surnamed Saito, came to Australia in 1996 through the husband's corporate assignment at a Japanese company. After five years, he quit his job to work at a Japanese restaurant in Melbourne, where he learned to cook. It was common, he noted, for nonchefs from Japan to open *izakaya*s because they only required very general culinary training.[45]

Despite a relatively shallow culinary background, the Saito couple strove to produce a Japanese style of cuisine distinct from local competitors. This strategy arose because, by the 2010s, the two hundred Japanese restaurants in Melbourne's central business district were almost entirely owned by non-Japanese Asian migrants. For example, Motoki Saito proudly said that his *izakaya* did not offer US-style roll sushi, which, in his view, was not really Japanese food. Dishes prepared by non-Japanese chefs might have looked Japanese but often lacked the umami taste of properly prepared dashi broth, he said. He emphasized that his service was traditional Japanese *izakaya*-style, whereas many local *izakaya*s followed the Western order of soup, appetizer, main dish, and dessert.

The restaurant had two floors, with a small sushi bar on the first. Like many *izakaya*s in Tokyo, it was a bright and lively space decorated with red lanterns and posters from beverage companies. To maintain a Japanese atmosphere, Saito hired as many Japanese staff as possible. The service staff members were all young Japanese. Japanese heavy metal music imparted a bit of party atmosphere. Saito and his wife prepared hot dishes and hired a sushi chef. Although most of Hachibeh's sushi chefs were Japanese, when we visited in 2018, the sushi chef was Mr. Kim, an ethnically Korean forty-one-year-old with dual Australian-US citizenship. He studied sushi making at a culinary school in Korea and then worked as a sushi chef at Korean-run Japanese sushi restaurants in California for ten years. In 2012, he came to Melbourne to work as a sushi chef. His "play" on sashimi—tossing fish slices and decorative herbs onto plates with a smooth flick of his hands—both showcased his skill and entertained customers. To his regular customers, his fancy knife work at the sushi counter embodied Japanese authenticity. As this American-inspired performance of Japaneseness illustrates, the presentation of ethnic authenticity is always a negotiation between customers and producers and is not based on an absolute standard.[46]

São Paulo is another market where we see attempts by some *izakaya* owners to use Japanese authenticity to distinguish their establishments from other, more localized Japanese restaurants. The *izakaya* in Brazil is both an extension and evolution in the Japanese food boom, introducing diners to a broader range of hot dishes and Japanese alcohol than typically found in the familiar "sushi-sashimi" combos served in Brazilian Japanese restaurants. Through dining in *izakaya*s, the Brazilian public came to know new dishes such as *katsu sando* (cutlet sandwiches), *buta no kakuni* (stewed pork belly), and *karaage*. The popularization of the *boteco japonês* (Japanese taverns), as *izakaya*s in São Paulo were called, was confirmed by the creation of a specific category for "best *izakaya*" in one of the most prized gastronomic awards, the VEJA São Paulo listings.

While there are many cheap localized *izakaya*s in São Paulo, higher-end *izakaya*s typically emphasize "authenticity" over localization. An instance is Yorimichi Izakaya, nominated as the best *izakaya* in São Paulo in 2017. Located in the upscale residential Paraíso neighborhood, it aimed to replicate a Tokyo *izakaya*'s "authentic feel." Its manager and part-owner, Nikkei Brazilian Ken Mizumoto, lived for eleven years in Japan. Yorimichi served small-plate dishes prepared on a charcoal grill in the center of the dining room with the smoke sucked up by a rectangular hood in the ceiling. A U-shaped counter with fifteen seats encircled the cooking space for customers to enjoy the spectacle. The menu listed dozens of brands of Japanese *sake* and *shōchū,* as well as whiskeys, beers, and Chilean and Argentinian wines. Bottles bore the names of patrons, according to Japan's bottle-keep custom. A cozy counter on the first floor and a private tatami room on the second floor were often booked by employees of East Asian multinationals.[47]

Such spaces emphasized Japaneseness by organizing the restaurant space around the performance of skilled Japanese chefs cooking in a style represented as authentically Japanese. This strategy was most often pursued by ethnic Japanese, though non-Japanese operators could also attempt it. Some hired Japanese managers and cooks. For example, the French-owned Izakaya Isse in Paris and the Vietnamese-owned Iro Izakaya in Berlin both hired Japanese chefs as well as front-of-house staff to give their places the taste and feel of Japan. In both cases, the managers explained this as a strategy to distinguish their offerings from the mass-market sushi restaurants run by Chinese or Vietnamese migrant entrepreneurs (see Chapter 5).[48] However, as the next section illustrates, emphasizing Japaneseness through ethnic and place-based authenticity was not the only way restaurateurs could market genuine *izakaya* cuisine.

Playing with the *Izakaya* Menu

Especially for non-Japanese restaurateurs, the *izakaya* concept also could invite innovations that played with ideas of Japaneseness. As described earlier, even in Japan a mix of cuisines is common on the *izakaya* menu, encouraging syncretism and hybridity of preparations. The open-endedness of the *izakaya* culinary imaginary thus allowed for Japanese elements to be decentered or translated in innovative ways. This decentered Japaneseness could reflect transnational Japanese culinary traditions (e.g., Nikkei cuisines), personal journeys of the chef (e.g., sojourns in Japan), or ironic and irreverent evocations of Japaneseness, such as we saw in Kenka in New York.

The *izakaya* was thus an open invitation for restaurateurs of many backgrounds to play with notions of Japanese culinary authenticity, without discarding them altogether. As Gabriel Stulman, owner of a half dozen restaurants in New York's West Village, said in an interview, "I would be paralyzed by the idea of opening a sushi bar. . . . But an *izakaya* was easy for me to wrap my head around."[49] In 2012, his group opened Chez Sardine with Canadian chef Mehdi Brunet-Benkritly. Its creative menu included Canadian-Japanese fusions, such as miso-and-maple-glazed salmon head and breakfast pancakes, a stack of silver-dollar-size pancakes layered with chopped fluke, copious salmon roe, and spicy yogurt sauce, as well as such non-Japanese fusions as foie gras and smoked-cheddar grilled-cheese sandwich. (After two years, Stulman ditched the *izakaya* concept for a classic American casual bar, underscoring the rapidity of restaurant trends.)

Hong Kong is an established culinary global city with customers from around the world willing to try new restaurant concepts, enabling chefs to innovate with *izakaya* cuisine. Some of the prominent promoters of *izakaya*s in the city were Western chefs. One was Max Levy, an American chef whose first experience in Japan was working in the Tsukiji fish market, then in restaurants in Tokyo. After college, he moved to New York, training at the Asian-influenced French restaurant Jean Georges and Bond Street, a nightclub-like Japanese restaurant featuring sushi. Eventually, he became the only non-Japanese sushi chef at New York's venerable Sushi Yasuda. After opening the first Okra in Beijing in 2012, in 2015 Levy opened a second in Sai Ying Pun, an upcoming Hong Kong food district better known for its wet markets. The restaurant featured a casual downstairs *izakaya*, Okra Kitchen, and an upstairs *omakase* sushi bar, Okra Bar. Some dishes used ingredients and techniques from China, while others drew on Levy's Jewish and Louisiana roots and frequent travel to Japan. In Okra Kitchen, innovative dishes included country-style homemade tofu with North China soybeans, Guizhou-style andouille sausage, and a grilled fish head (not just the usual jaw). Another was beef tongue salted with a traditional Jewish technique for making corned beef and then aged and smoked. He also served a brown rice *sake* aged five years with the bouquet of light Chinese rice wine. The restaurant appealed to expatriates and local gastronomes intrigued by Levy's stories of sourcing ingredients and learning new techniques.[50] Authenticity, in his case, was grounded in his personal culinary journey, in which Japan was but one stop, albeit an important one. Unfortunately for Levy, the dual impact of pandemic lockdowns and the months-long street battles surrounding the national security law in Hong Kong severely impacted the international clientele supporting such restaurants in Hong Kong. Okra closed in July 2021.[51]

Japanese chefs were also attracted to the *izakaya* form because of the license for innovation. However, when working abroad, they could be trapped in the expectations of the "ethnic restaurateur" to produce "authentic" (and familiar) dishes rather than innovate in unexpected ways.[52] We observed this dilemma with the creative *izakaya* Adjito, which was opened in Düsseldorf in 2015 by Yasu Umezaki, from Matsuyama in Shikoku. An artist by training, Umezaki worked as a designer for Japanese restaurateurs (including for the popular Düsseldorf *izakaya* Kushi-tei described earlier). With no training in cuisine, Umezaki drove a Japanese food truck around Europe for two years, developing a repertoire of unique Japanese-European fusion specialties. Adjito's dishes challenged German understandings of Japanese (and Western) food. A "gyoza hamburger" was based on a Japanese manga and used *gyōza*-style meat and a fluffy milk roll baked by a Japanese bakery. An "udon carbonara" was flavored with dashi and miso rather than cream. Unlike the "authentic Japanese" ambience of Düsseldorf's Kushi-tei, Adjito's interior design was edgy, even sinister. It included such gothic flourishes as beetles inlaid in wooden dining tables. With its creative design and menu, Adjito faced online complaints from some diners that the cuisine was not "authentic." It closed in 2019. While the reasons for its failure could be multiple, Adjito illustrates how Japanese chefs had difficulty marketing innovative *izakaya* cuisine to customers with fixed expectations. The fact that Umezaki was ethnically Japanese only confused diners who expected a familiar "Japanese" menu from a Japanese chef (a complaint also voiced about Japanese-American cuisine in Chapter 4).[53]

Creating Global "Japanese" Drinking Spaces

Like its open-ended food menu, the marketing of alcohol through the *izakaya* imaginary also could be realized in different ways. In top-tier global cities, the *izakaya* was a vehicle to promote a new high-end Japanese-inflected drinking culture encompassing Japanese *sake*, whiskey, cocktails, and craft beers. In cities with vibrant urban nightlife, *izakaya*s were presented as a new style of nightspot. In North American cities, the *izakaya* could be a setting for hard drinking and partying, activities not usually associated with Asian dining. In some Asian markets, in contrast, the *izakaya* represented an invitation to alcohol connoisseurship and intimate sociability, an imaginary that appealed to women. The *izakaya* thus represented a novel "Japanese style" of drinking experience reaching new types of customers.

The *Izakaya* as Urban Nightlife Spot

Some restaurateurs, taking a cue from "wild" spaces like New York's Kenka or the Blue Ribbon Izakaya, marketed the *izakaya* as a space for people to party while drinking high-margin *sake* bombs and cocktails. This is illustrated by Yakitori Boy and Japas Lounge in Philadelphia, founded as a partnership between a Taiwanese owner of a Chinese restaurant and a Japanese chef-owner of a sushi restaurant in the city. In the early 2000s, they often went to New York to check out restaurants. After visiting several *izakayas*, they decided to set one up in Philadelphia. In 2008, they opened Yakitori Boy and Japas Lounge in Chinatown. Their *izakaya* specialized in yakitori skewers, sushi rolls, and small dishes—called Japas, short for "Japanese tapas"—that included tempura and teriyaki lamb chops. They marketed the *izakaya* as a place for individuals and small groups, as well as large celebrations, such as bachelor or bachelorette and birthday parties. The first-floor Yakitori Boy resembled a chain *izakaya* in Japan, with its yakitori and sushi bars, booths, and dark wood accents. The second-floor Japas Lounge had a large standing bar, lounge, and karaoke rooms. This rendering of the *izakaya* as an Asian-themed destination for partying appealed to the city's sizable urban youth market.

Momotaro in Chicago pursued a strategy of marketing alcohol to customers who viewed *izakayas* primarily as restaurants. It was owned by the Chicago-based Boka group, which, since 2002, had opened over a dozen restaurants. The restaurants, each partnered with a celebrity chef, spanned the tastes of new American cuisine, winning national awards. Momotaro, founded in 2012 as Boka's first foray into Japanese cuisine, was an upscale fusion restaurant with a basement *izakaya*. When we visited in 2017, it was overseen by chef Mark Hellyar, who had worked in Japan for several years, including at the Japanese restaurant Shunbou at Tokyo's Park Hyatt Hotel. The Japanese government had even given him a Taste of Japan award in 2016 for promoting Japanese cuisine in the West.[54] Its manager Anna Shin told us of the challenge to sell the *izakaya* concept to Chicagoans. They already had their favorite bars and were not easily enticed by the Japanese character of what appeared to be yet another drinking place.[55] The basement *izakaya*, echoing New York's Village Yokocho, had Japanese-themed *yokochō* décor. Its website described it as a "narrow lounge-inspired 'alley' around a central bar detached with hand-painted Japanese menus, moody neon signs, and vintage Tokyo street signs [that] set the scene for the *izakaya*'s direct reference to Tokyo's most famous post-war black markets."[56] This décor was also a nod to Chicago's gangster era, making the underground *izakaya* more legible to locals.

Izakaya in some European cities also used an edgy, underworld décor to introduce more alcohol and nightlife patronage into the Japanese-themed venues. An example is Berlin's Ryotei 893, on Kantstrasse. Opened in 2017, it was created by Vietnamese German restaurateur The Duc Ngo, the so-called Duke of Kantstrasse, who, as described in Chapter 5, introduced hipster Japanese cuisine to Berlin in his four other restaurants. Ryotei 893 was an upscale establishment that dispensed with pub-style warmth to embrace the darker Berliner aesthetic of an underground club. The numbers 893 also read in Japanese as "*ya-ku-za*," which meant gangster. Early in the evening, customers lined up to enter in front of a single red neon lamp above the facade of the former pharmacy, its one-way mirrored glass windows intentionally etched with bold graffiti. Inside, the wall art evoked yakuza tattoos. Halogen lamps over each table lit just enough space to see and photograph the food. A circular light-green marble table in a corner "for special guests and after hour's [sic] poker" mimicked the VIP area of a high-end club.[57] The establishment was more a laid-back lounge bar than a loud party spot, and most tables were occupied by youngish couples on dates when we visited. The menu was inspired by the fusion cuisine of Noboyuki "Nobu" Matsuhisa, alongside the roll sushi and other items that Berliners had come to expect at Ngo's other restaurants.[58] Especially in cities such as New York, Philadelphia, and Berlin, with flourishing nighttime economies, there was money to be made in promoting the *izakaya* as a novel nightlife experience and not simply a restaurant.

Promoting a Global *Sake* Boom

Beyond a boisterous nightlife image, the *izakaya* drinking style could also be directed toward connoisseurship. A chief focus was premium craft *sake*, made of highly polished rice by small brewers in Japan, and increasingly by *sake* brewers in other countries (though these were still a small part of the global market). While expensive in comparison to local beverages, craft *sake* found a market in global culinary cities with big-spending gourmets. This was especially true in Asia, where the price of *sake* and the price of wine (its chief competition) were more on a level field. From 2007 to 2017, Japan's worldwide *sake* exports increased sharply from 11,334 kiloliters to 169,023 kiloliters. In 2020, the top four importers of *sake* by volume were Taiwan, mainland China, the United States, and South Korea.[59] High-end *izakaya*s were both products of and promoters of this global *sake* boom.

New York City was the US center of the global *sake* boom. In the 1990s, Bon Yagi, a founder of Little Tokyo (see Chapter 3), saw the potential for marketing premium *sake* to Americans but realized that its high import costs would raise the price, making it a hard sell. So he opened the *izakaya* Sakagura in 1997 in Midtown, where high-earning, trend-conscious professionals were willing to pay for premium drinks. Sakagura was perhaps the city's first "*sake izakaya*." In 2018, he opened a second branch in the East Village, by which time wealthy finance industry types had displaced the bohemian "starving artists" who once populated the area. When we visited the East Village Sakagura in September 2019, a young Nepali *sake* sommelier avidly explained the tasting profiles of various craft *sake*s. She said that she had never tasted *sake* before taking this job but gained expertise at events hosted by *sake* vendors and through the guidance of senior staff. Offering over two hundred brands of *sake,* Sakagura represented another variation in the global *izakaya* imaginary—namely, the "*sake* temple" for tasting and marketing high-end *sake* to aspiring connoisseurs.[60]

In Asia, *sake* found a market among Asia's nouveau riche in the 2000s, many of whom were already familiar with local rice-based alcoholic drinks. In Taipei, culturally and geographically close to Japan, the associations of the *izakaya* were richer and more complicated than in Europe or the United States. From the colonial times in the early twentieth century, there were already "Taiwan-style *izakaya*s" (*taishi jūjiuwu*) selling a few Japanese dishes among mostly Taiwanese offerings.[61] Taipei residents saw these establishments as an old-fashioned type of Taiwan restaurant with some Japanese links. However, the global *izakaya* boom beginning in the early 2000s stimulated the rise of modernized "Japanese-style *izakaya*s" (*rishi jūjiuwu*), offering a wide selection of Japanese *sake* and food. Unlike older Taiwan-style *izakaya*s, the new ones were tied to recent trends in Japan and globally, serving high-quality Japanese food and *sake*. Their sophisticated décor and menus made them popular with image-conscious young women.

One such establishment was Hana Bi, which opened in Taipei in 2007. It was marketed as a "Japanese tapas *izakaya*" to distinguish it from Taiwan-style *izakaya*s, with the term "tapas" linking it to global *izakaya* culture.[62] Its owner, Michael Ou, had spent his youth in the United Kingdom and New Zealand, trained as a French-cuisine chef, and went to Japan to study Japanese language and cuisine, where he qualified as a "*sake* master" (*kikizakeshi*). In 2015, he started *sake* festivals in Taipei and Shanghai, and gave lectures on *sake*, including one at an exhibition in a high-end *izakaya* in Shanghai we attended with representatives of Michelin and World's 50 Best Restaurants.[63] The Japanese government recognized him for promoting Japanese *sake* culture in Taiwan. When we visited Hana Bi in 2018, we stepped into a *sake* temple serving over forty brands of Japanese *sake*, along with *kamameshi* (rice casseroles) and small plates of Japanese regional food. Hana Bi aspired to "authentic" Japanese *izakaya* culture, which Ou interpreted as pairing quality Japanese *sake* with Japanese cuisine. He said that Taipei residents went out either to eat or to drink without thinking of doing both. So Ou promoted his Japanese tapas *izakaya* as a place to savor both Japanese *sake* and food. Given Taipei's proximity to Japan, culinary trends there hewed closer to Japan than in Europe or America, while attracting the same well-heeled clientele who knew tapas and other global culinary trends.

With a soft wooden interior and warm yellow lighting, the atmosphere of Hana Bi resembled an upscale modern *izakaya* in Tokyo. The display of menu books, chopsticks, and plates on each table was similar to practices in Japan, such as the folded menu book covering the wooden chopsticks. It was written in Japanese with the colloquial statement, "Let's drink up!" (*Omoikiri nonjaou ka, pātto!*). There were many table seats, with a seatless counter separating the dining hall from the open kitchen. (The purpose of this unusual design, Ou explained, was to prevent locals from asking the staff behind the counter to drink with them.) During our four-hour visit, all customers were women in their twenties or thirties. This was not unusual, Ou said. Japanese *izakaya*s like Hana Bi were more expensive than Taiwan-style *izakaya*s, so men intent on heavy drinking avoided them. Instead, it appealed to middle-class young women looking for a quiet environment to enjoy good food and drink in a sophisticated and urbane atmosphere. When men came, they were accompanying female friends, girlfriends, or wives, said Ou. This pattern suggests that the Japanese *izakaya* imaginary in some Asian markets like Taipei is a feminized version of Japanese drinking culture.[64]

Local and Transnational Spaces of Sociability

In addition to eating and drinking, the *izakaya* carries an expectation of nocturnal sociability and communal life. Beyond the scenes of boisterous partying and alcohol connoisseurship already described, we introduce two other scenes of conviviality and sociability in the *izakaya*. One is an urban third place for Chinese women; the other is an expatriate retreat in an emerging African global city. Both examples show how the *izakaya* is simultaneously a local community spot and a transnational imaginary bringing consumers together locally and connecting them to the image and experience of *izakaya*s in other cities.

The *Izakaya* as a Feminized Urban Third Place

While the image of the *izakaya* in Japan has been that of a male-oriented watering hole, this is less the case in Asian countries with their own male-dominated drinking cultures. Instead, the *izakaya* form has been adopted by urban Asian women as a fashionable, refined, even feminized drinking space for consuming light foods and low-percentage alcoholic beverages. This can be seen in places like Hana Bi in Taiwan and similar spots in Seoul and Hong Kong. In general, Asian consumers seem more familiar with representations of the small-scale *izakaya* frequented by a community of regular customers. This ideal of intimate *izakaya* sociability has been transmitted through Japanese manga and television serials, especially *Midnight Diner* (*Shinya shokudo*), a manga and then a television program that depicts a late-night *izakaya* where customers share their emotional ups and downs over small-plate dishes and drinks prepared by a patient bar master. This series was widely available on streaming services (such as Netflix) in some countries. In China, it played on television screens in *izakaya*s we visited, conveying the scenes of cozy familiarity. This section focuses on *izakaya* in Tianjin, where this ideal was adopted by many female customers.

In the 2010s, Shanxi Road, the former Japanese colonial concession in Tianjin's city center, became known for *izakaya*s owned and run by Chinese who had never been to Japan. Still, some had experience learning from Japanese chefs in China.[65] The *izakaya*s were not refined establishments serving connoisseurs, such as Hana Bi in Taipei, but rather cozy spots for young middle-income Tianjin urbanites. These *izakaya*s were spaces for ca-

FIGURE 7.2 Young Chinese women enjoying a night out at Izakaya Er Fan Hive after 10 p.m. in downtown Tianjin, China. The male chef-owner was busy preparing food and beverages behind the bar counter. (Photo by Chuanfei Wang, March 16, 2017)

sual dining rather than for heavy drinking, with menus that placed food ahead of the alcohol. The food emphasis could also be seen in the practice in these *izakaya*s of delivering lunch bento (*biandang*), while students from a nearby middle school even ate lunch in them. This idea of the *izakaya* as an everyday space drew on cultural familiarity with Japan's *izakaya* culture. As Japan was the most popular overseas tourist destination for middle-class residents in China's coastal cities, many *izakaya* patrons had visited it.

The *izakaya*s on Shanxi Road formed a particular niche in Tianjin's restaurant market for youthful consumers. According to our informants, Chinese restaurants were generally regarded as noisy and unsophisticated, and Western restaurants as expensive venues for conspicuous consumption but lacking in intimacy. In contrast, young consumers saw *izakaya*s as affordable places to hang out or go on a date, and a "safe" space for young women to avoid drinking pressures and male harassment while meeting with friends late at night. The space of the *izakaya* represented a type of lifestyle that was characterized by respect for individual preferences, a carefree atmosphere, and coziness associated with urban Japan, while the moderately priced meals attracted younger consumers.[66] We observed that the customers of the Tianjin *izakaya*s, as in Taipei, were mainly young women in small groups.[67]

An exemplar of this kind of *izakaya* is Erfanzhu, housed in a two-story Japanese-style structure built during the colonial era in the 1930s. On our visit late one Friday evening in 2017, the *izakaya* tables were crowded with women in their twenties. The restaurant had two cooking areas, an outside grill and an inside kitchen for preparing salads and cooked food. On the first floor was a bar counter with six seats and a table with two sofas for four people. The two women sitting at the bar beside us were former university classmates working at companies. They frequented Erfanzhu, where they felt comfortable chatting with female friends late into the night. On the second floor were two low tables for tatami seating, one occupied by five women and the other by four women and two men.[68] Conspicuously absent were male-dominated drinking rituals typical at Chinese restaurants—toasting with hard liquor (*baijiu*) and exhortations to "drink up" (*ganbei*)—which often alienated young women who were treated as decorative accessories at such events.[69] At Erfanzhu, a cup of *sake* or a cocktail was the companion for a meal. The beverages were sweet and low in alcohol, such as a lychee-flavored beer or a mixed-fruits *sake* cocktail. The light-tasting food had less spice, oil, and salt than typical Tianjin fare and included such Japanese dishes as sashimi, yakitori, and tempura, as well as Korean and Western dishes. House specialties included "Erfan *paocai*" (similar to kimchi) and "house-made pickles" (*zijiazhi xiancai*), a selection of Western pickles, spicy *paocai,* and Japanese daikon pickles.

Erfanzhu was opened in 2011 by a university graduate from Tianjin in his late twenties who had never been to Japan or studied Japanese cooking. He told us that he was motivated by a desire to own a business and an interest in Japanese culture. Though his young kitchen staff lacked professional culinary training, they learned from the internet, cookbooks, and Japanese television programs. They aimed to reproduce the *izakaya* atmosphere and dishes seen on these transnational media, a self-teaching method common among the Chinese operators of *izakaya* on Shanxi Road. These young entrepreneurs took advantage of the *izakaya*'s flexible menus and cozy image to create their own version of the "late-night diner"—a third place between home and work—for Tianjin women.

The *Izakaya* as a Transnational Expatriate Space

In the 2010s, the growing global *izakaya* fashion led to their establishment in places where there were few Japanese restaurants. This was similar to the Irish pub that, as a global form, could be established practically anywhere to attract a diverse clientele. In Nairobi, Cheka Japanese Izakaya Restaurant, founded in 2015, the only *izakaya* in the city, was an expatriate community space attracting many elite migrants living in the city. It was too expensive for most Kenyans, but some urban professionals and businesspeople patronized it on special occasions. To appeal to expatriates and distinguish it from other Asian restaurants in the city, its thirty-two-year-old founder, Yuki Kashiwagi, emphasized both its Japaneseness and its local mission.[70]

Kashiwagi had a social agenda for the restaurant. Originally from Osaka, he had been raised by a single mother and came to Africa ten years earlier as a Japan International Cooperation Agency volunteer in Zambia. The hospitality and help from local people had left a lasting impression on

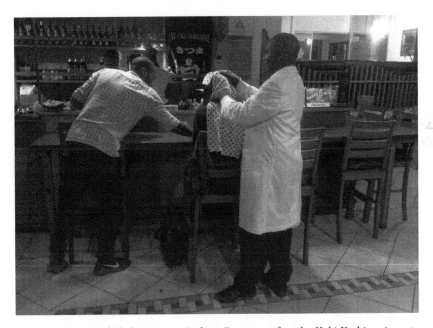

FIGURE 7.3 A goal of Cheka Japanese Izakaya Restaurant founder Yuki Kashiwagi was to provide jobs for disadvantaged Kenyans. One strategy was to employ blind masseurs to give customers massages at the restaurant. (Photo by Lisa Yajun Hu, November 5, 2017)

him. After completing his tour in Zambia, he sought to repay the hospitality by working to increase employment opportunities for poor Africans. He opened his *izakaya* in Lavington, a high-income residential area, with a staff of thirty Kenyans, mainly single mothers from the Kangemi and Kiberia slums. For them, this was a chance to have stable employment, said Kashiwagi. Hence the name of the *izakaya*, because *cheka* means "smiling and laughing" in Swahili. Kashiwagi saw the *izakaya* as a virtuous cycle; growing numbers of happy customers generated profits that enabled him to hire and help more people. Additionally, as the only Japanese running a Japanese restaurant in Nairobi, he wanted his *izakaya* to be authentic. "This is the concept of a bar-restaurant, drinking and eating, *izakaya* style," Kashiwagi explained. "They share everything. This is the positive thing. You want to share the food, pan-fried, sashimi, sushi, tempura, so let's go to Cheka."[71]

Most customers were well-paid professionals, including international aid workers from Japan and other countries. According to Kashiwagi, the customers included Europeans (40 percent), Japanese (30 percent), other Asians (20 percent), and Kenyans (10 percent). He observed that Kenyan customers were the least familiar with Japanese cuisine and seafood, mainly ordering grilled chicken and other cooked meat dishes. They expected restaurants to serve large portions and thus found the small plates off-putting. In contrast, the expatriate customers seemed to understand the small-plate *izakaya* concept. Many ordered Japanese beer and *sake*, with Japanese customers partial to the *shōchū*.

Cheka Japanese Izakaya Restaurant was a community space, not for the Japanese migrant community, as in an earlier era, but rather for a cosmopolitan community of well-paid migrants from around the world. In this sense, the *izakaya* was akin to Irish pubs that functioned as gathering places for expatriates in similar cities, underscoring the *izakaya*'s transformation from an ethnic Japanese imaginary to a global one. However, Kashiwagi still saw himself as a cultural intermediary. He took customers' questions, such as, "Why you don't have California rolls?" and "Why isn't your ginger pink?" as opportunities to educate them about Japanese food in Japan.[72] At the same time, he strove to meet multiple customer expectations to represent a "local" *izakaya* for Kenyans, a "global" *izakaya* with diverse customers, and a "Japanese" *izakaya* with authenticity claims. Such negotiations are part of the cultural bricolage of running an *izakaya*—or any similar space—in an emerging global city.

The Japanese Restaurant as Global Imaginary

*Izakaya*s have been opening in cities around the world since the early 2000s. The spread was driven less by consumer demand—they had to be taught what the word "*izakaya*" meant—than by the business strategies of restaurateurs. Strategies included promoting alcohol, especially high-end *sake* and cocktails, to new consumer groups, such as women; casualizing service by emphasizing small plates served in no particular order; and deskilling the cooking process with easily cooked dishes. While the manifestation of the *izakaya* imaginary varied locally, they shared an image as sites for fun, sharing food, and conviviality. Outside Japanese immigrant communities, Japanese restaurants had seldom had an image as a space for drinking, partying, or hanging out late into the evening. As such, *izakaya*s were a new type of urban third place that fostered social interactions ranging from boisterous partying to intimate conversations, depending on the context. And while the *izakaya* could be regarded as twenty-first-century japonaiserie, or another celebration of Asian exoticism, the leading performers in this space were the customers themselves, not staff members performing as ethnic "others." Perhaps this transposition of the customer into performer also indicates how this Japanese restaurant space has become familiar and comfortable to a wide variety of consumers.

Even in the relatively short duration of the *izakaya* fashion trend (a little over two decades), we see significant transformations of its form. While earlier *izakaya*s were independently owned by adventurous chefs and lifestyle migrants, corporate chains have been increasing. This shows how McDonaldization processes, described in Chapter 6, are also shaping midrange Japanese dining. And while some Japanese migrant chef-owners seek to promote an authentic Japanese dining experience, this chapter shows the growing presence of non-Japanese restaurateurs who, as in Chapters 5 and 6, are creating more flexible and open-ended forms and functions of the Japanese restaurant. These trends of innovation and hybridization in global Japanese restaurant cuisine are amplified in the high-end restaurant scenes described in the next chapter.

Notes

1. Chris Hudson, "The 'Craic' Goes Global: Irish Pubs and the Global Imaginary," in *Revisiting the Global Imaginary: Theories, Ideologies, Subjectivities: Essays in Honor*

of Manfred Steger, ed. Chris Hudson and Erin K. Wilson (New York: Palgrave Macmillan, 2019), 155–173.

2. Alice Bosio et al., *"Izakaya:* Le Japon à petit plats" [*Izakaya:* Japan with small plates], *Le Figaro,* October 2, 2013, https://www.lefigaro.fr/sortir-paris/2013/10/02 /30004-20131002ARTFIG00311-izakaya-le-japon-a-petits-plats.php; Dean Kuipers, "We're Way Past Sushi," *Los Angeles Times,* March 30, 2006, E26; Julia Moskin, "Soaking Up the Sake," *New York Times,* April 9, 2013, https://nyti.ms/12GlQZj.

3. Taro Futamura and Kazuaki Sugiyama, "The Dark Side of the Nightscape: The Growth of *Izakaya* Chains and the Changing Landscapes of Evening Eateries in Japanese Cities," *Food, Culture and Society* 21, no. 1 (2018): 101–117.

4. Hashimoto Kenji (橋本健二), *Izakaya no sengoshi* (居酒屋の戦後史) [Postwar history of *izakaya*] (Tokyo: Shodensha, 2015), 52–58.

5. James Farrer, "Grimy Heritage: Organic Bar Streets in Shanghai and Tokyo," *Built Heritage* 3, no. 3 (2019): 73–85.

6. James Farrer, "The Space-Time Compression of Tokyo Street Drinking," *Food, Culture and Society* 24, no. 1 (2021): 49–65.

7. James A. Foley, "Kenka Is a Wild and Freaky Ride," *Village Voice,* June 5, 2013, https://www.villagevoice.com/2013/06/05/kenka-is-a-wild-and-freaky-carnival-ride/.

8. The aesthetic of "erotic grotesque nonsense" emerged in prewar Japan in the 1920s and 1930s as an artistic movement focusing on grotesque visuals and bizarre humor. See Miriam Silverberg, *Erotic Grotesque Nonsense* (Berkeley: University of California Press, 2007).

9. Yudai Kanayama, interview by James Farrer, April 20, 2019.

10. Yudai Kanayama, interview by James Farrer, April 20, 2019.

11. Yudai Kanayama, interview by James Farrer, April 20, 2019.

12. Moskin, "Soaking Up the Sake."

13. Max Jacobson, "Daruma: Slow Grazing at the Most Authentic *Izakaya* Around," *Los Angeles Times,* July 23, 1989, https://www.latimes.com/archives/la-xpm-1989-07-23 -ca-397-story.html.

14. Peter Meehan, "Tokyo Nights, without the Smoke," *New York Times,* August 30, 2006, F8.

15. "Alles im Ramen: Zu Besuch bei Saeki Haruhiko von Takumi" [Everything in ramen: visiting Haruhiko Saeki of Takumi], RP-Online (Rheinische Post), November 8, 2018, https://rp-online.de/nrw/staedte/duesseldorf/alles-im-ramen_aid-24311915.

16. Haruhiko Saeki, interview by James Farrer, August 28, 2017; fieldwork by James Farrer, 2016, 2017, and 2018.

17. Haruhiko Saeki, interview by James Farrer, August 28, 2017.

18. Haruhiko Saeki, interview by James Farrer, August 28, 2017.

19. Fieldwork by James Farrer, 2017.

20. In all these places, poor language skills and weak knowledge of labor regulations opened these young migrants to exploitation in terms of pay and work hours. Fieldwork by James Farrer, 2016, 2017, and 2018; fieldwork by Chuanfei Wang, 2017.

21. Bosio et al., *"Izakaya."*

22. Patrick Duval, interview by Chuanfei Wang, August 31, 2018; fieldwork by Chuanfei Wang, August 31, 2018.

23. BYO CO LTD accessed December 4, 2020, https://byo.co.jp.

24. "Yō Reika shi intabyū: Nyūyōku no serebu ga tsudou EN Japanese Brasserie no wakaki josei ōnā" (楊麗華氏インタビュー: ニューヨークのセレブが集うEN Japanese

Brasserie の若き女性オーナー) [Reika Yo interview: A young female owner of EN Japanese Brasserie where celebrities from New York gather], *HuffPost,* November 15, 2013, https://www.huffingtonpost.jp/artinfo-japan/en-japanese-brasserie_b_4279920.html.

25. Frank Bruni, "A Paean to Tofu in a Japanese Pub," *New York Times,* November 24, 2004, F8.

26. Adam Pratt, "En Style," *New York Magazine,* November 11, 2004, https://nymag.com/nymetro/food/reviews/restaurant/10383/.

27. Akiko Thurnauer, conversation with James Farrer, August 23, 2019; Peter Wells, "Cha Kee Is a Beacon in Chinatown's Revival," *New York Times,* November 23, 2021, https://www.nytimes.com/2021/11/23/dining/restaurant-review-cha-kee-chinatown.html?smid=url-share.

28. Blue Ribbon Restaurants accessed June 1, 2020, https://www.blueribbonrestaurants.com/.

29. Fieldwork by James Farrer, January 5, 2018.

30. Caroline Pardilla, "An Ode to the Sake Bomb," *Los Angeles Times,* April 22, 2013, https://www.lamag.com/digestblog/an-ode-to-the-sake-bomb/.

31. Zuma accessed December 11, 2020, https://www.zumarestaurant.com.

32. Aby Sam Thomas, "Cooking Up a Win: Zuma Co-founder Rainer Becker," *Entrepreneur,* September 23, 2018, https://www.entrepreneur.com/article/320537.

33. "A Fashionable Modern Japanese Restaurant in Knightsbridge," *Time Out,* August 1, 2019, https://www.timeout.com/london/restaurants/zuma; fieldwork by Chuanfei Wang, August 2018.

34. Thomas, "Cooking Up a Win."

35. *The Caterer,* "Caterer and Hotelkeeper 100: Rainer Becker, Zuma, Roka," July 11, 2011, https://www.thecaterer.com/news/restaurant/caterer-and-hotelkeeper-100-rainer-becker-zuma-roka.

36. "Watami hisutori" (ワタミヒストリー) [Watami history], Watami, accessed November 28, 2020, https://www.watami.co.jp/corporate/history/.

37. Watami accessed October 2, 2020, https://www.watami.co.jp/group/restaurant/international.html.

38. Watami accessed November 28, 2020, https://www.watami.co.jp/group/restaurant/international.html.

39. "Watami hisutori."

40. Kawabata Motoo (川端基夫), *Gaishoku kokusaika no dainamizumu: Atarashī "ekkyō no katachi"* (外食国際化のダイナミズム: 新しい "越境のかたち") [The dynamism of the internationalization of the restaurant industry: The new "transnational pattern"] (Tokyo: Shinhyoron, 2016), 91–94.

41. Kawabata, 91.

42. Elizabeth Rosen, "Japanese Restaurants Feed Their Global Ambitions with New York Branches," *Nikkei Weekly,* September 22, 2016, https://asia.nikkei.com/NAR/Articles/Japanese-restaurants-feed-their-global-ambitions-with-New-York-branches.

43. Michael Kaminer, "Resaurant Review: Ootoya," *Daily News,* August 1, 2012, https://www.nydailynews.com/life-style/eats/restaurant-review-ootoya-article-1.1125959.

44. Shun Lu and Gary Alan Fine, "The Presentation of Ethnic Authenticity: Chinese Food as a Social Accomplishment," *Sociological Quarterly* 36, no. 3 (1995): 535–553.

45. Motoki Saito, interview by Chuanfei Wang, February 2018.

46. Fieldwork by Chuanfei Wang, February 2018. For the idea of authenticity as a negotiation, see Lu and Fine, "Presentation of Ethnic Authenticity."

47. Fieldwork by Mônica Carvalho, November 28, 2018.

48. Patrick Duval, interview by Chuanfei Wang at Izakaya Isse, August 31, 2018; fieldwork by Chuanfei Wang, August 31, 2018; manager Nobu, interview by James Farrer at Iro Izakaya, July 18, 2019; fieldwork by James Farrer, July 18, 2019.

49. Moskin, "Soaking Up the Sake."

50. Max Levy, interview by James Farrer, May 9, 2019.

51. Gavin Yeung, "Okra Hong Kong Is Closing In July," *The Tatler*, June 1, 2021, https://www.tatlerasia.com/dining/the-industry/okra-hong-kong-closure.

52. This is a phenomenon discussed in Krishnendu Ray, *The Ethnic Restaurateur* (New York: Bloomsbury, 2016).

53. Fieldwork by James Farrer, August 2017; Yasu Umezaki, interview by James Farrer, August 24, 2017.

54. "Taste of Japan Honorary Award," *Japan Now*, Embassy of Japan newsletter, February 17, 2016, https://www.us.emb-japan.go.jp/jicc/japan-now/EJN_vol12_no3.html.

55. Anna Shin, interview by David Wank, March 3, 2017.

56. Momotaro accessed October 31, 2020, https://www.momotarochicago.com.

57. "893 Ryotei Bar / Allenkaufmann Studio," Arch Daily, August 30, 2020, https://www.archdaily.com/946014/893-ryotei-bar-allenkaufmann-studio.

58. Fieldwork by James Farrer, October 31, 2017.

59. "Shurui no yushutsu sūryō jōi 20-kakoku chiiki (reiwa 2nen 12getsu)" (酒類の輸出数量上位 20 か国・地域 (令和 2 年 12 月)) [20 countries/regions with the highest export volume of alcoholic beverages (December 2020)], 国税庁 (Koku zei chō) [National tax agency], accessed December 5, 2022, https://www.nta.go.jp/taxes/sake/yushutsu/yushutsu_tokei/r02.htm.

60. Bon Yagi and Sakura Yagi, interview by James Farrer, April 17, 2019; fieldwork by James Farrer, April 17, 2019; Nancy Matsumoto, "Bon Yagi: Emperor of New York's Japanese East Village—Part 2," Discover Nikkei, November 6, 2015, http://www.discovernikkei.org/en/journal/2015/11/6/bon-yagi-2/.

61. The word "*jüjiuwu*" is the Chinese pronunciation of the Japanese characters for "*izakaya*." It is a loanword from Japanese.

62. "Taipei shinai ni aru nichishiki tapasu *izakaya* kamameshi senmon-ten 'HanaBi' de kamameshi to nihonshu wo tan'nō!" (台北市内にある日式 Tapas 居酒屋釜飯専門店 "HanaBi" で釜飯と日本酒を堪能!) [Enjoy Kamameshi and *sake* at the Japanese-style Tapas Izakaya and Kamameshi Restaurant "HanaBi" in Taipei City!], *Sake meguri*, January 19, 2019, https://sakemeguri.com/taipei-zhongshan-hanabi/.

63. Fieldwork by James Farrer, March 2018.

64. Michael Ou, interview by Chuanfei Wang, May 9, 2018; fieldwork by Chuanfei Wang, May 2018.

65. Fieldwork by Chuanfei Wang, March 2017.

66. Naoki Inoue, editor of *Jin Magazine,* interview by Chuanfei Wang, March 2017.

67. Fieldwork by Chuanfei Wang, March 2017.

68. Fieldwork by Chuanfei Wang, March 2017.

69. For a discussion of the subordinate position of women in Chinese banquet drinking culture, see Yan Ge, "How to Survive as a Woman at a Chinese Banquet," *New York Times*, November 30, 2019, https://nyti.ms/2OyZ3za.

70. Yuki Kashiwagi, interview by Yajun (Lisa) Hu, October 8, 2017.

71. Yuki Kashiwagi, interview by Yajun (Lisa) Hu, October 8, 2017.

72. Yuki Kashiwagi, interview by Yajun (Lisa) Hu, October 8, 2017.

8 | Reinventing Japanese Fine Dining in Culinary Global Cities

JAMES FARRER, MÔNICA R. DE CARVALHO, AND CHUANFEI WANG

J apanese fine dining restaurants around the world are redefining Japanese cuisine in the twenty-first century. This chapter highlights the mobile careers of the Japanese and non-Japanese chefs who animate these highly acclaimed restaurants. The individual stories of the chefs, most of whom are multiple migrants, illuminate the importance of cross-border mobility for developing creative culinary repertoires. Their collective narrative illustrates the agglomeration effects of culinary global cities where creative professionals work in close proximity, innovating and sharing knowledge. The chapter shows the importance of these urban culinary contact zones, the rise of gourmet tourism and internet media, and the culinary politics redefining high-end Japanese cuisine within them.

Saskia Sassen characterizes global cities as sites where business activities with a transnational scope foster agglomeration economies at a local urban scale. The mechanism of agglomeration is information exchange: "The mix of firms, talents, and expertise from a broad range of specialized fields makes a particular type of urban environment function as an information center. Being in a city becomes synonymous with being in an extremely intense and dense information loop."[1] Although the transnational organization of cuisine is far less concentrated in a few cities than the financial industry that is Sassen's focus, similar agglomeration effects shape the information exchanges, personnel flows, and influences in the culinary field. Culinary global cities such as New York, Hong Kong, and Tokyo are hotspots where star chefs seek to make a mark, food writers search for nov-elties, and supply chains of fine dining ingredients converge.[2] Kitchens in these cities are contact zones where ideas are created, mastered, and mim-icked by a diverse staff.[3] While Japan could largely be regarded as a send-ing region for migrant Japanese chefs in the past, in the twenty-first century Japan's culinary global cities—Tokyo in particular—also have become nodes in the more complex mobilities of chefs through multiple cities across con-tinents. This type of circulation of talent is reshaping high-end Japanese cui-sine not only outside Japan but in Tokyo itself. At the same time, the concentration of international gourmet tourism produces a wealthy and de-manding audience for Japanese restaurants, one that is increasingly di-verse in any given city but increasingly similar around the world.

This chapter explores the processes that are transforming Japanese fine dining in this culinary global city network. These include mobilities of people, ideas, authorities, organizations, and influence. The sections in this chapter focus on these processes roughly in the order in which they histori-cally became salient in global Japanese fine dining: the reinvention of tra-dition, culinary migration, hybridization, culinary boundary crossing, the globalization of culinary authorities, corporatization, mediazation, and na-tion (re)branding. Each section uses case studies in one or two cities to il-lustrate each process, even though all the processes are global and cumulative in their effects. Hence, they are not exclusive to the cases here but rather patterns that interact in reshaping fine dining on a world-wide scale.

The Reinvention of Culinary Tradition: *Kaiseki* in Tokyo and Hong Kong

Japanese high cuisine has been continuously reinvented in Japan, and these reinvented traditions are now being repackaged and exported to overseas markets, particularly in Asia. There is no better representative of "tradi-tional" Japanese high cuisine than *kaiseki,* but it is also itself a multiply reinvented tradition. Its origins are often attributed to the simple meals served at tea ceremonies in the seventeenth century, but even this idea seems to have been a reinvention of writers nearly a century later.[4] According to food historians, the term "*kaiseki*" only came into common use in the nineteenth century. By then, it was associated with a "flamboyant and extravagant series of dishes" served at *ryōtei* (fine dining restaurants with entertainment) in Tokyo and other cities, an idea far removed from any early associations with tea cuisine.[5] In its contemporary form, *kaiseki* is defined by food scholar Nancy Stalker as "a formal multicourse dinner that usually employs fresh seasonal ingredients and strives to balance the taste, texture, appearance and colors of food."[6] As food historian Eric Rath points out, many of *kaiseki*'s ideals are rather recent inventions, including the central concept of "seasonality" (which only became salient when technology and transport made eating foods out of season possible).[7] *Kaiseki*, as just defined—a marriage of seasonality, tableware, refined presentation, and atmosphere—thus only took shape in the twentieth century.

In essence, contemporary *kaiseki*—like New Nordic cuisine or the paleo diet—is a modern fantasy of a culinary past, whose most famous reinvention is associated with the activities of a single chef, restaurateur, and artisan—Kitaōji Rosanjin (1883–1953).[8] Rosanjin, his artistic name, was a culinary and cultural nationalist but also a well-traveled observer of foreign foodways. In Rosanjin's Meiji-era youth, European cuisine was increasingly popular in Japan and the country was expressing its status as an imperial power by embracing Western foodways. Rosanjin broke with this trend toward culinary Occidentalism by defining Japanese cuisine through a juxtaposition with both Western and Chinese cooking.[9] In his *kaiseki* cuisine, he emphasized seasonality and meticulous sourcing of ingredients with a focus on the visual design of a dish (now called presentation). In his prewar *ryōtei* Hoshigaoka, he showed a fastidiousness for distinctive ceramics, especially Chinese antiques collected on his travels throughout the Japanese empire. Not satisfied with Chinese aesthetics, he started making his own tableware, reportedly over two hundred thousand pieces. As Stalker writes, Rosanjin's obsession with authenticity was a paradox. "Rosanjin became an ultimate arbiter of Japaneseness in culinary culture by violating the norms of Japanese traditions of art and cuisine."[10] He personified the idea that Japanese fine dining, especially *kaiseki*, was aesthetically superior to Western foods and considered French cuisine particularly overrated. Infamously, in 1954 he ordered his duck raw at an acclaimed Paris restaurant because he did not trust the French chefs to cook it properly.[11] As Stalker shows, Rosanjin was a contradiction: a modernist disguised as a traditionalist and a culinary chauvinist obsessed with Japan's global reputation.

A contemporary Tokyo restaurant that represents the ongoing reinvention of *kaiseki* in the spirit of Rosanjin is RyuGin, which opened in 2003. Over the next ten years, it became among the most expensive and lauded restaurants in the city, with three Michelin stars and a listing on the World's 50 Best Restaurants (or World's 50 Best).[12] A fixed-course meal with drinks and service fees started at USD 450 in a posh dining room where diners could peer down on the Imperial Palace. Sounding at times like a Rosanjin disciple, chef-owner Seiji Yamamoto adamantly defended Japanese culinary tradition in his 2018 interview with us: "It is meaningless if the person who is making Japanese food cannot answer the question of what Japanese food is. My definition is 'that which expresses the richness of the Japanese natural environment through food.' Therefore, it is not possible to admit something as Japanese cuisine that does not reflect the richness of the natural environment in Japan."[13] Despite Yamamoto's advocacy of an essential Japaneseness based on Japan's terroir, unique products, and specialized technique, he achieved culinary notoriety by embracing the high-tech artistry of molecular gastronomy pioneered by Ferran Adrià in Spain's legendary El Bulli restaurant. At the 2008 International Chefs Congress in New York City, a young Yamamoto wowed an audience of chefs and food writers by silk-screening a QR code onto a plate using squid ink and showing videos of a refrigerator that made "liquid ice." Anointed "Japan's kaiseki king" by the World's 50 Best list for Asia in 2019, Yamamoto followed a classic *kaiseki* format of menu and presentation.[14] Yet even some of his first signature dishes employed Western ingredients or preparations, including a sweet and crunchy foie gras presented with fresh fig and served with cognac and a vintage port. His desserts were molecular experimentations, including the famous Minus-196° Candy Apple, which enveloped nitrogen-frozen ice cream in a toffee shell.[15]

Yamamoto is ambivalent about his reputation for eclectic technique, which he attributes to food bloggers latching onto his flashiest molecular dishes. He has since dropped his famed candy apple dessert. Much in the spirit of Rosanjin, Yamamoto served his artful dishes on antique ceramics so precious that he banned cameras, lest one drop on a dish. When asked about the importance of his persona as a chef, he disagreed with the idea that diners go to a restaurant to consume the "personality" or a "message" from a creative chef. He insisted that the "spirit of Japanese cuisine" lay in expressing the essence of ingredients and a firm mastery of technique. "Picking something from here and there" with a "hybrid spirit" is just "fakery," he said.[16] Despite his emphasis on Japaneseness, Yamamoto depends on high-spending foreign customers for his business. He also has opened branches of his *kaiseki* restaurant in Hong Kong and Taiwan. RyuGin is an expression of Japanese reinvented tradition in ways that clearly appealed to global arbiters of culinary taste, such as Michelin and the World's 50 Best.

Noting the fast-developing market for Japanese fine dining in East Asia, many top Japanese restaurants have chosen Hong Kong or Shanghai to open their first overseas branches. The creative goal is to evoke the parent restaurant in Japan without appearing as a lesser copy. RyuGin in Hong Kong is one such venture. As Yamamoto told us, "true Japanese cuisine" does not copy menus or replicate tastes. Instead, it "uses Japanese techniques to give expression to the ingredients from that place." Given the importance of seafood in Hong Kong, he explained, "the most important thing is to prove how wonderful Hong Kong seafood is by using Japanese cooking techniques."[17]

To head his restaurant Tenku RyuGin in Hong Kong, Yamamoto dispatched two Tokyo employees, head chef Hidemichi Seki and pastry chef Mizuho Seki, a married couple who met at Tokyo's RyuGin. Both had extensive experience in Japanese and French cuisines, a mix reflected on the menu. Most dishes could be considered traditional Tokyo *kaiseki,* while some—especially Mizuho Seki's dessert creations—used molecular gastronomy techniques. Some ingredients were specific to the local context, while others were imported from Japan. On the winter 2019 menu, this mix was seen in the *hassun* (the first course in a *kaiseki* meal) that combined regional Japanese and Chinese ingredients. It consisted of Japanese agar jelly and *shirako* (codfish milt), a "spring roll" wrapped with Yunnan ham and shiso leaf, and *tokoroten* (seaweed noodles) in tomato juice. The dessert was a blend of Chinese and Japanese elements using foaming techniques from molecular gastronomy: airy bubbles of Mount Wuyi Lapsang souchong smoked tea and dried Kyoto persimmon in an almond sorbet with a milky queen rice espuma.[18]

Both the Taipei and Hong Kong RyuGins have received critical acclaim. Yamamoto described his relationship to these overseas restaurants as a branding and consulting contract. The restaurants were owned by local partners, with Yamamoto dispatching chefs whom he trained. This was a model followed by other Japanese restaurants in Asia. It showed how repackaged Japanese traditions were exported directly by ambitious chefs to promising urban markets facilitated by transnational business connections.

Culinary Migrations: Creating a Brazilian Culture of Japanese Fine Dining

Culinary migration consists of chefs and restaurateurs moving across borders, absorbing influences, and remaking cuisines grounded in these migration experiences. To use terms from earlier chapters, this migration fosters both the deterritorialization and reterritorialization of culinary ideas. Such international migration has only recently become a defining feature of the careers of elite chefs. Previously, culinary careers were established largely on a national scale, with the assumption being that the best French chefs were trained in France and worked in Paris, or that the best Japanese chefs were trained in Japan and worked in Tokyo or Kyoto. Now, with the rise of globe-spanning culinary fields, such as the one we describe for Japanese cuisine, cross-border mobility has become a common feature of elite culinary career making.[19] However, different patterns of culinary migration may still be associated with distinct forms of culinary reterritorialization or innovation. This section focuses on circular culinary migration centered on São Paulo, Brazil's main global food city. The examples highlight two paths of circular or return migration among Brazilian chefs and restaurateurs, one through Japan and another through the culinary centers of the Global North, illustrating how these two paths influence the reterritorialization, or glocalization, of Japanese fine dining in Brazil. While the first path reinforces the long-standing importance of Japan-based culinary authenticity in São Paulo, the second has brought in other globalized schemata, notably the locavore ideal, sustainability, and the cult of the creative chef. Both types of migrants contribute to a narrative of culinary glocalization; all the chefs we interviewed described striving to make a distinctly Brazilian contribution to Japanese cuisine, usually in terms of ingredients, and sometimes in preparation.

São Paulo's Japanese restaurant community, the largest outside Japan, has been shaped for a century by circular migrations of family members between Brazil and Japan. This can be seen in the career of Ricardo Yoshikawa. In 2016, at the age of thirty-nine, he opened Ryo, the first restaurant in Brazil specializing in *kaiseki* cuisine, which was awarded one Michelin star.[20] His family's relationship with Brazil began with an uncle who opened a cosmetic factory in the country after World War II. The uncle encouraged Yoshikawa's grandfather, who owned *ryōkan* (a hotel serving food) and *kaiseki* restaurants in Japan, to send his eldest son to Brazil to scout business opportunities in the hospitality sector. Yoshikawa's father migrated to São Paulo in the 1960s, where he acquired Buffet Colonial, one of the three biggest event spaces in the city. He then began expanding into new ventures. In 2015, Ricardo Yoshikawa and three friends opened the *kaiseki* restaurant Ryo. The four partners, all descendants of Japanese, had first met at a Buddhist temple in São Paulo. According to Yoshikawa, during his childhood, Brazilians knew little about Japanese food, but in the 1990s, Japanese food had become popular outside Japanese communities. Yoshikawa saw that the high-end market was short of options and decided to raise the bar for Japanese cuisine in Brazil. Already, he explained, the upper-class Brazilian clientele for Japanese food was well traveled and recognized high-level gastronomy, and many had visited Japan.[21]

Ryo's approach to *kaiseki* emphasized the distinct Brazilian context and ingredients while hewing to Japanese techniques. For example, the lack of four clearly defined seasons in Brazil meant that the idea of seasonality was translated into biweekly changes in the menu. The seven- or nine-course tasting menus included both local ingredients and imported ones from Japan and prioritized traditional *kaiseki* dishes. At the start of the typical two-hour meal, chef Edson Yamashita displayed the fresh fish to be served. One dinner in 2016 included grouper sashimi with sea urchin, bluefin tuna with nori seaweed jam, *karasumi* (cured mullet roe) with Brazilian Jataí honey, suckling pig belly cooked for six hours, and leek salad, radish, pea sprouts, and chrysanthemum flower. The finale was a sequence of sushi, including smoked grouper and seaweed-wrapped minced toro with turnips. Desserts used local flavors, such as the *cupuaçu* (an Amazonian fruit) and cocoa powder ice cream topped with Brazil nuts. This locavore *omakase* (chef's choice) menu costs BRL 450–650 (about USD 90–125). Ryo also offered Japanese beers and imported *sake* and wine. No juices, sodas, or other sugar-based items were allowed, and even the acidity of the water was lowered to provide ideal conditions for umami taste. Another local adaptation was a sweet variety of coffee harvested in the highlands of Minas Gerais.[22] As is common in São Paulo Japanese restaurants, all of Ryo's staff, including kitchen workers and service people, were Nikkei.

Another Japan-centric but also locavore approach to Japanese fine dining was seen at Aizomê, run by chef Telma Shiraishi, granddaughter of Japanese immigrants.[23] Aizomê, founded in 2007, showed the Japanese culinary tradition of refinement, comfort, and care through its private rooms, wood-crafted interiors, and central counter where patrons could observe

FIGURE 8.1 Chef Telma Shiraishi at Aizomê's original location in Jardins, São Paulo, 2018. (Photo by Grazielly Yumi Novais, courtesy of Telma Shirashi)

the "sushiman," the term for sushi chefs in Brazil, at work.[24] In the words of a journalistic reviewer, Shiraishi's *kaiseki* "unites the Japanese original concept to the particularities found in Brazilian ingredients."[25] The premium course included Chilean anchovy marinated in miso and grilled, pink shrimp breaded in crispy rice flakes and *ao nori* (dried laver), spicy mayonnaise sauce with sriracha and *masago* (smelt roe), grilled miso *picanha* (a fine Brazilian beef cut) with black rice, mushrooms and vegetables, and golden grilled squid in dashi with saffron. "My cuisine is authorial," she said, "a blend of traditional and contemporary influences. I am Brazilian, but I try to bring back my Japanese roots."[26]

The examples of Yoshizawa and Shiraishi show how the Japanese fine dining culture in São Paulo remains grounded in the migration of Nikkei chefs who had family ties and personal sojourns in Japan. In recent decades, however, the transnational mobilities of Japanese-cuisine chefs in the city have extended beyond Japan to other global cities, particularly New York. Among these chefs, we see the culinary influences on Brazilian Japanese cuisine are increasingly diverse, including a greater emphasis on the authority and biography of the chef and less emphasis on Japan as the touchstone of technique and style. The most prominent of these New York migrants was Jun Sakamoto, a Brazilian Nissei and star of Brazilian Japanese fine dining.

When we interviewed Sakamoto in 2016, he was fifty-one years old. His father was an agronomist engineer who, upon graduating from university in Japan, migrated to Brazil after World War II to live in the countryside of São Paulo State.[27] In the 1980s, Sakamoto traveled to New York to pursue his interest in photography, working in Japanese restaurants as a kitchen assistant and waiter, and then as an apprentice to a Japanese sushi master. "The old man was very rigid," Sakamoto said, and he had to learn the craft of sushi in his off-hours, picking up knowledge while visiting *izakaya*s with his more-senior colleagues. After returning to Brazil, he helped a friend design the trendy Japanese restaurant Sushi Leblon, which opened in 1986 in Rio de Janeiro, specializing in creative American-influenced roll sushi. Sakamoto enrolled in architecture school but eventually left to work in the restaurant. In 1998, he was invited to replace the deceased founder of Komazushi in São Paulo, a traditional sushi bar near Avenida Paulista, the heart of Brazil's financial district at the time. This marked his start as a professional sushiman. Then, in 2000, he used his family's savings to open his eponymous Sakamoto in Pinheiros, an upper-class neighborhood where he could pursue a larger non-Nikkei Brazilian market. Working with a brick-layer, he transformed a residential house in Rua Lisboa into a modern restaurant. With his architectural training, Sakamoto aimed to re-create the uncluttered Japanese-inspired interiors that he had seen in New York.

The restaurant is based on Sakamoto's "collection of dreams," he told us. "When a person goes to a restaurant, he or she wants to be rejuvenated, not just to eat! The ambiance, the service, the music, good utensils, excellence must be there. The care in the preparation of the rice, the details, but no fancy stuff is needed. . . . I did not want anything too modern. I wanted to see 'tradition' in every tiny corner."[28]

The restaurant had several tables where customers ordered from a limited menu and an L-shaped sushi bar where Sakamoto and his sous-chef served his *omakase* selection for up to a dozen diners seated in front of them. The *omakase* menu included sixteen pieces that used such seasonal products as grilled oysters, sea urchin, and high-grade local fish. The price for a typical meal in his restaurant ranged from BRL 350 to BRL 500 (about USD 70–100). The food served at tables was traditional Japanese dishes prepared by sous-chefs, including the acclaimed whiting fish *misoyaki* and such desserts as green apple ice cream with sweet *sake* gelatin. Sakamoto used many

imported ingredients, including vinegar and *katsuobushi* (fermented bonito) from Japan and California rice, while modifying some to suit his taste.
For example, he added his house-made dashi and nori to the soy sauce from
Japan. He had learned to make dashi from a Japanese chef at Liberdade, who
helped him find his distinctive personal flavors. In other dishes, he started
using imports but then switched to local ones. For example, he first made
miso soup with miso from Tokyo's Mitsukoshi Department Store but then
switched to miso made by an elderly Japanese woman in the São Paulo
countryside. In 2015 the restaurant received a star in the inaugural *Michelin
Guide Rio de Janeiro & São Paulo* and has kept it since.

Inspired by the creative Japanese cuisine he encountered in New York,
Sakamoto praised the development of a distinctive Brazilian-Japanese cuisine
based on the experience of Japanese culinary migrants to Brazil. He saw a
cuisine starting from what was immediately at hand, a pattern he had
observed in the improvisations of local sushimen in Brazil. He said, "I [be-
lieve] one day, the true fusion of these cultures [Brazilian and Japanese] will
happen. . . . I dream of a fusion of equals, where the best of the Japanese
cuisine will meet the best of the Brazilian cuisine. Then there will be a real
fusion."[29] Brazilian-style sushi was one such fusion, and he dreamed of
bringing it to New York:

> I want to move to the United States and retire there. I think, in an almost
> arrogant way, that my sushi will be more successful than the original Japa-
> nese there. Your affection for food modifies your perception of it. Your cul-
> ture influences your vision. My sushi is Brazilian! Sushi in Japan is more
> acidic; Japanese people like it but do not love what I do. Maybe Americans
> will. I do not think any cuisine belongs to its original place. Japanese cui-
> sine does not belong to Japan. It is a live being. Is a human being more blood
> or culture? I am Brazilian, I am Japanese, I have values of both cultures and
> I found in myself a balance of them. I feel privileged to have a lot of both
> cultures.[30]

Sakamoto's glocalizing vision garnered him accolades in the regional
Japanese culinary field as the best sushiman in South America and a place
in Japanese government gastrodiplomacy. He was the first chef to serve as
culinary curator for the Japan House, opened by the Japanese government
in São Paulo in 2017. As discussed later, this honor signified the Japanese
government's growing embrace of glocalized forms of Japanese cuisine represented by Sakamoto. At the same time, his story, including his aspira-

tions to open a restaurant in New York, showed the increased importance of mobility—not just through Japan but through other global cities where Japanese-cuisine chefs now made their careers. A stint in a Michelin-starred restaurant was a career maker, enabling a chef to move to other cities to work or open their own restaurants. The following examples elaborate on these multiple migrations increasingly shaping global Japanese cuisine.

Hybridization: Creating Global *Kaiseki* in the Culinary Contact Zones

Beyond building individual careers, culinary migration also has agglomerative effects, as the chefs working in global food cities meet, collaborate, and produce new genres of cuisine out of multiple influences. Thus, this process of culinary hybridization reflects both the accumulated experiences of individuals and their interactions in the culinary contact zones of global cities. In this section, we examine the transformation of *kaiseki* in culinary global cities.

Although representing tradition in Japan, *kaiseki*'s flexible format of seasonal dishes was seen by chefs in global cities as inviting experimentation within Japanese fine dining (especially compared to the narrower range of dishes in high-end sushi restaurants).[31] For aspiring creative chefs, *kaiseki* was more a grammar for a meal than a fixed repertoire of dishes, with the menu organized around varied cooking techniques rather than an established set of menu items or recipes. These techniques—simmering, grilling, steaming, frying—followed by steamed rice (or sometimes another starch) could be interpreted liberally by the chef. Borrowing from high-end sushi restaurants, many restaurateurs also employed a set menu formula, sometimes labeled "*omakase kaiseki*." Its fixed prices and dishes enabled the chefs to plan complex menus. This experimental *kaiseki* was especially embraced by non-Japanese chefs.

One New York restaurant that epitomized this pairing of culinary creativity and luxury was the Uchū Kaiseki Bar, manned by chef Samuel Clonts. Entering through the nondescript front of a shabby building on New York's Lower East Side, a visitor encountered a cozy dark wooden bar counter and liquor-bottle-laden shelves that evoked a high-end cocktail bar. This was the dining area of Uchū. As the kitchen and bar were in separate areas, Clonts only emerged periodically to deliver and explain courses. Customers at the counter interacted with the chatty sommelier Raymond Trinh, who introduced fine Japanese *sake* and whiskey while pushing champagne as the ideal pairing for sushi. (Champagne paired with sushi was a New York fixation, driven by high margins.) Whether through its wood-paneled gentleman's club interior, hefty champagne list, or copious portions of luxury ingredients, Uchū epitomized the money-driven excess of fine dining in New York City. A meal with *sake* could cost USD 400, and even more with champagne. The customers were diverse, said Clonts. When we visited in 2018, they included two older white financiers, one of them a regular, and two young Chinese women who said that their hobby was Japanese fine dining.[32]

Clonts interpreted *kaiseki* liberally, but its basic grammar was evident in the twelve-course meal that started with *sakizuke* (the *kaiseki* opener paired with *sake*) of Hokkaido sea urchin—a striking contrast of orange urchin and black soy over white diced scallops and cucumber. This was followed by a soup of *tairagai* (a razor clam imported from Japan) in a clam broth flavored by seared ramps that imparted a smoky taste. Then came three types of seafood that were, respectively, raw, grilled, and sautéed. Uchū's signature dish was *temaki* (cone-shaped sushi) hand-rolled by Clonts in front of the guests and topped with a glistening mound of golden Osetra caviar, an obscenely casual application of a pricey ingredient. A similarly ironic deployment of luxury ingredients was seen in the next dish, a steak *sando* (sandwich) made with hand-cut white bread and top-grade (very expensive) Miyazaki wagyu that mimicked the cheap convenience store sandwiches sold in Japan. Despite such showy culinary pop art, the extraordinary prices rankled even jaded New York food critics.[33] This performance gave Clonts his first Michelin star.[34]

A white American from Arizona, Clonts only briefly studied restaurants in Japan while preparing to open the restaurant. He picked up his hybrid cooking style at Brooklyn Fare, training under Cesar Ramirez, the acclaimed Mexican American chef who created his own Japanese-French fusion cuisine. One of only five New York restaurants awarded three Michelin stars in 2019 (along with Masa, described in Chapter 4), Brooklyn Fare was known for luxurious items packaged in novel ways. Many of its seafood ingredients came from Tokyo's Tsukiji fish market. "New York is about all the great things of the world coming together in one place," Clonts said. "That's what makes it New York." Disavowing the trendy locavore ethos, Clonts embraced the reality that global food cities have always been a nexus

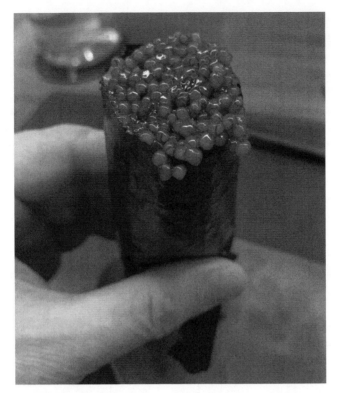

FIGURE 8.2 A signature dish at the Uchū Kaiseki Bar in New York City was a *temaki* sushi with glistening Osetra caviar made and presented to each diner personally by chef Samuel Clonts. (Photo by James Farrer, April 18, 2019)

of transnational migrant staff, wealthy mobile customers, and imported luxury ingredients with a hefty price tag. [35]

In Asia (outside Japan itself), some of the emerging urban nodes of hybrid Japanese fine dining in the 2010s were Hong Kong, Singapore, Shanghai, and Taipei. With relatively accessible labor markets for global culinary talents, these have become culinary global cities, each with its own red Michelin city guide and restaurants on the World's 50 Best list. Their relationships to Japanese food have been shaped by their large residential Japanese populations and proximity to Japan. Since the 2000s, there have been large flows of tourists and business travelers in both directions, and consequently, customers in East Asia are better versed in Japanese tastes and ingredients than in other regions. In all these cities, Japanese chefs from

Japan have worked closely with chefs from Chinese and other backgrounds.[36] At the same time, fine dining chefs have also been promoted as a new type of creative talent from whom innovation is expected.[37] As in New York, *kaiseki* has emerged as a new space for chef-led culinary innovations in Asian global cities. These restaurants are also culinary contact zones where menus are conceived, mastered, and eventually imitated by rising chefs.

Haku, a creative *kaiseki* restaurant on the Kowloon side of Hong Kong Bay, reflected the type of culinary mobilities and hybridization shaping global Japanese fine dining. Haku was a collaboration between a prominent Hong Kong restaurant group; Hideaki Matsuo, the chef-owner of the three-Michelin-starred Kashiwaya in Osaka; and the Argentinian head chef, Agustin Balbi. At Haku, Matsuo served as consulting executive chef, providing advice and training on an irregular basis. Balbi, in turn, pointed to his transnational biography when explaining his culinary career to us during an interview. He was raised by his Spanish grandmother, who influenced his tastes, as evident in the Spanish ingredients and flavors of his cooking. His exposure to Japanese food came in Chicago when he worked at the Japanese-influenced restaurant L2O. Then he moved to Japan, working at a Spanish restaurant, followed by two years at RyuGin, and then at the Cuisine Michel Troisgros, also a Japanese-influenced French restaurant in Tokyo. Having lived and worked for five years in Japan, he spoke fluent Japanese. (His wife also was Japanese.) His *kaiseki* dishes at Haku mostly used ingredients imported from Japan. They did, however, have Spanish inflections, such as the use of ham to make dashi, a foamed chorizo, and a nostalgic rice casserole based on his grandmother's recipe and employing select Spanish ham (*jamòn pata negra*).[38]

The name of the restaurant Haku came from the expression "*haku rai hin*" (literally, "imported goods") because the chef and his ideas had come from abroad. Despite its experimental menu and non-Japanese chef, the restaurant was well received by critics, as attested by Balbi's recognition in 2016 as "Best New Chef" by the *Tatler Hong Kong*.[39] Balbi opined that being a foreigner gave him more freedom than a Japanese chef. His Japanese customers recognized his dishes as Japanese but were intrigued by their creative flourishes.[40] In short, Balbi's hybrid cuisine was shaped by multiple sojourns in urban culinary contact zones.

Of course, not all experimental *kaiseki* was produced by white migrant chefs. One rising master of this genre was Hiroki Odo, whose two-Michelin-starred *kaiseki* restaurant opened in New York in 2019. Odo was an artistic partnership with Korean American sushi chef Seong Cheol Byun that mixed locavore New York *kaiseki* with a sushi *omakase* course based on local fish. Guests were welcomed into Odo with a chilled cup of craft *sake* from Brooklyn Kura proffered by Frank Cisneros, a Spanish sommelier who had spent years in Tokyo (and helped to found Uchū). "When you visit a place in Japan," Odo explained, "you are always welcomed with the local *sake*. This is our way of welcoming guests."[41]

Odo, a thirty-six-year-old from Kagoshima, emphasized how New York's varied culinary scene had influenced his approach. The food has to be daring, he said. "In New York, there are no rules. You can do anything. You can challenge yourself. Those who are good will survive and the bad will be eliminated."[42] Odo sought pronounced flavors that appealed to a New York palate, including marinating salmon in whiskey instead of *sake* and sneaking goat cheese into the tempura. He also favored crunchy textures over soft ones to satisfy a penchant for crispy foods that he had observed among New Yorkers. "More than traditional *kaiseki*," he said, "I am trying to make a *kaiseki* that fits the times, not only in terms of food but also the movement of fashion, a *kaiseki* for this era."[43] At the same time, he described himself as a "filter" for all ingredients and ideas to ensure they emerged with a Japanese taste. And while he acknowledged innovating, he stressed it was done in a Japanese way, such as producing five different types of dashi—based on matsutake, shellfish, *konbu* (dried seaweed), *katsuobushi*, and *umeboshi* (red pickled plum)—all of which appeared in the dinner course during our visit. In the middle of our *kaiseki* meal, Odo ceded the stage to chef Byun for a sushi intermezzo. Byun's signature *temaki* sushi incorporated house-made kimchi. For *nigiri* (hand pressed) sushi, he used only local fish caught on the US East Coast, some of which was aged and cured. "It's not traditional sushi," Odo explained. "When it passes through his filter, I think it becomes a new sushi culture. If that doesn't happen, then there is no meaning in what we are doing here."[44] Restaurant Odo's hybridized *kaiseki* was an outcome of the migrations of the two principal chefs but, even more so, of their interactions with customers and other cooks in New York City.

While all of these individual culinary biographies differ, in each case their hybrid cuisine reflects complex interactions in the culinary contact zones of global cities. This global culinary scene is created by ambitious chefs moving from city to city to build both knowledge and résumés, adding to the mix of ideas and experiences. As the next section explores more deeply, many are also moving between cuisines.

Crossing and Blurring Boundaries: French and Japanese Crossovers

Another process remaking Japanese cuisine is migration not across geographical borders but rather across the imagined—and often arbitrarily constructed—borders of national cuisines. Nowhere is this more evident than in the ongoing culinary osmosis of people and ideas between Japanese and French cuisine. This began as early as the Meiji period when elements of French cuisine became central to modern Japanese banquet dining.[45] In the twenty-first century, this boundary crossing (and boundary blurring) continued with the migration of chefs from Japanese to French cuisine and vice versa. French influences have seeped even into the more traditional practices of Kyoto cuisine.[46] In this section, we focus on chefs working at creative Franco-Japanese restaurants in Paris and Tokyo.

The presence of Japanese chefs in high-end French restaurants in France dates back to at least the 1980s, where they influenced the advent of lighter and innovative forms of nouvelle cuisine by using novel (often Asian) ingredients and plating (influenced partly by Japanese *kaiseki*).[47] A recent development in the 2010s has been the increasing number of French restaurants in Paris headed by Japanese chefs who now control the taste and identity of the restaurants.[48] A 2016 edition of the Parisian magazine *Le Fooding* included a "Japaname Tour" of Paris with an illustrated foldout map. It listed forty restaurants headed by Japanese chefs, twenty-eight of whom were classified as "Japarisienne," a term for ethnically Japanese chefs who cook French cuisine.[49]

Unlike the earlier Japanese chefs working in traditional French restaurants, Japarisienne chef-proprietors occupied a distinct space that sometimes blurred the boundaries between French and Japanese restaurants. We asked Patrick Duval, a leading expert on Japanese cuisine in France, how to position them. (He was editor of *Wasabi Magazine*, author of the "Gastronomy" chapters for Michelin guides in Japan, and owner of Izakaya Isse, described in Chapter 7.) Duval noted their "Japaneseness" as an original contribution to the Parisian culinary scene:

Actually, I think there is a French base, but the way they're doing it is very Japanese. . . . So, it's French food actually but made by Japanese; so, it's something new. . . . Japanese of course when they come with their own culture, will do it differently from a French chef, and actually, it's very tasty and very good, and also the way they present it is very beautiful. Food critics are very impressed by the way Japanese chefs are doing the frigid [cryogenic] food because it's something we have never seen, of course. It's our food culture but made in a way it's never been done before; so the food is very impressive.[50]

When we asked some Japarisienne chefs to describe their offerings, most said it was their "original cuisine." Many wanted to be free from the idea that they must be doing something "Japanese" simply because of their ethnicity. In reality, it was difficult to escape labelling as Japanese by consumers and critics, and some of these chefs embraced a Japanese identity and branded their cuisine and restaurants as Japanese in various ways.

We discussed these issues in 2018 with Atsushi Tanaka, one of the younger Franco-Japanese stars, who ran a small, modernist restaurant named by his initials, A.T., in the Latin Quarter. "Paris has a lot of Japanese chefs, and each has their own style," he said. "There are those who really love French cuisine and want to make French cuisine, and I guess I am part of this pattern. And then some do French cuisine and bring in an element of Japaneseness (*wa*) to their food. There are really all types."[51] Tanaka put himself on the "French" end of his spectrum, emphasizing his "original style," which included molecular gastronomy and cryogenic cooking techniques. When dining at his restaurant in summer and winter 2019, we noted significant but subtle Japanese elements. On both occasions, the menu was heavy on seafood, including razor clams and sea urchin. On the November visit, the razor clams had a hint of yuzu. The dessert called Hinoki was an art piece of sesame ice cream with aromatic hinoki leaves.[52] The 2019 *Michelin Guide,* which recommended A.T., described the restaurant's gray and beige minimalist interior as embodying "the quintessence of Japan."[53] Despite such framing by Michelin, Tanaka downplayed the importance of his Japanese background in his interview with us, emphasizing his affiliation with the natural wine movement and other broad culinary trends in Europe.[54]

Closer to the "Japanese" end of this spectrum lay the cooking of Taku Sekine at his casual bistro Dersou, also a recipient of one Michelin star. Compared with A.T., Dersou more clearly represented a fusion of Japanese and French tastes and techniques. Sekine, like Tanaka, worked his way through Michelin-starred kitchens in France, including that of Alain Ducasse, but in contrast to Tanaka, he decided to open a midmarket bistro. Dersou was on a quiet street of the eleventh arrondissement, where there are many Japanese eateries. It occupied a high-ceiling, garage-like space with blue walls, high stools facing a counter, and a burnt cement floor. Just as at counter-based restaurants in Tokyo, dishes were prepared in front of customers with the stove, ovens, and utensils in view. The tableware was Japanese ceramics. When we dined there in 2019, thirty-year-old sous-chef Yuri Maeda, originally from Kanagawa Prefecture, was managing the counter. She told us that the menu drew on Japanese, Taiwanese, Italian, and Korean cuisines. The Japanese elements in our dinner consisted of a combo of *onigiri* (rice balls) grilled with a paste of miso and shiso, *karaage* (fried chicken), hazelnut butter broth with nori and scallops, sashimi-*don* (sashimi bowl) with *ikura* (salmon roe) and miso soup, and beef ragoût *gyudon* (beef bowl) with egg yolk, rice, and miso soup. When we asked Maeda how "Japanese" she considered the menu, she replied that only "fifteen to twenty percent" of the dishes were "basically Japanese," while the ambiance was "eighty percent plus" Japanese.[55]

The Japarisiennes were also inspiring chefs working in more traditional Japanese kitchens around Europe and farther afield. For example, Toshiharu Minami of the celebrated Hamburg Japanese restaurant Zipang pointed to the inspiration of Paris in the making of his "nonnational" (*mu kokuseki*) menu, which incorporated French techniques.[56] As Keiichi Sawaguchi's sociological research shows, Japanese chefs working in French cuisine in Europe were less of a unified culinary community than a migrant culinary labor force following career pathways created by culinary schools and restaurants.[57] However, we also see how this labor mobility affected numerous cross-fertilizations of ideas, techniques, and tastes between French and Japanese cuisines and chefs of various nationalities. Moreover, many individual chefs working in this Franco-Japanese culinary borderland now felt free to migrate back into a notional "Japanese" culinary space.

While Japanese chefs working in Paris often resisted a Japanese label, in Tokyo, we saw more French-trained chefs assume the mantle of "Japanese cuisine" for personal and marketing reasons. This included Yoshihiro Narisawa, who was often mentioned, together with Seiji Yamamoto, as a leading chef of Tokyo's culinary scene. With a father who operated a Western-style bakery, Narisawa developed an early interest in French cuisine. He went to France at age nineteen and trained for eight years under renowned chefs, including Paul Bocuse, Frédy Girardet, and Joël Robuchon. Return-ing to Japan in 1996, he started his first restaurant in Odawara, Kanagawa Prefecture. After seven years, he moved to Tokyo to open Les Créations de Narisawa, later renamed Narisawa. In 2008, the restaurant received its first Michelin star, followed in 2013 by its second star and a ranking on the World's 50 Best list. Since 2013, it has remained on the list, sometimes top-ping the Asian rankings.

Narisawa's creative cuisine defied simple categorization as "French" or "Western." During our interview with him in 2018, he also called his cui-sine "Japanese."[58] He assumed the label because of his passion for Japanese ingredients, some obtained by foraging and others through his ties to farm-ers and fishermen. He also featured Japanese *sake*s and Japanese wines in his pairings. Echoing Rosanjin, tableware was made by craftsmen specifi-cally for Narisawa. He sees the "soul of Japanese cuisine" as lying in Japan's mountains and seashores, and his signature dishes included an edible land-scape that evoked the forests and fields of rural Japan, with a "soil" made of matcha, soy pulp, and black tea, and bamboo and crunchy "branches"

FIGURE 8.3 Chef Yoshihiro Narisawa's edible landscape appetizer is emblematic of his in-novative *satoyama* cuisine based on locally sourced organic ingredients. (Photo by James Farrer, June 3, 2017)

fashioned from ten ingredients. It was both culinary Japonisme and a close relative of the signature Edible Earth of Copenhagen's Noma, the temple of locavore gastronomy.

Narisawa calls his dishes "*satoyama* cuisine" (literally, "land and mountain cuisine"), a term that avoids conventional boundaries of national cuisine while still emphasizing Japaneseness. He explained the concept of *satoyama* cuisine to us:

> Of course, we are not traditional Japanese [cuisine]. But the question of genre, whether we are Japanese cuisine or Italian cuisine or French cuisine, or Chinese cuisine, doesn't interest me at all. What matters is that we are in Japan, I am Japanese, we use only Japanese products, ninety-five percent are Japanese.... All the meat, fish, vegetables, fruits are from Japan only. And we try to think of the most attractive way of preparing them. We use Japanese techniques, Italian techniques, Chinese techniques, all types. So, I do not use a little knife for a large daikon but rather a big cleaver. This is Chinese and Japanese technique. The way of thinking, the philosophy, my own rules about cuisine all reflect the traditional culture of *satoyama*. So it is difficult to say what kind of cuisine this is. I can only say it is Narisawa original. Maybe we can call it innovative *satoyama* cuisine.[59]

In fact, some prominent chefs we interviewed dismissed the idea that Narisawa's cuisine was even Japanese, pointing out that his training was in French kitchens. Narisawa, however, stressed that his early training was decades ago and that he was constantly learning. When asked about his technique, he replied, "I can say it is sixty or seventy percent Japanese technique," but included Chinese and other elements picked up on his frequent travel around the world.[60] Narisawa's idea of cuisine went beyond nationality to include the image of himself as a creative professional. He was a prototype of a chef-centered model of culinary authenticity, centered on artistry and originality. Yet his reputation also stemmed from having a foot in two easily recognized culinary traditions. This type of culinary border crossing has become less an aberration than a defining feature of modern Japanese (and French) fine dining.

Globalizing Culinary Authority: Michelin and the World's 50 Best

One of the most important transformations in the reception of Japanese restaurants around the world is the increasingly global scope of culinary authorities and audiences in the past decade.[61] These authorities include organizations that rank restaurants, most notably the rapidly expanding Michelin city guides and the World's 50 Best Restaurants list, as well as an increasingly globalized chorus of semiprofessional food bloggers, journalists, and gourmets who fly around the world in search of the best restaurants. These authorities have been very favorable to Japanese-cuisine restaurants. Rosanjin's view of the superiority of Japanese fine dining appeared vindicated in 2009, a half century after his death, when the arbiter of French culinary standards, the *Michelin Red Guide*, awarded 227 stars to restaurants in Tokyo in the inaugural guide to the city, compared with 59 for New York and 40 for Hong Kong. Suddenly, journalists anointed Tokyo the "focus of the culinary world" and "the undisputed world leader in fine dining."[62] At the same time, Japanese restaurants in New York, Hong Kong, and other culinary global cities were often among the most highly rated. This prompted gaggles of high-end culinary tourists to flock to the restaurants topping these lists. In some ways, the global culinary world has aligned itself to standards echoing Rosanjin's ideals of seasonality, locality, and aesthetic presentation. But now, these standards are applied and interpreted by global authorities alongside such new standards as sustainability and staff diversity (including hiring more women).

Many celebrity Japanese chefs we interviewed benefited from this new global restaurant rating regime. Narisawa argued that the globalization of fine dining audiences was fostering innovative cuisine. Especially significant, he felt, were the World's 50 Best designations, drawing attention to regions ignored by Michelin guides and motivating chefs to pursue the sort of boundary-crossing innovation that he achieved in his cuisine:

> Especially in Japanese cuisine, rather than the idea that Japanese cuisine is this fixed idea, and it must be done a particular way, there is the idea of, "hey, this is also good," or "hey, it could be more interesting this way," that has been a good influence. This is not only true of Japanese cuisine, but also of Chinese, traditional French. Of course, it is good that some traditional things survive and are handed down so that people can enjoy them. But we also have to think of how to make things that people today want to enjoy. And with climate change, with have to think about the environment. With the environment today, we can't just go on eating tuna all the time.[63]

He felt that health, environment, and sustainability concerns were challenging ideas of conventional standards in Japanese fine dining, particularly the emphasis on wild-caught fish in the sushi culture. "Of course, the traditional *sushiya* [sushi bar] is delicious," he said. "But how much are the traditional sushi artisans really thinking about the environment? If you think about the environment, it will be tough to continue with the current style."[64]

Reflecting the new global standards in fine dining, Narisawa positioned himself among chefs concerned about sustainable cooking in Japan by using organic ingredients and creating close ties with local producers. While some critics viewed these actions as environmental virtue signaling or greenwashing,[65] Narisawa's comments show how this rhetoric is now central to branding global Japanese cuisine. In 2021, the Michelin guide even began awarding green stars for sustainability, including one to Narisawa.[66] The Japanese government also incorporated sustainability into the definition of *"washoku"* (traditional Japanese cuisine) in its application submitted in 2013 to UNESCO for Japanese cuisine's recognition as an intangible cultural heritage.[67]

The growing global culinary accolades were tied to the rise of luxury food tourism, including in Tokyo. Narisawa's customers were 70 percent non-Japanese, he said in our 2018 interview, driven by his restaurant's accolades in the World's 50 Best.[68] This indicated that the same type of highly mobile and affluent people dining in New York and London were also supping in Tokyo. The homogenization of this elite consumer base furthers the global fine dining culture crossing culinary and national borders.

Corporatization: Traveling with Nobu

The growing presence of corporate actors in Japanese high-end fine dining has mirrored the evolution of mass-market Japanese cuisine described in Chapters 5, 6, and 7. Markets for Japanese cuisine created by entrepreneurial chef-owners and their independent restaurants became increasingly penetrated by large corporations using economies of scale and standardization to expand them. Some fine dining companies began as corporate ventures. An example is the Japan-based Suntory Group, which founded high-end restaurants in the 1970s in New York and São Paulo and then created the subsidiary Sun with Aqua in 2002 to operate pricey restaurants in Singapore, Shanghai, and Hawai'i.[69] More often, high-end restaurant corporations have emerged through entrepreneurial expansion by individual chef-proprietors. In these, the chefs themselves most often became the brand. An exemplar is David Chang, whose Momofuku group grew from a single ramen shop in New York in 2004 to sixteen restaurants, including fine dining outlets, in 2019.[70] In Japanese cuisine, the epitome of the corporate celebrity chef was Nobuyuki "Nobu" Matsuhisa, whose global licensing operation of his eponymous Nobu group has created new transnational career paths for chefs to accumulate experience as producers and mediators of tastes in global Japanese cuisine.[71] Nobu-trained chefs have increasingly staffed the kitchens of high-end Japanese restaurants worldwide, powerfully influencing the taste and appearance of global Japanese cuisine. Put differently, whether a city had a branch of Nobu could be one of its qualifications as a culinary global city.[72]

Chef-owner Nobu Matsuhisa is himself a pioneering culinary migrant. His corporation began as a restaurant founded in Los Angeles in 1994 and grew to become the most prominent global brand in Japanese fine dining. In 2019, there were forty-five Nobu restaurants in fifteen countries on all five continents.[73] In his memoir, Matsuhisa described Nobu-style Japanese cuisine as a compilation of culinary inspirations gained through his experiences around the world, including formative years in Peru and California in the 1980s.[74] As he told a reporter in 2018 at the opening of a Nobu outlet in Houston, "It started with Peruvian and Japanese, but today you will see how we are inspired by lots of other cuisines, too. Our chefs are from all over the world, so we have Filipino, British, Italian, French, American . . . all kinds of cultures and chefs creating dishes with their knowledge and passion."[75]

The Nobu corporation represents not only culinary fusion and creativity but also processes of standardization, systematization, and labor mobility. Nobu's signature dishes, all created by Matsuhisa, form the core of the menu found in every Nobu restaurant and include his black cod miso (perhaps his most famous dish), yellowtail sashimi with jalapeño, and chocolate bento box. Additionally, chefs in each Nobu restaurant create new specialties using local ingredients that are served only in their outlets, such as wagyu tacos (Los Angeles), monkfish pâté (Tokyo), and *hirame* (flounder) with XO salsa (Hong Kong). Nobu corporate chefs teach chain-wide recipes to executive and sushi chefs at branches owned by licensees.[76] Despite these innovations, Matsuhisa insists that he maintains the Japaneseness of his dishes.[77] In this way, Nobu-style cuisine exists in a network of hundreds of chefs in Nobu outlets in numerous global cities.

The company has created mobility opportunities within the Nobu global network to retain footloose personnel. Even a person hired as a dishwasher can work their way up to the professional position of sushi chef and find work in locations throughout the network. The career of Nikkei Brazilian Letícia Shiotsuka, whom we interviewed in 2018 at Nobu São Paulo, illustrates the possibilities in the Nobu global network.[78] She studied gastronomy in São Paulo and became a professional chef at a renowned local catering service firm before joining Nobu in Miami. In her training at Nobu, she worked at every station in the Miami branch, including back-office activities, to learn all details of its operation. Along the way, she worked her way up from junior sous-chef to hot kitchen head chef in Miami. When a Nobu outlet opened in São Paulo, she returned to her home city as executive chef. Such mobility within the network ensured worldwide consistency for Nobu restaurants run by different licensees.

This mobility within the Nobu network enabled widely distributed resources to be brought together to found a new restaurant as seen at Nobu São Paulo. Typical of Nobu operations outside the United States and Japan, Nobu São Paulo was licensed to local investors, with Nobu US headquarters providing consulting services and ensuring brand consistency through its global network.[79] The restaurant was financed by Grupo Trabuca Bar, which operated other Japanese bars and restaurants in the city, while the launch was coordinated by Nobu's US headquarters. The general manager was Andrew Ishiki, who had worked for Nobu Australia and reported directly to US headquarters. Marketing was also organized by US headquarters with a local publicity team handling press relations.[80] All Nobu restaurants had a common staffing pattern, with an executive chef who ran the hot kitchen, a sushi chef overseeing the counter, a floor manager in charge of service, and a back-house manager for inventory.[81] While the staff was employed by local partners, they were often people who had worked in other Nobu branches. In São Paulo, the head sushi chef was a Brazilian Nikkei chef who had worked at Nobu outlets in Miami, New York, Moscow, and Perth. Nobu also had a team of corporate chefs based in each region who traveled among outlets to ensure quality and consistency. For the São Paulo opening, the corporate head chef came from the Miami outlet and the corporate sushi chef from Las Vegas.

Executive chef Shiotsuka explained the global and local aspects of the organization and menu in Nobu in São Paulo. A month before the outlet's 2018 opening, the corporate chef and corporate sushi chef came from the United States to do market research, identify local producers of ingredients, and set the menu and prices. The menu featured Nobu's cuisine, and all tableware was Nobu branded. Many ingredients were imported, such as yuzu juice, dry miso, and soy sauce from Japan and rice from California. Fish came from Alaska and Chile, as well as Brazil. There were two food preparation areas, the sushi bar and the "hot dishes" kitchen, where the workspace was organized like a traditional French kitchen, Shiotsuka explained. "On the preparation side, there are touches of international (French) cuisine, but Nobu's cuisine is predominantly Japanese, especially the cuts," she said.[82]

Shiotsuka explained that Brazilian twists to dishes were created by adding local ingredients. This was done cautiously because most customers expected to eat Nobu's standard signature dishes. Brazilian twists were first applied to desserts. Some were hybrids, such as a *kakigori* (shaved ice) called Scratchpad and made with laminated ice and Brazilian caipirinha syrup. Other desserts were reinvented and upscaled local sweets, an example being guava tart. It was based on the Brazilian dessert *goiabada com queijo*, which in Brazil typically consists of a thick slice of semicured Canastra cheese from Minas Gerais topped by a generous portion of guava jam. At Nobu, it was transformed into a sablé topped with guava compote mousseline and mascarpone cream cheese. The chefs at Nobu São Paulo thought of naming their creation Mineirinho in homage to the Brazilian dessert but ended up following Nobu's corporate practice of "international" (mostly English) naming by calling it simply guava tart.

Nobu actively facilitated knowledge sharing in its global network. In 2019, the corporation implemented World of Nobu, an online learning management system to circulate knowledge of Nobu's cuisine and operations among all employees. The system shared dishes created at a Nobu restaurant with other outlets, inspiring chefs to develop new ones to enhance the menus of their outlets. According to a video introducing World of Nobu, the learning management system was moving corporate instructional materials and testing to this online format. The system's heaviest users were chefs and front-of-the-house staff.[83] In this way, Nobu sought to channel the local creations of chefs reflecting their personal mobilities into flows of information and inspiration throughout its worldwide network.

The corporate organization maintained consistency in the menu and service. Corporate chefs based in five regional headquarters enforced brand standards, as mentioned above. Matsuhisa also traveled constantly, aiming to visit each restaurant annually.[84] To further ensure a "Japanese taste," he sought to pair a local with a Japanese chef in each restaurant. As he explained in his memoir, "There are some things about the spirit of Japanese cuisine that it takes a Japanese mind to understand. Likewise, it takes a local chef to understand the preferences of the people who live in that region."[85]

It is the daily responsibility of executive chefs to maintain the Nobu style, as we learned during our 2018 visit to Nobu Melbourne (opened a decade earlier). Executive chef Sean Tan told us that his role was "to maintain the taste of Nobu" in the restaurant by monitoring the forty cooks working under him: "My job is to make sure consistency is there. Wherever I look, I taste everything, I check the way they look, like I said, as a head chef, it's not only a sharp knife, but your eyes need to be sharp. You need to see before they do something if they are doing it the right way or the wrong way. If they are doing it the wrong way, you know the flavor won't be there." Tan ensured that chefs' creativity hewed to the Nobu style. "I used to like other gastronomic ideas, but if I work for Nobu-san, I should spend more time to fully understand his philosophy. It's the same when I hire new people. They like to bring in their knowledge, and when they do something, they like to put extra, always extra, extra. It is my job to guide them into Nobu."[86] Tan said that Nobu's recipes avoided complex cooking techniques, comparing the cuisine to Italian cuisine, which prioritized simplicity over the complexities of French cooking. Each dish used five ingredients at most, and their preparation utilized basic kitchen skills rather than specifically Japanese ones. This enabled newly hired chefs to learn Nobu's tastes on the job quickly. Standardization of tastes was further achieved by the use of master recipes for sauces and dressings in Nobu's signature dishes across all outlets. An example was New Style Salmon Sashimi, which used local salmon with the same sauce across all outlets. However, outlets used both local and imported ingredients depending on the possibilities for local sourcing. Tan said that 90 percent of the ingredients at his restaurant were sourced in Australia, while 10 percent were imported, such as the locally unavailable yuzu juice.

Nobu promoted the globalization of taste and style through standardization, simplification, and the mobility of staff. In particular, the mobile knowledge and movement of its chefs inspired many imitators around the world. These included scores of Nobu chefs who left to open independent restaurants, such as Yoshizumi Nagaya, whose restaurant Nagaya serving Nobu-style fusion dishes in Düsseldorf was Germany's only Michelin-starred Japanese restaurant.[87]

Mediazation: *Kaiseki* for China's WeChat Generation

The rise of social media, especially platforms for sharing photos and videos among consumers, has changed restaurant dining around the world. No market has embraced the internet more powerfully than China. The emerging consumer group of young, wealthy Chinese consumers—the so-called second-generation rich (*fuerdai*)—no longer looked for the showy luxury ingredients valued by their parents. Instead, they expected innovative and, above all, visually exciting products they could photograph to share with friends on social media. New Japanese fine dining restaurants in Chinese cities, focused on social media marketing and food as fashion, have emphasized WeChatable aesthetics.

One such restaurant in Shanghai was the innovative *kaiseki* restaurant Anthologia. Opened in 2016, this high-end eatery, whose Chinese name translates as Global Gourmet Theater (Diqiu meishi juchang), was a forty-six-seat venue for staging Japanese food culture that resembled a small IMAX theater. A set menu cost CNY 1,080 per person (USD 166) for eight courses following *kaiseki* service. Each course featured an appearance by the chef or an assistant with a video presentation on a massive screen that all the diners faced. On our visit, one video starred owner Naoya Hirano and the restaurant staff in a boat fishing off the coast of Nagasaki. Diners received a piece of tender and sweet *hiramasa* (gold-striped amberjack) presented by the sous-chef while watching the same sous-chef pull a similar writhing fish out of the bay. This display sought to convince diners they were eating a genuine product while inspiring them to travel to Nagasaki, where the fish was caught. As we talked over dinner and cups of *sake,* Hirano expressed his hope to open a boutique hotel near this fishing area in Japan. He wanted to ride the global boom in gastrotourism by appealing to his well-off Shanghai customer base interested in traveling to Japan. Thus, a longing to travel to exotic places and experience fresh and natural tastes merged in the visual spectacle of the restaurant service. The chefs were literally performers, as well as cooks. At one point in our meal, Chef Bulizo (whose real name was Terada) presented dishes while dressed as a Kabuki performer, slicing fish in one scene and performing ikebana in another.[88]

Hirano saw this type of theatrical restaurant marketing as befitting the adventurous spirit of Shanghai diners. "You have to be willing to do something outrageous to succeed in China," Hirano said. "This is what the

Chinese expect. It has to be an interesting experience. The food must be good, but it doesn't need to be spectacular."[89] The theater-restaurant was also a smart business model because of its small staff, single seating, and simultaneous service of the same dish to all diners. Anthologia was inspired by Paul Pairet's Shanghai restaurant Ultraviolet, which pioneered the multisensory, three-dimensional food theater experience and received three Michelin stars and recognition by the World's 50 Best. Such successful innovations in Shanghai influenced developments in the rest of Asia since many chefs passed through the city's restaurants, picking up influences, including this restaurant theater model.

Beyond Shanghai, the mediazation of cuisine was influencing fine dining everywhere. Contemporary *kaiseki* restaurants were particularly amenable to elaborate WeChatable (or Instagrammable) presentations, another reason for the rising popularity of this new format. While a few *kaiseki* restaurants, such as RyuGin in Tokyo, resisted this trend by banning cameras in the dining room, others installed table lighting for food photography, such as the lights suspended over the counters in Hong Kong's Haku and New York's Uchū.

Nation Branding: How Japanese Gastropolitics Broadens Japanese Cuisine

The Japanese government has played a significant role in defining and expanding the scope of Japanese fine dining through its intertwined aims to expand Japanese soft power and stimulate the global market for Japanese agricultural and service products. Much has been written about the abortive attempts by the Japanese government in the early 2000s to "police" the boundaries of a rapidly globalizing Japanese cuisine by certifying restaurants abroad. This public criticism of nationalistic culinary politics seems to have engendered a shift away from policing culinary boundaries to promoting "*washoku*" as a global luxury brand.[90] One such effort is the Washoku World Challenge, a competition organized by the Ministry of Agriculture, Forestry and Fisheries of Japan for non-Japanese chefs working abroad in Japanese cuisine. The 2019 competition results mentioned the winning chef from Shanghai's Sun with Aqua (owned by Suntory):

> "This 7th edition demonstrates that the finalists' technical level keeps improving every year," said the judges. "Creating Japanese dishes that incor-

porate the characteristics and unique ideas of other countries' culinary cultures, while respecting the fundamentals of Japanese cuisine built on the concept of umami, expands the potential of Japanese cuisine. The creations of each one of the finalists embodied this notion." On their decision to award the top prize to Wang Wei Ping, the judges said: "Wang's use of Chinese black vinegar in the preparation of the rice for hamaguri clam sushi was a magnificent idea that brought a Chinese touch to Japanese cuisine."[91]

This more recent approach to culinary branding indicated the fundamental goal of Japanese gastropolitics as maintaining the value of the Japan brand in the culinary field. The point is for chefs' culinary creations to reinforce the exclusive and refined image of Japanese cuisine, so the actual recipes are less important than the buzz that they generate. As part of this initiative, the judges saw it as meritorious for foreign chefs to "[expand] the potential of Japanese cuisine," even by giving it "a Chinese touch."

One of the most ambitious projects in Japan's culinary politics is Japan House, a joint venture of the Ministry of Foreign Affairs of Japan and the Japan External Trade Organization to strengthen the position of Japanese culture (including cuisine) in key regional global cities. There are now three Japan Houses, in São Paulo, Los Angeles, and London, all multipurpose structures hosting Japan-centered events throughout the year. Food is a central theme, and each Japan House hosts multiple eateries managed by local restaurateurs chosen by their organizing committees. Japan House also provides a window into the state-sponsored politics of Japanese cuisine.

We visited all three sites, although only the São Paulo site was already operating during our visits. It featured various spaces, including art exhibition floors, a restaurant, and a Japanese-style café. Nikkei Brazilian Angela Hirata was the project developer and its first president, headhunted by Dentsu Japan, a leading marketing and consulting firm with close ties to the Japanese government.[92] She said that Japan House São Paulo served to intensify commercial and cultural ties between the two countries. "We are not here to attract more Japanese descendants (even though, of course, they are very welcome) to our space. We are here to make all Brazilians feel at home at the JH." To select the head of Japan House's gastronomy section, she said that a group of Ministry of Foreign Affairs officials and Dentsu executives went incognito to the city's top Japanese-food restaurants to evaluate which best represented the "traditional values of high-end gastronomy in Japan." They selected the much-celebrated chef Jun Sakamoto, owner of

FIGURE 8.4 Japan House entrance in São Paulo, seen from the second floor, 2019. (Photo by Estevam Romera, courtesy of Japan House, original in full color)

Jun Sakamoto and Junji restaurants, followed in 2019 by Telma Shiraishi's Aizomê (see our earlier discussion of these two chefs).

Japan House São Paulo held lectures, exhibits, and tastings regarding cuisine, some of which we attended. On September 29, 2017, Narisawa Yo-shihiro lectured on "the *satoyama* philosophy in Narisawa's kitchen." It was part of the launch for a book that was a photographic account of his journey as a chef throughout Japan with Brazilian photographer Sergio Coimbra. Narisawa's lecture conveyed his idea of *satoyama* cuisine by recounting vis-its to spots where Narisawa gathered exquisite ingredients during all four seasons. The pair traveled for a year, collecting views and stories on Japan's local food cultures. An accompanying exhibition displayed about eighty photographs, as well as objects and videos representing the gastronomy de-scribed by Narisawa as "food for the body and soul."[93] Although Narisawa was one of the most prominent Japanese-French chefs (and some critics even

FIGURE 8.5 View of Telma Shiraishi's Aizomê restaurant on the second floor of the Japan House in São Paulo, 2019. The space is surrounded by large windows overlooking a bamboo garden. (Photo by Grazielly Yumi Novais, courtesy of Telma Shirashi)

disputed the idea that his gastronomy was "Japanese"), he appeared at Japan House to represent Japanese culinary culture through *satoyama* cuisine—defined not only by Japanese technique but by a strong locavore ethos.

Another event we attended was a lecture and workshop on August 25, 2017, with chef Zaiyu Hasegawa on dashi and the essential features of Japanese cuisine. Hasegawa ranks, along with Narisawa and RyuGin's Yamamoto Seiji, as a preeminent representative of global Japanese cuisine. In 2019, his Tokyo restaurant Den placed first on Asia's 50 Best (and eleventh on the World's 50 Best). Hasegawa's ideal was that a fine dining restaurant should be fun, and Den was well known for its culinary playfulness. It resembled a small family *izakaya* where Hasegawa and his wife greeted each guest and pulled out the laid-back family dog Puchi for photo-ops with guests. Den's most famous dishes were a foie gras *monaka* (a rice flour shell with sweet filling) and Dentucky Fried Chicken (a deboned fried chicken wing stuffed with seasonal ingredients). Hasegawa said he designed this latter dish to connect his cuisine with the experiences of foreign guests by serving it in a KFC-style cardboard box emblazoned with Hasegawa's smiling face in a playful imitation of KFC's Colonel Sanders.[94] Den was a pioneer of this type of culinary pop art in Japanese fine dining, using luxurious and complex techniques to create fast-food-like dishes.

Hasegawa's lecture at Japan House addressed the inherent tensions in the globalization of a national cuisine defined through local ingredients, techniques, and habitus. About fifty chefs and restaurateurs attended, mostly Brazilians. He encouraged his audience to mix local and Japanese ingredients to train the public's palate to identify a "true" Japanese flavor in homemade dashi. His discussion of using local ingredients for cooking Japanese recipes resonated with the audience, given that geographic distance made imports from Japan prohibitively expensive. He noted that dashi could be made from any ingredient, described preparing it from raw ham, and expressed his wish to cook it in Japan with such Brazilian ingredients as *palmito* (palm heart) and cassava. This point echoed the statement in his book on Den, "It is possible to create a Japanese cuisine with local ingredients. It may not be an authentic Japanese cuisine, but I see it as a Japanese cuisine of the global era."[95] Ultimately, the "magic" of a good chef was to surprise customers, he said.[96]

For Hasegawa, however, there was an important distinction between Japanese and other cuisines as an accumulation of techniques, ingredients, and personal experiences. As an example of the former, in his lecture, he mentioned the Japanese practice of removing all fluids from a fish to render it usable for five days. Also, the source of an ingredient could be reflected in its taste, even with an ingredient as basic as water. In preparing dashi, for example, using Brazilian water is "good" as a use of local ingredients but, "despite the good result, it will never taste the same [as in Japan]." He noted that foreigners often asked what "is rightfully Japanese [cuisine]?" In response, he drew on a place-based definition that entailed exposure to cooking in Japan; chefs who prepared dishes closer to Japanese cuisine had personally experienced Japanese culture. Thus, Hasegawa waffled on the possibilities and limitations of creating Japanese cuisine abroad. His definitions on culinary authenticity reflect the competing tendencies of, on the one hand, an essentialist notion that Japanese cuisine was grounded in Japan's traditional foodways and, on the other, an eclecticism and emphasis on creativity that was also evident in his own cooking. In his lecture we thus see the fluid coexistence of both ideals of Japanese cuisine: a grounding in place and a newfound global openness.[97]

Such fluidity (or slippage) in what is regarded as Japanese cuisine even occurred in official banquets hosted by the Japanese government. A much-reported banquet at the G20 Osaka Summit in June 2019 was prepared by Yoshihiro Narisawa and Seiji Yamamoto of RyuGin. The banquet showcased the high-quality fare of Tokyo restaurants. Narisawa was the apparent lead chef, as many dishes resembled those in his restaurants, including the colorful eggplant dish Summer Matsuri, topped with fresh flowers in shiso-flavored tomato-based gelatin. Other dishes were from the menu of RyuGin. With Narisawa and Yamamoto as the core, a group of chef-teachers from Japan's venerable Tsuji Culinary Institute in Osaka cooked dinner for the heads of state on June 28. In his opening remarks, Japanese prime minister Shinzo Abe said, "The concept of tonight's dinner is *'satoyama'* based on the idea to integrate sustainability and gastronomy."[98] The statement coincided with the conference theme of a sustainable world. It also represented the flexibility and transcendence of contemporary Japanese cuisine, which could adapt to the diversity of peoples with different dietary preferences while reflecting Japanese cuisine's seasonal essence. For example, the second dish, called Temari, was made for vegetarian diners and resembled a traditional Japanese ball toy. The brochure accompanying the banquet described its *satoyama* cuisine as "world standard Japanese cuisine."[99]

The events at Japan House and the G20 banquet highlighted the Japanese government's efforts to go beyond promoting an ahistorical and fixed idea of *washoku*.[100] Instead, the cutting edge of fine dining in Tokyo was represented by chefs known for their heterodox approaches, such as Hasegawa, or interlopers in the Japanese culinary field, such as Narisawa. What they had in common was global recognition earned through acknowledgment by the World's 50 Best list, Michelin stars, and other accolades. Flexible use of the Japan brand is hardly surprising in this type of culinary nation branding since it seeks to sustain brand value rather than specify its contents. In practice, Japanese cuisine has long been a flexible construct, and *satoyama* cuisine and Dentucky Fried Chicken may just be the latest variants. By looking at these official culinary activities, we can see that even the state politics of nation branding are constantly shifting and expanding the boundaries of "Japanese" culinary imaginary.

The Tensions Inherent in a Global-National Cuisine

From Odo's New York *kaiseki* to Matsuhisa's Nobu style to Narisawa's *satoyama* cuisine, a new global Japanese cuisine has emerged at the top rung of the ladder of prestige and acclaim in the world's culinary capitals. This is not a culinary movement in the typical sense, as few if any culinary principles unify the creations of these chefs. What they do share is the experience of mobility among the multicultural kitchens and dining rooms of global cities. Staff are mobile, and so are customers, creating a globalized condition of diversity. Through this mobility, culinary hybridization and boundary crossing become norms. These patterns of mobility—and the mixing and borrowing of techniques and flavors—are accelerated by processes of corporate expansion, the growth of internet media, the idolization of the celebrity chef, the rise of a foodie plutocracy, and state-led culinary politics aiming to enlarge the reputation of Japanese cuisine.

Despite this mobility and mixing, chefs also share the brand—and burden—of "Japaneseness," the need to represent Japan to customers while constantly reinventing the contents of its associated culinary imaginaries. We could try to locate these chefs on a continuum bounded by, on the one hand, traditional or conventional Japanese and, on the other, original, eclectic, or fusion, but such an exercise in categorization would obscure how they all productively played off the paradoxes and tensions inherent to a globalized national cuisine. Most found themselves alternately defending and defying a nation-based label of "Japanese" and its associated traditions and conventions. While doing so, they also embraced global norms that increasingly concerned their customers, such as sustainability and local sourcing. For example, Odo grounded his cuisine in his knowledge of Japanese techniques but worked intensively with local staff to produce a *kaiseki* meal with New York characteristics. Narisawa, who employed a diversity of techniques in the kitchen, strove for creations in Tokyo that were innovative while grounded in Japanese terroir—a possible translation of "*satoyama*."

The emergence of global Japanese cuisine traced in this chapter illustrates how the globalization of any "national cuisine" both undermines and reifies the imagined boundaries of the "national." A celebrity chef such as Narisawa may artfully dodge questions about the nationality of his "original cuisine" by creating his own *satoyama* label. Yet even he is drawn into the nation branding of "Japanese" cuisine by government schemes, such as Japan House or the G20 banquet, that seek to sustain the Japan brand by incorporating the value of *satoyama*. This incorporation involves appropriating the newly rising global value of sustainability into the Japan brand. Nevertheless, despite the ample documentation in this chapter of a cuisine defined by boundary crossing, it is still delimited as "Japanese" in various ways by chefs, the Japanese government, consumers, and the reviewing media. This is not a novel phenomenon. Our initial discussion of *kaiseki* shows that "Japanese cuisine" was a continually reinvented and imagined tradition even in Japan. The novelty documented in this chapter is how, in the twenty-first century, reinvention is produced by multiple mobile actors, from individual chefs and restaurateurs to critics and government officials, in transnational networks connecting cities around the world.

Notes

1. Saskia Sassen, "The Global City: Introducing a Concept," *Brown Journal of World Affairs* 11, no. 2 (2005): 29.

2. Vanina Leschziner, *At the Chef's Table: Culinary Creativity in Elite Restaurants* (Stanford, CA: Stanford University Press, 2015), 45.

3. James Farrer, "Shanghai's Western Restaurants as Culinary Contact Zones in a Transnational Culinary Field," in *Globalization and Asian Cuisines: Transnational Networks and Contact Zones,* ed. James Farrer (New York: Palgrave Macmillan, 2015), 103–124.

4. Eric C. Rath, "Reevaluating Rikyū: *Kaiseki* and the Origins of Japanese Cuisine," *Journal of Japanese Studies* 39, no. 1 (2013): 67–96.

5. Eric C. Rath, *Japan's Cuisines: Food, Place and Identity* (London: Reaktion Books, 2016), 43; Nancy K. Stalker, "Rosanjin: The Roots of Japanese Gourmet Nationalism," in *Devouring Japan: Global Perspectives on Japanese Culinary Identity,* ed. Nancy K. Stalker (Oxford: Oxford University Press, 2018), 134; Katarzyna Joanna Cwiertka and Yasuhara Miho, *Branding Japanese Food: From Meibutsu to Washoku* (Honolulu: University of Hawai'i Press, 2020), 102.

6. Courses generally include an appetizer (*sakizuke*), sashimi (*mukōsuke*), a simmered dish (*takiawase*), a grilled dish (*yakimono*), and a hearty course such as a hotpot (*shiizakana*), along with soups, palate cleansers, pickles, and desserts at the chef's discretion. Stalker, *Devouring Japan,* 349.

7. Rath, *Japan's Cuisines,* 53.

8. His given name was Kitaōji Fusajirō. Kitaōji Rosanjin was an artistic name, usually shortened to Rosanjin, which is our usage here.

9. Kitaōji Rosanjin (北大路魯山人), "Nihonryōri no kiso gainen" (日本料理の基礎概念) [The basic concepts of Japanese cuisine], in *Rosanjin ajidō* (魯山人味道) [Rosanjin's way of taste], ed. Hirano Masaki (1936; reis., Tokyo: Chuokoronsha, 1980), 272–283.

10. Stalker, "Rosanjin," 141.

11. Stalker, 143.

12. RyuGin occupied place forty-one on the list in 2018 and sixty-two in 2019; Hillary Dixler Canavan, "Everyone Congratulate the World's 50 Best for Including Six Women on Its New, Longer Long List," Eater, January 18, 2019, https://www.eater.com /worlds-50-best-restaurants-awards/2019/6/18/18683686/worlds-50-best-restaurants -2019-51-to-120-female-chefs-diversity-problems.

13. Seiji Yamamoto, interview by James Farrer and Chuanfei Wang, December 9, 2018.

14. Asia's 50 Best 2019. https://www.theworlds50best.com/asia/en/ (accessed March 20, 2020).

15. Yukari Pratt, "Molecular Morsels," *Japan Times,* January 11, 2008, https://www.japantimes.co.jp/life/2008/01/11/food/molecular-morsels.

16. Seiji Yamamoto, interview by James Farrer and Chuanfei Wang, December 9, 2018.

17. Seiji Yamamoto, interview by James Farrer and Chuanfei Wang, December 9, 2018.

18. Fieldwork by James Farrer, May 2019.

19. James Farrer, "From Cooks to Chefs: Skilled Migrants in a Globalising Culinary Field," *Journal of Ethnic and Migration Studies* 47, no. 10 (2021): 2359–2375; Priscilla Parkurst Ferguson and Sharon Zukin, "The Careers of Chefs," in *Eating Culture,* ed. Ron Scapp and Brian Seitz (Albany: State University of New York Press, 1998), 92–111.

20. Ricardo Yoshikawa, interview by Mônica Carvalho, December 2016 (one month after opening).

21. Ricardo Yoshikawa, interview by Mônica Carvalho, December 2016.

22. Arnaldo Lorençato and Saulo Yassuda, "Ryo," *Veja São Paulo,* October 2019, https://vejasp.abril.com.br/estabelecimento/ryo/.

23. Telma Shiraishi, interview by Mônica Carvalho, August 29, 2017; Marcelo Katsuki, "Restaurante Aizome comemora dez anos," *Folha de São Paulo,* March 10, 2017, https://marcelokatsuki.blogfolha.uol.com.br/2017/03/03/restaurante-aizome-comemora-10-anos-com-eventos-e-menu-de-favoritos/.

24. Telma Shiraishi, interview by Mônica Carvalho, August 29, 2017.

25. Katsuki, "Restaurante Aizome comemora dez anos."

26. Katsuki; Telma Shiraishi, interview by Mônica Carvalho, August 29, 2017.

27. Jun Sakamoto, interview by Mônica Carvalho, December 12, 2016.

28. Jun Sakamoto, interview by Mônica Carvalho, December 12, 2016.

29. Jun Sakamoto, interview by Mônica Carvalho, December 12, 2016.

30. Jun Sakamoto, interview by Mônica Carvalho, December 12, 2016.

31. Adam Platt, "Ichimura Raises Its Prices and Loses Some of Its Charm after Declaring Independence from Brushstroke," Grub Street, May 7, 2017, https://www.grubstreet.com/2017/05/ichimura-nyc-restaurant-review.html.

32. Samuel Clonts, interview by James Farrer, April 19, 2019.

33. Ryan Sutton, "Upscale Uchū Makes Old-School Luxuries Feel Tired: The Lower East Side Kaiseki Spot Packs in the Extravagances, but Little Punch," Eater, January 23, 2018, https://ny.eater.com/2018/1/23/16912880/Uchū-nyc-review-kaiseki.

34. Uchū closed in September 2019, an unusual development for a restaurant that had just acquired a Michelin star, but according to informants, not so unusual in Feldman's chaotic company.

35. Samuel Clonts, interview by James Farrer, April 19, 2019.

36. Farrer, "From Cooks to Chefs."

37. Meryl Koh, "10 for 10: Hong Kong's Top Chefs Reflect on the Local Dining Scene Then and Now," Michelin Guide November 15, 2017, https://guide.michelin.com/en/article/features/10-for-10-hong-kong-s-top-chefs-reflect-on-the-local-dining-scene-then-and-now.

38. Agustin Balbi, interview by James Farrer, May 13, 2019.

39. Charmaine Mok, "What's the Best New Restaurant of 2017?" *Tatler Hong Kong,* October 31, 2017, https://hk.asiatatler.com/dining/t-dining-best-new-restaurant-readers-choice-2017.

40. Agustin Balbi, interview by James Farrer, May 13, 2019.

41. Hiroki Odo, interview by James Farrer, September 24, 2019; fieldwork by James Farrer, April 17, 2019.

42. Hiroki Odo, interview by James Farrer, September 24, 2019.

43. Hiroki Odo, interview by James Farrer, September 24, 2019.

44. Hiroki Odo, interview by James Farrer, September 24, 2019.

45. Katarzyna Joanna Cwiertka, *Modern Japanese Cuisine: Food, Power and National Identity* (London: Reaktion Books, 2006).

46. Greg de St. Maurice, "KYOTO CUISINE GONE GLOBAL," *Gastronomica* 17, no. 3 (2017): 36–48.

47. Ligaya Mishan, "The New Generation of Chefs Pushing Japanese Food in Unexpected Directions," *New York Times Magazine,* September 2, 2019, https://nyti.ms/2loL9U1.

48. Samuel H. Yamashita, "The 'Japanese Turn' in Fine Dining in the United States, 1980–2020," *Gastronomica* 20, no. 2 (2020): 45–54.

49. Oliver Strand, "Japanese Chefs Make Their Mark in Paris," *New York Times,* March 29, 2016, https://nyti.ms/22YJLCT.

50. Patrick Duval, interview by Chuanfei Wang, August 2018.

51. Atsushi Tanaka, interview by James Farrer, July 28, 2018; fieldwork by Chuanfei Wang, August 2018.

52. Fieldwork by Mônica Carvalho, November 25, 2019.

53. "AT," Michelin Guide France, accessed June 1, 2020, https://www.viamichelin.com/web/Restaurant/Paris-75005-AT-9ier21bt.

54. Atsushi Tanaka, interview by James Farrer, July 28, 2018; fieldwork by Chuanfei Wang, August 2018.

55. Yuri Maeda, interview by Mônica R. de Carvalho, November 29, 2019.

56. Toshiharu Minami, interview by James Farrer, August 17, 2016.

57. Sawaguchi Kei'ichi (澤口恵一), "Nihon seiyōryōri no hatten keiro to resutoran wākā no rōdōshi" (日本西洋料理の発展経路とレストランワーカーの労働史) [The developmental pathways of European cuisines in Japan and the labor history of restaurant workers], Kaken kenkyūhi joseijigyō kenkyū seika hōkokusho [Grant-in-aid for scientific research: Research results report], June 22, 2017, https://kaken.nii.ac.jp/ja/file/KAKENHI-PROJECT-26380700/26380700seika.pdf.

58. Yoshihiro Narisawa, interview by Mônica R. de Carvalho, James Farrer, and Chuanfei Wang, June 29, 2018.

59. Yoshihiro Narisawa, interview by Mônica R. de Carvalho, James Farrer, and Chuanfei Wang, June 29, 2018.

60. Yoshihiro Narisawa, interview by Mônica R. de Carvalho, James Farrer, and Chuanfei Wang, June 29, 2018.

61. James Farrer, "Red (Michelin) Stars over China: Seeking Recognition in a Transnational Culinary Field," in *Culinary Nationalism in Asia,* ed. Michelle King (London: Bloomsbury Academic, 2019), 193–213.

62. James Farrer, "Eating the West and Beating the Rest: Culinary Occidentalism and Urban Soft Power in Asia's Global Food Cities," in *Globalization, Food and Social Identities in the Asia Pacific Region,* ed. James Farrer (Tokyo: Sophia University Institute of Comparative Culture, 2010), 129.

63. Yoshihiro Narisawa, interview by Mônica R. de Carvalho, James Farrer, and Chuanfei Wang, June 29, 2018.

64. Yoshihiro Narisawa, interview by Mônica R. de Carvalho, James Farrer, and Chuanfei Wang, June 29, 2018.

65. Chefs making such claims are criticized for failing to take a strong stand on sustainable fishing, particularly overfishing of tuna. Concerns about the sincerity of celebrity chefs' sustainability rhetoric were voiced by the founder of "Chefs for the Blue" Hiroki Sasaki; Hiroki Sasaki, conversation with Mônica R. de Carvalho, James Farrer, and Chuanfei Wang, May 18, 2018. Also see Melinda Joe, "Calling on Chefs to Lead the Charge against Overfishing," *Japan Times,* May 26, 2018, https://www.japantimes.co.jp/life/2018/05/26/food/calling-chefs-lead-charge-overfishing/.

66. Jessica Thompson, "Tokyo Still Has More Michelin-Starred Restaurants," *Time Out,* December 8, 2020, https://www.timeout.com/tokyo/news/tokyo-still-has-more-michelin-starred-restaurants-than-any-other-city-in-the-world-120820.

67. "Washoku, Traditional Dietary Cultures of the Japanese, Notably for the Celebration of New Year," UNESCO, Intangible Cultural Heritage, December 2–7, 2013, https://ich.unesco.org/en/RL/washoku-traditional-dietary-cultures-of-the-japanese-notably-for-the-celebration-of-new-year-00869.

68. Yoshihiro Narisawa, interview by Mônica R. de Carvalho, James Farrer, and Chuanfei Wang, June 29, 2018.

69. "Company Profile," Sun with Aqua, accessed December 14, 2020, http://sunwithaqua.com/company-profile/?lang=en.

70. Momofuku accessed September 15, 2019, https://momofuku.com/.

71. Farrer, "From Cooks to Chefs."

72. See Shoko Imai, "Umami Abroad: Taste, Authenticity, and the Global Urban Network," in *The Globalization of Asian Cuisines: Transnational Networks and Culinary Contact Zones,* ed. James Farrer (New York: Palgrave Macmillan, 2015), 57–78.

73. Nobu Group accessed November 5, 2020, https://www.noburestaurants.com/.

74. Nobuyuki Matsuhisa, *Nobu: A Memoir* (New York: Simon and Schuster, 2017).

75. Greg Morago, "5 Questions to Nobu Matsuhisa, Who Recently Opened Houston's First Nobu Restaurant," *Houston Chronicle,* June 7, 2018, https://www.houstonchronicle.com/entertainment/restaurants-bars/article/5-questions-to-Nobu-Matsuhisa-who-recently-12976436.php.

76. Matsuhisa, *Nobu,* 111.

77. Matsuhisa, 119. See also Imai, "Umami Abroad."

78. Letícia Shiotsuka, interview by Mônica R. de Carvalho, November 2018.

79. Matsuhisa, *Nobu,* 104.

80. Andre Ishiki, interview by Mônica R. de Carvalho, November 2018.

81. Matsuhisa, *Nobu,* 108–109.

82. Letícia Shiotsuka, interview by Mônica R. de Carvalho, November 2018.

83. "World of Nobu: Why Creating a Great Learner Experience Matters," Wisetail, accessed December 18, 2020, https://www.wisetail.com/world-of-nobu-why-creating-a-great-learner-experience-matters-webinar/.

84. Matsuhisa, *Nobu,* 115–117.

85. Matsuhisa, 108–109.

86. Sean Tan, interview by Chuanfei Wang, March 4, 2018.

87. Yoshizumi Nagaya, interview by James Farrer, September 17, 2017; fieldwork by James Farrer, September 17, 2017.

88. Fieldwork by James Farrer, March 5, 2017.

89. Naoya Hirano, interview by James Farrer, March 5, 2017.

90. See, for example, Rumi Sakamoto and Matthew Allen, "There's Something Fishy about That Sushi: How Japan Interprets the Global Sushi Boom," *Japan Forum* 23, no. 1 (2011): 99–121; Cwiertka and Yasuhara, *Branding Japanese Food.*

91. "Washoku World Challenge Final: The Winner Is Wang Wei Ping," Taste of Japan, February 22, 2020, https://tasteofjapan.maff.go.jp/en/topics/detail/98.html.

92. Angela Hirata, interview by Mônica R. de Carvalho, September 17, 2017.

93. Fieldwork by Mônica R. de Carvalho, October, 2017.

94. Zaiyu Hasegawa, conversation with James Farrer at Den, September 19, 2020. The cartoon-like image of KFC's founder Colonel Harland Sanders has been very well known in Japan since the 1980s.

95. Hasegawa Zaiyu (長谷川在佑), *Den: Shinkasuru Tōkyō nihon ryōri* (傳: 進化するトーキョー日本料理) [Den: The evolving Tokyo-Japanese cuisine] (Tokyo: Shibata shoten, 2017), 20.

96. Notes from Zaiyu Hasegawa's talk at Japan House São Paulo by Mônica R. de Carvalho, August 25, 2017.

97. Notes from Zaiyu Hasegawa's talk at the Japan House São Paulo by Mônica R. de Carvalho, August 25, 2017.

98. Komatsu Hiroko (小松宏子), "Nihon no shoku bunka wo sekai ni! Sekai no shunō wo unaraseta, G20 yūshokukai no menyū no uragawa to wa?" (日本の食文化を世界に! 世界の首脳を唸らせた, G20 夕食会のメニューの裏側とは?) [Bringing Japanese food culture to the world! What is behind the menu of the G20 dinner that made the world leaders exclaim?], *Hitosara Magazine*, August 16, 2019, https://magazine.hitosara.com/article/1712/.

99. Komatsu.

100. For a detailed discussion of this promotion of *washoku* and the problems with it, see Cwiertka and Yasuhara, *Branding Japanese Food.*

9 | Reflecting on the Global Japanese Restaurant

JAMES FARRER AND DAVID L. WANK

This book describes how, over 150 years, Japanese cuisine has gone from being consumed only in Japan to being served in restaurants in almost every country. Even as the cuisine has acquired new tastes, appearances, and attributes while spreading far outside Japan's borders, it has remained a cultural product touted and consumed precisely because it is considered "Japanese." To explain this, we have adopted a global perspective, defined by several characteristics. The first is a focus on restaurants as the intersection of the mobilities, imaginaries, and politics that have conveyed the cuisine to an expanding global dining public. The second is a global multiscalar analysis (local, national, regional, international, transnational, global) to explain the networked interactions of multiple actors (entrepreneurs, chefs, migrants, critics, corporations, and states, to name a few) that have established Japanese restaurants in urban centers and peripheries. Third is the historical layering of the cultural, political, economic, and social contexts and practices that have continuously enlarged the presence of Japanese restaurants and stimulated innovations in their menus. Therefore, this book is not only a new narrative of Japanese cuisine "going global," but also a distinct explanation of global cultural production in the modern world.

As a study of globalizing process, this book comes out at an extraordinary time. The pandemic that erupted in early 2020 and tore through so many lives also upended the globalized culinary world described in its pages. Even as we wrote our final chapters, disruptions of supply lines and the reassertion of national borders through travel restrictions challenged our premise of global mobilities and related politics and imaginaries. In spring 2020, we received dozens of emails from restaurateurs we had interviewed in New York and other culinary global cities soliciting donations to keep staff employed or announcing temporary (and some permanent) closings. We wondered if our book would be an epitaph for the global Japanese restaurant. Now, two years later, we see the pandemic not as an ending but an inflection point, one intertwined with other global crises, especially the war in Ukraine. In the conclusion of this final chapter, we also consider the impact of COVID-19, and these other global crises, on processes we have identified.

The Global Scope of the Japanese Culinary Field

Our global perspective has focused on restaurants serving Japanese cuisine outside Japan. This perspective has let us identify historical processes of the globalization of Japanese cuisine. First, our narrative challenges the typical story that the worldwide spread of Japanese cuisine seemingly started in California in the 1960s. Instead, we have argued that the globalization of Japanese cuisine did not begin with the sushi boom in the West in the mid-twentieth century but rather in the late nineteenth century with the Japanese empire in East Asia and the creation of settler colonies in the Americas. Second, we have shown how the globalization of Japanese cuisine is not simply a collection of local and regional narratives but rather one of successive food fashions with a global scope. In this succession, earlier restaurant fashions enabled those that came later. Thus, the Japanese tearooms and sukiyaki restaurants in the late nineteenth- and early twentieth-century Japanese empire helped lay the basis for the mid-twentieth-century booms of teppanyaki steak houses and sushi restaurants in other contexts. This succession is not linear but layered: older trends do not disappear but survive on the culinary peripheries and fringes, such as teppanyaki restaurants in the rural regions of the southern United States. Third, the history of specific restaurant forms is deeply intertwined with broader phenomena, including the nineteenth-century fashion of *Japonisme,* changing policies toward immigrants and citizens of Japanese descent, and the shifting political and economic status of Japan, as well as such historical processes and events as colonialism, World War II, financial bubbles and bursts, and, most recently, the global pandemic. All of these are implicated in and reflected in culinary history.

In terms of spatial scale, our research has highlighted global urban hierarchies that amalgamate prestige, wealth, and power. Culinary global cities have an outsize influence on restaurant fashions and trends in other cities. In particular, our study has highlighted the substantial role of New York in everything from sukiyaki restaurants to sushi-centered pan-Asian restaurants to teppanyaki steak houses and fusion *kaiseki* (formal cuisine). However, the position of New York as the preeminent global food city is not immutable, especially with the rise of East Asia as the largest overseas market for Japanese cuisine. In the 2010s, for example, we saw Shanghai challenging New York due to its vast flows of financial capital and a fashion-conscious population that made the city a magnet for star chefs from around the world. During this period, Shanghai became the city outside Japan with the most Japanese restaurants.[1] However, China's increasingly authoritarian and nationalist politics may dampen enthusiasm for innovative cosmopolitanism and the migrant entrepreneurship that drives cultural production in the restaurant industry. These trends have been exacerbated by COVID-19 travel restrictions that have been longer lasting and stricter than in any other country. We also see the rise of other regional centers, such as Singapore in Southeast Asia, Dubai in the Middle East, and Nairobi in East Africa. These cities are growing as amalgamators of globalizing restaurant trends and allocators of capital and kitchen talent to their hinterlands.

Another factor in the shifting geography of the globalized Japanese culinary field is the rise of the internet as a source of knowledge and influence. This enables entrepreneurs with no knowledge of Japanese cuisine and who have never been to Japan to self-teach on the internet by watching videos detailing the step-by-step preparation of dishes. Our study suggests that this is furthering the establishment of Japanese restaurants by restaurateurs outside larger urban centers, such as Julienne Sushi Bar in Elizabethtown, Pennsylvania, or the small *izakaya*s (pubs) we visited in Tianjin, China. In various places throughout the world, we heard stories of restaurateurs and chefs picking up skills on the internet rather than by travel. In this sense, the internet is a force for flattening the urban hierarchies in the culinary field.

In particular, we see how Tokyo has been significantly repositioned to be more central in the networks of culinary global cities in the twenty-first century. In the late nineteenth and early twentieth centuries, Japan was primarily a sender of immigrants who founded Japanese restaurants abroad. This has changed sharply in the twenty-first century. We now see more culinary mobilities centered on Japanese cities. One pattern is the circular migration patterns in East Asia, such as Chinese who study and work in Japan returning to China and opening restaurants there. Another is chefs in the fine dining sector sojourning in Japan to pick up skills through stints in restaurants. And significantly, the centrality of Tokyo can be seen its growing number of Michelin-starred restaurants and listings on the World's 50 Best Restaurants list, attracting the world's gourmets and aspiring chefs to the city. This has encouraged Japanese chefs to open innovative restaurants that appeal not only to Japanese diners but also to well-to-do culinary tourists. Thus, global culinary mobilities—of producers, consumers, and cultural intermediaries—have situated Tokyo, and to a lesser extent Kyoto, more fully in a globalizing culinary field and elevated their positions in culinary urban hierarchies. These shifting networks and hierarchies of culinary global cities—especially in Asia—remain an intriguing area of study, and not just in the field of Japanese cuisine.

The global scope of our research methodology also suggests a new characterization of the organization of cuisine in general, including the processes of culinary innovation and culinary influence. The interactions among actors who produce, consume, and evaluate restaurants (chefs, diners, critics, suppliers, restaurateurs, corporations) constitute a transnational culinary field on an increasingly global scale.[2] Previous research has typically focused on the scope of the culinary field at the urban and national scales.[3] In particular, chefs were seen as making their careers locally in urban markets or in national fields and largely learning from and reacting to local or national peers. International standards—such as Michelin stars—were seen as becoming relevant to most markets only in the past ten to twenty years. Our research has shown that there is a transnational culinary Japanese field organized in networks connecting to and concentrated in culinary global cities. This is not unique to Japanese cuisine. Other contemporary culinary fields, such as French fine dining or Mexican fast food, also have an emergent global scale.[4]

Culinary global cities are sites of change and interaction. Influences not only are shared within individual cities but are accelerated by the circulation of various culinary actors among cities. Moreover, while previous research has emphasized culinary innovation mostly in high-end restaurants, we have stressed innovation in the midrange and low-end restaurants. In the midrange sector, our narrative highlights the culinary innovations of people working in transnational migrant networks, such as the hipster restaurants designed by Vietnamese migrants in Berlin and the wok-sushi format created by Chinese migrants in northern Italy. We have seen the importance of Little Fuzhou in New York City as a node of connections for creating a sushi-roll-centered form of Japanese restaurant that has influenced Japanese restaurants worldwide. Innovation in networks is also reflected in the personal migration experiences of cooks. Migrant cooks at all price levels acquire ideas as they move among restaurants and cities, adding dishes to the menus of their Japanese restaurants that reflect their prior family histories and work experiences. We also find that innovations are at the heart of corporate gastronomy, producing newfangled dishes to appeal to a mass market. These innovations, too, involve trends such as the poke bowl that rapidly spread worldwide.

Another globalizing trend is a shift away from individual proprietorship to corporate ownership. Most overseas Japanese restaurants throughout the twentieth century were small-scale family businesses. Corporate ownership became increasingly common in the late twentieth century, mainly through the spread of mass-market fast-food chains. By the early twenty-first century, corporatized restaurants competed against single proprietor-owned establishments at every price level, from mass-market chains to fine dining restaurants. Their investments on all six continents were creating Japanese restaurants in new markets, such as Africa, Southeast Asia, and the Middle East. While corporatization may signal the decline of Japanese cuisine as a migrant-led ethnic business, it has not eliminated the importance of the "Japan brand" as a marker of distinction and taste.

Why Has Japanese Cuisine Remained Fashionable?

This book has portrayed the global Japanese restaurant as a sequence of culinary fashions spanning more than a hundred years. These restaurants have been patronized by an expanding variety of consumers, spreading from colonial cities of Japan's East Asian empire to cities and their hinterlands on six continents. Now, Japanese restaurants may not represent the most popular culinary genre in all the world's cities, but they are usually among the most expensive and fashionable. Here, we draw on our narrative to explain this ongoing and expanding appeal of Japanese cuisine outside the borders of Japan. This appeal is rooted in late nineteenth-century Japanese imperialism in East Asia and the aesthetics of *Japonisme* in Europe and North America, which created an allure for Japanese cuisine. Be it a response to Japanese hegemony (East Asia) or Western Orientalism (Europe and North America), elites consumed Japanese cuisine as a marker of social distinction. As a global fashion, Japanese food began spreading in the 1920s starting with sukiyaki. Since then, despite the waxing and waning of specific fashions, consuming Japanese cuisine has remained a mark of distinction, becoming a symbol of urban sophistication from Berlin to Singapore by the mid-twentieth century.[5] In the twenty-first century, the allure of Japanese cuisine expanded to the lower ends of the market, as seen in the popularity of poke and ramen.

In explaining the relatively persistent appeal of Japanese cuisine, we build on this book's basic premise that its globalization was due not simply to the allure of the dishes but also to the restaurant forms in which they were consumed. Based on this insight, we argue that certain characteristics of the global Japanese restaurant have lent themselves to successive Japanese-cuisine booms. For a fashion to globalize at multiple levels of the market, it requires certain factors: novelty, familiarity, replicability, and missionaries.

First, Japan's long history of urbanization produced a variegated restaurant scene that provided a basis for novelty in later overseas restaurant ventures. By around 1800, Edo (now called Tokyo) was one of the largest cities in the world, with reportedly six thousand restaurants, including the early *izakaya*, *ryōtei* (fine dining restaurants with entertainment), and sushi stands.[6] Over the next century, this repertoire expanded to include hybridized Chinese and Western restaurant forms, such as the Japanese-style café, the sushi bar, the teppanyaki steak house, and the ramen bar, each embodying characteristic dishes, service styles, and décor. Beginning in the late nineteenth century, entrepreneurial restaurateurs began introducing these forms to the global dining public. We argue that this variety of extant Japanese restaurant forms enabled Japanese cuisine to avoid the fate of singular food fashions, which die because they lose their distinctiveness as they spread.[7] The forms constituted a rich cultural repertoire that has continuously replenished the distinctive "newness" of Japanese cuisine. In our data, this is seen clearly in the early twenty-first century in the rise of ramen, which was touted as a novel dish in Japanese cuisine—the "new sushi."

The fact that it was served in a restaurant with a form similar to that of the sushi bar underscores how the "novelty" of the product that makes for distinction is cloaked in the familiarity of the past.[8]

Second, Japanese restaurants invoked familiar imaginaries and patterns of consumption. The "new" was paradoxically familiar. The various novel forms of Japanese restaurants have successively replenished the appeal of Japanese cuisine while embodying a familiar imaginary of "Japan." This imaginary encompasses the Japanese culinary aesthetics promulgated since the nineteenth century and later values of health and freshness that became deeply associated with Japanese food. Regarding the service style, Japanese restaurants hired and assigned staff in ways that could be represented as stereotypically Japanese while according with changing gender norms. Thus, feminized servers and masculinized, Japanese-appearing chefs made these spaces both exotic and easy to navigate socially for diners worldwide. In this regard, the gendering of the consumer experience in Japanese restaurants closely tracked the historical shift globally from a focus on male clientele socializing over alcohol to a focus on women seeking lighter and healthier meals, a pattern that was already visible in the early twentieth-century teahouses, with their female-friendly décor and staffing. (A similar shift can be seen in Western restaurants with the advent of early twentieth-century cafeterias and department store restaurants friendly to women.)[9] Also, many dishes served in the various Japanese restaurant forms were already products of culinary contacts between Chinese, Westerners, and Japanese in Japanese cities, creating an easily translatable flavor profile. In our study, the paradoxically exotic and the familiar appeal is perhaps best articulated by the assurances that restaurateur Rocky Aoki gave diners at Benihana Steakhouse that they would have a Japanese experience with no surprises (see Chapter 4).

Third, despite the reputation of Japan for culinary artisanry, what stands out in most of the restaurants in this book is the easy replicability of the dishes. Many were initially street foods or fast foods and not based on elaborate court or banquet cuisines. While *kaiseki* is an obvious exception, it remains a rarified (and relatively rare) foodie fashion. A process of replication (and deskilling) is described throughout this book, as restaurateurs of many backgrounds quickly learned to produce teppanyaki, sushi, yakitori, or ramen. Such replicability and flexibility are also characteristic of many other global restaurant fashions. The pizzeria and taqueria are two prominent examples of restaurants serving signature dishes that are relatively easy to make and infinitely adaptable to local ingredients and consumer tastes. This feature of Japanese food fashions is not unique, but it runs against the perception that Japanese food requires esoteric or specialized skills. Perhaps the most explicit expression of this view is Yoshiharu Sato's statement that the ramen sold in his Menya Musashi chain is nothing but a "Japanese brand" that is surprisingly easy to produce (see Chapter 6).

Fourth, Japanese cuisine and restaurants have been promoted by a wide range of cultural intermediaries. The earliest ones were Japanese who, as the first people from Asia to "modernize," were often insecure about the status of Japan in the world.[10] Some wanted foreigners, especially Europeans and Americans, to appreciate Japanese culture, thereby positioning Japan as equal to the West with its own rich culture and not just a cheap imitator of Western modernity. This can be seen in Moto Saito's story and her desire to earn the respect of Western audiences, first in Shanghai and later in New York. After World War II, restaurant projects as varied as Nippon-Kan in Düsseldorf and Dosanko Ramen in New York were founded by Japanese business communities to impress and educate foreigners about Japanese culture while also making money. This study has also described a host of non-Japanese cultural intermediaries. Many prominent early food writers were women possibly drawn to the refined aesthetics of the Japanese restaurant, an image first established through the feminized aesthetics of the Japanese tearoom in the late nineteenth century. In the twenty-first century, culinary intermediaries include celebrity chefs who invested in new food fashions. The participation of intermediaries from a wide variety of ethnicities and nationalities helped ensure the continued expansion of these fashions. The discussion of cultural intermediaries raises the issue taken up in the following section, of what about Japan, Japanese cuisine, or Japanese culture they have been claiming to convey as culinary ambassadors and missionaries.

What Is Japanese about the Global Japanese Restaurant?

Even as Japanese cuisine has been globalized, localized, hybridized, and reinvented in restaurants around the world, ideas of Japaneseness—or authenticity—have remained central to the imaginary of the global Japanese restaurant. Many producers and consumers around the world explained to us how a restaurant or its food was (or wasn't) *prave* (in Czech), *zhen-zong* (in Chinese), or *autêntico* (in Portuguese). They used such terms—for "genuineness" or "authenticity"—to distinguish "real" Japanese foods and restaurants from "counterfeit" ones. This idea of authenticity represents standards—normative touchstones—of Japaneseness that are conveyed in both discourses and practices. Our finding that people of many backgrounds and positions were deeply concerned about something called authenticity challenges the argument by some scholars that authenticity in cuisine is primarily a concern of majority (usually white) consumers.[11] Producers—of many ethnicities—have a major stake in producing authenticity. Japanese restaurateurs, in particular, played a key and early role in articulating and establishing standards of authenticity that were discursive as well as practical. And Japanese informants have remained vocal about these standards into the twenty-first century. Restaurant owners and chefs made authenticity claims to add economic value to their restaurants, but many also linked their personal and social identities to these claims.[12] Of course, authenticity also represents attempts to define who can legitimately operate a Japanese restaurant by valuing some participants in the Japanese culinary field and excluding others.[13] From our study, we identify three long-existing standards for claiming or disputing authenticity in the Japanese restaurant: people, place, and practices. We also identify a fourth expectation for creativity that can be regarded as a new standard of culinary authenticity, but one that also exists in tension with the others.

These discourses of authenticity are not unique to Japanese cuisine. Ideas of place-based authenticity are the basis of the notion of terroir (literally the taste of a place) and the influential "geographical indication" system of the European Union (EU) (which defines specific products as belonging to a region).[14] Notions of process-based authenticity lie behind many regional cookbooks and are also the basis of the "traditional specialty guaranteed" designation of the EU (which protects a traditional way of making a product).[15] People-based standards of culinary authenticity refer to who is "allowed" to make a cuisine. Such discriminatory notions are unlikely to be enshrined in formal regulations. Nonetheless, people-based (often ethnic) standards of authenticity are common in discussions about cultural appropriation (when members of one group are accused of "stealing" the cuisine of another) or the practice of racialized hiring in kitchen work and the exclusion of migrants from representations of authentic local products.[16] Finally, creativity is increasingly a standard of authenticity in contemporary restaurants, especially in fine dining. A chef's capacity to innovate is a defining element of professional competence.[17] While creativity may be seen as contrary to the traditional people-place-process standards of authenticity, we have found it to be a central expectation of restaurant cuisines at all levels of production. In short, restaurant cuisine should be both "true" and "new," or familiar and innovative, which forms an essential tension driving food fashions, as discussed in the previous section.

It is easy to dismiss all four such notions of authenticity as strategies of social exclusion, and not only the person-based ones. Notions of terroir, for example, were promulgated in France to defend French wines from cheaper but tasty colonial imports.[18] Notions of process and creativity exclude those who fail to master the appropriate techniques or who fail to use them in novel ways. Seen more positively, however, culinary authenticity signifies ways in which people seek connections to places, peoples, and lifeways through foods, either their own or those of people they seek to engage with.[19] Geographic mobility pulls apart the ties among foods, producers, places, and practices, making authenticity an urgent issue for many producers and consumers of "traveling cuisines," including overseas Japanese cuisine.

In the case of Japanese cuisine, increasingly explicit claims about authenticity arose as Japanese restaurants opened in places distant from Japan, as different types of people began operating them, and as the processes they used gradually changed. Initially, the first three touchstones of places, people, and practices reflected the tacit culture, or habitus, of the Japanese migrants who ran and patronized the earliest restaurants outside Japan. As these restaurateurs came to face a broader non-Japanese public and intensifying competition, they became more explicit in expressing these standards to their audiences. Our narrative has featured Moto Saito, who opened restaurants beginning in the 1930s aimed at non-Japanese customers (see Chapters 1 and 4). Facing an elite non-Japanese audience, she articulated Japanese authenticity in terms of the first three standards—namely, foods made in a Japanese way by Japanese cooks with at least some key Japanese ingredients and techniques, served in a space designed according to Japanese norms, and embodying a Japanese style of service. Her standards were clearly stated on her menu, although she made compromises on all fronts. Such claims continue in Japanese restaurants today, though with a greater emphasis on creativity and innovation as part of the value of a restaurant meal.

The first standard of authenticity concerns who is cooking and serving the food. Although explicitly ethnic standards are muted in multicultural societies, we found almost everywhere an assumption that Japanese cooks would produce the most authentic Japanese food.[20] One expression of this was to hire Japanese head chefs. This practice was even advocated by celebrity chef "Nobu" Matsuhisa, who described the role of these hires as maintaining a Japanese taste in kitchens with many non-Japanese cooks.[21] Another practice of person-based authenticity was an emphasis on the physical and performative aspects of race and ethnicity. Some restaurateurs allocated non-Japanese personnel, typically other East Asians, with putative Japanese features to visible positions. Common in North America and Europe, such placement was intended to assure customers of the authenticity of the restaurant's food and enhance its Japanese imagery. Still, such practices were discriminatory, as seen in the experiences of the Hispanic male and mixed-race female sushi chef mentioned in Chapter 5.[22] The salience of ethnicity (and gender) may be seen even in the selections in the Michelin guides, as practically all Michelin-starred Japanese restaurants remain headed by ethnic Japanese (male) chefs. For example, in the 2018 guides for London, Singapore, New York, Hong Kong, and San Francisco, forty Japanese restaurants received stars, with thirty-six headed by chefs with Japanese surnames and only one woman.[23] Although the authors of guidebooks would argue this reflects the cooking skills of ethnically Japanese chefs, the result appears exclusionary.

A second authenticity standard is place, typically with Japan as the touchstone. For overseas restaurants, it is impossible to actually be in Japan. Japanese restaurants abroad use multiple methods to establish place-based connections to Japan. The most common is using interior design to evoke a Japanese space. Higher-end restaurants import expensive furnishing from Japan and hire artisans from Japan to build their spaces. Restaurants toward the lower end may only place a Japanese painting on the wall and lucky cat (*maneki neko*) figurine by the cash register. Another common strategy is importing ingredients, beverages, and seasonings from Japan. Thus, top sushi bars fly in fish from the Tsukiji market in Tokyo. The fact that the fish might have been caught in the Indian or Atlantic Ocean is less significant than its having touched base in Tokyo. Spending time in Japan also authenticates staff. For non-Japanese chefs, a short sojourn in Japan can embellish their culinary capital as cooks of Japanese cuisine and the reputations of the restaurants where they work. For chefs who did not work in Japan, there is the reflected glory of working under those who did. Conversely, for restaurateurs working in Japan, the place-based definition of authenticity gives them broad latitude to ignore other authenticity standards. It allows creative chefs in Tokyo, such as Yoshihiro Narisawa, to claim Japaneseness through locally sourced ingredients, regardless of the various Western or Chinese techniques he applies to them (see Chapter 8). Finally, it is important to note that place-based claims can be arbitrary, especially for multiply reterritorialized dishes. Thus, teriyaki can be tied to Japan, Seattle, and the US Pacific Northwest depending on a restaurant's context, imaginary, and strategy (see Chapter 6). This indicates that place, as with race, is a negotiated standard of culinary authenticity but still very salient for both producers and consumers since personal stories and identities are easily tied to places.

The third notion of culinary authenticity centers on practices seen as characteristic of a Japanese restaurant. A clear example is cooking techniques, which are especially relevant for chefs who lack an ethnic association with Japan. This standard of culinary authenticity is exemplified by non-Japanese chefs such as Ivan Orkin, Max Levy, and Agustin Balbi (discussed in Chapters 4, 7, and 8, respectively), who boast of their years working in Japanese kitchens as a testimony to their skill level. It is also seen in the practice at corporate restaurants, such as Nobu, of giving specialized but relatively quick training to chefs and servers. Japanese practices are equally important in the front-of-house service, from Japanese-style uniforms to shouts of "*irasshaimase*" (welcome) to guests, heard around the world even from servers who cannot speak any other Japanese. Service rituals may include elaborate acts such as the comedic knife routines seen at Benihana and widely mimicked in teppanyaki restaurants outside Japan. These practices have driven claims and counterclaims regarding authenticity. Some diners have seen the acts as authentic Japanese techniques, while others have disputed their provenance, even dismissing them as "minstrel shows" (see Chapter 4). Many chefs and restaurateurs criticized competitors for inauthentic cooking techniques and service practices during our interviews with them. We see these critiques as reflecting fears that the competitors (typically "outsiders") were lowering industry standards, leading to intensified competition, and depressing profit margins.

Finally, our study has identified creativity, or innovation, as an increasingly important standard of culinary authenticity in Japanese restaurants. This standard is not unique to Japanese cuisine and is strongly influenced by both fast-food marketing and the mid-twentieth-century "modernist" trend in European fine dining. Based on the idea of novelty as an intrinsic good, modernism in cuisine created an expectation of frequent menu changes, novel ingredients, and exotic preparations. Innovation has long characterized the fast-food industry, where securing brand loyalty entails constantly offering surprising iterations of signature dishes and time-limited specials. Thus, Yoshinoya has produced a continuous stream of new bowl dishes, often localized for specific overseas markets. As a movement in refined dining, culinary modernism was exemplified by chefs such as Ferran Adrià at El Bulli in Spain since the late 1980s and appeared in the 2000s in global Japanese restaurants (see Chapter 8).[24] A fine dining Japanese restaurant is now seen as inauthentic if it fails to regularly update the menu with surprising dishes. This standard has even permeated to lower market levels. In restaurants in the rural United States, one can find chefs boasting about their "original" sauces for roll sushi and hibachi. At all market levels, however, this standard of innovativeness exists in tension with other standards—whether people, place, or technique. Managers of Japanese restaurants must balance between signaling creativity and evoking familiar Japanese elements. Through the processes we described in previous chapters—corporatization, diversification, agglomeration, and borrowings from other cuisines—the standard of creativity has gained ground in the transnational Japanese cuisine field over the decades. Some highly innovative restaurateurs even say that they ignore authenticity (in terms of the other three standards). Yet in abandoning these standards, they may alienate customers seeking a genuine "Japanese" restaurant.

Over the time frame of our narrative, the standards for creating and operating a Japanese restaurant moved from the implicit culture of Japanese immigrants in overseas communities to the increasingly explicit discourses and practices of authenticity in the transnational Japanese culinary field. The salience of these ideas became evident to us throughout fieldwork visits to hundreds of restaurants, many owned and operated by non-Japanese, that displayed Japan imaginaries in their décor, staffing, and markers of ties to Japan. From time to time, iconoclast restaurateurs have come along whose seeming disregard for ties to Japan actually expanded ways of showing such ties. They thus broadened the scope of "Japanese" cuisine. They did so by associating their restaurants with new media images of Japan circulating in a broader public sphere. The forerunners were arguably the owners of tearooms in the early twentieth century who based their décor on images from world expositions and reproductions of Japanese woodblock prints. Rocky Aoki at Benihana in the 1960s conveyed Japaneseness by pandering to US consumers' image of Japan gained through samurai movies. In the 1990s, Simon Woodroffe based his futuristic design for Yo! Sushi on images of "high-tech" Japan circulating among young Brits. In the 2000s, Serge Lee in Paris marketed restaurants in Little Tokyo that evoked Japanese manga and anime to young French fans of these genres. And in the 2010s, Naoya Hirano played on Shanghai diners' images of Japan as a luxury tourist destination. This shows that authenticity claims based on ideas of Japaneseness are both very persistent and very flexible. Even as their sources shifted from classical woodblock prints to anime and digital media, imaginaries of Japan remained the touchstone of authenticity. Increasingly, however, these imaginaries are being created outside of Japan itself.

COVID-19 and the Global Japanese Restaurant

The lockdowns, social-distancing practices, and closure of national borders to migrants in response to the COVID-19 pandemic have disrupted many of the culinary mobilities described in this book. They have stunted the flows of workers and customers into the middle-market segments described in Chapters 5, 6, and 7 and truncated the travels of the one-percenters who fueled the high-end dining described in Chapter 8. As the pandemic becomes endemic, it is uncertain how patterns of mobility will change. In many markets, particularly the United States and Europe, the exit of workers from the restaurant industry has led to a severe shortage of restaurant staff. Breakdowns in logistics created unprecedented shortages of Japanese ingredients, including soba, *sake*, yellowtail, and Japanese sweets.[25] Prices of many ingredients increased globally. In many countries, the pandemic amplified right-wing populism and antimigration politics that may normalize lower levels of transnational mobility. The effects have been immediate and—most likely—long term.

Already the consequences of decreased mobility seem especially dire for several types of restaurants discussed in this book. For one, the pandemic seems to have accelerated the decline of Japantowns, dragging down independent restaurants that served as community social centers. As described in Chapter 3, Japantown restaurants in many cities were already experiencing economic and demographic challenges before the pandemic, including the aging of owners and patrons and replacement of the original Japanese migrants with those from other Asian countries. According to media reports, the pandemic accelerated these trends by closing some long-established Japanese family-owned businesses, including Benkyodo in San Francisco and Village Yokocho in New York City, both iconic eateries discussed in Chapter 3.[26] More broadly, the pandemic seemed to disproportionately cause problems for the independent chef-owned restaurants featured in most chapters of this book. Even as they cut back on labor costs and relied on takeout, they could not pay rent and other fixed costs. Industry analysts predicted that chain restaurants would better survive the greatly reduced business during COVID-19.[27] Larger chains generally had better access to credit, brand recognition, digital know-how, and other resources to weather business downturns and even take advantage of them. They had more administrative resources than small (often immigrant-owned) businesses to handle the paperwork to get government aid.[28] Thus, the pandemic seemed to accelerate the corporatization of the global Japanese restaurant already described in Chapters 6 and 7.

FIGURE 9.1 The future of Japanese restaurant cuisine may lie in delivery, an emerging fast-service trend accelerated by the COVID-19 pandemic. Dondon was an early entrant in the sushi delivery business in Denmark. (Photo by James Farrer, April 2, 2012)

FIGURE 9.2 During the COVID-19 pandemic, many restaurants in the United States developed outdoor dining areas, including the *izakaya* Shibuya in the Adams Morgan district of Washington, DC. (Photo by James Farrer, July 29, 2021)

Actors in the Japanese culinary field have responded to these challenges by creating novel restaurant forms. One example is the rise of the "ghost kitchen," a restaurant with no dining room and all service done by delivery. During the pandemic, consumers in social isolation ordered online, with food delivered by third parties such as UberEats. Sushi ghost restaurants already existed in Japan, with delivery services dramatically increasing during the pandemic. Restaurant-industry insiders we spoke with around the world reported an increase in delivery business during the pandemic, which they felt was permanent.[29] Another pandemic-related trend that may have a lasting impact is the more physically open Japanese restaurant. The street-side restaurant, introduced as a survival strategy for the industry in many global cities during the pandemic, has gained popularity and may remain. Curbside, terrace, or garden-like Japanese restaurants have always existed in tropical regions but were not common in Japan or in other markets in the global North. Their advent in cities from Berlin to San Francisco could represent a lasting change. Finally, many high-end restaurants have had to search for new local clienteles to replace the global gourmets and business travelers who filled their dining rooms before the pandemic. This has resulted in creative midrange ventures by fine dining chefs introduced in this book, including, for example, a casual bar from Narisawa that also served shaved ice.[30] For a time at least, the movement was toward simpler, more affordable restaurant meals. In markets facing labor shortages, menus were adjusted to feature items easier to prepare by a downsized and less-experienced staff. Finally, although many restaurants closed, according to informants in Tokyo, the pandemic also presented an opportunity for new restaurateurs to open in empty locations now available at cheaper rents.[31]

The pandemic, interacting with other crises such as the war in Ukraine, may continue to disrupt the broader patterns of mobility and influence among global cities. We see several possible scenarios for post-pandemic culinary mobilities. One is the rebound of transnational mobility but re-centered on a different set of cities more open to migration, investments, and tourism. Russian and Chinese cities have seen drastic decreases in inbound travel during the pandemic and war. A long-term decline in flows of people and capital in some cities could accelerate a shift in influence in the culinary field toward cities with greater ease of investment and travel. Singapore could be one beneficiary of China's lockdowns and broader patterns of economic delinking from China. Finally, with labor shortages overall, cities that cultivate skilled labor through culinary education and through migration will develop more vibrant restaurant scenes.

The other scenario is that culinary mobilities across national borders will not return to pre-pandemic levels. This could result in the worldwide decline of the cross-border flows of investments, ideas, and peoples among cities that have sustained the globalized urban culinary scene described in this book. In this case, the circulations of influence within Japanese cuisine—and transnational restaurant cultures more generally—could become more regional or even national and local. We would likely see greater indigenization of labor forces, supply chains, and ownership. We already have seen this in Shanghai, for example, where "zero COVID" policies have drastically restricted flows of foreign workers and travelers, leading to the closure of many restaurants that were oriented toward expatriate consumers amid a shrinking pool of foreign culinary talent.[32] More dramatically, culinary developments in Ukraine have been disconnected from the regional circulation of talent and investment with St. Petersburg and Moscow we observed before the annexation of Crimea in 2014.

Another likely scenario is the shift of culinary influences to online conversations and influencers, making cities less privileged spaces of culinary influence and exchange. A flatter culinary world of dispersed influencers with a global following is clearly in the making. These are not mutually exclusive developments, since online flows of information could increase at the same time material mobilities decline, a pattern we have seen during the pandemic in many regions, including China.[33] All of these scenarios would entail a shift in the spatial organization of Japanese and other cuisines.

Thirty years ago it was written that the world's culture was being "remade in Japan;" now we can see that "Japan" is also being remade in the world.[34] The pandemic looks increasingly like an inflection point rather than a rupture in this process of remaking Japanese cuisine through global mobilities, culinary politics, and new imaginaries. The global Japanese restaurant will undoubtedly survive the pandemic, regional wars, and pauses in human mobility, while the geographies of its ongoing transformations will keep shifting. As before, new restaurant fashions, innovative Japan imaginaries, and agents of cultural mediation will continue reinventing the global Japanese restaurant.

Notes

1. James Farrer, "Domesticating the Japanese Culinary Field in Shanghai," in *Feeding Japan: The Cultural and Political Issues of Dependency and Risk,* ed. Andreas Niehaus and Tine Walravens (New York: Palgrave Macmillan, 2017), 287–312.

2. Our concept of transnational culinary fields was developed in James Farrer, "Introduction: Travelling Cuisines in and out of Asia: Towards a Framework for Studying Culinary Globalization," in *The Globalization of Asian Cuisines: Transnational Networks and Culinary Contact Zones,* ed. James Farrer (New York: Palgrave Macmillan, 2015), 1–20; James Farrer, "From Cooks to Chefs: Skilled Migrants in a Globalising Culinary Field," *Journal of Ethnic and Migration Studies* 47, no. 10 (2021): 2359–2375; James Farrer, "Red (Michelin) Stars over China: Seeking Recognition in a Transnational Culinary Field," in *Culinary Nationalism in Asia,* ed. Michelle King (London: Bloomsbury Academic, 2019), 193–213.

3. Christel Lane, *The Cultivation of Taste: Chefs and the Organization of Fine Dining* (Oxford: Oxford University Press, 2014); Vanina Leschziner, *At the Chef's Table: Culinary Creativity in Elite Restaurants* (Stanford, CA: Stanford University Press, 2015).

4. Priscilla Parkhurst Ferguson, "A Cultural Field in the Making: Gastronomy in 19th-Century France," *American Journal of Sociology* 104, no. 3 (1998): 597–641; Priscilla Parkurst Ferguson and Sharon Zukin, "The Careers of Chefs," in *Eating Culture,* ed. Ron Scapp and Brian Seitz (Albany: State University of New York Press, 1998), 92–111; Jeffrey M. Pilcher, *Planet Taco: A Global History of Mexican Food* (Oxford: Oxford University Press, 2017).

5. Katarzyna Joanna Cwiertka, "From Ethnic to Hip: Circuits of Japanese Cuisine in Europe," *Food and Foodways: Explorations in the History and Culture of Human*

Nourishment 13, no. 4 (2006): 241–272; Sasha Issenberg, *The Sushi Economy: Globalization and the Making of a Modern Delicacy* (New York: Gotham Books, 2007); Irmela Hijiya-Kirschnereit, "Das Sushi-Sakrileg: Zur Verbreitung von Sushi in Mitteleuropa" [The sushi sacrilege: The spread of sushi in Central Europe], *Jahrbuch für Kulinaristik* 2 (2018): 134–165; Lynn Nakano, "Eating One's Way to Sophistication: Japanese Food, Transnational Flows, and Social Mobility in Hong Kong," in *Transnational Trajectories in East Asia: Nation, Citizenship, and Region,* ed. Yasemin N. Soysal (Abingdon, UK: Routledge, 2014), 106–129; Wai-Ming Ng, "Popularization and Localization of Sushi in Singapore: An Ethnographic Survey," *New Zealand Journal of Asian Studies* 3, no. 1 (2001): 7–19.

6. Iino Ryōichi (飯野亮一), *Izakaya no tanjō: Edo no nomidaore bunka* (居酒屋の誕生: 江戸の呑みだおれ文化) [Birth of the *izakaya*: Edo's drinking culture] (Tokyo: Sakuma shobo, 2014), 16. For the history of the emergence of specific types of Japanese restaurants, see Okubo Hiroko (大久保洋子), *Edo no shoku kūkan—Yatai kara nihonryōri e* (江戸の食空間―屋台から日本料理へ) [The eating spaces of Edo: From street stalls to Japanese cuisine] (Tokyo: Kodansha, 2012).

7. "As fashion spreads, it gradually goes to its doom. The distinctiveness which in the early stages of a set fashion assures for it a certain distribution is destroyed as the fashion spreads, and as this element wanes, the fashion also is bound to die." Georg Simmel, "Fashion," *American Journal of Sociology* 62, no. 6 (1957): 547.

8. Simmel, 547.

9. Katie Rawson and Elliott Shore, *Dining Out: A Global History of Restaurants* (London: Reaktion Books, 2019), 53, 89–90.

10. This sense of insecurity was also evident in the articles in Japanese American newspapers when reporting—as newsworthy—that white people (often described as "Americans") reacted favorably to various forms of Japanese cuisine, such as sukiyaki.

11. See Lisa Heldke, *Exotic Appetites: Ruminations of a Food Adventurer* (Abingdon, UK: Routledge, 2015).

12. Satomi Fukutomi, "From 'Isn't It Raw?' to Everyday Food: Authenticating Japanese Food in Perth, Australia," *Gastronomica: The Journal for Food Studies* 22, no. 1 (2022): 34–43; Cornelia Reiher, "Negotiating Authenticity: Berlin's Japanese Food Producers and the Vegan/vegetarian Consumer," *Food, Culture & Society* (2022), DOI :10.1080/15528014.2022.2076028.

13. James Farrer and Chuanfei Wang, "Who Owns a Cuisine? The Grassroots Politics of Japanese Food in Europe," *Asian Anthropology* 20, no. 1 (2021): 12–29.

14. Rachel Laudan, "Slow Food: The French Terroir Strategy, and Culinary Modernism," *Food, Culture & Society* 7, no. 2 (2004): 133–44; Amy B. Trubek, *The Taste of Place: A Cultural Journey into Terroir* (Berkeley: University of California Press, 2008).

15. Fabio Parasecoli, *Knowing Where It Comes from: Labeling Traditional Foods to Compete in a Global Market* (Iowa City: University of Iowa Press, 2017), 40.

16. Jillian Cavanaugh, "Authenticity and its Perils: Who is Left out when Food is 'Authentic'?" *Gastronomica: The Journal for Food Studies* 23, no.1 (2023): 28–37.; Farrer and Wang, "Who Owns A Cuisine?"; Hirose Akihiko and Kay Kei-Ho Pih, "'No Asians Working Here': Racialized Otherness and Authenticity in Gastronomical Orientalism," *Ethnic and Racial Studies* 34, no. 9 (2011): 1482–1501.

17. Leschziner, *At the Chef's Table.*

18. Laudan, "Slow Food."

19. Lauren Crossland-Marr and Elizabeth Krause, "Theorizing Authenticity," *Gastronomica: The Journal for Food Studies* 23, no. 1 (2023): 5–12.; Brad Weiss, "Configuring the Authentic Value of Real Food: Farm-to-fork, Snout-to-tail, and Local Food Movements," *American Ethnologist* 39, no. 3 (2012): 614–626.

20. Farrer and Wang, "Who Owns A Cuisine"; Fukutomi, "From 'Isn't it Raw?'".

21. Nobuyuki Matsuhisa, *Nobu: A Memoir* (New York: Simon and Schuster, 2017), 108–109.

22. The experienced male Mexican American sushi chef working in New York City pointed out the extra effort required for a Hispanic man to prove himself in the kitchen. The much younger Filipino white female assistant sushi chef working in Tennessee stated her intention to quit the industry since she was neither male nor Japanese and saw no future in this field. Fieldwork by James Farrer, 2019.

23. The breakdown by city for starred Japanese restaurants in the 2018 Michelin city guides is as follows: Singapore—five starred Japanese restaurants, all with Japanese head chefs; San Francisco—nine starred restaurants, seven with Japanese head chefs; New York—ten starred restaurants, nine with Japanese head chefs; London—two starred Japanese restaurants, all with Japanese head chefs; Hong Kong—eight starred restaurants, seven with Japanese head chefs; and São Paulo—six starred Japanese restaurants, all with Japanese head chefs (three of these were Nikkei Brazilians, judging by names alone). The ethnicity of chefs is judged based on surnames and may include local citizens of Japanese ancestry. Only one chef (in San Francisco) was female, also Japanese. Of the four non-Japanese, three had Chinese surnames, and one was Mexican American.

24. Constant menu updates, borrowings from other culinary traditions, and the implementation of technology from the fast-food industry are all hallmarks of the global modernist culinary movement. This trend was itself influenced by Japanese cuisine, including notions of presentation and seasonality borrowed from *kaiseki*. So these influences go both ways. Nathan Myhrvold, Chris Young, and Maxime Bilet, *Modernist Cuisine* (London: Taschen, 2011); Samuel H. Yamashita, "The 'Japanese Turn' in Fine Dining in the United States, 1980–2020," *Gastronomica: The Journal for Food Studies* 20, no. 2 (2020): 45–54.

25. Makai Takao (真海喬生), "Beikoku de kūzen no nihon shokuzai busoku: Soba ya hamachi, okashi made" (米国で空前の日本食材不足：そばやハマチ、お菓子まで) [Unprecedented shortage of Japanese ingredients in the United States, including soba, yellowtail, and even sweets], *Asahi Shinbun,* August 26, 2021, https://digital.asahi.com/articles/ASP8R7GKZP8LULFA005.html?ref=mor_mail_topix1.

26. Claire Wong, "How the Pandemic Threatens to Destroy America's Three Remaining Japantowns," NBC News, December 17, 2020, https://www.nbcnews.com/news/asian-america/how-pandemic-threatens-destroy-america-s-three-remaining-japantowns-n1251290; Robert Simonson, "The Mysterious Man Who Built (and Then Lost) Little Tokyo," New York Times (April 8, 2022), https://www.nytimes.com/2022/04/08/nyregion/tony-yoshida-japan-village-angels-share.html.

27. Stacey Haas et al., "How Restaurants Can Thrive in the Next Normal," McKinsey Insights, May 2020, https://www.mckinsey.com/industries/retail/our-insights/how-restaurants-can-thrive-in-the-next-normal.

28. Jenny Zhang, "The Path to Survival Is Even More Complicated for Immigrant-Owned Mom-and-Pop Restaurants," Eater, May 6, 2020, https://www.eater.com/2020/5/6/21240280/immigrant-owned-mom-and-pop-restaurants-struggle-to-survive-coronavirus.

29. Interviews conducted by James Farrer and Krishnendu Ray for the "The Future of Eating Out Lecture Series," Institute of Comparative Culture Sophia University (accessed Nov. 24, 2022), https://www.icc-sophia.com/the-future-of-eating-out-lecture-series; James Farrer, "A Tokyo Restaurant Community Faces Covid-19," *Etnografia e ricerca qualitativa* 13, no. 2 (2020): 245–254; Cornelia Reiher, "Berlin's Japanese Foodscapes During the Covid-19 Crisis: Restaurateurs' Experiences and Practices During the Spring 2020 Restaurant Shutdown," *Berliner Blätter* 86 (2022): 105–122.

30. Bees Bar homepage, accessed January 23, 2022, https://www.beesbar-narisawa-jp.com/.

31. Fieldwork by James Farrer in Tokyo, 2021 and 2022; see also "The Future of Eating Out Lecture Series."

32. This generalization is based on discussions with informants in Shanghai. A list of closed venues appears here: "The Great List of Closed Venues," *Smart Shanghai,* January 2, 2022, http://www.smartshanghai.com/specials/closed-venues/.

33. Anthony Zhao, a Shanghai restaurateur turned food blogger, describes how Chinese restaurants increasingly depended on social media during the COVID-19 period. See James Farrer, "On the Other Side of the Curve: China's Restaurateurs Face an Uphill Battle," *Gastronomica: The Journal for Food Studies* 20, no. 3 (2020): 24–25.

34. Joseph Jay Tobin, ed., *Re-Made in Japan: Everyday Life and Consumer Taste in a Changing Society* (New Haven, CT: Yale University Press, 1992).

Bibliography

This bibliography consolidates the secondary sources and reference works that are used in the book. All other sources, such as websites, news articles, and interviews, are listed in the endnotes of each chapter.

Appadurai, Arjun. "How to Make a National Cuisine: Cookbooks in Contemporary India." *Comparative Studies in Society and History* 30, no. 1 (1988): 3–24.
———. "On Culinary Authenticity." *Anthropology Today* 2 (1986): 24–25.
Arnold, Bruce Makoto, Tanfer Emin Tunç, and Raymond Douglas Chong, eds. *Chop Suey and Sushi from Sea to Shining Sea: Chinese and Japanese Restaurants in the United States.* Little Rock: University of Arkansas Press, 2018.
Arnold, Hugo. *The Wagamama Cookbook.* 2004; reis., New York: Metro Books, 2010.
Asakura, Toshio. "Cultural Heritage in Korea—from a Japanese Perspective." In *Reconsidering Cultural Heritage in East Asia,* edited by A. Matsuda and L. E. Mengoni, 105–106. London: Ubiquity Press, 2016.
Assmann, Stephanie. "Global Engagement for Local and Indigenous Tastes: Culinary Globalization in East Asia." *Gastronomica: The Journal for Food Studies* 17, no. 3 (2017): 1–3.
Austin, Leonard. *Around the World in San Francisco.* Stanford, CA: James Ladd, 1940.
Baldwin, Watson. "The Restauranteurship of Hong Kong's Premium Japanese Restaurant Market." *International Hospitality Review* 32, no. 1 (2018): 8–25.
Befu, Harumi. "The Global Context of Japan Outside Japan." In *Globalizing Japan: Ethnography of the Japanese Presence in Asia, Europe, and America,* edited by Harumi Befu and Sylvie Guichard-Anguis, 25–44. London: Routledge, 2003.
Berg, Shelley C. "Sada Yacco in London and Paris, 1900: Le rêve réalisé." *Dance Chronicle* 18, no. 3 (1995): 343–404.
Beriss, David, and David Sutton, eds. *The Restaurants Book: Ethnographies of Where We Eat.* Oxford: Berg, 2007.
Beriss, David, and David Sutton. "Restaurants, Ideal Postmodern Institutions." In *The Restaurants Book: Ethnographies of Where We Eat,* edited by David Beriss and David Sutton, 1–13. Oxford: Berg, 2007.

Bestor, Theodore C. "Most F(l)avored Nation Status: The Gastrodiplomacy of Japan's Global Promotion of Cuisine." *Public Diplomacy Magazine* 11 (2014): 57–60.

———. "Supply-Side Sushi: Commodity, Market, and the Global City." *American Anthropologist* 103, no. 1 (2001): 76–95.

Bonacich, Edna, Sabrina Alimahomed, and Jake B. Wilson. "The Racialization of Global Labor." *American Behavioral Scientists* 52, no. 3 (2008): 342–355.

Bourdieu, Pierre. *Distinction: A Social Critique of the Judgement of Taste.* Cambridge, MA: Harvard University Press, 1984.

Bradach, Jeffry L. *Franchise Organizations.* Boston: Harvard Business School Press, 1998.

Brandimarte, Cynthia A. "'To Make the Whole World Homelike': Gender, Space, and America's Tea Room Movement." *Winterthur Portfolio* 30, no. 1 (1995): 1–19.

Burget, Eduard. "Čajovna Yokohama, villa Sakura a Joe Hloucha" [Tearoom Yokohama, villa Sakura and Joe Hloucha]. *Dějiny a Současnost* 7 (2006): 12–14.

Cang, Voltaire. "Sushi Leaves Home: Japanese Food and Identity Abroad." In *Food Identities at Home and on the Move: Explorations at the Intersection of Food, Belonging and Dwelling,* edited by Raul Matta, Charles-Edouard de Suremain, and Chantal Crenn, 19–33. Abingdon, UK: Routledge, 2020.

Cavanaugh, Jillian. "Authenticity and its Perils: Who is Left out when Food is 'Authentic'?" *Gastronomica: The Journal for Food Studies* 23, no.1 (2023): 28–37.

Ceccagno, Antonella. "The Chinese in Italy at a Crossroads: The Economic Crisis." In *Beyond Chinatown: New Chinese Migration and the Global Expansion of China,* edited by Mette Thunø, 115–136. Copenhagen: NIAS Press, 2007.

Ceng Pingcang (曾品滄). "Ri-shi liaoli zai Taiwan: Chushao yu Taiwan zhishi jieceng de shequn shenghuo" (日式料理在台灣：鋤燒與台灣知識階層的社群生活) [Japanese cuisine in Taiwan: *Sukiyaki* and social life of the Taiwan intellectual class]. *Taiwan shi yanjiu* 22, no. 4 (2015): 1–34.

Chang, David. *Eat a Peach.* New York: Clarkson Potter, 2020.

Chang, David, and Peter Meehan. *Momofuku.* New York: Clarkson Potter, 2009.

Chang, Tou Chuang. "Theming Cities, Taming Places: Insights from Singapore." *Geografiska Annaler: Series B, Human Geography* 82, no. 1 (2000): 35–54.

Chen, Yong. *Chop Suey, USA: The Story of Chinese Food in America.* New York: Columbia University Press, 2014.

Chen Yu-Jen (陳玉箴). "Shiwu xiaofei zhong de guojiai, jieji yu wenhua to zhanyan, rizhi yu zhanhou chuqi de 'Taiwan cai'" (食物消費中的國家階級與文化展演：日治與戰後初期的臺灣菜) [National, class, and cultural expression in food consumption: Japanese occupation and "Taiwanese cuisine" in the early postwar era]. *Taiwan shi yanjiu* 15, no. 39 (2008): 141–188.

———. *Taiwan cai de wenhuashi: Shiwu xiaofei zhong de guojia tixian* (台灣菜的文化史：食物消費中的國家體現) [The cultural history of "Taiwanese cuisine": Expressing the nation through food consumption]. Taipei: Lianjing chubanshe, 2020. Kindle edition.

Chesneau, Ernest. "Le Japon à Paris" [Japan in Paris]. *Gazette des Beaux-Arts,* July 1, 1878, 387.

Chevallier, Jim. *A History of the Food of Paris: From Roast Mammoth to Steak Frites.* New York: Rowman and Littlefield, 2018.

Chin, Gabriel J., and John Ormonde. "The War against Chinese Restaurants." *Duke Law Journal* 67, no. 4 (2018): 681–741.

Ching, Leo T. S. *Becoming Japanese: Colonial Taiwan and the Politics of Identity Formation.* Berkeley: University of California Press, 2001.

Coates, Jamie. "Between Product and Cuisine: The Moral Economies of Food among Young Chinese People in Japan." *Journal of Current Chinese Affairs* 48, no. 3 (2020): 1–19.

Coe, Andrew. *Chop Suey: A Cultural History of Chinese Food in the United States.* Oxford: Oxford University Press, 2009.

Collins, Jock. "Australia's New Guest Workers: Opportunity or Exploitation?" In *Critical Reflections on Migration, "Race" and Multiculturalism,* edited by Martina Boese and Vince Marotta, 71–87. Abingdon, UK: Routledge, 2017.

Conklin, David P. "The Traditional and the Modern: The History of Japanese Food Culture in Oregon and How It Did and Did Not Integrate with American Food Culture." MA thesis, Portland State University, 2009.

Crossland-Marr, Lauren, and Elizabeth Krause. "Theorizing Authenticity." *Gastronomica: The Journal for Food Studies* 23, no. 1 (2023): 5–12.

Cwiertka, Katarzyna Joanna. *Cuisine, Colonialism and Cold War: Food in Twentieth-Century Korea.* London: Reaktion Books, 2012.

———. "Eating the Homeland: Japanese Expatriates in the Netherlands." In *Asian Food: The Global and the Local,* edited by Katarzyna J. Cwiertka and Boudewijn C. C. Walraven, 133–152. Abingdon, UK: Routledge, 2015.

———. "From Ethnic to Hip: Circuits of Japanese Cuisine in Europe." *Food and Foodways: Explorations in the History and Culture of Human Nourishment* 13, no. 4 (2006): 241–272.

———. *Modern Japanese Cuisine: Food, Power and National Identity.* London: Reaktion Books, 2006.

Cwiertka, Katarzyna Joanna, and Yasuhara Miho. *Branding Japanese Food: From Meibutsu to Washoku.* Honolulu: University of Hawai'i Press, 2020.

Donovan, Frances R. *The Woman Who Waits.* Boston: Richard G. Badger, 1920.

Düsseldorf Japan Club. *Rain no nagare: Shakai, rekishi hen* (ラインの流れ: 社会, 歴史編) [The flow of the Rhine: Society and history volume]. Düsseldorf: Japan Club, 1990.

Duruz, Jean. "Adventuring and Belonging: An Appetite for Markets." *Space and Culture* 7, no. 4 (2004): 427–445.

———. "The Travels of Kitty's Love Cake: A Tale of Spices, 'Asian' Flavors, and Cuisine Sans Frontières?" In *The Globalization of Asian Cuisines: Transnational Networks and Culinary Contact Zones,* edited by James Farrer, 37–56. New York: Palgrave Macmillan, 2015.

Fairlie, Robert W. "Immigrant Entrepreneurs and Small Business Owners, and Their Access to Financial Capital." *Small Business Administration* 396 (2012): 1–46.

Farina, Felice. "Japan's Gastrodiplomacy as Soft Power: Global Washoku and National Food Security." *Journal of Contemporary Eastern Asia* 17, no. 1 (2018): 131–146.

Farrer, James. "Culinary Globalization from Above and Below: Culinary Migrants in Urban Place Making in Shanghai." In *Destination China: Immigration to China in the Post-reform Era,* edited by Angela Lehmann and Pauline Leonard, 175–199. New York: Palgrave Macmillan, 2019.

———. "Domesticating the Japanese Culinary Field in Shanghai." In *Feeding Japan: The Cultural and Political Issues of Dependency and Risk,* edited by Andreas Niehaus and Tine Walravens, 287–312. New York: Palgrave Macmillan, 2017.

———. "Eating the West and Beating the Rest: Culinary Occidentalism and Urban Soft Power in Asia's Global Food Cities." In *Globalization, Food and Social Identities in the Asia Pacific Region,* edited by James Farrer, 128–149. Tokyo: Sophia University Institute of Comparative Culture, 2010.

———. "From Cooks to Chefs: Skilled Migrants in a Globalising Culinary Field." *Journal of Ethnic and Migration Studies* 47, no. 10 (2021): 2359–2375.

———. "Grimy Heritage: Organic Bar Streets in Shanghai and Tokyo." *Built Heritage* 3, no. 3 (2019): 73–85.

———. "Imported Culinary Heritage: The Case of Localized Western Cuisine in Shanghai." In *Rethinking Asian Food Heritage,* edited by Sidney Cheung, 75–104. Taipei: Foundation of Chinese Dietary Culture, 2014.

———. "Introduction: Travelling Cuisines in and out of Asia: Towards a Framework for Studying Culinary Globalization." In *The Globalization of Asian Cuisines: Transnational Networks and Culinary Contact Zones,* edited by James Farrer, 1–20. New York: Palgrave Macmillan, 2015.

———. "The Multiple Contexts of Protest: Reflections on the Reception of the MIT Visualizing Cultures Project and the Anti-Right Japanese Demonstration in Shanghai." *Positions: East Asian Cultural Critique* 23, no. 1 (2015): 59–90.

———. "On the Other Side of the Curve: China's Restaurateurs Face an Uphill Battle." *Gastronomica: The Journal for Food Studies* 20, no. 3 (2020): 24–25.

———. "Red (Michelin) Stars over China: Seeking Recognition in a Transnational Culinary Field." In *Culinary Nationalism in Asia,* edited by Michelle King, 193–213. London: Bloomsbury Academic, 2019.

———. "Shanghai's Western Restaurants as Culinary Contact Zones in a Transnational Culinary Field." In *Globalization and Asian Cuisines: Transnational Networks and Contact Zones,* edited by James Farrer, 103–24. New York: Palgrave Macmillan, 2015.

———. "The Space-Time Compression of Tokyo Street Drinking." *Food, Culture and Society* 24, no. 1 (2021): 49–65.

———. "A Tokyo Restaurant Community Faces Covid-19." *Etnografia e ricerca qualitativa* 13, no. 2 (2020): 245–254.

Farrer, James, and Andrew David Field. *Shanghai Nightscapes: A Nocturnal Biography of a Global City.* Chicago: University of Chicago Press, 2015.

Farrer, James, Christian Hess, Mônica R. de Carvalho, Chuanfei Wang, and David Wank. "Japanese Culinary Mobilities: The Multiple Globalizations of Japanese Cuisine." In *Routledge Handbook of Food in Asia,* edited by Cecilia Leong-Salobir, 39–57. Abingdon, UK: Routledge, 2019.

Farrer, James, and Chuanfei Wang. "Who Owns a Cuisine? The Grassroots Politics of Japanese Food in Europe." *Asian Anthropology* 20, no. 1 (2021): 12–29.

Ferguson, Priscilla Parkhurst. "A Cultural Field in the Making: Gastronomy in 19th-Century France." *American Journal of Sociology* 104, no. 3 (1998): 597–641.

Ferguson, Priscilla Parkhurst, and Sharon Zukin. "The Careers of Chefs." In *Eating Culture,* edited by Ron Scapp and Brian Seitz, 92–111. Albany: State University of New York Press, 1998.

Fine, Gary Alan. *Kitchens: The Culture of Restaurant Work.* Berkeley: University of California Press, 1996.

Fogel, Joshua A. *Articulating the Sinosphere.* Cambridge, MA: Harvard University Press, 2009.

———. "'Shanghai-Japan': The Japanese Residents' Association of Shanghai." *Journal of Asian Studies* 59, no. 4 (2000): 927–950.

Freedman, Paul. *Ten Restaurants That Changed America.* New York: Liveright, 2016.

Fukutomi, Satomi. "From 'Isn't It Raw?'" to Everyday Food: Authenticating Japanese Food in Perth, Australia." *Gastronomica: The Journal for Food Studies* 22, no. 1 (2022): 34–43.

Gabaccia, Donna R. *We are What We Eat. Ethnic Food and the Making of Americans.* Cambridge, MA: Harvard University Press, 1998.

Gaik Cheng Khoo. "The Hansik Globalization Campaign: A Malaysian Critique." *Gastronomica: The Journal for Food Studies* 19, no. 1 (2019): 65–78.

Gans-Morse, Jordan. "Demand for Law and the Security of Property Rights: The Case of Post-Soviet Russia." *American Political Science Review* 111, no. 2 (2017): 338–359.

Glebe, Günther. "Segregation and the Ethnoscape: The Japanese Business Community in Düsseldorf." In *Global Japan: The Experience of Japan's New Immigrant and Overseas Communities,* edited by Roger Goodman, Ceri Peach, Ayumi Takenaka, and Paul White, 110–127. Abingdon, UK: Routledge, 2005.

Gmelch, George. "Return Migration." *Annual Review of Anthropology* 9, no. 1 (1980): 135–159.

Grantham, Bill. "Craic in a Box: Commodifying and Exporting the Irish Pub." *Continuum* 23, no. 2 (2009): 257–267.

Guest, Kenneth J. "From Mott Street to East Broadway: Fuzhounese Immigrants and the Revitalization of New York's Chinatown." *Journal of Chinese Overseas* 7 (2011): 24–44.

Hannerz, Ulf. *Cultural Complexity: Studies in the Complexity of Meaning.* New York: Columbia University Press, 1993.

Hanyu, Noboru. "Japantown in the 20s and 30s." *Nikkei Heritage* 12, no. 3 (2000): 14–16.

Hasegawa Zaiyu (長谷川在佑). *Den: Shinkasuru Tōkyō nihon ryōri* (傳: 進化するトーキョー日本料理) [Den: The evolving Tokyo-Japanese cuisine]. Tokyo: Shibata shoten, 2017.

Hashimoto Kenji (橋本健二). *Izakaya no sengoshi* (居酒屋の戦後史) [Postwar history of izakaya]. Tokyo: Shodensha, 2015.

Hegwood, Robert "Sukiyaki and the Prewar Japanese Community in New York." Unpublished paper presented at the Columbia Graduate Student Conference, 2014.

Heldke, Lisa *Exotic Appetites: Ruminations of a Food Adventurer.* Abingdon, UK: Routledge, 2015.

Hess, Christian A. "From Colonial Port to Socialist Metropolis: Imperialist Legacies and the Making of 'New Dalian.'" *Urban History* 38, no. 3 (2011): 373–390.

Hijiya-Kirschnereit, Irmela. "Das Sushi-Sakrileg: Zur Verbreitung von Sushi in Mitteleuropa" [The sushi sacrilege: The spread of sushi in Central Europe]. *Jahrbuch für Kulinaristik* 2 (2018): 134–165.

Hirose Akihiko, and Kay Kei-Ho Pih. "'No Asians Working Here': Racialized Otherness and Authenticity in Gastronomical Orientalism." *Ethnic and Racial Studies* 34, no. 9 (2011): 1482–1501.

Hudson, Chris. "The 'Craic' Goes Global: Irish Pubs and the Global Imaginary." In *Revisiting the Global Imaginary: Theories, Ideologies, Subjectivities: Essays in Honor of Manfred Steger,* edited by Chris Hudson and Erin K. Wilson, 155–173. New York: Palgrave Macmillan, 2019.

Ichijo, Atsuko, Venetia Johannes, and Ronald Ranta, eds., *The Emergence of National Food: The Dynamics of Food and Nationalism.* New York: Bloomsbury, 2019.

Ichioka, Yuji. *The Issei: The World of the First Generation Japanese Immigrants, 1895–1924.* New York: Free Press, 1988.

Iino Ryōichi (飯野亮一). *Izakaya no tanjō: Edo no nomidaore bunka* (居酒屋の誕生: 江戸の呑みだおれ文化) [Birth of the *izakaya*: Edo's drinking culture]. Tokyo: Sakuma shobo, 2014.

Ikeda Tōsen (池田桃川). *Shanhai hyakuwa* (上海百話) [A hundred tales of Shanghai]. Shanghai: Nihontō, 1926.

Ikegami Akira (池上彰). *Sō datta no ka! Chūgoku* (そうだったのか！中国) [Is that so! China]. Tokyo: Shūeisha, 2010.

Ikezawa Yasushi (池澤康). *Amerika nihonshoku uōzu* (アメリカ日本食ウォーズ) [American Japanese food wars]. Tokyo: Toshibaya, 2005.

Imai, Shoko. "Umami Abroad: Taste, Authenticity, and the Global Urban Network." In *The Globalization of Asian Cuisines: Transnational Networks and Culinary Contact Zones,* edited by James Farrer, 57–78. New York: Palgrave Macmillan, 2015.

Inouye, Daniel H. *Distant Islands: The Japanese American Community in New York City, 1876–1930s.* Boulder: University Press of Colorado, 2018.

Ishige Naomichi (石毛直道), Koyama Shūzō (小山修三), Yamaguchi Masatomo (山口昌伴), and Ekuan Shōji (栄久庵祥二). *Rosuanjerusu no nihon ryōriten—sono bunka jinruigakuteki kenkyū* (ロスアンジェルスの日本料理店—その文化人類学的研究) [Japanese restaurants in Los Angeles—an anthropological research]. Tokyo: Domesu, 1985.

Issenberg, Sasha. *The Sushi Economy: Globalization and the Making of a Modern Delicacy.* New York: Gotham Books, 2007.

Ito, Kazuo. *Issei: A History of Japanese Immigrants in North America.* Seattle: Japanese Community Service, 1973.

Itoh, Keiko. *The Japanese Community in Prewar Britain: From Integration to Disintegration.* Abingdon, UK: Routledge, 2001.

Iwabuchi, Koichi. *Recentering Globalization: Popular Culture and Japanese Transnationalism.* Durham, NC: Duke University Press, 2002.

Iwama Kazuhiro (岩間一弘). "Shanghai no nihonshokubunka: Menyū no genchika ni kansuru hiaringu chōsa hōkoku" (上海の日本食文化：メニューの現地化に関するヒア

リング調査報告) [Shanghai's Japanese food culture: A hearing survey report of menu localization]. *Chiba shōdai kiyō* 51, no. 1 (2013): 1–54.

Iwaya Sazanami (巌谷小波). *Sazanami yōkōmiyage gekan* (小波洋行土産 下巻) [Sazanami Western tour memoir Volume 2]. Tokyo: Hakubunkan, 1905.

Jacob, Frank. "'Foreign, Brackish, and Exotic': Japanese Food in the American Press, 1853–1918." In *Chop Suey and Sushi from Sea to Shining Sea: Chinese and Japanese Restaurants in the United States,* edited by Bruce Makoto Arnold, Tanfer Emin Tunç, and Raymond Douglas Chong, 151–164. Little Rock: University of Arkansas Press, 2018.

Jakle, John A. "Roadside Restaurants and Place-Product-Packaging." *Journal of Cultural Geography* 3, no. 1 (1982): 76–93.

Jakle, John A., and Keith A. Sculle. *Fast Food: Roadside Restaurants in the Age of the Automobile.* Baltimore, MD: Johns Hopkins University Press, 1999.

Jasanoff, Sheila, and Sang Hyun Kim. *Dreamscape of Modernity: Sociotechnical Imaginaries and the Fabrication of Power.* Chicago: University of Chicago Press, 2015.

Joo Young-ha (주영하). *Sigtag wiui Hangugsa: Menyulo bon 20 segi Hangug eumsig munhwasa* (식탁 위의 한국사: 메뉴로 본 20 세기 한국음식문화사) [History of Korea on the table: Understanding Korean food cultural history of the 20th century through menu]. Seoul: Humanist, 2013.

Katakura Yoshifumi (片倉佳史). "Kōwan toshi kiryū o tazune" (港湾都市基隆を訪ね) [Visit the port city of Keelung]. *Nihon Taiwan kōryū kyōkai* 1, no. 898 (2016): 18–27.

Kawabata Motoo (川端基夫). *Gaishoku kokusaika no dainamizumu: Atarashii "ekkyō no katachi"* (外食国際化のダイナミズム: 新しい "越境のかたち") [The dynamism of the internationalization of the restaurant industry: The new "pattern of transnationalism"]. Tokyo: Shinhyoron, 2016.

Kawaguchi, Gary, and Shizue Seigel. "San Francisco's Japantown: The Shaping of a Community." *Nikkei Heritage* 12, no. 3 (Summer 2000): 4–7.

Kawamori Yoshizō (河盛好蔵). *Pari kōjitsu* (巴里好日) [Good days in Paris]. Tokyo: Kawade Bunko, 1984.

Kawashima, Kumiko. "Japanese Labour Migration to China and IT Service Outsourcing: The Case of Dalian." In *Destination China: Immigration to China in the Postreform Era,* edited by Angela Lehmann and Pauline Leonard, 123–145. New York: Palgrave Macmillan, 2019.

———. "Service Outsourcing and Labour Mobility in a Digital Age: Transnational Linkages between Japan and Dalian, China." *Global Networks* 17, no. 4 (2017): 483–499.

Keßler, Sandra. "Japanisch, exotisch, kosmopolitisch, modern: Sushi als Global Food in Deutschland" [Japanese, exotic, cosmopolitan, modern: Sushi as global food in Germany]. In *Interkulturalität und Alltag* [Interculturality and the everyday], edited by Judith Schmidt, Sandra Keßler, and Michael Simon, 148–161. Münster: Waxmann, 2012.

King, Michelle, ed., *Culinary Nationalism in Asia.* London: Bloomsbury Academic, 2019.

Kishida Kunio (岸田國士). *Kitashi Monojō* (北支物情) [About northern China]. Tokyo: Hakusuisha, 1938.

Kitaōji Rosanjin (北大路魯山人). "Nihonryōri no kiso gainen" (日本料理の基礎概念) [The basic concepts of Japanese cuisine]. In *Rosanjin ajidō* (魯山人味道) [Rosanjin's way of taste], edited by Hirano Masaki, 272–283. First published 1936. Tokyo: Chuokoronsha, 1980.

Koga, Yukiko. *Inheritance of Loss: China, Japan, and the Political Economy of Redemption after Empire*. Chicago: University of Chicago Press, 2016.

Kojima, Shigeru. "The Immigrants Who Introduced Japanese Cuisine to the Americas (Part 2: South America)." *Food Culture: Journal of the Kikkoman Institute for International Food Culture*, no. 23 (2013): 3–10.

Kottman, Nora. "Japanese Women on the Move: Working and (Not) Belonging in Düsseldorf's Japanese (Food) Community." In *Food Identities at Home and on the Move: Explorations at the Intersection of Food, Belonging and Dwelling*, edited by Raul Matta, Charles-Edouard de Suremain, and Chantal Crenn, 175–187. Abingdon, UK: Routledge, 2020.

Ku, Robert Ji-Song. *Dubious Gastronomy: The Cultural Politics of Eating Asian in the USA*. Honolulu: University of Hawai'i Press, 2013.

Kumakura, Isao. "The Globalization of Japanese Food Culture." *Food Culture* 1 (2000): 7–8.

Kushner, Barak. *Slurp! A Social and Culinary History of Ramen—Japan's Favorite Noodle Soup*. London: Global Oriental, 2012.

Lane, Christel. *The Cultivation of Taste: Chefs and the Organization of Fine Dining*. Oxford: Oxford University Press, 2014.

Laudan, Rachel. *The Food of Paradise: Exploring Hawaii's Culinary Heritage*. Honolulu: University of Hawai'i Press, 1996.

———. "Slow Food: The French Terroir Strategy, and Culinary Modernism." *Food, Culture & Society* 7, no. 2 (2004): 133–44.

Leschziner, Vanina. *At the Chef's Table: Culinary Creativity in Elite Restaurants*. Stanford, CA: Stanford University Press, 2015.

Lie, John. *Multi-ethnic Japan*. Cambridge, MA: Harvard University Press, 1972.

Light, Ivan H. *Ethnic Enterprise in America: Business and Welfare among Chinese, Japanese, and Blacks*. Berkeley: University of California Press, 1972.

Liu-Farrer, Gracia. *Labor Migration from China to Japan: International Students, Transnational Migrants*. Abingdon, UK: Routledge, 2011.

Lone, Stewart. *The Japanese Community in Brazil, 1908–1940: Between Samurai and Carnival*. New York: Palgrave Macmillan, 2001.

Low, Morris. *Japan on Display: Photography and the Emperor*. Abingdon, UK: Routledge, 2006.

Lu, Shun, and Gary Alan Fine. "The Presentation of Ethnic Authenticity: Chinese Food as a Social Accomplishment." *Sociological Quarterly* 36, no. 3 (1995): 535–553.

Machimura, Takashi. "Living in a Transnational Community within a Multi-ethnic City." In *Global Japan: The Experience of Japan's New Immigrant and Overseas Communities*, edited by Roger Goodman, Ceri Peach, Ayumi Takenaka, and Paul White, 147–156. Abingdon, UK: Routledge, 2005.

Maguire, Jennifer Smith, and Julian Matthews. "Are We All Cultural Intermediaries Now? An Introduction to Cultural Intermediaries in Context." *European Journal of Cultural Studies* 15 (2012): 551–562.

Mansfield, Becky. "'Imitation Crab' and the Material Culture of Commodity Production." *Cultural Geographies* 10, no. 2 (2003): 176–195.

Marsden, Anna. "Second-Generation Chinese and New Processes of Social Integration in Italy." In *Chinese Migration to Europe: Prato, Italy and Beyond,* edited by Loretta Baldassar, Graeme Johanson, Narelle McAuliffe, and Massimo Bressan, 101–118. London: Palgrave Macmillan, 2015.

Massey, Douglas S. "Racial Formation in Theory and Practice: The Case of Mexicans in the United States." *Race and Social Problems* 1, no. 1 (2009): 12–26.

Matsuhisa, Nobuyuki. *Nobu: A Memoir.* New York: Simon and Schuster, 2017.

Matsui, Shichiro, "Economic Aspects of the Japanese Situation in California." MA thesis, University of California at Berkeley, 1922.

Matsumoto Hirotaka (松本紘宇). *Nyūyōku Take Sushi monogatari* (ニューヨーク竹寿司物語) [New York Take Sushi tale]. Tokyo: Asahi shinbunsha, 1995.

Matsumura Shigeki (松村茂樹). "Rokusanen ibun" (六三園逸聞) [Memories of Rokusan]. *Otsuma kokubun* 28 (1997): 195–206.

Matsumura, Mitsunobu (松村光庸). "1930-nendai ni okeru Tenshin Nihon sokai kyoryūmin no kōzōteki tokushitsu" (年代における天津日本租界居留民の構造的特質) [Structural features of Tianjin Japanese concession residents in the 1930s]. *Kaikō toshikenkyū* 6 (2011): 73–90.

McNamara, Dennis L. "Comparative Colonial Response: Korea and Taiwan." *Korean Studies* 10 (1986): 54–68.

Milikowski, Marisca. "Exploring a Model of De-ethnicization: The Case of Turkish Television in the Netherlands." *European Journal of Communication* 15, no. 4 (2000): 443–468.

Miyake Koken (三宅孤軒). *Shanhai inshōki* (上海印象記) [Shanghai retrospective]. Tokyo: Ryōri shinbunsha, 1923.

Mladenova, Dorothea. "Sushi global: Zwischen J-branding und kulinarischem Nationalismus" [Sushi global: Between J-branding and culinary nationalism]. In *Japan: Politik, Wirtschaft und Gesellschaft* [Japan: Politics, economy and society], edited by David Chiavacci and Iris Wieczorek, 275–297. Berlin: Vereinigung für sozialwissenschaftliche Japanforschung, 2013.

Mohabir, Nalini, YenpengJiang, and Renfeng Ma. "Chinese Floating Migrants: Rural-Urban Migrant Labourer's Intentions to Stay or Return." *Habitat International* 60 (2017): 101–110.

Möhring, Maren. *Fremdes Essen: Die Geschichte der ausländischen Gastronomie in der Bundesrepublik Deutschland* [Strange foods: The history of foreign gastronomy in the Federal Republic of Germany]. Berlin: Walter de Gruyter, 2012.

———. "Von Schwalbennestern und neuen Fingerfertigkeiten: Globalisierung und esskulturelle Transfers am Beispiel asiatischer Küchen in Deutschland" [Globalization and food culture transfers using the example of Asian kitchens in Germany]. *Jahrbuch für Kulinaristik* 2 (2018): 31–51.

Mori Koichi (森幸一). "Sanpauroshi ni okeru nihonryōri(ten) no ichi, imēji, juyō no katachi" (サンパウロ市における日本料理 (店)の位置, イメージ, 受容のかたち) [Japanese restaurants in Saõ Paulo City: The market, image and the forms of acceptance]. *JICA: Yokohama kaigai iju shiryōkan kiyō* 9 (2014): 21–57.

Mori, Koichi. "As condições de aceitação da culinária japonesa na cidade de São Paulo— por que os brasileiros começaram a apreciar a culinária japonesa?" [Conditions for acceptance of Japanese cuisine in the city of São Paulo—why did Brazilians begin to appreciate Japanese cuisine?]. *Estudos Japoneses* 23 (2003): 7–22.

Myhrvold, Nathan, Chris Young, and Maxime Bilet. *Modernist Cuisine.* London: Taschen, 2011.

Nakano, Lynn. "Eating One's Way to Sophistication: Japanese Food, Transnational Flows, and Social Mobility in Hong Kong." In *Transnational Trajectories in East Asia: Nation, Citizenship, and Region,* edited by Yasemin N. Soysal, 106–129. Abingdon, UK: Routledge, 2014.

Ng, Wai-Ming. "Popularization and Localization of Sushi in Singapore: An Ethnographic Survey." *New Zealand Journal of Asian Studies* 3, no. 1 (2001): 7–19.

Nodera, Isamu, "A Survey of the Vocational Activities of the Japanese in the City of Los Angeles." PhD. diss., University of Southern California, 1936.

Nogueira, Arlinda Rocha, "São Paulo, Algodão e o Japonês na Década de 1930" [São Paulo, cotton and the Japanese in the 1930s]. *Revista do Instituto de Estudos Brasileiros* 26 (1986): 9–26.

Ocejo, Richard E. *Masters of Craft: Old Jobs in the New Urban Economy.* Princeton, NJ: Princeton University Press, 2017.

Ōhori Sō (大堀聰). *Dainijisekaitaisen shita no ōshū hōjin (Doitsu Suisu)* (第二次世界大戦下の欧州邦人[ドイツ・スイス]) [The Japanese in Europe in World War II (Germany and Switzerland)]. Tokyo: Ginga shoseki, 2021.

Okubo Hiroko (大久保洋子). *Edo no shoku kūkan—Yatai kara nihonryōri e* (江戸の食空間―屋台から日本料理へ) [The eating spaces of Edo—from street stalls to Japanese cuisine]. Tokyo: Kodansha, 2012.

Oldenburg, Ray. *The Great Good Place: Cafes, Coffee Shops, Bookstores, Bars, Hair Salons, and Other Hangouts at the Heart of a Community.* Boston: Da Capo, 1999.

Omi, Michael, and Howard Winant. *Racial Formation in the United States,* 3rd ed. New York: Routledge, 2015.

Onozawa, Nitaya. "Immigration from Japan to the U.S.A., Historical Trends and Background." *Tokyo Home Economics Bulletin/Tsukuba Women's University Bulletin,* no. 7 (2003): 115–125.

Orkin, Ivan, and Chris Ying. *Ivan Ramen: Love, Obsession, and Recipes from Tokyo's Most Unlikely Noodle Joint.* Berkeley: Ten Speed, 2013.

Ottati, Gabi Dei, and Daniele Brigadoi Cologna. "The Chinese in Prato and the Current Outlook on the Chinese-Italian Experience." In *Chinese Migration to Europe: Prato, Italy and Beyond,* edited by Loretta Baldassar, Graeme Johanson, Narelle McAuliffe, and Massimo Bressan, 29–48. London: Palgrave Macmillan, 2015.

Panibratov, Andrei. "Russian Restaurant with Japanese Cuisine Makes Foreign Markets' Selection: The Case of Two Sticks." *Asian Case Research Journal* 16, no. 2 (2012): 335–346.

Parasecoli, Fabio. *Knowing Where It Comes from: Labeling Traditional Foods to Compete in a Global Market.* Iowa City: University of Iowa Press, 2017.

Pilcher, Jeffrey M. "Culinary Infrastructure: How Facilities and Technologies Create Value and Meaning Around Food." *Global Food History* 2, no. 2 (2016): 105–131.

———. *Planet Taco: A Global History of Mexican Food.* Oxford: Oxford University Press, 2017.

Rath, Eric C. *Japan's Cuisines: Food, Place and Identity.* London: Reaktion Books, 2016.

———. *Oishii: The History of Sushi.* London: Reaktion Books, 2021.

———. "Reevaluating Rikyū: *Kaiseki* and the Origins of Japanese Cuisine." *Journal of Japanese Studies* 39, no. 1 (2013): 67–96.

Rawson, Katie, and Elliott Shore. *Dining Out: A Global History of Restaurants.* London: Reaktion Books, 2019.

Ray, Krishnendu. *The Ethnic Restaurateur.* New York: Bloomsbury, 2016.

———. "Ethnic Succession: A Review Essay." *Food, Culture & Society,* 8, no. 1 (2005): 124–131.

———. "The Immigrant Restaurateur and the American City: Taste, Toil, and the Politics of Inhabitation." *Social Research* 81, no. 2 (2014): 373–396.

Reichl, Christopher A. "Stages in the Historical Process of Ethnicity: The Japanese in Brazil, 1908–1988." *Ethnohistory* 42, no. 1 (1995): 31–62.

Reiher, Cornelia. "Berlin's Japanese Foodscapes During the Covid-19 Crisis: Restaurateurs' Experiences and Practices During the Spring 2020 Restaurant Shutdown." *Berliner Blätter* 86 (2022): 105–122.

———. "Negotiating Authenticity: Berlin's Japanese Food Producers and the Vegan/vegetarian Consumer." *Food, Culture & Society* (2022), DOI:10.1080/15528014.2022.2076028.

Ritzer, George. *The McDonaldization of Society: An Investigation into the Changing Character of Contemporary Social Life.* Newbury Park, CA: Pine Forge, 1993.

Rouff, Kenneth. "Japanese Tourism to Mukden, Nanjing, and Qufu, 1938–1943." *Japan Review* 27 (2014): 171–200.

Rousseau, Signe. *Food Media: Celebrity Chefs and the Politics of Everyday Interference.* London: Berg, 2013.

Russek, Audrey. "Appetites Without Prejudice: U.S. Foreign Restaurants and the Globalization of American Food Between the Wars." *Food and Foodways* 19, no. 1–2 (2011): 34–55.

Saitō Kiyoe (斉藤清衛). *Tōyō hito no tabi: Yōroppa kikō* (東洋人の旅: 欧羅巴紀行) [A trip to Europe: A journey of an Oriental person]. Tokyo: Shun'yō-dō shoten, 1937.

Saitō Moto (斎藤もと). *Nyūyōku no koinobori* (ニューヨークの鯉のぼり) [A carp flag in New York]. Tokyo: PHP Press, 1988.

Sassen, Saskia. *Global City: New York, London, Tokyo.* Princeton, NJ: Princeton University Press, 1991.

———. "The Global City: Introducing a Concept." *Brown Journal of World Affairs* 11, no. 2 (2005): 27–43.

———. "Researching the Localizations of the Global." In *The Oxford Handbook of Global Studies,* edited by Mark Juergensmeyer, Saskia Sassen, and Manfred Steger, 73–92. New York: Oxford University Press, 2018.

Schaland, Ann-Julia. *The Vietnamese Diaspora in Germany*. Berlin: Deutsche Gesellschaft für Internationale Zusammenarbeit, 2015.

Sewell, Bill. "Reconsidering the Modern in Japanese History: Modernity in the Service of the Prewar Japanese Empire." *Japan Review* 16 (2004): 213–258.

Shigemitsu Katsuaki (重光克昭). *Chūgoku de ichiban seikō shite iru Nihon no gaishoku chēn wa Kumamoto no chīsana rāmenya datte shittemasuka?* (中国で一番成功している日本の外食チェーンは熊本の小さなラーメン屋だって知ってますか?) [Do you know that the most successful Japanese chain restaurant in China is a small ramen shop from Kumamoto?]. Tokyo: Daiyamondosha, 2010.

Silverberg, Miriam. *Erotic Grotesque Nonsense*. Berkeley: University of California Press, 2007.

Simmel, Georg. "Fashion." *American Journal of Sociology* 62, no. 6 (1957): 541–558.

Smith, Kate. *Travel and the Social Imagination in Imperial Japan*. Berkeley: University of California Press, 2017.

Solt, George. *The Untold History of Ramen: How Political Crisis in Japan Spawned a Global Food Craze*. Berkeley: University of California Press, 2014.

Song, Changzoo. "Transcultural Business Practices of Korean Diaspora and Identity Politics: Korean Sushi Business and the Emergence of 'Asian' Identity." *Studies of Koreans Abroad* 32, no. 3 (2014): 1–23.

Souther, Mark J. "The Disneyfication of New Orleans: The French Quarter as Facade in a Divided City." *Journal of American History* 94, no. 3 (2007): 804–811.

Spang, Rebecca. *The Invention of the Restaurant: Paris and Modern Gastronomic Culture*. 2nd ed. Cambridge, MA: Harvard University Press, 2020.

Stalker, Nancy K. "Introduction: Japanese Culinary Capital." In *Devouring Japan: Global Perspectives on Japanese Culinary Identity*, edited by Nancy K. Stalker, 1–31. Oxford: Oxford University Press, 2018.

———. "Rosanjin: The Roots of Japanese Gourmet Nationalism." In *Devouring Japan: Global Perspectives on Japanese Culinary Identity*, edited by Nancy K. Stalker, 133–150. Oxford: Oxford University Press, 2018.

Suzuki, D. T. 1994. *Essays in Zen Buddhism*. New York: Grove Press.

Swislocki, Mark. *Culinary Nostalgia: Regional Food Culture and the Urban Experience in Shanghai*. Stanford, CA: Stanford University Press, 2008.

Tagsold, Christian. *Spaces in Translation: Japanese Gardens and the West*. Philadelphia: University of Pennsylvania Press, 2017.

Takahashi Hayato (高橋勇人), ed. *Dairenshi* (大連市) [The city of Dalian]. Dalian, China: Tairiku shuppan kyōkai, 1931.

Tanabe Hiragaku (田辺平学). *Doitsu: Bōkū kagaku kokumin seikatsu* (ドイツ: 防空, 科学, 国民生活) [Germany: Air defense, science, national life]. Tokyo: Sagami shobo, 1942.

Taro Futamura and Kazuaki Sugiyama. "The Dark Side of the Nightscape: The Growth of *Izakaya* Chains and the Changing Landscapes of Evening Eateries in Japanese Cities." *Food, Culture and Society* 21, no. 1 (2018): 101–117.

Terry, T. Philip. *Terry's Guide to the Japanese Empire: Including Korea and Formosa, with Chapters on Manchuria, the Trans-Siberian Railway, and the Chief Ocean Routes*. Rev. ed. Boston: Houghton Mifflin, 1930.

Thirion, Yvonne. "Le japonisme en France dans la seconde moitié du XIXe siècle à la faveur de la diffusion de l'estampe japonaise" [*Japonisme* in France in the second half of the 19th century thanks to the spread of the Japanese prints]. *Cahiers de l'Association internationale des études françaises,* no. 13 (1961): 117–130.

Tianjin's Japanese Society (天津居留民団). *Tenshin kyoryū mindan nijū shūnen kinen shi* (天津居留民団二十周年記念誌) [Special Issue of 20th Anniversary of Tianjin's Japanese Society]. Tianjin: Tenshin kyoryū mindan, 1930.

Tobin, Joseph Jay ed. *Re-Made in Japan: Everyday Life and Consumer Taste in a Changing Society.* New Haven, CT: Yale University Press, 1992.

Tominari Ichiji (富成一二). *Tenshin annai* (天津案内) [Tianjin guidebook]. Tianjin: Chūtō sekiyin kyoku, 1913.

Tomlinson, John. *Globalization and Culture.* Chicago: University of Chicago Press, 1999.

Toyoshima, Noboru. "Japanese Restaurants in Thailand: Dining in the Ambience of Japanese Culture." *Journal of Asia-Pacific Studies* 19 (2013): 279–296.

Trubek, Amy B. *Haute Cuisine: How the French Invented the Culinary Profession.* Philadelphia: University of Pennsylvania Press, 2000.

———. *The Taste of Place: A Cultural Journey into Terroir.* Berkeley: University of California Press, 2008.

Ujita Norihiko (宇治田憲彦). *Amerika ni nihon shoku bunka wo kaika saseta samuraitachi* (アメリカに日本食文化を開花させたサムライたち) [The samurai who popularized Japanese food culture to the United States]. Tokyo: Sanyo shuppansha, 2008.

Urry, John. *Sociology beyond Societies: Mobilities for the Twenty-First Century.* Abingdon, UK: Routledge, 2012.

Waldinger, Roger, Howard Aldrich, and Robin Ward. *Ethnic Entrepreneurs:Immigrant Business in Industrial Societies.* Newbury Park, CA: Sage, 1990.

Wan Lujian (万鲁健). *Jindai Tianjin riben qiaomin yanjiu* (近代天津日本侨民研究) [A research on Japanese migrants in modern Tianjin]. Tianjin: Tianjin renmin chubanshe, 2010.

Wang Haofan (王昊凡). "Shanghai no taishū sushiten ni okeru rōkaruka to 'sushishokunin' no seiritu oyobi sono yakuwari" (上海の大衆寿司店におけるローカル化と'寿司職人'の成立及びその役割) [Localization in Shanghai's popular sushi restaurants and the establishment of "sushi chefs" and their roles]. *Nihon rōdō shakai gakkai nenpō* 27 (2016): 132–158.

Wank, David L., and James Farrer. "Chinese Immigrants and Japanese Cuisine in the United States: A Case of Culinary Glocalization." In *The Globalization of Asian Cuisines: Transnational Networks and Culinary Contact Zones,* edited by James Farrer, 79–99. New York: Palgrave Macmillan, 2015.

Warde, Alan, and Lydia Martens. *Eating Out: Social Differentiation, Consumption and Pleasure.* Cambridge: Cambridge University Press, 2000.

Weiss, Brad. "Configuring the Authentic Value of Real Food: Farm-to-fork, Snout-to-tail, and Local Food Movements." *American Ethnologist* 39, no. 3 (2012): 614–626.

Whitaker, Jan. *Tea at the Blue Lantern Inn: A Social History of the Tea Room Craze in America.* New York: St. Martin's, 2015. Kindle edition.

White, Merry. *Coffee Life in Japan.* Berkeley: University of California Press, 2012.

White, Paul. "The Japanese in London: From Transience to Settlement?" In *Global Japan: The Experience of Japan's New Immigrant and Overseas Communities,* edited by Roger Goodman, Ceri Peach, Ayumi Takenaka, and Paul White, 79–97. Abingdon, UK: Routledge, 2005.

Wildie, Kevin. *Sacramento's Historic Japantown: Legacy of a Lost Neighborhood.* Charleston: History Press, 2013.

Wilson, Katherine. *Golden Gate: The Park of a Thousand Vistas.* Caldwell, ID: Caxton Printers, 1950.

Wu, David Y. H. "Cultural Nostalgia and Global Imagination: Japanese Cuisine in Taiwan." In *Re-Orienting Cuisine: East Asian Foodways in the Twenty-First Century,* edited by Kwang Ok Kim, 119–122. New York: Berghahn Books, 2015.

Yamamoto Takatsugu (山元貴継). "Nihon tōchi jidai no chōsenhantō ni okeru nihonhondo shusshinsha no tenkai—tochi shoyū to no kakawari o chūshin ni" (日本統治時代の朝鮮半島における日本本土出身者の展開― 土地所有との関わりを中心に) [Development of people from mainland Japan on the Korean Peninsula during the Japanese colonial era—focusing on the relationship with land ownership]. *Rekishi chiri gaku* 45, no. 1 (2003): 3–19.

Yamashita, Samuel H. "The 'Japanese Turn' in Fine Dining in the United States, 1980–2020." *Gastronomica: The Journal for Food Studies* 20, no. 2 (2020): 45–54.

Yano, Christine R. "Side-Dish Kitchen." In *The Restaurants Book: Ethnographies of Where We Eat,* edited by David Beriss and David Sutton, 47–64. Oxford: Berg, 2007.

Yaury, James. "How to Win in the Indonesian Market: Case Analyses on the Pair of Competitors." MBA thesis, Waseda Business School, 2019.

Yokoyama Hiroaki (横山宏章). *Shanhai no nihonjinmachi—Honkō: Mōhitotsu no Nagasaki* (上海の日本人街― 虹口: もう一つの長崎) [Shanghai's Japantown: Another Nagasaki]. Tokyo: Sairyusha, 2017.

Zelinsky, Wilbur. "The Roving Palate: North America's Ethnic Restaurant Cuisines." *Geoforum* 16, no. 1 (1985): 51–72.

Zeng, Guojun, Henk J. De Vries, and Frank M. Go. *Restaurant Chains in China: The Dilemma of Standardisation versus Authenticity.* Singapore: Palgrave Macmillan, 2017.

Zhang, Xiang. "Spatial Patterns and Social/Cultural Implications of Japanese Fast-Food Chains in China." *Asian Geographer* 35, no. 1 (2018): 15–34.

Zheng, Tiantian. *Red Lights: The Lives of Sex Workers in China.* Minneapolis: University of Minnesota Press, 2009.

Contributors

Mônica R. de Carvalho earned her PhD in global studies from Sophia University, where she is a collaborative research fellow at the Institute of Comparative Culture, having coauthored articles and book chapters as contributions to the Global Japanese Cuisine Project. After living for more than twelve years in Japan and China, she has returned to Brazil, where she is an associate professor at SKEMA Business School. She teaches graduate-level courses in Brazil, France, and China on international business development and global environmental, social, and governance issues.

James Farrer is professor of sociology and director of the Graduate Program in Global Studies at Sophia University in Tokyo. His research focuses on the contact zones of global cities, including ethnographic studies of sexuality, nightlife, expatriate communities, and urban food cultures. Recent publications include *International Migrants in China's Global City: The New Shanghailanders, Shanghai Nightscapes: A Nocturnal Biography of a Global City* (with Andrew David Field), and *The Globalization of Asian Cuisines: Transnational Networks and Culinary Contact Zones*. His current projects investigate community foodways in Tokyo and urban nightlife and restaurant cultures in diverse world regions. Originally from Tennessee, he has conducted research in China and Japan for nearly thirty years.

Christian A. Hess is associate professor of history at Sophia University. His research focuses on Japanese colonialism in Northeast China and its legacies after 1945. His current project *From Colonial Port to Socialist Metropolis* is an urban history of Dalian as it developed from a Japanese colonial center to a socialist production city in the People's Republic of China. Recent publications include "Sino-Soviet City: Dalian between Socialist Worlds, 1945–1955," in the *Journal of Urban History;* and "Securing the City, Securing the Nation: Militarization and Urban Police Work in Dalian, 1949–1953," in *The Habitable City in China: Urban History in the Twentieth Century,* edited by Toby Lincoln and Xu Tao. A native of California, he also has an interest in the history of Japanese and Chinese cuisine in the state.

Lenka Vyletalova earned her PhD in global studies from Sophia University, where she is collaborative research fellow at the Institute of Comparative Culture. She is adjunct professor at Prague University of Economics and Business and Palacky University Olomouc. Her research focuses on the relationships between labor mobility, gender and social change. She has been active in nurturing strategic partnerships between civil society, academia, and private and public organizations through community development projects in Japan, the Czech Republic, Ukraine, and Switzerland.

Chuanfei Wang earned her PhD in global studies from Sophia University, where she is collaborative research fellow at the Institute of Comparative Culture. She is assistant professor of sociology and sustainability studies at Hosei University. She is the author of numerous articles and book chapters on the Japanese wine industry, the globalization of Japanese culinary culture, and international wine tourism. Originally from Tianjin, China, she has lived in Tokyo for two decades.

David L. Wank is professor of sociology and dean of the Graduate School of Global Studies at Sophia University. His research focuses on social transformations in state and society of networks, power, and values, with a focus on China. Book publications include *Commodifying Communism: Business, Trust, and Politics in a Chinese City; The Space of Religion: Temple, State, and Communities of Buddhism in Modern China* (with Yoshiko Ashiwa, forthcoming); and *Dynamics of Global Society: Theory and Prospects* (in Japanese, with Yoshinori Murai and Tadashi Anno). His ongoing projects investigate the globalization of Chinese Buddhism as both religion and culture that is proceeding with China's growing political and economic power in the twenty-first century. Originally from Pennsylvania, he has lived in China and Japan for forty years.

Index

Page numbers in **boldface** type refer to illustrations

labor: in expatriate Japantowns, 87–88; family, 170–171, 185; immigration, migrants, and, 69–72, 74, 86, 87–88, 95, 170–171, 194–199, 204–206; race and, 183, 210n77; restaurant management and, 178–179, 264–265; shortages, 204, 344; wages and, 170–171, 197, 201, 204
labor market, 51
Lancaster, Pennsylvania, 171–172, 174–175
language, 43, 215, 229–230, 247n14, 263
Lee, Serge, 103–104
Levy, Max, 274
Li, Qiankai, 171–172
Liberdade, Brazil, **84**, 84–87, **87**
Li family, 177–179, **178**
Little Club, 128–129
Little Fuzhou, 173, 177–178
Little Tokyo: in Los Angeles, 79, 85, 135; in New York's East Village, 104–108, 257–261, 278
Liu, Tanxiang, 230–231
Liu, Tehmin, 37
localist imaginary, 41–42
localization: authenticity and, 272–273; in Brazil, 226–227; globalization and, 216–217, 233–234, 294, 298–299
local research, 6–7
Lofgren, Kristofor, 237–238
London, 89, 267–268
Los Angeles: Little Tokyo, 79, 85, 135; sukiyaki, 127–128, 130–131; sushi bars in, 138–139
Lunchbox, 243–244

manga, 96–99, 104, 140, 275, 280, 341
market competition: authenticity and, 271–273; culinary politics and, 11–12
Marold, Jan, 124
marriage migration, 149–152
Marsh, Dorothy, 126
Marufuku, 81
Maruyasu, 95–96
massification, 117–118, 129
mass market: entrepreneurship and, 164–165; ethnic succession and, 166–182; Japanese cuisine, 164–182; migration and, 164–182. *See also* Fuzhou Chinese restauranteurs

Matsuhisa, Nobu, 311–314, 338
Matsui, Hideki, 224
Matsumoto, Hirotaka, 136–138
Matsuo, Hideaki, 302
Matsuya, 77–78
Matsuzaki, Minesaku, **84**
Maxim Group, 51
McDonaldization, 213–214, 228, 285; of *izakaya*, 256, 269
McDonald's, 212–213, 218, 220
media: food bloggers and, 118, 154, 169; manga, 96–99, 104, 140, 275, 280, 341; social, 229, 315–316, 344–345, 348n33; World's 50 Best Restaurants list and, 308–310. *See also* Michelin stars
mediazation, 315–316
Meehan, Peter, 141–142
Meiguanyuan, 42
memory, 40–42. *See also* nostalgia
Menya Musashi, 234–239
methodology. *See* fieldwork
Michelin stars, 12, 142, 233; celebrity chefs and, 309–310; fine dining and, 298, 302–305, 308–310; tourism and, 309–310; World's 50 Best Restaurants list and, 308–310
Midwest Japantowns, 75–78
migrants, 2; in Brazil, 82–83; in China, 185, 194–198; ethnic succession and, 166–192; Fuzhou Chinese restauranteurs and, 169–179, 207n15; Japantowns and, 67–71; labor and, 69–72, 74, 86, 87–88, 95, 170–171, 194–199, 204–206; in Nairobi, 202–205; new migrant faces of global Japanese cuisine, 205–206; racism toward, 71–72, 75; refugees and, 37, 40, 61n72, 166–168, 182, 187–188; in Shanghai, 32; social capital and, 240–241; in Sri Lanka, 199–202; Vietnamese, 187–188; women, 28
migration: authenticity and, 149–154; from China, 171–175, 207n15; circular, 193, 194–196; COVID-19 and, 341–342; culinary global cities and, 294–299, 306–307; marriage, 149–152; mass market and, 164–182; mobility and, 8, 164–165, 193–205, 311–313, 341–344;

Osaka, 186–187
Ou, Michael, 278–279
outdoor dining, **343**
ownership, 53–54, 64n120, 158n46, 265;
    chef-owners, 164–165, 167–168, 182–185;
    corporatization and, 230–243, 332; in
    Japantowns, 79–81, 96–97; race and, 181,
    182–184; social identity and, 79

Paddleford, Clementine, 132
pan-Asian menus, 168–169
Papa Nô, 189, **189**
Paris, France: ethnic succession in,
    182–185; Japanese teahouses in,
    119–121; Japantown in, 90–91, 98,
    101–104
Paris International Exposition, 119, 120
Pennsylvania, 171–172, 174–175, 180, 276
People's Republic of China (PRC), 37, 42,
    52–54, 169
Perera, Chamila Lakshitha, 201
Philadelphia roll, 136, 172
Pierce, Anne Lewis, 126
Platt, Adam, 140
poke bowls, 201–202, 245, 254n153;
    authenticity and culinary politics of,
    228–230
politics, 3; anti-Japanese, 38–39, 43, 52–54;
    in China, 40–41, 52–54; cultural politics
    of ethnic succession, 182–192; expatriate
    Japantowns and, 97; geopolitical
    competition and, 55–56; in Germany,
    187; identity and, 12; open border
    policies and, 7; postcolonial culinary
    politics and imperialism, 52–56. *See also*
    culinary politics
popular culture, 101–104, 107, 128–129,
    300; authenticity and, 340–341
postcolonialism: culinary imperialism and
    its postcolonial culinary imaginaries,
    56–57; in Korea, 40, 43–44; nostalgia
    and, 57; postcolonial culinary politics,
    52–56; in Taiwan, 40–42, 57
postmodernism, 219–220
postwar urbanization, 78, 79–80
Prague, 99, **123**, 123–124
PRC. *See* People's Republic of China

Prohibition era, 72–73, 258
prostitution. *See* sexual services
Pu Yi (Emperor), 28

race: authenticity and, 181–182, 190–192;
    ethnicity and, 12, 180–182, 190–192,
    205–206; labor and, 183, 210n77;
    ownership and, 181, 182–184; servers
    and, 173–175; "whitening" of Japanese
    restaurants and, 180
racial stereotyping, 12, 181–182, 190–192
racism, 82; discrimination and, 71–72,
    158n46; toward Japanese migrants,
    71–72, 74
railway restaurant cars, 23–24, **24**
ramen noodle restaurants, 44, 46, 80–81,
    118; Ajisen Ramen, 230–232; Ando
    Momofuku and, 162n117; authenticity
    and, 141–142, 153–154, 214–216; Chang
    and, 141–142, 153–154; culture and,
    214–215; Dosanko Ramen, 214–216;
    fashions and growing popularity of,
    140–144; "first," 247n12; mobilities and,
    140–141; in themed Japantowns,
    103–104
Rath, Eric, 291
raw fish, 36, 134–137. *See also* sushi
    restaurants
Ray, Krishnendu, 154, 167
refugees, 37, 40, 61n72, 166–168, 182,
    187–188
reinvention, 290–293
religion, 95, 105, 220, 240–241
restaurant forms, 3–5, 7, 15, 117–118, 151,
    156, 329–334, 343
restaurant management: corporatization
    and, 313–314; *kaizen* and, 219–220; labor
    and, 178–179, 264–265; styles, 50–51,
    64n128, 267; in Vietnam, 100–101
Restaurant Queen, 145–146
restaurants: authenticity and success of,
    168–169; collaborative fieldwork and
    research visits to, 13–14, 20n45;
    corporate restaurant groups and, 51–52;
    in department stores, 24–25; ethnic
    succession, hiring, and competition in,
    190–192; immigration and, 164–166;

sociability: femininity and, 279, 280–282; *izakayas* and, 255–285; local and transnational spaces of, 280–284
social capital, 166, 236–237, 239–243
social identity, 3, 79
social media, 229, 315–316, 348n33; influencers, 344–345
social relationships, 51
Song (Chef of Misono, Nairobi), 203–204
sourcing ingredients, 291, 314, 320, 334, 339
South America, 82–87. *See also* Brazil
soy sauce, 133, 147
Spain, 292
Sri Lanka, 211n100; migrants in, 199–202; mobilities in, 199–202
Stalker, Nancy, 291
status, 187. *See also* elite culture
Stulman, Gabriel, 273–274
Suehiro, 80
Sugimoto, Kuichi, 89–90, 113n91
sukiyaki, 69, 117–118; decline of, 130–131; as earliest global Japanese cuisine, 39–40; fashions of, 73–74, 75, 80, 125–131; in Germany, 130; growth and popularity of, 73–74, **74,** 80, 125–131; in Los Angeles, 127–128, 130–131; national identity and, 39–40; in New York City, 126–128, **127,** 130–131; nighttime economy and, 128–129; sexual services and, 125; in Shanghai, 36, 39–40, 64n123, 128–129, 158n46
Sumi, 150
Sunshine Café, 76–77
Suntory Group, 310
suppliers, 183, 196
Sushi Leblon, 297
Sushi Nozawa, 138
sushi restaurants: authenticity and, 136–137; California sushi roll trend and, 46, 100, 102–103, 135–137, 213; Chinese views on, 36; in Dalian, 29; by Fuzhou Chinese restauranteurs, 170, 172; in Germany, 96; health and, 174; hipster Japanese cuisine and, 188–190; in Japantowns, 78; multiculturalism and, 180–181; *omakase* menu and, 134,

138–140; Philadelphia roll and, 136, 172; raw fish and, 36, 134–137; in Shanghai, 64n123; in Sri Lanka, 200–201; sushi bar origins and fashions, 134–140; sushi chefs and, 172, 181; sustainability and, 237–238; in Taiwan, 30–31; in US, 135–140; wok sushi and, 185; women sushi chefs and, 181
sustainability, 237–238, 309–310, 326n65
Sweetfin, 229
Syvochub, Artem, 236

Taipei, Taiwan: culinary imaginaries in, 41–42; culinary politics in, 41–42; Japanizing population through cuisine in, 30–31; *sake* boom in, 278–279
Taiwan: culinary politics in, 40–42; elite culture in, 41–42; Japanese restaurants in, 30–31; nationalism in, 44; postcolonialism in, 40–42, 57
Taiwanese cuisine, 30–31, 41–42
Taiwan Lou, 30
Takada, Tomonori, 270
Takara, 102–103
Takayama, Hiroshi, 149
Takayama, Masayoshi "Masa," 138–139
takeout, 174
takoyaki shops, 48
Takumi, 49–51, **50**
Takumi Ramen, 240
Tan, Sean, 314
Tanaka, Atsushi, 305
Tang, Tao, 49–51
Tangu Road (Rokusantei), 34, 60n60
teahouses. *See* Japanese teahouses
technology, 220, 225; social media and, 229, 315–316, 344–345, 348n33
television, 103–104, 142–143, 204, 257. *See also* manga
temaki, 213; *temakeria,* 226–228
Teng, Jan, 173
Tenkin, 73
teppanyaki. *See* Japanese steak houses
teriyaki, 224–226
Teriyaki Boy, 237
Teriyaki Japan, **244,** 244–245
Teriyaki Madness, 225